DATE DUE

DEMCO 38-296

MULTIMEDIA NETWORKING HANDBOOK
1999

MULTIMEDIA NETWORKING HANDBOOK 1999

James Trulove, *Editor*

AUERBACH

Boca Raton   London   New York   Washington, D.C.

Library of Congress Cataloging-in-Publication Data

Catalog record is available from the Library of Congress.

Contributors

DAVID H. AXNER, President, DAX Associates, Oreland PA

DANIEL BAHR, Director of Technology, Virtual Resources, Atlanta GA

GERALD L. BAHR, Networking Consultant, Roswell GA, jbahr@avana.net

FRANK J. BOURNE, Senior Applications Engineer, StrataCom, Atlanta GA

JAMES W. CONARD, President, Conard Associates, Venice FL

G. THOMAS DES JARDINS, Senior Software Engineer, Inbound Technology Group, FORE Systems, Inc., Warrendale PA

PHIL EVANS, Director of Telecommunications, Perot Systems Corp., Dallas TX

MATTHEW FELDMAN, Chief Technology Officer, Intelect Visual Communications, New York NY

ERIK FRETHEIM, Senior Manager, Systems Design and Planning, Data Services Division, MCI Communications, Richardson TX

JOHN GALGAY, Principal Consultant, Bay Networks, Atlanta GA

ROOHOLLAH HAJBANDEH, Manager of Business Development, American Communications Consultants, Inc., Madison WI

GILBERT HELD, Director, 4-Degree Consulting, Macon GA

TIM KELLY, Vice President, Cygnus Communications, Battleground WA

KEITH G. KNIGHTSON, Technology Consultant, Kanata, Ontario, Canada

DANIEL A. KOSEK, Principal, Fountain Rock Technologies, Inc., Walkersville MD

ARMIN R. MIKLER, PhD Candidate, Department of Computer Science, Iowa State University, Ames IA

NATHAN J. MULLER, Consultant, The Oxford Group, Huntsville AL

LUC T. NGUYEN, Area Consulting Manager, Bay Networks, Atlanta GA

CHRISTINE PEREY, Independent Consultant, PEREY Communications & Consulting, Placerville CA, cperey@spiter.lloyd.com

WENDY ROBERTS, Principal Consultant, Virtual Resources, Atlanta GA

FREDERICK W. SCHOLL, President, Monarch Information Networks, Inc., New York NY

DALE SMITH, National Professional Services Manager, Bay Networks, Birmingham AL

MARTIN TAYLOR, Vice President of Technology Strategy, Madge Networks, San Jose CA

JAMES TRULOVE, Data Networking Systems Manager, Lucent Technologies, Austin TX

Contributors

GOPALA KRISHNA TUMULURI, *Software Test Engineer, FORE Systems, Pittsburgh PA*
PRERANA VAIDYA, *Member, Technical Staff, Phillips Research Laboratory, New York NY*
JEFFREY WEISS, *Vice President of Technology, Telco Systems, Norwood MA*
JOHNNY S. K. WONG, *Professor of Computer Science, Iowa State University, Ames IA*

Contents

Contents

Introduction
Multimedia Networking: New Perspectives

Multimedia networking has begun to truly come of age in the modern business world. Although traditional "pure" networks still exist for the separate delivery of voice, data, and video, new networks are often implemented as a combination of all three types of remote communications merged into one delivery system. Indeed, many legacy networks are seeing the addition of multimedia applications as the greatest pressure to effective network throughput.

In the recent past, the innovations in multimedia communication have been brought to us primarily through encapsulation in data networks and multiplexed wide area transport. Thus we have voice and video over IP data networks, voice over frame relay, and video through ISDN basic rate and primary rate services. Now, in addition to these methods, the cell-based switching of ATM offers a simple means to mix the high quality-of-service demands of voice and video with the more delay-tolerant data services.

Image transmission, with its commensurate high bandwidth requirements, occupies an increasing portion of available network bandwidth, both on the local and global levels. Without considering the Internet for the moment, one can easily name myriad innovative applications that involve image transmission. For example, the image storage and the retrieval of photographs, scanned documents, medical images, maps, and even bank checks are common in today's network environment. Videoconferencing over local and remote networks is in a very rapid phase of deployment, providing new opportunities in education, medicine, project collaboration, and management. The world benefits enormously from this new interactive video technology. Important applications encompass a range of uses from distance learning to medical expert assistance for remote areas to instant "distant" meetings.

The advent of the Internet adds several additional layers to the above uses for networked image transmission. Virtually all modern Web sites contain rich graphic and image content, and many add simple animation and real-time audio. Real-time, ad-hoc, voice, and video transmission are already feasible over the Internet. Point-to-point and point-to-multipoint transmission is easily accomplished for both audio and video, and multipoint conferences can be provided with little additional equipment. Broadcast, or so-called "net-cast," media has begun to provide streaming information content for such applications as news, financial data, and weather with multimedia.

The addition of audio and video entertainment "channels" has begun in earnest on the Internet. At the present time, while sitting comfortably at your computer, you can tune in to your favorite jazz, classical, rock, easy listening, or alternative music from a variety of audio net-casters around the globe. Special-purpose audio feeds are often available from live concerts. Video servers are now offering image transmission that includes periodic, still images as well as an increasing number of full-motion (more or less) video feeds that may be broadcast to thousands. One can easily "see" live images of the current ski conditions in Vail, the beach in Malibu, and the traffic conditions in Phoenix. Similar images are available from Sweden to Sydney. Even music concerts may now have a low-bandwidth video feed to the Internet.

These audio and video transmissions require substantial amounts of network bandwidth and have specific transmission-delay parameters to achieve reasonable quality. This bandwidth requirement stresses virtually every component in the super-network that is comprised of a chain of image servers, routers, switches, backbones, local networks, and premise connections. Bandwidth allocation, quality of service, compression techniques, transport technologies, and network management are all critically important considerations in the implementation of successful multimedia networking. Delivery of the multimedia content to the customer premise is another bandwidth-constrained system component that must be properly provisioned to support quality multimedia communication.

The *Multimedia Networking Handbook* is intended to address all these issues that must be faced to implement satisfactory multimedia installations. It provides overview, insight, and details by subject-matter experts on each of the crucial aspects of multimedia networking. The book is organized into eight sections, each of which covers an important portion of multimedia networking issues. The reader is free to proceed in a straightforward manner through the individual chapters or to browse a particular topic in depth. Many of the chapters provide important reference information that will be consulted often.

JAMES TRULOVE

jtru@realtime.net

Section I
Multimedia Networking: A Status Report

Modern networking is a potpourri of mixed-media applications with vast differences in transmission requirements. The staid, traditional data networks of the past are being forcibly made obsolete by requirements for combined data and video delivery. In addition, voice networks are moving past their isolation from local and wide area data into a brave new world of data/voice/video integration. What is in store is far more than the combination of voice and data delivery to a call-center work station. It is a leveling of the transport method field so that all forms of remote communication coexist in the same information stream.

Any significant change to the communications infrastructure has wide-reaching implications for business. Business users will be required to make significant decisions regarding their multimedia networking policies. At the local level, transport of multimedia applications causes intermittent to severe congestion on the pervasive 10M to 16M bps shared networks. Increasing effective bandwidth to the work station level can partially be accomplished by adding port switching to concentration hubs and/or jumping the speed to 10/100/1000M bps. However, that is not the whole picture.

We need to be prepared for the shift to multimedia by exploring the business implications, the technology requirements, and the delivery needs of the worldwide expansion of our communications consciousness. It can certainly be argued that multimedia applications are a market-driven commodity. As such, the expansion to multimedia networking is governed by economic realities of price vs. performance and is dependent upon the availability of multimedia applications and content. Few business and technology managers want to incur the expense, manage the disruption, or deal with the competing issues involved in the rush to multimedia.

Despite the technical complexities, favorable economic factors and the expanding availability of information content are producing a market convergence that will fuel explosive growth in multimedia networking. The user community, from business sector managers to consumers, will continue to demand greater multimedia capabilities, speed, and performance. We must have the answers they need.

Much of this handbook concentrates on very narrowly focused slices of the overall multimedia networking pie. While these tight subject matter constraints allow us to more easily present the in-depth material that is the trademark of this series, it presupposes we have a general framework within which to relate the detailed subjects. This first section provides an overview of some of the broader issues in multimedia networking.

Chapter 1

Business Impact and Implications of Multimedia

Phil Evans

Multimedia is becoming so pervasive that many businesses have little choice but to incorporate it. In the near future, multimedia applications will affect both how businesses operate internally and how they compete for market share.

The opportunities are enormous for developers of multimedia-related software and hardware, telecommunications services, systems integrators, consultants, and the related installation, operation, and maintenance service providers. One research firm, Market Intelligence, predicts multimedia users worldwide will spend up to $24 billion on multimedia applications by the year 2000. The frenzy of alliances, acquisitions, and cooperative forums prove the commitment of leading companies to multimedia.

MULTIMEDIA'S IMPACT

"Multimedia communications," as used throughout this book, refers to an information transport methodology in which traffic of many kinds can share a common network without compromising the quality of information being transported. Through combinations of telephone company and cable company broadband access into homes and businesses across the nation, the leading multimedia transport technologies — synchronous optical network (SONET), fiber distributed data interface (FDDI), switched multimegabit data service (SMDS), and asynchronous transfer mode (ATM) — are being employed to provide services only dreamed of in the past.

The delivery of broadband communications into living rooms and offices will affect people's home lives and work habits. Home shopping, education, access to a massive range of third-party data bases, interactive entertainment and games, connection to an employer's data bases, video-conferences, and applications not yet imagined will become commonplace.

Imagine rising in the morning to a personal selection of music, news, entertainment, or to an old-fashioned alarm, on TV or radio, then washing the sleep from your eyes and checking the TV screen for late-breaking events of personal interest. Overnight, your "electronic agent" monitored all available sources of information — stock prices and volumes, a favorite team's score from the late game, world and national news — recording those items of specified interest so you could review them in the morning. You decide to buy a stock, based on current information, so you speak into the computer (or use the "point and click" method if you cannot break the habit) to define the number of shares and the price. The order goes to the exchange and to the bank for financial approval. You browse updated information on the companies you intend to visit later and effectively plan the day's business activities.

Just before going out the door, you load all pertinent data the agent has gathered into your personal digital assistant (PDA). The PDA contains your personal computer, address and telephone list, maps, calendar, cellular telephone, pager, fax, wireless and wired modems, and files so you can perform your job as a mobile professional. Returning home that night, you turn on the TV for a repeat of the morning's update activity (compliments of your electronic agent). You make your buy/sell decisions and execute, check the scores and the news of interest, and surf the entertainment channels to select a program to enjoy with dinner. You are current with all work because you communicated it as it happened throughout the day. Your company and clients have been updated in real time. A toast to technology.

This new world is inevitable because of the simultaneous convergence of a set of four powerful factors: technology, business, sociopolitics, and legislation/regulation (see Exhibit 1). This convergence is more prevalent in technologically advanced nations, but through telecommunications its impact will be worldwide.

MULTIMEDIA ENABLERS

Technology. Technological advancements enabling multimedia include fast-packet transmission protocols like ATM and SMDS; computer advancements such as massively parallel processing, client/server platforms, and relational data bases; and infrastructure enhancements based on fiber optics. In the near future, low earth orbiting satellites (LEOS) and the digitization of information — whether in voice, video, image, text, or data format — will enable the creation of compound electronic documents (e.g., an e-mail message with a voice explanation appended to it).

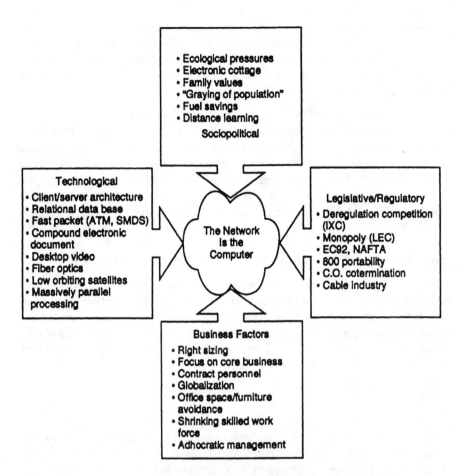

Ecological pressures
- Ecological pressures
- Electronic cottage
- Family values
- "Graying of population"
- Fuel savings
- Distance learning

Sociopolitical

Technological
- Client/server architecture
- Relational data base
- Fast packet (ATM, SMDS)
- Compound electronic document
- Desktop video
- Fiber optics
- Low orbiting satellites
- Massively parallel processing

The Network Is the Computer

Legislative/Regulatory
- Deregulation competition (IXC)
- Monopoly (LEC)
- EC92, NAFTA
- 800 portability
- C.O. cotermination
- Cable Industry

Business Factors
- Right sizing
- Focus on core business
- Contract personnel
- Globalization
- Office space/furniture avoidance
- Shrinking skilled work force
- Adhocratic management

Exhibit 1.   Factors Affecting the Development of Multimedia Applications

Business. Dominating business factors that encourage the widespread incorporation of multimedia are "rightsizing" and, concurrently, the use of more contract personnel; the drive to reduce the expense of office space, furniture, supplies, and related utilities, which encourages more work from home; and the growing requirement to more effectively use the skills of technically competent personnel.

Process reengineering is the popular trend for meeting business challenges with technology, and multimedia is appropriate in many applications. Business, government, and education are employing technology to change the way work is performed and services are delivered. Technology is being used to improve and expand services and reduce costs and delivery times. Multimedia technology is integral to business reengineering.

Sociopolitics. Sociopolitical challenges to conserve energy and reduce pollution are answered by multimedia applications that allow one or more adults to work from home instead of an office building. Distance learning, home shopping, telemedicine, and the "electronic cottage" industry are all enabled and enhanced by multimedia.

Legislation/Regulation. Privatization and deregulation are converting staid, monopolistic environments into dynamos of competition, with all of the attendant benefits of choice, quality, and value. Acquisitions of cable companies by telephone companies, and vice versa, are in full swing now that constraints have been lifted. Other initiatives encouraging the adaptation of multimedia are federal and state government mandates requiring businesses to establish car or van pools, work-at-home jobs, and neighborhood satellite offices.

MULTIMEDIA APPLICATIONS FOR BUSINESSES AND CONSUMERS

Emerging applications of multimedia tend toward entertainment, education, shopping, dissemination of information, and cooperative work environments. As technology, services, user expectations, and experiences mature in multimedia, applications that have yet to be envisioned are also expected to emerge. Some will become immensely popular while others languish; but through the increasing levels of sophistication in multimedia that come with experience, the winners will progressively outnumber the losers.

Consumers, many of whom can remain in their homes or businesses and still shop for services, will have better products and services at competitive prices when and where they want them. Businesses will understand their markets in more intimate detail than ever before, thereby being able to refine the production and delivery of quality products and services tailored to specific segments of their markets. Waste will be reduced, deliveries optimized, and consumers' wants and demands satisfied.

Education and Training

Education is a major concern in the U.S. and many other nations. CDROM-equipped personal computers are one way to deliver interactive training. Students can interact with the course as they have time, need, and motivation. Specific course areas can be accessed and reviewed as often as needed, irrelevant topics can be skipped, and basic to advanced study levels can be selected.

Opportunities abound for course developers and educators to create materials that satisfy business, government, medical, and educational needs. Benefits also accrue to those who implement such training. According to one insurance company, compared with the traditional instructor-led course, its multimedia version produced graduates who had better retention of course materials in half the study time.

Distance Learning. Distance-learning applications of multimedia allow teachers to reach students at different locations by means of video, audio and interactive data connections. Shared video screens let teachers and students alike see changes to course materials as they are made. It is on such capabilities that the hopes of education are riding in many nations, with entrepreneurs ready to enhance and exploit these capabilities. A business can, for example, show tens of thousands of K-12 students the merits of the company's products while simultaneously helping to underwrite education, or receive instantaneous reactions to product surveys as they appear on students' PCs.

Information Dissemination

Kiosks equipped with PCs that have touchscreens and keyboards for data entry, as well as printers, are already popular for numerous applications. The state of Oregon uses such kiosks to provide information on available jobs and unemployment benefits. The Ontario Ministry of Transportation in Canada has an application that allows drivers to easily renew licenses, make address and name changes, and pay fines. Northwest Natural Gas Company uses similar devices to disseminate company information and news in the form of a full-motion, color newsletter for employees and customers.

Another application under consideration for kiosks is issuance of building permits for routine projects. Governments, businesses, hospitals, and universities have many opportunities to provide fast, efficient services by substituting conveniently located kiosks at crowded offices with long lines and, in some cases, inefficient personnel. New business ventures await entrepreneurs who are able to identify applications and create the hardware, software, and telecommunications systems to serve them.

Cooperative Work Environments

Multimedia combined with groupware is a formidable business weapon that allows knowledgeable personnel to contribute to the problem-solving and decision-making challenges of business, almost without respect for physical location. Remote users communicate by voice, handwritten notes, fax, and full-motion video while simultaneously sharing applications and data. PCs and workstations are equipped with digital video cameras, microphones, digitizing tablets, and associated coder/decoders and software that enable such cooperative capabilities.

Personnel so equipped can work as effectively from home or the mountain cabin as they can from the next-door office. These work arrangements permit companies to optimize the usefulness of their scarce technical professionals and guard against burnout or loss of personnel to competitors. Multimedia- enabled cooperative work environments will do much to keep professionals happy (they can work from wherever they work best) and productive (they are in contact through the network and their multimedia terminal).

Offering employees the chance to work from home is not just a generous gesture to the technical professional, or the talented employee who also wants to be an at-home parent, or the valuable person who is physically home-bound. It is also a way for a business to meet government mandates, such as the state of Colorado's directive, stemming from clean-air rules, that 10% of all employees telecommute, or Japan's directive for large companies to establish neighborhood satellite offices around Tokyo.

Energy, environmental, and family considerations are emerging as never before to challenge how business is conducted. Such challenges are actually opportunities for those with the imagination and competency to apply the full capabilities of multimedia made possible by computer networks of unprecedented quantity and quality.

Entertainment

Entertainment is most often cited when multimedia and the information superhighway are discussed. It remains to be seen whether the market can match the media hype that claims 500+ channels can be brought to the home in vivid digital images for entertainment and interactive games of every description. Irrespective of the uncertainties, there is real commitment on the part of entertainment production companies, cable companies, telecommunications companies, electronics manufacturers, and financiers the world over. Related business opportunities exist for the creation of billing and collection systems in various levels of the entertainment industry. For example, a consumer receiving an advertisement-free movie at 8:00 p.m. on a Saturday night might be billed more than the viewer who requests the same movie on another night, with 15 minutes of advertisements interspersed. Likewise, the same movie received on a high-definition television (HDTV) set should cost more than if it were received on a standard small-screen television.

The Marketer's Dream. Another potential of multimedia entertainment is accurate information on service subscribers, down to the family or individual level. Such granularity is significantly valuable to anyone interested in selective marketing, and that applies to almost every business. This capability can be exceptionally refined through audience interaction with infomercials, with participation encouraged in numerous ways, from "free" movies to sweepstakes.

1-6

Home Shopping

Enhanced shopping through multimedia applications has piqued the interest of many business professionals. People are increasingly motivated to shop from home, citing reasons from concern for personal safety to dissatisfaction with sales personnel.

Virtual Shopping Malls. One option shoppers have is to wander a virtual electronic mall, moving in and out of boutiques that provide choice and specialization as never before imagined. Products can be examined in three-dimensional color visualizations; availability and warranty information can be obtained, along with prices and terms; and all information can be compared to competitive offerings within the same virtual mall.

Depending on their preferences, more skilled or less enthusiastic shoppers can employ software agents to do their shopping for them. These agents, programmed with information on buyer preferences and spending limits, will sort through the maze of competitive offerings to select the best buys, thereby leaving the virtual shopper free to pursue other endeavors. Business will discover opportunities to market products and services, build and sell agents to be virtual personal shoppers, develop the credit checking, billing, and collections systems, create the electronic malls and boutiques, and enlist companies to participate in the malls.

READYING YOUR COMPANY FOR MULTIMEDIA

A few innovative businesses are already incorporating multimedia applications; most businesses, however, are on the periphery, watching and wondering.

In the current business climate of doing more with less, technology managers must identify those areas to which their restricted budgets and staffs can be optimally applied. Multimedia should be included among the top two or three technologies to be studied, planned, and implemented.

In working with business managers, specific areas must be identified as candidates for the application of multimedia. Then a plan that addresses the specifics of software, hardware, transport, applications, training, operation and maintenance, management, and backup must be developed, refined, and sold to executive management.

Publications, educational companies that develop specialized seminars and short courses, consulting companies, and systems integrators are increasingly engaged in multimedia projects. Technology managers must stay aware of the experiences, reputations, and customers of these resources so that they will know the resources on which they can depend when the time comes to initiate multimedia applications of their own.

SUMMARY

Multimedia is an enabling technology that itself is being enabled by advances in networking and software. Technology managers face a growing number of opportunities — and demands — to employ multimedia as their businesses strive to gain market share and meet competition from around the globe. Therefore, technology managers must make a concerted effort to learn, plan for, and implement multimedia applications that grow with the business.

Executives and entrepreneurs can profitably exploit multimedia through innovative applications that satisfy customer wants and government mandates. Budget-minded government officials can enhance provision of services through applications of multimedia. Educators can also greatly enhance the quality and quantity of education and training programs through networked multimedia. The implications of multimedia will affect our lives well into the 21st century.

Chapter 2
Broadband Applications and Technology Requirements
James W. Conard

Communications technology has become the core of the distributed information system so vital to the modern enterprise. Information, in the form of data, voice, and, increasingly, graphics and images, is transported among users by the vast array of public and private communications networks. These networks are evolving toward much higher speeds and significantly lower transit delays. Broadband networks, which is what these high-speed networks are called, are not being designed as an exercise to demonstrate engineering capability. They are being developed and deployed only because network service providers see an increasing demand for communications services that can only be met with a low-latency, very fast, high-capacity network infrastructure.

This chapter reviews the justification for this perception. First the trends, forces, generic applications, and user needs that are driving the development of broadband communications are examined, and the enabling technologies that will provide the foundation for broadband products and services are introduced. The chapter concludes with an overview of the broadband standards and architectures that are prerequisites to the global availability of broadband communications.

TECHNOLOGY INTERRELATIONSHIPS

Ultimately it will be the broadband marketplace, whose structure is illustrated in Exhibit 1, that will determine the success or failure of broadband networking, vendors, services, and products. This marketplace is characterized by its diverse but interrelated elements. It includes:

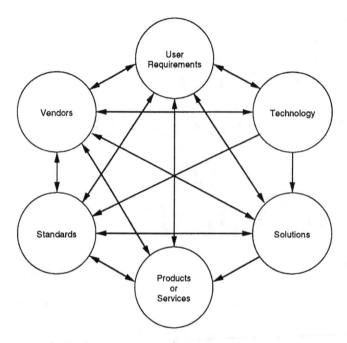

Exhibit 1.   The Broadband Marketplace

- *Users.* They require cost-effective solutions to networking problems.
- *Technologies.* The basis for network product development.
- *Standards.* These are intended to stabilize the market and thereby make life easier and products cheaper for users and vendors.
- *Products and services.* The goal is to increase revenue for the producer by solving users' problems.
- *Vendors.* They are trying to survive and thrive in a complex and dynamic environment.
- *Solutions.* These use the technologies to create products and services.

The market interrelationships for broadband networking, at least initially, seem ideal. The requirement to move increasingly large amounts of information in ever-decreasing periods of time is certainly real. At the same time, the technologies that can be applied to meeting this requirement are either here or just over the horizon.

USER NEEDS

Users do not, in general, care about technology. Users simply want cost-effective solutions to their problems. The user's ideal communications system is a single high-performance, economical network utility that accommodates all types of traffic and that provides the following:

- *Improved performance.* To be useful this must translate into improved productivity. It takes 15 minutes to transfer a 1M-byte file at 9,600 bps but only 4 seconds at 2M bps.
- *Better bandwidth use.* Bandwidth costs are 70 to 80% of communications system life cycle costs. Effective use of expensive resources is important.
- *More reliability.* Users recognize that resilience is an expensive quality if it is obtained with fully meshed networks; a solution is bandwidth on demand.
- *More flexibility.* This means being able to reassign capacity to different applications and different types of information as the requirements change.
- *Economies of scale.* Possible when one transport mechanism is used for all information types.
- *Data integrity.* Error-ridden information is often worse than no information.
- *Management capability.* Users need sophisticated management tools for operations, administration, and failure reporting and recovery.
- *Real-time interaction.* Information often has to be timely to be useful.

These requirements are quite general. They apply to any network, not just high-speed networks. Users are often at a loss to quantify these requirements, because it is extremely difficult to predict the future in other than very general terms. Users are unanimous, however, in predicting that future networks will have to move more information more quickly and, of course, less expensively.

Parallel Forces

The industry is being driven toward high-capacity, fast-response communications networks by three parallel forces. The first is a very rapid increase in the number of small traffic streams, those generating less than 64K bps, a result of the expanding numbers of LANs and microcomputers. There is also a huge installed base of synchronous and asynchronous terminals and devices generating traffic at rates of 600 bps to 19.2K bps. Many small streams of information begin to add up to large bandwidth needs.

A second force is the increase in the number of graphic work stations, image and video transfer, and networked mainframes, all of which generate large streams of data. The increase in both large data streams and aggregated small streams is, in large part, the result of distributed services being created by distributed applications.

A final but often overlooked contributor is the desire to leverage communications investment by integrating voice traffic with the data traffic on the network. Voice will remain, by far, the largest source of information to be carried by broadband networks.

High-Bandwidth Applications

As bandwidth-intensive computer applications increase in popularity, so rises the need for broadband networks. Surveys project that installed computer power will grow by a factor of 20 during the 1990s. The percent of this communications computational power that is interconnected by communications is expected to increase from 25% to 50%, leading to a 40-fold increase in communications capacity requirements. The use of high-capacity circuits (e.g., T1 and T3) is already increasing by 25% per year.

The rise in distributed computing environments will certainly be a factor. The purpose of distributed computing is to enable a community of users to share geographically separate resources. Client work stations can access remote servers shared by all. Distributed computing puts users at more sites, needing to communicate with each other and generating more traffic between sites.

There is increasing demand for image transfer, which includes everything from X-rays to photographs. To avoid the need for tremendous bandwidth, an image such as an X-ray is an obvious candidate for data compression. Radiologists, however, will not base a diagnosis on a compressed and expanded X-ray; they do not trust them. Remote diagnostics and other medical imaging technologies (e.g., monograms and CAT scans) are high-bandwidth requirements.

The limits of computer effectiveness using text displays alone have been reached. This is causing a movement from text to graphics in computer interfaces (i.e., the so-called graphical user interfaces), which require much more bandwidth. Transfer of a high-resolution screen requires moving 64K to 300K bytes compared with the 2K bytes required for a 3270-type transfer.

But the most important broadband application is the exchange of data at high speeds. This includes document exchange, host networking, and use of computer-aided design and manufacturing systems. There is, in general, an increase in applications that require more storage and more retrieval of remote documents and other information. This creates the need for a fast, high-capacity delivery service to accommodate bursty, interactive requirements.

Integrated, mixed-media desktop applications are sometimes referred to as the innovation that necessitates high-speed networking. Natural human communication makes use of speech, visual cues, graphics, and text. Combining these in work station and other computer interfaces is, therefore, an obvious requirement but has been restrained by lack of an adequate appropriate technology. Now that the interface technology is available, the communications network must be expanded to support the high-bandwidth, real-time transmissions associated with mixed media applications.

LAN Applications

Broadband networks are needed to directly interconnect local area networks (LANs). LANs are already, in terms of speed, broadband high-speed networks because they operate in the range of 4M to 100M bps. Installation numbers for LANs are also impressive. A recent AT&T survey predicts that, in the U.S., there will be 5 million LANs serving 40 million devices by 1993. Giving users of these LANs access to distributed resources and to remote hosts will require that the LANs be interconnected.

Such applications as X.400, X.500, and electronic data interchange will make it necessary for the connections to operate over long distances. Downsizing also contributes to increased LAN-to-LAN traffic because applications that were formerly on mainframes will be distributed among work stations and require access to shared data bases.

LAN-to-LAN applications currently operate over leased lines, using bridges and routers. These solutions are expensive, especially when modifications to the network are necessary. They are hard to manage, and their performance is not all that efficient. Packet switching, for example, is too slow for high-resolution graphics. Circuit switching is fast but has low bandwidth efficiency. Neither is ideal for LAN-to-LAN traffic. Broadband networking, on the other hand, offers frame relay as an immediate solution, switched multimegabit data service (SMDS) as an intermediate-range solution, and broadband integrated services digital network (ISDN) as a longer-term LAN-to-LAN solution.

Residential Applications

Potentially the greatest revenue-producing broadband application is often overlooked. There are more than 80 million U.S. households with telephone service and more than 90 million with over-the-air or cable television service. Each of these homes is a potential user of high-speed networking services.

The most obvious residential application is entertainment. On-demand movies, for example, are already available in broadband ISDN trials. Conversational services such as video telephony and video mail are high-bandwidth consumers. Distributed services being discussed include electronic publishing and high-fidelity music. Retrieval services would include library searches that would deliver still pictures, graphics, and video. A service is in existence that allows a customer to browse over a digital network

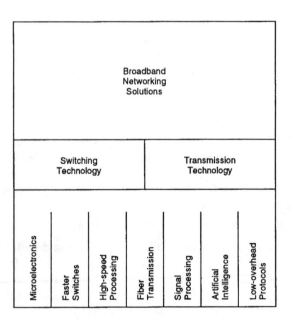

Exhibit 2.   Enabling Technologies

through the equivalent of a real estate multiple listing — complete with full-color photographs.

Security services, remote appliance and utility control, and home shopping are other residential applications that, in the aggregate, will require more bandwidth than currently available. Early planning for broadband networking is aimed at providing 150M-bps service to each residence.

ENABLING TECHNOLOGIES

The existence of broadband applications requirements does not guarantee the development of communications solutions. There must also exist the underlying basic technologies on which to build the solutions.

Connections have always been at the heart of networking, and broadband networking is aimed at providing high-capacity connections between users. What has changed is the technology. New switching technologies have lowered the time it takes to establish connections, and new transmission technologies have raised the rate at which information is transferred over connections. These improvements to switching and transmission technologies have been made possible by advances in microelectronics, high-speed processing, signal processing, fiber-optic transmission, and research into efficient protocols and artificial intelligence. Exhibit 2 summarizes these technology relationships.

Digital Switching

Because it is impractical to build a fully meshed network on a global scale, an efficient switching technology (needed to direct information through a multinodal network) is critical to cost-effective, responsive networking.

Switches are predominantly installed in central, tandem, or regional switching offices that are owned by telephone companies, but many private networks also contain switching mechanisms. Switches may operate in the space, frequency, or time domains and may switch circuits, messages, packets, or cells.

In the switching sense, circuits are connections that exist between users for a user-defined duration. Messages are relatively large, variable-length, user-defined information streams. Packets are relatively small, variable-length data units that are switched without regard for their relationship to other packets. Cells are fixed-length packets, designed to accommodate such bursty variable-rate information sources as computers and work stations as well as continuous bit-rate isochronous sources such as voice and video.

Communications switching technology has been under continual development. Electromechanical switching, the mainstay technology for many years, began to decline in use during the 1970s and will be mostly phased out by 1995. Analog program-controlled switching succeeded electromechanical switching but peaked in use during the 1980s and has given way to digital stored-program-controlled switching.

For many reasons, relating both to economics and performance, only digital switching meets the requirements of high-speed networking. Digital stored-program control permits service features and modifications to be effected through changes to software rather than redesign of hardware.

Fast Packet Switching and Services

Achieving high-speed networking requires increases in both transmission rate and switching speed. To increase the switching speed, the amount of time that a unit of user data spends in the switching process at a node in the communications path must be reduced. This concept goes by the generic name *fast packet switching*.

Fast packet switching is a concept, not a service or a product. It is basically similar to the familiar X.25 packet switching but is characterized by much higher throughput and much lower node delay because the switching occurs at a lower layer of the network's architecture. Fast packet services take for granted the low-error-rate connections that are characteristic of digital switching and transmission. They are like packet switching in that virtual circuits are established. Fast packet techniques

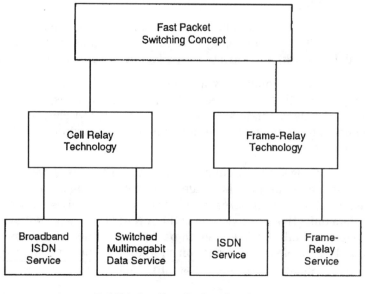

Exhibit 3. Fast Packet Services

can also be compared to digital multiplexing, in that the high speed permits voice, data, and images to share the same transmission resource.

In the near future, fast packet switching will be enhanced with the development of new high-speed switching fabrics. Fabric refers to the design and structure of the switching activity. The new switching fabrics are designed to support on-the-fly switching, wherein the switching stages are implemented as very fast silicon gates. The switching process is triggered by tag bits, which are associated with a virtual channel number or a connection address. A three-stage switch requires a three-bit tag. A packet arriving on any input line and carrying the same tag will be directed to the same output line. This technique is much faster and more efficient than software switching. Further in the future lies probably the fastest possible, at least with our current physics, switching technology — photonic switching.

The fast packet concept has spawned two different major technology approaches and a number of product and service solutions. As illustrated in Exhibit 3, these are called frame relay and cell relay.

Both terms refer to fast packet–based technologies. From an architectural perspective, frame relay is a data link layer service and cell relay is a physical layer service. Frame relay solutions for public (e.g., ISDN) and private networks (e.g., those composed of leased digital lines) have been developed. There are two cell relay solutions currently available or planned. The SMDS based on the Institute of Electrical and Electronic Engineers (IEEE) 802.6 metropolitan area network standards is now available in selected locations. Broadband ISDN services using the asynchronous transfer mode (ATM) over cell relay will begin appearing later in the decade.

Fiber-Based Digital Transmission

Digital, stored program control switches are being rapidly deployed in the switching centers of public and private networks. Simultaneously, and even more rapidly, digital transmission facilities are replacing analog facilities in the links between switching centers. Already 80% of the long-haul trunks interconnecting U.S. switching offices are digital and, increasingly, fiber. An all-fiber long-haul network will probably be in place around the turn of the century.

Fiber transmission facilities are critical to high-speed networks because broadband communications require very high information transfer rates and very low error rates. These quality and speed requirements cannot be satisfied by such mature technologies as coaxial cable, microwave, and satellite communications.

Fiber-optic transmission is capable of very high speeds. Rates exceeding 200M bps over distances of 60 kilometers without the use of repeaters have been routinely achieved. Fiber exhibits excellent immunity to electromagnetic and radio frequency interference. Typical error rates are less than 1 in 10^9 bits. Fiber is electrically isolated and, as a result, there are no problems with ground loops, cross-talk, lightning, or sparks. Because fiber cable is difficult to tap, it is relatively secure. Light weight and small size result in reduced installation costs. And optical fiber cable, although it lends itself most easily to point-to-point architectures, can be deployed in any desired topology.

The deployment of fiber in the long-haul wide area telephone company transmission plant is being coordinated under the umbrella of a set of standards called the synchronous optical network (SONET). SONET standardization is being performed in the U.S. under the aegis of the American National Standards Institute (ANSI) and abroad by the International Telephone and Telegraph Consultative Committee (CCITT) under the name synchronous digital hierarchy (SDH).

SONET was originally proposed by Bell Communications Research during the late 1980s as a means of providing the regional Bell operating companies with an infrastructure that would support multivendor, multicarrier broadband services.

SONET defines standard physical optical interfaces in modules from 51.84M bps to 2.5G bps. SONET is now in the early stages of deployment and is being supported by vendors and networks around the world.

High-Speed Networking Standards

If broadband communications networking is to achieve any major success, the associated services must be available virtually everywhere, and products must connect to virtually any network. Ensuring that this will be possible is the purpose of broadband standards.

ANSI and CCITT are only two of many organizations around the world that are heavily engaged in trying to establish broadband standards. The effort is spread across many networking disciplines, involving the creation of standards for architecture, access, transmission, switching, and management.

The architecture for broadband networking will conform to the International Standards Organization reference model for open systems interconnection (OSI). Early broadband interfaces are being derived from the work of the IEEE on local and metropolitan networks and from the work of ANSI and the CCITT on ISDN. Switching and transmission standards such as ATM and SONET continue to be defined.

Broadband standards, as well as broadband development, can be structured as shown in Exhibit 4. The most important characteristics of this model are:

- It follows the framework of the lower three layers of the OSI reference model.
- It recognizes the existence of three major function sets, called planes: a user plane, a control plane, and a management plane.
- It recognizes the need to accommodate both variable and continuous bit rate services (i.e., data and voice).

SUMMARY

The reason for the existence of multiple broadband approaches is that users are not yet pushing a particular broadband solution. They are simply pushing in the direction of higher speed services, and there are not yet enough users of broadband services to have established which services are best. (Because additional approaches are on the drawing board, there is not, and probably never will be, just a single broadband solution.)

As a result, the strategy of network providers seems to be to not attempt to predict which services might be feasible in the future. Instead, the strategy is to develop an infrastructure based on continually improving switching technology and fiber transmission. The use of cell switching permits

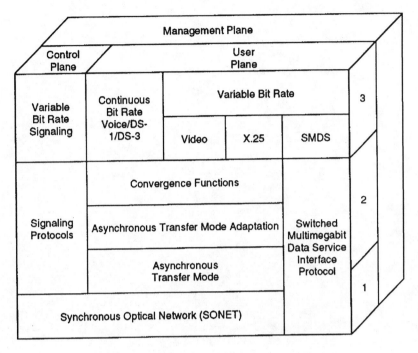

Exhibit 4. Broadband Service Structure

any user-generated information stream to be mapped to cells for switching and delivery. This approach makes the network transparent to the services offered at the user interface.

There remains little doubt that high-speed networks are necessary. There is also little doubt that network service providers are eager to supply high-speed services. What is in doubt is exactly what form the network will take or exactly what services will be offered. At the moment, a number of different trial approaches are being deployed.

Chapter 3
Global Multimedia Networking: A Web of Controversy

KEITH G. KNIGHTSON

Many countries and organizations have developed initiatives aimed at establishing an electronic highway such as the National Information Infrastructure (NII) in the U.S. and the European Information Infrastructure (EII). To cover global aspects, a Global Information Infrastructure (GII) is being developed.

The outcome of these initiatives depends on the changes taking place in the information and communications industries because of converging technologies, deregulation, and business restructuring or reorganization based on economic considerations. In short, establishing an infrastructure that integrates communications, computer, and entertainment technology requires the cooperation of industry, government, and standards bodies.

This chapter explores some of the possibilities and problems associated with information infrastructures worldwide. Special attention is given to the role of, and impact on, corporate network users.

WHAT IS AN INFORMATION INFRASTRUCTURE?

The term *information infrastructure,* which is used interchangeably with the term *information superhighway* in this chapter, describes a collection of technologies that relate to the storage and transfer of electronic information, including voice, data, and images. It is often illustrated as a technology cloud with user devices attached, including broadband networks, the Internet, and high-definition TV (HDTV).

However, problems emerge when users attempt to fit technologies together. For example, in the case of videophone service and on-demand video service, it is not clear whether the same display screen technology can be used, or whether a videophone call can be recorded on a locally available VCR. This example illustrates the need for consistency between similar technologies and functions.

Relevance of Information infrastructures

The information infrastructure is important because it provides an opportunity to integrate technologies that have traditionally belonged to specific industry domains, such as telecommunications, computers, and entertainment. (Integration details are discussed later in this chapter.) The information infrastructure also presents an opportunity to greatly improve the sharing and transferring of information. New business opportunities abound related to the delivery of new and innovative services to users.

Goals and Objectives of Information Infrastructures

The goals of most information infrastructures are to achieve universal access and global interoperability. Without corporate initiatives, the information infrastructure could result in conflicting and localized services, inefficient use of technology, and greater costs for fewer services. Some of the elements necessary to achieve such goals, including standards and open technical specifications that ensure fair competition and safeguard user interests, have yet to be adequately addressed.

BACKGROUND: TECHNOLOGY TRENDS

Two factors are often cited as driving the technology boom: the increase in computer processing power and the increase in the amount of available memory. Advances in these areas make a greater number of electronic services available for lower costs. This trend is expected to continue.

Bandwidth Pricing

Unfortunately, comparable gains of higher bandwidths and decreasing costs are not as evident in the communications arena. Whether this is because of the actual price of technology or because of pricing strategies is debatable. Many applications requiring relatively high bandwidths have yet to be tariffed.

On-demand video is an interesting test case for the pricing issue. To be attractive, this service would have to be priced to compete with the cost of renting a videotape. However, such a relatively low price for high bandwidth would make the price of traditional low-bandwidth phone services seem extremely expensive by comparison. ATM-based broadband ISDN is likely to emerge as the vehicle for high-speed, real-time applications where constant propagation delay is required.

The lack of higher bandwidths at inexpensive prices has inhibited the growth of certain applications that are in demand. The availability of

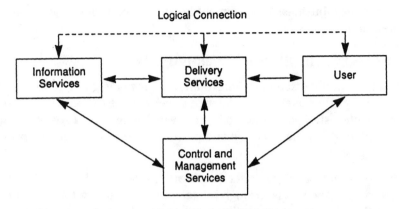

Exhibit 1. Service-Oriented Architecture

inexpensive high bandwidth could revolutionize real-time, on-demand applications, not only in the video entertainment area but also in the electronic publishing area.

Decoupling Networks and Their Payloads

One factor that is influencing the shape of the superhighway is the move toward digitization of information, particularly audio and video. Digitization represents a total decoupling between networks and their payloads.

Traditionally, networks have been designed for specific payloads, such as voice, video, or data. Digital networks may become general-purpose carriers of bit streams. In theory, any type of digital network can carry any and all types of information in digital format, such as voice, video, or computer data, thus banishing the tradition of video being carried on special-purpose cable TV networks and telephone service being carried only over phone company networks. All forms of information are simply reduced to bit streams.

The Service-Oriented Architecture

The separation of information services from bit-delivery services leads to the concept of a new service-oriented architecture as shown in Exhibit 1. The most striking aspect of this service-oriented architecture is that the control and management entity may be provided by a separate service organization or by a distributed set of cooperating entities from different service organizations. The architecture represents a move away from the current world of vertical integration toward one of horizontal integration.

Deregulation of communications also plays a part in this scenario. Deregulation often forces an unbundling of components and services, which creates a business environment ideally suited to a service-oriented architecture.

KEY ISSUES IN BUILDING THE SUPERHIGHWAY

Achieving a singular, seamless information highway is going to be a challenge, and whether users can influence development remains to be seen. Unless all interested parties act in harmony on the technical specifications (i.e., standards), market sharing, and partnering issues, the end user may be the biggest loser.

For provision of a given service (e.g., voice or data), it should not matter whether a user's access is through the telephone company, the cable company, or the satellite company. Similarly, it should not matter whether the remote party with whom a user wants to communicate has the same access method or a different one.

Several common elements exist in any end-to-end service. For example, there is a need for agreed-on access mechanisms, network platforms, addressing schemes, resolution of inter-provider requirements, and definition of universal services. The development of a generic framework would help to ensure that service requirements are developed equitably and to introduce innovative new services.

The User's Role

Users are becoming more technology literate. The use of technology in the home in recent years has increased. Many users already benefit from what can be achieved through the convergence and integration of user-friendly technologies. User perspectives, rather than those of a single industry or company, should be thoroughly considered in the development of infrastructure initiatives.

Government's Role

The private sector takes most of the risks and reaps most of the rewards for development of the information superhighway. However, government should assert some influence over the development of universally beneficial user services. The role of the government mainly involves:

- Encouraging industry to collaborate and develop universally beneficial user services.
- Mediating between competing industry factions.
- Solving problems involving cultural content, cross-border and customs issues, protection of the individual, obscene or illegal material, and intellectual property and copyrights.

Industry's Role

Three dominant technology areas — telecommunications, computers and related communications, and the entertainment industry — are converging. Although there has already been some sharing of technology among industries, a single integrated system has not been created.

For example, many existing or planned implementations of videophone service invariably involve a special-purpose terminal with its own display screen and camera. For a home or office already equipped with screens and loudspeakers for use with multimedia-capable computers, the need for yet another imaging system with speakers is a waste of technology.

Apart from the cost of duplication associated with the industry separations, there is the problem of the lack of flexibility. For example, if a VCR is connected to a regular TV, it should also be able to be used to record the videophone calls.

Plug-and-Play Integration. A plug-and-play solution may soon be possible in which the components are all part of an integrated system. In such a case, screens, speakers, recording devices, computers, and printers could be used in combination for a specific application. The components would be networked and addressed for the purposes of directing and exchanging information among them.

Similar considerations apply to computing components and security systems. Using the videophone example, if the remote videophone user puts a document in front of the camera, the receiving party should be able to capture the image and print it on the laser printer.

Plug-and-play integration is not simple; yet if the convergence is not addressed, the result will be disastrous for end users, who will be faced with a plethora of similar but incompatible equipment that still fails to satisfy their needs.

The Dream Integration Scenario

Exhibit 2 shows what the ideal configuration might look like when a high degree of convergence has been achieved. Ideally, there would be only one pipe into the customer's premises, over which all services — voice, video, and data — are delivered. User appliances can be used interchangeably. In this scenario, videophone calls could be received on the home theater or personal computer and recorded on the VCR.

The Nightmare Scenario

Exhibit 3 shows what user networks might look like if convergence is not achieved. Customer premises would include many pipes. Some services

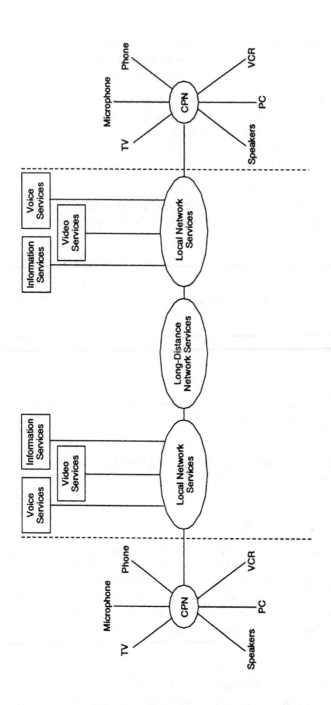

Exhibit 2. The Dream Integration Scenario

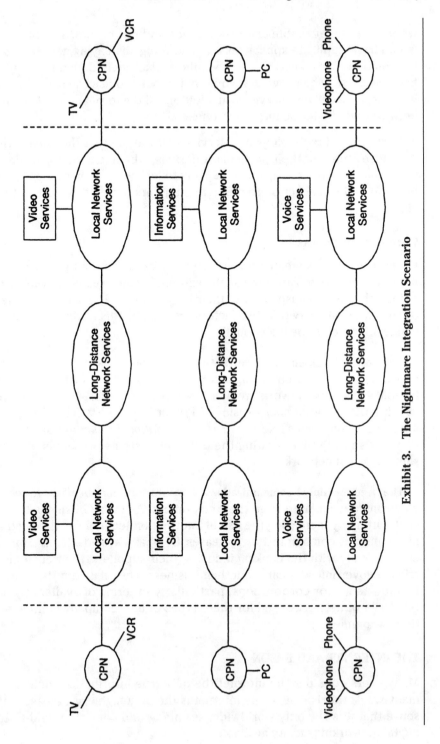

Exhibit 3. The Nightmare Integration Scenario

would only be available on certain pipes and not others. The premises would have duplicate appliances for generating, displaying, and recording information. End-to-end services would be extremely difficult to achieve because all service providers would not choose to use the same local or long-distance delivery services. In addition, all the local and long-distance networks would not be fully interconnected.

Purveyors of technology and services may argue that this means they can all sell more of their particular offerings, which is good for business. Users, on the other hand, are more likely to feel cheated, because they are being forced to subscribe to different suppliers for slightly different services.

Corporate Networks

Large corporations create networks that are based on their preferred supplier of technology. They are usually extremely conservative in their technology choices because many of their business operations depend totally on the corporate network. Two factors are causing this traditional, conservative approach to be questioned.

The Cost of Maintaining Private Networks. In many cases, several private networks operate within a single corporation, such as one for voice, one for IBM's Systems Network Architecture (SNA) network, and one for a private internet — or *intranet* — using TCP/IP or Novell's IPX. The change taking place is sometimes referred to as *consolidation*. Consolidation involves network sharing by operating the different systems protocols over the same physical network.

The Need for Global Communications. Corporations cannot afford to remain electronically isolated from their customers. As every business tackles cost cutting by increasing the use of information technology, the need for intercompany communication increases. Companies need to communicate electronically with the banking industry, their suppliers, their customers, and the government to carry out their business. The GII is going to increase in importance for corporations, particularly in terms of availability and reliability of networks used for these types of intercompany communication or commerce.

THE INTERNET AND B-ISDN

Many users consider the Internet the only true information highway. In many ways, this is true — the Internet is the only highway, at least in the sense that it is the only worldwide, seamless, and consistent end-to-end digital networking facility available.

In addition, the Internet has become a place where certain standardized applications can be used. It has a globally unique, centrally administered address space. The Internet provides national and international switched data services on a scale that would usually be associated with the major telecommunications carriers.

Not surprisingly, not everyone agrees that the Internet is the only highway. Technically, the Internet is a connectionless packet network overlaid on a variety of network technologies, such as leased lines, frame relay, asynchronous transfer mode (ATM), and LANs. However, it is difficult to imagine that at some point in the future, all voice and video traffic would be carried over such a network rather than directly over a broadband integrated services digital network (B-ISDN).

Thus, there may be a battle between the Internet and the traditional telecommunications carriers for control of the primary switching of data. The carriers may try to establish broadband ISDN as the primary method of switching data end to end, using telephone company-oriented number/addressing plans such as E.164. The Internet community is interested in the use of broadband ISDN, primarily as a replacement for leased lines between Internet switching nodes (i.e., routers) where the real switching occurs.

The deployment of broadband ISDN within the Internet may result in the migration of routers to the edges of the Internet, eliminating the need for intermediate routers. In any event, the interaction between the traditional router-based Internet style of operation and the emerging broadband ISDN switched services will be closely watched by corporate users.

The anarchic nature of the Internet will also be put to the test by commercial users who will want better service guarantees and accountability for maintenance and recovery. Despite these known deficiencies, the Internet remains the predominant information highway, and it is difficult to imagine that it will lose its dominance in the near future.

TELECOMMUNICATIONS AND CABLE TV

Deregulation in many countries now permits cable TV companies to offer services traditionally offered by the telephone companies. One of the scenarios under consideration in many countries is shown in Exhibit 4.

The cable companies are just beginning to form plans on how new two-way services should be offered. Access to the telephone company network would also provide access to other services, such as the Internet.

A major issue is the kind of interface to be provided on the cable network for associated telephone apparatus. It is not clear whether a traditional phone could simply be plugged into the cable system. Other issues, such as numbering and access to 800 service, need to be resolved.

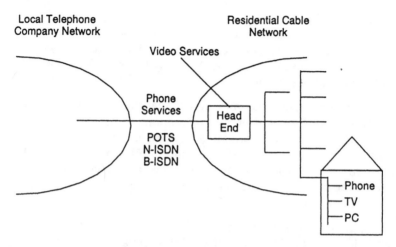

Exhibit 4. **Telephone Company and Cable TV Network Interconnection**

Whether traditional modem, telephony, or ISDN interfaces could be used or whether new cable-specific interfaces would be developed is also under consideration. Both solutions could coexist through provision of appropriate conversion units.

Cable systems usually consist of a headend with a one-way subtending tree and branch structure. Whether the headend would provide local switching within the residential area has not been determined. Other topologies, such as rings, may be more appropriate for new services.

Conversely, deregulation also permits the telephone companies to offer services previously offered by the cable companies. In such a case, a video server would be accessed by the telephone company network, probably using broadband ISDN and ATM technology, as shown in Exhibit 5.

COMPUTER-INTEGRATED TELEPHONY

Computing and telecommunications are coming together in several ways. Computers can now be attached to telecommunications lines to become sophisticated answering machines, autodialers, and fax machines. The availability of calling and called-line identification permits data bases to be associated with telephone calls. For example, the calling line identification can be used to automatically extract the appropriate customer record from a data base so that when the call is answered the appropriate customer information becomes available on a screen.

Computer-integrated telephony allows a variety of telephone service features to be controlled by the customer's computers. Intelligent network

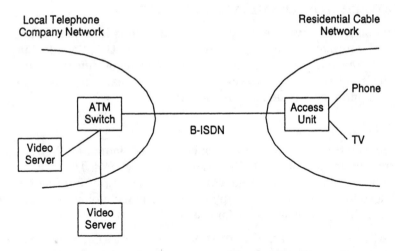

Exhibit 5.   Telephone Company-Provided Video Services

architectures that facilitate the separation of management and control are ideally suited to external computer control.

Public switched data networks have not been very efficient because of the costs of building separate networks and because the scale and demand for data proved nothing like that for voice services. A single digital network such as narrowband ISDN (N-ISDN) or broadband ISDN changes the picture significantly when coupled with the new demand for digital services.

COMPUTING AND ENTERTAINMENT

Most personal computers on the market have audiovisual capabilities. Movies and audio clips can be combined with text for a variety of multimedia applications. Video or images can be edited as easily as text.

With the advent of high-definition TV and digital encoding of TV signals, it is easy to imagine a system in which the traditional TV screen and the PC monitor would be interchangeable. Computers are already being used to produce movies and as a playback medium, even providing the possibility of real-time interaction with the users.

Integrating all the appliances into a single architecture is the difficult part. Home theater systems provide simple forms of switching between components — for example, video to TV or VCR, or audio from TV to remote speakers. Soon, no doubt, the personal computer will be part of this system.

NATIONAL AND INTERNATIONAL INITIATIVES

Many countries have prepared recommendations for their respective national information infrastructures, including the U.S., Canada, Europe, Japan, Korea, and Australia, among others. The major differences in each country's initiatives seem to revolve around to what extent government will fund and regulate the information infrastructure.

The U.S.

The Information Infrastructure Task Force (IITF) launched the National Information Infrastructure (NII) initiative in early 1993. The IITF is composed of an advisory council and committees on security, information policy, telecommunications policy, applications, and technology. Government funding is being made available for the development of NII applications.

The IITF's goal is that the information infrastructure become a seamless web of communications networks, computers, data bases, and consumer electronics. The NII initiative is also closely associated with the passage of a new telecommunications act, which outlines principles for the involvement of the government in the communications industry. According to the Telecommunications Act of 1996, the government should:

- Promote private sector investment.
- Extend the universal service concept to ensure that information resources are available at affordable prices.
- Promote technological innovation and new applications.
- Promote seamless, interactive, user-driven operation.
- Ensure information security and reliability.
- Improve management of the radio frequency spectrum.
- Protect intellectual property rights.
- Coordinate with other levels of government and with other nations.
- Provide access to government information and improve government procurement.

International Initiatives

The G7 countries (Britain, Canada, France, Germany, Italy, Japan, and the U.S.) are considering developing an information infrastructure that would offer, among others, the following services:

- Global inventory.
- Global interoperability for broadband networks.
- Cross-cultural education and training.
- Electronic museums and galleries.
- Environment and natural resources management.
- Global emergency management.
- Global health care applications.

- Government services on-line.
- Maritime information systems.

STANDARDS AND STANDARDS ORGANIZATIONS

It is difficult to imagine how objectives such as universal access, universal service, and global interoperability can be achieved without an agreed-on set of standards. However, some sectors of industry prefer that fewer standards are established because this gives them the opportunity to capture a share of the market with proprietary solutions. Regardless, several national and international standards development organizations (SDOs) throughout the world are initiating activities related to the information infrastructure.

ISO and ITU

Both the International Standards Organization (ISO) and the International Telecommunications Union (ITU — formerly the CCITT) are embarking on information infrastructure standards initiatives. The ISO and ITU have planned a joint workshop to address standards issues.

American National Standards Institute Information Infrastructure Standards Panel (ANSI IISP)

The ANSI IISP goals are to identify the requirements for standardization of critical interfaces (i.e., connection points) and other attributes and compare them to national and international standards already in place. Where standards gaps exist, standards development organizations will be asked to develop new standards or update existing standards as required.

ANSI IISP is developing a data base to make standards information publicly available. The process of identification and the structure of the IISP is illustrated in Exhibit 6. In its deliberations, the ANSI IISP has been reluctant to identify specific networking architectures or interconnection arrangements and appears to be confining its efforts to a cataloging process.

Telecommunications Standards Advisory Council of Canada (TSACC)

The TSACC is an umbrella organization for all the standards organizations in Canada. It is a forum where all parties can meet to discuss strategic issues.

The objectives of TSACC, in respect to the Canadian Information Infrastructure and the GII, are similar to those of the ANSI IISP. However, TSACC considers the identification of specific networking architectures and associated specific access and interconnection points essential to achieving the goals of universal access, universal service, and interoperability.

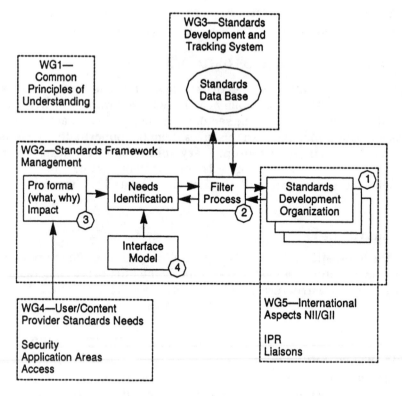

Exhibit 6.   ANSI IISP Structure and Process

European Telecommunications Standards Institute (ETSI)

The Sixth Review Committee (SRC6) of ETSI published a report on the European Information Infrastructure (EII) that emphasizes the standardization of the EII. Many of the recommendations in the report concern the development of reference models for defining the particular services and identifying important standards-based interface points. Broadband ISDN is recommended as the core technology for the EII.

The Digital Audio Visual Interface Council (DAVIC)

DAVIC was established in Switzerland to promote emerging digital audiovisual applications and services for broadcast and interactive use. DAVIC, which has a very pro-consumer slant, believes that these services will only be affordable through sufficient standardization. DAVIC may be the only forum in which home convergence issues can be solved. The council has formed technical committees in the following five areas:

- Set-top units.
- Video servers.
- Networks.
- Systems and applications.
- General technology.

ALTERNATIVE INITIATIVES

Two interesting U.S.-based information infrastructure initiatives are also worth mentioning.

EIA/TIA

The Electronic Industries Association (EIA) and its affiliate Telecommunications Industry Association (TIA) have just released version 2 of their white paper titled "Global Information Infrastructure: Principles and Promise." The basic principles conclude that:

- The private sector must play the lead role in development.
- Enlightened regulation is essential.
- The role of global standards is critical.
- Universal service and access must support competitive, market-driven solutions.
- Security and privacy are essential.
- Intellectual property rights must support new technologies.

The Computer Systems Policy Project (CSPP)

The CSPP is not a standards organization but an affiliation of the chief executive officers of several American computer companies. The CSPP has published a document titled "Perspectives on the National Information Infrastructure: Ensuring Interoperability." The CSPP document identifies the following four key points-of-presence as candidates for standardization:

- The interface between an information appliance and a network service provider.
- The applications programming interface between an information appliance and emerging NII applications.
- The protocols that one NII application, service, or system uses to communicate with another application, service, or system.
- The interfaces among and between network service providers.

SUMMARY

The technical challenges of creating a Global Information Infrastructure are not insurmountable. The main difficulties arise from industries competing for the same business rather than sharing an expanding business, and from the lack of agreement on necessary open standards to achieve universal access and global interoperability that would expand the total business.

Interoperability requires agreed-on network architectures and the associated standards that could, in some cases, stifle innovation. A balance must also be struck between government regulation and private sector control over GII development. However, if each camp can cooperate, it is possible that in the future the communications, information, and entertainment industries could merge technology to provide plug-and-play components integrated into a single, coherent system that offers exciting new services that exist now in only the wildest imaginations.

Section II
Voice Communications over Multimedia Networks

Our initial exploration of the details of multimedia networking will concentrate on the three general applications for remote communications: voice, video, and data transmission. This section will concentrate primarily on voice communications.

Voice and video are related, despite their bandwidth differences, in the need for on-time delivery of the communication content. Unlike routine data transmission, which can tolerate wide delivery delays and unpredictability, voice and video must have a guaranteed delivery schedule. The adjacent packets of information have an inherent time value which must be preserved to be satisfactorily reconstructed at the destination.

In a word, these time-sensitive applications are bandwidth happy. To preserve their precious temporal requirements, we could simply provide unlimited bandwidth. In fact, this is exactly how the original voice-over-the-network applications were handled. A typical 10M-bps LAN may operate at 5 to 10% of its theoretical maximum operating throughput. A small number of voice transmissions, properly packetized, over such a network will have negligible impact. However, if we expand that number of simultaneous conversations, and throw in an occasional large data file transmission, the voice transmission will start to fail. Failure of a voice transmission is actually a time slippage, as it matters more that the digitized voice got to the distant end at the right time than that it simply arrived unadulterated.

On comparatively large-bandwidth transport media such as the LAN, small numbers of voice connections can be accommodated by excess bandwidth. However, distant transmission of voice is another matter. The available bandwidth on a typical frame relay or Internet connection is far less than on the LAN. In the past, large users with multicity locations bought a moderate bandwidth "pipe" between the locations and used channelized T1/FT1 multiplexing to provide both data and voice transmissions. However, this method is not practical for more economical low-bandwidth point-to-point connections, such as 56K-bps dedicated circuits, and it is very wasteful of bandwidth, as channels often lie unused. It is also not practical for businesses that must communicate with a multiplicity of locations. These applications are better served by frame relay or virtual private networking (VPN) over the Internet, both of which are stochastic transport technologies. However, neither of these methods natively offers time guarantees, and voice adapters must provide a range of accommodation to the packets during the reconversion to analog voice.

To be truly efficient and meet the delivery constraints, then, voice-over-data systems must provide some sort of "quality of service" (QOS) method. In cases where the intermittent delays are minimal, an ersatz QOS can be provided by delay compensation and packet ordering in the end devices. True QOS methods over data networks involve complicated methods such as IP's RSVP or ATM's constant bit rate (CBR) circuits. Many of these transport issues are covered in this and later sections.

In this section, we will cover voice-centric aspects of transport over the local area, the wide area, and a special case of both, the Internet. In some instances, we must necessarily broaden our focus to include the common aspects of video transmission to our subject of voice communication. We will begin with an excellent introduction to the implications of placing both voice and video on the LAN. This is followed by a discussion of Internet and frame relay voice applications. Finally, a technical discussion of voice compression methods and silence idle-time utilization is presented.

Chapter 4
Voice and Video on the LAN

Martin Taylor

Voice and data convergence in the LAN is about to become a hot topic in the industry, thanks to advances in switching and processors, as well as the H.323 standard. This chapter first looks at the business reasons for considering the deployment of voice and video over the LAN and then discusses the technical issues and requirements. Topics include the value of voice and video on the LAN, infrastructure efficiencies, LAN technologies for integrated voice and video, and standards for LAN-based voice and video applications

Most desktops in enterprises today are equipped with two network connections: a LAN connection to the PC or work station for data communications and a phone connection to the PBX for voice communications. The LAN and the PBX exist as two separate networks with little or no connectivity between them. Each has evolved to meet the very specific and differing needs of data and voice communications, respectively.

Despite much talk in the industry about the convergence of computers and communications, LANs and PBXs have not really moved any closer together during the last decade. In the mid-1980s, some PBX vendors sought to bring data services to the desktop via ISDN technology, but the advent of PCs requiring far more than 64K-bps communications bandwidth favored the emerging LAN standards of Ethernet and Token Ring. So far, most LAN vendors have not attempted to support voice communications on the LAN. But all this is about to change.

There are three key factors at work today that suggest that voice and data convergence in the LAN is about to become a hot topic in the industry:

- The widespread acceptance of advanced LAN switching technologies, including ATM, which makes it possible for the first time to deliver reliable, high-quality, low-delay voice transmissions over the LAN.

- The emergence of the first standard for LAN-based videoconferencing and voice telephony, H.323, which removes objections about the use of proprietary protocols for voice and video over the LAN.
- The deployment of the latest generation of Intel processors, featuring MMX technology, which makes high-quality software-based real-time voice and video processing feasible for the first time, and the new PC hardware architectures with Universal Serial Bus that permit voice and video peripherals to be attached without additional hardware inside the PC.

This chapter first looks at the business reasons for considering the deployment of voice and video over the LAN and then discusses the technical issues and requirements.

THE VALUE OF VOICE AND VIDEO ON THE LAN

There are essentially two main kinds of motivation for considering voice and/or video on the LAN: the need to support new types of applications that involve real-time communications and the desire to improve the overall cost effectiveness of the local communications infrastructure.

New Types of Applications

Desktop videoconferencing, real-time multimedia collaboration, and video-based training are all examples of new kinds of applications that can benefit from the delivery of voice and video over the LAN.

The uptake of desktop videoconferencing has been held back by a combination of high costs and the difficulty of delivering appropriate network services to the desktop. Standards-based H.320 desktop videoconferencing systems require costly video compression and ISDN interface hardware, as well as the provision of new ISDN connections at the desktop alongside the LAN and the phone system. New systems based on the H.323 standard and designed to run over the LAN will leverage the processing power of the latest PCs and the existing switched LAN infrastructure, to lower cost and simplify deployment dramatically.

Desktop videoconferencing may be used either to support internal meetings and discussions between groups located at remote sites or to support direct interaction with customers and clients. For example, some enterprises in the mortgage lending business use videoconferencing to conduct mortgage approval interviews with potential borrowers, so as to greatly reduce the overall time to complete a mortgage sale.

Real-time collaboration applications, involving any mix of video and voice with data conferencing to support application sharing and interactive whiteboarding, provide a new way for individuals and small groups to collaborate and work together remotely in real time. This emerging class of applications, typified by Microsoft NetMeeting, is being evaluated by many enterprises, particularly for help desk applications.

By contrast, video-based training is already widely used in enterprise LANs. By delivering self-paced video learning materials to the desktop, training needs can be met in a more timely and less disruptive fashion than traditional classroom methods.

The growing popularity of these kinds of applications should be noted by network planners and designers. A preplanned strategy for local LAN upgrades to support voice and video will reduce the lead time for the deployment of these applications and enable the enterprise to move swiftly when the application need has been identified, to obtain the business benefits with the least possible delay.

Infrastructure Efficiencies

A single local communications infrastructure based on a LAN that handles data, voice, and video has the potential to cost less to own and operate than separate PBX and data-only LAN infrastructures.

The average capital cost of a fully featured PBX for large enterprises is between $700 and $750 per user, according to TEQConsult Group, a leading U.S. telecommunications consultancy. Furthermore, this is expected to rise slightly over the next few years as users demand more sophisticated features from their phone systems. It is not difficult to see how a switched LAN that has been enhanced to handle voice could provide a solution for telephony at a fraction of this cost.

Most large PBX installations are equipped with additional facilities such as voice mail and Interactive Voice Response systems for auto-attendant operation. These systems are typically connected directly to the PBX via proprietary interfaces, and they, too, represent major capital investments. With voice on the LAN, such voice-processing applications could be based on open server platforms and leverage the low-cost processing power and disk storage that is a feature of today's PC server market, thereby lowering the system's capital cost still further.

Separate PBX and LAN infrastructures each incur their own management and operational costs. For example, moves, adds, and changes require separate actions to patch physical LAN and voice connections and to update LAN log-on and voice directories. With telephony provided over a voice-enabled LAN supporting combined directory services, the management effort required to administer moves and changes would be substantially reduced.

These cost of ownership benefits come with a raft of usability improvements for telephony. The PC (with phone handset attached) becomes the communications terminal for making and receiving phone calls, and the processing power and graphical user interface of the PC can be leveraged to provide point-and-click call launch and manipulation. Features of PBXs such as call transfer, divert, and hold, which are hard to invoke from a phone keypad, become very easy to use from a Windows interface.

Incoming callers can be identified on the PC display by matching Calling Line Identifier with directory entries. And with voice mail and e-mail supported on a unified messaging platform such as Microsoft Exchange or Lotus Notes, all messages are accessible and manageable via a single user interface.

These usability benefits for voice telephony over the LAN also extend to videoconferencing — a single consistent user interface may be applied to both video and voice-only calls.

LAN TECHNOLOGIES FOR INTEGRATED VOICE AND VIDEO

The LAN technologies in widespread use today — Ethernet, Fast Ethernet, FDDI, and Token Ring — were not designed with the needs of real-time voice and video in mind. These LAN technologies provide "best effort" delivery of data packets, but offer no guarantees about how long delivery will take. Interactive real-time voice and video communications over the LAN require the delivery of a steady stream of packets with very low end-to-end delay, and this cannot generally be achieved with the current LAN technologies as they stand.

Asynchronous Transfer Mode (ATM)

At one time, there was a belief that ATM networking to the desktop would be embraced by LAN users to solve this problem. ATM is a networking technology that was designed specifically to handle a combination of the low-delay steady-stream characteristics of voice and video and the bursty, intermittent characteristics of data communications.

The ATM Forum, the industry body responsible for publishing ATM specifications, has developed a number of standards that enable desktops connected directly to ATM networks to support existing LAN data applications as well as voice telephony and videoconferencing. The ATM Forum standards for the support of voice and video over ATM to the desktop typically avoid the use of traditional LAN protocols such as IP, and instead place the voice or video streams directly over the ATM protocols.

While it is clear that ATM to the desktop provides an elegant and effective solution for combining voice, video, and data over the LAN, this approach does imply a "forklift" to the LAN infrastructure and the end station connection. The cost and disruptive impact of such an upgrade tend to limit its appeal, and as a result desktop ATM is not expected to be widely adopted.

However, the ability of ATM to provide "quality of service" — that is, to deliver real-time voice or video streams with a guaranteed upper bound on delay — makes it an excellent choice for the LAN backbone where voice and video over the LAN is needed.

Shared and Switched LANs

It is generally accepted that shared LANs are unsuitable for handling real-time voice and video because of the widely varying delays that are seen when multiple stations are contending for access to the transmission medium. The CSMA/CD access method used in shared Ethernet is particularly poor in this respect. Token Ring, on the other hand, is based on a token-passing access method with multiple levels of priority. Stations waiting to send data packets can be preempted by other stations on the ring with higher priority voice or video packets to send. As a result, Token Ring has excellent potential to handle real-time voice and video traffic, though this potential has yet to be realized in currently available networking products.

LAN switching does much to overcome the limitations of shared LANs, although today's products are still a long way from providing an answer for voice and video over the LAN. It is now cost effective to provide users with dedicated 10M-bps Ethernet connections to the desktop and 100M-bps Fast Ethernet uplinks from the wiring closet to the backbone.

However, despite the vast increase in bandwidth provision per user that this represents over and above a shared LAN scenario, there is still contention in the network leading to unacceptable delay characteristics. For example, multiple users connected to the switch may demand file transfers from several servers connected via 100M-bps Fast Ethernet to the backbone. Each server may send a burst of packets that temporarily overwhelms the Fast Ethernet uplink to the wiring closet. A queue will form in the backbone switch that is driving this link, and any voice or video packets being sent to the same wiring closet will have to wait their turn behind the data packets in this queue. The resultant delays will compromise the perceived quality of the voice or video transmission.

The only way to overcome this problem is to find a way of treating real-time voice and video packets differently from data packets in the network and to give them preferential treatment when transient data overloads cause queues to form on busy network links. In practice, this means that

LAN packets must be tagged with some kind of priority information that enables switches to identify which packets need to jump the queue

The IEEE 802, which oversees standards for LAN technologies, has initiated a project identified as 802.1p, which is concerned with "Traffic Class Expediting" in LAN switches.

The principal problem faced by 802.1p is that there is no spare information field in the standard Ethernet packet format that could carry the required priority tag. As a result, it has been necessary to propose a new Ethernet packet format with an additional 4 bytes of information in the packet header that can contain a 3-bit priority tag field (offering eight levels of priority), together with some other information concerned with virtual LANs.

With the new Ethernet packet format containing a priority tag, end station applications can identify real-time voice or video packets by assigning them a high-priority value in the tag. LAN switches that have been enhanced to process the priority tags can separate high- and low-priority traffic in the switching fabric and place them in separate queues at outgoing switch ports. The LAN switches need to implement a queue scheduling algorithm that gives preference to the higher priority queues on outgoing ports, and by this means it is hoped that real-time voice and video can be carried over the LAN without incurring unacceptable delays during periods of heavy data traffic.

As of July 1997, the 802.1p standard was still in draft form and the standard is not expected to be completed until 1998. Ethernet switches that support the 802.1p priority tags with multiple internal queuing structures will require a new generation of switching silicon, and the earliest we could expect to see products that conform to the standard would be late 1998 or into 1999. Surprisingly, we may see Token Ring switches that handle multiple priority levels before that time, leveraging the capabilities of the existing Token Ring standard that supports eight levels of priority.

Hybrid ATM Networks

The discussion of ATM described how it offers guaranteed quality of service for real-time voice and video streams. Today, ATM is increasingly used as a LAN backbone for pure data applications, because it offers greater scalability and fault tolerance than other LAN technologies. Ethernet and Token Ring LANs are connected to ATM via "edge switches" equipped with ATM uplinks, typically supporting the ATM Forum standard for carrying LAN traffic over ATM, know as LAN emulation.

It is possible to enhance ATM edge switches to enable desktops connected via Ethernet or Token Ring to enjoy the benefits of ATM quality of service across the LAN backbone. Two techniques have been proposed to achieve this.

The first technique, known as "Cell-in-Frame," extends the native ATM signaling protocols over dedicated Ethernet connections from the edge switch to the end station. The voice or video application in the end station places the voice or video stream in ATM cells using the ATM Forum standards for native ATM transport, and then encapsulates the ATM cells in Ethernet packets for transport to the edge switch for onward transmission onto the ATM network. Effectively, this is ATM to the desktop, but using physical Ethernet with standard Ethernet adapter cards as a kind of physical transport layer for ATM traffic.

The second technique makes use of an emerging standard protocol for end stations to request quality of service for IP-based voice or video applications, known as the Resource Reservation Protocol, or RSVP. The enhanced edge switch intercepts RSVP requests originated by end stations and converts them into ATM signaling to request the setup of connections across the ATM backbone with the appropriate quality of service. The edge switch then distinguishes between IP packets containing data and those containing voice or video, using the information provided by RSVP, and steers voice and video packets onto ATM connections that have quality of service.

At the time of writing, the technique described here for RSVP-to-ATM mapping enjoys somewhat broader industry support than cell-in-frame, perhaps because of its relationship with Internet technology.

Until LAN switches supporting 802.1p priority tagging have proved themselves capable of meeting the very stringent end-to-end delay requirements for real-time voice and video communications, hybrid approaches based on ATM in the backbone and switched Ethernet or Token Ring to the desktop are likely to find acceptance as the solution of choice for voice and video over the LAN.

Standards for LAN-Based Voice and Video Applications

Standards for voice and video over the LAN fall into two categories: those designed for native ATM protocols and those intended for general-purpose LAN protocols, particularly IP.

Standards for native ATM protocols, such as the ATM Forum's Voice Telephony over ATM (VTOA), are appropriate only for ATM-connected desktops or desktops running Cell-in-Frame over Ethernet.

Standards for applications that run over IP are applicable both to ATM-connected desktops as well as desktops in general Ethernet or Token Ring environments. The most important standard in this space is H.323, which was developed by the International Telecommunications Union. While H.323 is designed to be independent of the underlying networking protocol, it will most often be deployed running over IP.

H.323 references other existing standards for the digital encoding and compression of voice and video signals and describes how audio and video streams are carried in the payload of IP packets with the aid of the Real Time Protocol (RTP), which provides timing and synchronization information. H.323 also covers the handling of data streams for application sharing, shared whiteboarding, and real-time file transfer (referencing the T.120 standard) and includes signaling based on ISDN messaging protocols for call setup and teardown.

The H.323 standard is flexible and accommodates any combination of real-time voice, video, and data as part of a single point-to-point or multipoint conference call. It may be used with a voice stream alone as the basis of a LAN telephony solution. H.323 enjoys the broadest support in the industry as a proposed standard for Internet telephony.

Additional Components: Gateways and Gatekeepers

Creating a LAN infrastructure that can consistently deliver voice and video streams with sufficiently low delay is an absolute prerequisite for integrating voice and video on the LAN, but it is by no means the complete answer to the problem. There are two other key components of a complete voice and video solution, which in H.323 parlance are known as the gateway and the gatekeeper.

An H.323 gateway provides interconnection between voice and video services on the LAN and external voice and video services typically provided over circuit-switched networks such as ISDN and the public telephone network. The gateway terminates the IP and RTP protocols carrying the voice and video streams and converts them to appropriate formats for external networks. For videoconferencing, the conversion is most likely to be to H.320, another ITU standard that specifies how voice and video are carried over ISDN connections. For voice-only connections, the conversion will be to the G.711 standard for digital telephony. This allows voice interworking with any phone on a public network or connected to a PBX.

An H.323 gatekeeper is a pure software function that provides central call control services. While it is possible to run H.323 voice and video communications over the LAN without a gatekeeper, in practice this function is extremely useful. At the most basic level, the gatekeeper provides directory services and policy-based controls applied to the use of voice and video communications. For example, the gatekeeper can bar stations from accessing certain types of external phone numbers at certain times of day.

The gatekeeper can be thought of as the "server" in a client/server model of LAN-based telephony and videoconferencing.

At a more sophisticated level, the gatekeeper may be able to support supplementary services, including call transfer, hold and divert, hunt groups, pickup groups, attendant operation and so on — features that are typically found in high-end PBXs for controlling and managing voice calls. While the H.323 standard does not explicitly describe how supplementary call control features may be supported, the standard does provide a framework for the addition of these advanced capabilities.

CONCLUSION

This chapter has explained the value of voice and video integration on the LAN in terms of both application-driven needs and the desire for infrastructure efficiencies. It has looked at the technology issues surrounding the transport of real-time voice and video streams over LAN infrastructures and concluded that ATM backbones provide a solution in the near term, with the possibility of a later solution based entirely on switched Ethernet or Token Ring.

Finally, the chapter has described some additional functional elements, such as gateways and gatekeepers, that are an essential part of a complete solution for voice and video over the LAN. Over the last decade, the open standards-based environment typified by PCs and LANs has revolutionized the way data is handled and processed in enterprise environments. Now this open and standards-based approach is set to tackle the challenge of voice and video, formerly the exclusive domain of the PBX. The history of LAN evolution is set to repeat itself, and we can expect the traditional proprietary mainframe PBX to diminish in importance to the enterprise, giving way to client/server telephony and videoconferencing, just as the mainframe computer has been pushed into the background by client/server techniques for data processing.

Chapter 5
Internet Voice Applications

FRANK J. BOURNE

Of the more intriguing technologies to be hurled into the networking universe from the Internet "big bang" phenomenon, Internet telephony and audio transport seem to be garnering the lion's share of consumer attention.

Home and business users are eagerly delving into a dream world filled with unlimited free long-distance telephone calls, teleconferencing, and real-time audio Web applications. While direct experience with these fledgling applications often pales when compared with the promise, adventurous users are nonetheless happily exploring creative ways to apply new technologies to everyday problems.

A BRIEF HISTORY OF VOICE COMMUNICATIONS

Communications via telegraph, radio, telephone, and cellular technology each struggled through an early period of disbelief, limited acceptance, and technical hurdles. Each communication medium also had the potential to provide substantive solutions to real needs. Commercial acceptance and widespread deployment came only with the creative and effective application of these technologies.

For the moment, available Internet telephony packages have captured the curiosity and excitement of consumers in the same manner citizens band (CB) radio entranced the American public in the 1970s. CB was a convenience technology that lured users by the millions with the promise of free and easy communication with friends, family, and business associates. Demand grew so dramatically that the Federal Communications Commission (FCC) was forced to open the citizens band spectrum from 23 to 40 channels.

While CB is still active as a commercial and emergency communications tool, the vast majority of radios built now lie dormant in closets, garages, radio repair shop parts bins, and landfills. What happened?

How Unpredictable Service Can Doom a Good Idea

Congestion happened, among other things. For many once-impassioned CB cowboys, cowgirls, and rangers, the thrill of the fad wore off quickly with the realities of use. The excitement of anonymous pranksterism was dulled when users became equally susceptible to the same.

Security was nonexistent. Solar noise often relegated useful medium- and long-range communications to late-night hours. Hackers with illegal 100-watt linear amplifiers would dominate the channels with the best propagation and flame anyone who dared to talk. The inconveniences of terrain, keeping antennae properly tuned, and coordinating important calls were also discouraging to many once enthusiastic CD users.

Worse, there simply was too much demand for limited bandwidth. The sheer number of simultaneous users on a given channel produced background noise levels that were difficult or impossible to communicate over, even using the best equipment at short range.

The unregulated load placed on the spectrum resulted, effectively, in lost or errored information that made the medium nearly unusable. Without quality of service guarantees, commercial implementation was limited to the very few whose needs were well-suited by this unpredictable service.

STATE OF INTERNET TELEPHONY TODAY

The Evolution

Internet telephony is evolving through a period of CB radio-like application. Wander into one of the Internet Relay Chat (IRC)-based voice call servers and you will find hundreds of users chatting about a wide variety of interests.

Some users coordinate off-line to meet in private conversations in lieu of a standard telephone call. Many congregate in multiuser chat sessions on numerous topics of common interest — a natural evolution of the IRC relay chat channels. A few, cutting their teeth on limited demo versions of software, place calls randomly into any open channel in search of a modern "radio check."

Current Audio Products and Applications

But these applications represent old technology now. In fact, updated, improved versions of Internet audio and telephony software surface almost daily.

The energy in this industry manifests itself with an intense competitive urgency. New players and products are introduced and fade, accepted, rejected, or absorbed. The dominant vendors seek to outpace each other and grab market share. Alliances are struck, technologies acquired, and Web page press releases trumpet feature lists that would make a PBX salesperson envious. This industry is vibrant, alive, and here to stay — but in what form?

There are three basic audio product types approaching maturity on the Internet:

- *Audio broadcast.* Products in this category provide real-time, one-way transmission of press conferences, announcements, or entertainment such as music and talk radio.
- *Group conferencing.*These products enable multiuser voice conferencing.
- *Telephony.* Such products enable person-to-person telephony via a personal computer or workstation, conference calling, and voice mail. Some products provide whiteboarding capabilities, permit multiple simultaneous calls, and support collaborative computing.

THE WORKINGS OF INTERNET VOICE TECHNOLOGIES

Internet audio and telephony applications employ efficient software-driven codecs on a personal computer or workstation to digitize and packetize voice information for transport via internetwork protocols such as SLIP, PPP, TOP, or UDP. These applications use the computer's multimedia hardware for input/output devices (e.g., microphones and speakers) and analog-digital conversion.

Delay. Delay-handling mechanisms are implemented in most commercially available packages, since voice communications are particularly intolerant of delay and delay variation. While not as disconcerting as propagation delay over satellite, significant but tolerable delay is noticeable in these applications at most connection speeds. Delay is only significant in two-way communications.

Delay is accounted for by buffering a certain amount of voice information in order to compensate for variations in network transit time between callers. While this actually adds slightly to the overall delay perceived by the user, it is a necessary acknowledgment of the random, unpredictable delay present in today's Internet.

One-Way Audio Broadcasts. Broadcast applications enable entities such as radio stations, news services, or corporations to transmit one-way audio to a potentially unlimited number of users. A centralized server digitizes the audio and either transmits it in real time to Internet-attached users, or stores the compressed audio on the server.

If users are unable to attend the broadcast, they may later access a compressed audio file on the server. Users are not required to download the file to their local workstation in order to listen; the file may be played out in real time by the server, avoiding a long, unproductive wait.

Several Internet-only "radio stations" have already sprung into existence, offering an eclectic variety of music, talk, and commentary programming. One intriguing advantage of Internet-based audio programming is the ability to archive shows for access when the user finds it convenient to listen. If a favorite show or episode is missed at broadcast time, it may be accessed remotely at a later time or even downloaded to the user's local disk drive for repeated listening.

Two-Way Conferences. Two-way conferencing applications are very popular among noncommercial users. A modified chat-server implementation is used to connect multiple users. Half-duplex communication is the norm, but some available applications allow limited whiteboard and collaborative computing capabilities.

Connection Speeds and Sampling Rates. Voice quality is directly affected by connection speed and the quality of the codec design. While some of the available codecs are capable of sampling rates above 35 KHz, only a minority of users currently have Internet access speeds that top 14,400 bps. All available software specifies a minimum connection rate of 14,400 bps, which provides usable but grainy voice quality.

With the better codec implementations, voice quality approaches then surpasses that of toll-quality conventional public telephony because higher connection speeds allow greater sampling rates. This is an exciting promise when contrasted with the fixed 300 Hz to 3,000 Hz bandpass and 8 KHz sampling rate used in conventional telephony.

Software Enhancements. Because Internet telephony applications are software-based, creative enhancements to the virtual telephone set are possible. These enhancements come in the form of integration of familiar tools, such as autodialing, address lists, directory services, caller ID, notepads, and voice mail. More sophisticated users may opt for concurrent support of whiteboarding and other image transfer and collaborative computing. The potential for integration with other software applications also warrants consideration.

USAGE ISSUES AND IMPEDIMENTS

Several success factors have been achieved as Internet voice applications have matured. Codec design, voice quality potential, and usability have been well-received if shelf sales and trial downloads are any indication of market interest.

The response of power users and techno-junkies does not, however, necessarily indicate a broad, long-term acceptance of these technologies. For Internet voice products to continue to thrive, several obstacles have yet to be overcome.

Support for Full-Duplex Operation. Only a small portion of existing sound cards support full-duplex operation, limiting even full-duplex-enabled telephony software to half-duplex capability. Given the rapid growth in home computer sales, and the dearth of installed multimedia hardware in existing business computers, this should not be a long-term concern.

Likewise, 28.8K bps modems are rapidly becoming the norm, and high-speed cable access technology trials promise greater availability of usable multimedia bandwidth over the next two to three years. (What user wants to abandon a multiuser role-playing Net game or telecommuting session to take an Internet phone call?)

Interoperability Standards. Of greater concern is the general lack of standardization in codec and transport implementations. Few Internet voice implementations interoperate, requiring callers to use the same software to communicate.

Ease of use leaves much to be desired. Currently, both users must have an active Internet connection in order to place a call, which for many requires that a dial-up modem connection be made to the Internet before attempting to locate and connect a voice call to another user. One notable exception at this time is an Internet service provider (ISP) that proposes to allow a user to connect across the Internet through a server to a conventional telephone switch, from which users of traditional telephones may be dialed.

IP Addresses. Divining a user's Internet "telephone number" can also be challenging. All of the approaches currently available require significantly more coordination between users than conventional telephony.

Some products currently require users of a given application to use a private IRC-based server network. Some products allow "dialing" of a specific IP address, which gives more universal access to other users, should their client software be compatible with yours and they have a fixed address. Newer releases allow scanning a wide range of IP addresses for user IDs, which makes it possible to locate a specific called party, should they actually be on-line with their ISP at the time you wish to call.

An alternative approach to locating users with dynamically assigned public IP addresses employs an e-mail page to notify the called party that you wish to place a call to them.

Unpredictable Nature of the Internet. Perhaps the greatest limiting factor is the unpredictability of the Internet itself.

Traffic management is almost nonexistent, providing little or no quality of service guarantees to users. The vast majority of Internet voice applications are designed to manage delay and traffic loss only within strictly defined limits.

Internet provisioning practices do not account sufficiently for traffic loss, congestion, and delay. Current practices almost universally involve throwing more bandwidth and routers at the problem, which only provides temporary relief and does not ensure fairness among users. Retransmission of lost broadcast audio packets is somewhat acceptable within strict limits, but multisecond delays and large-scale discards render two-way voice communications unusable.

Multiplatform Support. Support for non-PC platforms is currently very limited, though it is only a matter of time before broader support of Macintosh and UNIX-based platforms is common.

Internet access capabilities are also being delivered in PBX platforms and PC-based telephony servers. While the PBX approaches are primarily aimed at 56K bps integrated services digital network (ISDN) Internet data access, it is only a small jump to providing Internet voice services on the same platform.

FUTURE DIRECTIONS

Technology Outlook

Rapid advances in hardware and software technology offer much hope for Internet telephony. Faster, more capable platforms will enable more sophisticated codec implementations, and improvements in peripherals such as sound cards, microphones, and modem speed will enhance voice quality. Multitasking and collaborative applications will benefit from increased platform capacity and connection speed as well.

Given sufficient processor power and connection bandwidth, sophisticated multimedia capabilities may be integrated with Internet telephony, bringing the capabilities of the corporate conferencing center to the desktop.

In addition to conversation, applications that employ images, video, whiteboarding, and console-sharing may be performed in real-time. Newer high-end home and business PCs approach these capacities today. Internet access speeds are increasing steadily and will achieve widespread availability in megabit increments within the next 10 years.

The growing acceptance of telecommuting will have a complementary impact upon the acceptance and deployment of Internet voice applications.

Success Factors

If Internet voice is to gain broad and permanent acceptance, it must offer value equivalent or superior to the existing public switched telephone network. Like the common telephone, interoperability must be universal and without question. Directory services, numbering, and billing must be effectively dealt with. Dialing must be effortless and intuitive, and feature sets must be standardized. While competitive pressures are understandably high, vendors and service providers must come to agreement on core standards and interoperability issues.

ALL-IMPORTANT INFRASTRUCTURE ISSUES

Quality of Service Is Everything

Commercial radio, the public switched telephone network, and cellular telephony have survived because commercial providers have taken the steps necessary to ensure that a minimum quality of service (QOS) can be guaranteed of their respective offerings.

Quality of service encompasses many factors that vary by the service offered. For voice communications, the most important factors are:

- *Reliability.* The service must be functioning at least 99.8% of the time. Users must have an extremely high degree of confidence that the network will function and provide the desired service every time it is used.
- *Performance.* The service must provide a minimum guaranteed level of performance that the user finds desirable and of value.
- *Predictability.* The service must provide consistent, predictable performance at or above a specified minimum level of quality.
- *Fairness.* The service must provide fair, equal access to network resources for all users.
- *Accessibility.* The service must be readily and easily available to a number of users sufficient to make the service of value to subscribers.

Each of these quality of service factors is affected by a number of infrastructure design issues that require analysis, planning, and monitoring by the service provider in order to ensure the long-term viability of the service.

Becoming as Reliable as the Telephone. During the years of federal regulation of the public telephone network, the telephone came to be considered an essential item of daily life for more than conversation. To be more than another household or business accessory, Internet telephony must at least come close to meeting the reliability of the conventional telephone.

Telephone networks have been designed and built for decades to have sufficient redundancy to function in all but the most catastrophic circumstances. Floods, earthquakes, tornadoes, hurricanes, and other natural disasters are examples of conditions that challenge even minimal network operation yet place a terrible urgency upon the provision of at least a marginal level of service. Telephone switch central offices operate on self-sustaining, battery-backed power systems for this reason.

Redundancy in power systems, switching hardware, cable capacity, and cable paths are all considered to be essential and critical baseline design criteria for any public telephone system. While federal deregulation has somewhat eased the metrics by which public telephone networks are built, a deeply ingrained cultural design ethic exists within the telephony community that preserves such conservative design practices.

Likewise, the public customer base has for generations grown up with an unquestioning dependence upon the reliability of the network. If the power goes out, one generally expects to be able to pick up the telephone and notify the power company. Day after day, customers depend on the telephone and think nothing of it, unless it fails to function.

Responsibilities of Service Providers. Despite federal deregulation, the telephone service industry remains heavily regulated. Service providers are required to contribute significantly to infrastructure development, to maintain minimum service levels, and to guarantee universal access to all users, including accommodation of special needs such as TDD terminals for the hearing-impaired or low-cost basic service to the infirm.

As of this writing, the rapid rise in Internet telephony has caused many public telephone service providers to protest to regulatory bodies. The perception is that if Internet telephony is to be given a free ride without contribution to infrastructure pools such as the Universal Service Fund, conventional service providers will be at a competitive disadvantage.

Notably absent from the protest are telephone service providers who were adventurous enough to also have well-established Internet service offerings. These regulatory issues are sure to be addressed as the Internet matures.

It seems unlikely that Internet telephony will completely supplant the existing telephone network for quite some time. Internet voice quality and service levels require dramatic improvement. To achieve this level of quality and service, massive investments made over decades by the public telephone service providers would need to be matched. Internet access devices and circuits must be simplified to an appliance level and match the reliability and survivability of the existing network.

Moreover, the core infrastructure of the Internet itself requires switching equipment and design practices that make efficient use of wide-area bandwidth while providing redundancy in switching capacity, sub-second rerouting, and intelligent, dynamic bandwidth allocation. All of these core network factors depend on the inclination and ability of the service providers to develop the Internet infrastructure to such a level.

Performance Metrics — Quantifying "Perception." Service performance includes many elements, such as the time required to connect a call, peak instantaneous call capacity, voice quality, noise levels, and the ability to support enhanced services. The capacity of the overall network to support calls at a guaranteed minimum level of quality under normal and disaster conditions is also significant.

Traditional metrics used in the design and benchmarking of data network performance focus on objective factors such as error rate, throughput, and latency. Voice networking exposes an entirely different range of subjective, human perception factors that are difficult to quantify yet are critical to the practicality of a commercial voice offering.

Bell Labs long ago developed a standard, the Overall Reference Equivalent (ORE), to attempt to bring the human factor to bear in the design of the public telephone network. The ORE metric quantifies the user's tolerance for circumstances, such as time to connect to another user, blocked calls due to network overload, echo, volume, and noise. These metrics are a fundamental component of all current voice network design and testing processes.

A successful mass deployment of Internet telephony will hinge on the same factors. The Internet infrastructure and user devices will require low delay to inhibit echo and double-talk. Low delay variation and low data loss will be necessary to avoid distortion and noise.

High-performance switching and efficient utilization of switching, trunking, and access capacity in the Internet backbone will be essential to achieving these goals. Backbone switching hardware and software must be scalable to accommodate high-capacity, long-term growth of the network that will be necessary to effectively meet user demand.

Predictability — Key to a Universal Service. While performance and reliability are paramount, consistent performance of the network is also of extreme importance.

Users will expect a universal service to perform in essentially the same manner every time it is called upon. If a significant variance in performance exists from call to call, the lower range of performance will be perceived as unacceptable. This will be cause for contention between service providers and clients and can only be addressed through effective service network design and provisioning practices.

As Internet access and traffic grow, we are already witnessing dramatic variances in a given server's performance as a consequence of demand on the host processor and contention for transport bandwidth. Much like today's commercial telephone switches, sufficient resources must be provisioned at the host site to ensure that the desired level of service is provided to users.

In addition, wide-area transport and switching capacity in the Internet backbone require significant improvement in order to avoid the unpredictable network overloads and outages seen today. Delay, throughput, and error rate must remain relatively consistent not only throughout a call, but from call to call.

Fairness — Meeting Guaranteed QOS Levels. What is fairness? Users should be able to depend on a level of service proportional to their investment in the service, regardless of the state of the network at any given moment.

For example, a user with an expensive high-speed connection should expect more total throughput during network congestion or impairment than a user with a less expensive low-speed connection. Each user should receive a degree of service that is directly proportional at all times to their contracted quality of service.

In a similar fashion, active user connections should not have their throughput, delay, or error rate reduced below minimum guaranteed levels at any time as a result of new connection requests or variance in demand by other established connections.

Fairness also includes the assurance that once a call is placed and in progress, quality of service cannot be disrupted or usurped by new calls. Fairness of this sort equates to an "all circuits are busy" message from the public switched telephone network. The implicit message is that other users were there first, and courtesy (quality of service) dictates that an in-progress call may not be disconnected or impaired in preference for a new call.

The current frame-switched Internet backbone architecture generally allows unfair, unpredictable degradation of service to established connections due to its minimal support and enforcement of quality of service metrics.

Accessibility to a Broad User Base. Virtually universal access exists in today's public switched telephone networks. Practically anyone in the world desiring connection to telephone service may obtain it.

Likewise, while the worldwide telephone network is composed of multitudes of independent local, regional, national, and international service providers, interoperability is truly universal. Any caller on any telephone service may connect to anyone in the world with a telephone, including cellular and commercial mobile-radio telephones. Internet telephony requires the same degree of interoperability.

Of course, public telephone networks were of value long before such wide access was provisioned. Internet access is today sufficiently broad to support an Internet telephony user base. The promise of interoperability with the billions of installed conventional telephones is extremely encouraging. In fact, Internet-style telephony seems to have quite a strong chance of becoming the dominant voice communications medium in the next century. Instrument costs (e.g., PC sound cards and software) will certainly be driven continually downward, and stand-alone consumer Internet telephone instruments are absolutely feasible.

SUMMARY

An advanced, cell-based asynchronous transfer mode (ATM) backbone is an absolute requirement for a profitable, efficient, high-performance public multimedia network. Frame-switching technology cannot guarantee the distinct quality of service requirements of mixed voice, video, and data without costly over-provisioning of bandwidth and switching capacity.

Conversely, profitable operation of a frame-switched architecture in an intensely competitive deregulated environment will beg oversubscription by service providers, resulting in poor performance, unpredictability, and unfairness to users — as is increasingly seen in today's Internet.

A well-designed ATM infrastructure with low delay, large per-virtual circuit and by-traffic-class buffering, advanced adaptive queue service algorithms, scalable capacity, and effective, closed-loop traffic management will be mandatory for the continued growth of the Internet as a profitable, commercially feasible service.

The same switching infrastructure can provide not only extremely high-performance Internet services, but also guaranteed performance for conventional and packetized voice services, all manner of data delivery services, video broadcast and conference services, and true multimedia service across the wide area.

Chapter 6
Voice over Frame Relay
Daniel Bahr and Wendy Roberts

Frame relay is becoming the transmission technology of choice for wide area network (WAN) users worldwide who are looking for a WAN technology that is low cost, fast, flexible, and standards based. Vendors and carriers have both reported growth rates of 350% from 1994 to 1995.

ADDING VOICE TO DATA NETWORK USER ISSUES

Optimized for data traffic, frame relay's explosive growth has been driven predominantly by local area network (LAN) internetworking, SNA migration, and remote access. As customers continue to express interest in frame relay, vendors and customers are pushing for other applications and traffic to run over a frame relay network.

In 1995 the first generation of equipment was introduced that supported voice over frame relay. These offerings met with moderate acceptance due largely to a lack of standards and lack of support. A year later, new vendors have begun supporting voice over frame relay and a new wave of customers has emerged who want to realize the financial benefit of incorporating voice/fax along with data into their frame relay networks.

The second generation of equipment does a better job of addressing the quality issues associated with voice compression. Additional buffer space to help with jitter, coupled with more advanced compression algorithms and better prioritization schemes, have alleviated some of the issues. However, there is still a lack of standards. As of this writing, this lack of standards makes all voice-over-frame relay (VOF) offerings proprietary solutions and, consequently, an issue for many end users.

In the 1990s, when the corporate world is downsizing and rightsizing, the prospect of lowering monthly telecommunications infrastructure costs is economically very attractive to many businesses. In many cases the cost issues are paramount, but there are other issues to be addressed as well — among them, ongoing infrastructure requirements, business continuity, and network management. A brief discussion of when it may be appropriate to incorporate voice into the data network will address many of these issues.

Business Perspective on Frame Relay

Frame relay today provides primary connectivity for LAN-to-LAN and IBM SNA/SDLC (System Network Architecture/synchronous data link control) connectivity, accounting for almost 95% of current network utilization. Unfortunately, many users of frame relay technology have yet to recognize the full economic advantage of its architecture.

Business Continuity Concerns. Combining voice over frame and potentially eliminating a major portion of the network is financially attractive. In fact, with the latest compression techniques it can cost as little as half a cent per minute. However, users must consider that if the frame relay link is lost, then both voice and data communication is now lost and a remote site is potentially without any communications.

Business continuity and application criticality must be considered. Many dial backup solutions may be applicable — integrated services digital network (ISDN), in many cases, or plain old telephone service, for example. In addition, for truly critical sites, users should consider multiple access paths for the cable into the building.

Network Management. Network management must also be considered when users look to combine multiple networks into one. The combination of voice/fax/data over the same physical link elevates the need for a robust network management system and for working with a carrier who provides valuable network information. Some carriers are expanding this part of their business and are offering access to their network management data.

The best candidates for voice over frame relay today are customers with existing frame relay data networks whose data requirements are a few DS0s, allowing them to take a relatively simple approach of looking at the equipment costs and the additional DS0 cost for adding voice.

For many of the carriers, combining voice traffic over the frame relay network presents issues of pricing as well as network management.

CARRIER SERVICE OFFERINGS AND IMPACT ON VOICE AND DATA DELIVERY

For public network frame relay service, many carriers have chosen a cautious approach to promoting and supporting VOF technology. This is due primarily to concerns about guaranteeing quality of service (QOS) specifications associated with voice traffic.

Exhibit 1. Frame Relay Providers

Carrier	Frame Relay Access Speeds	Geographic Coverage	Voice over Frame Relay
Ameritech	DS0, DS1		No
AT&T	DS0, DS1, DS3	USA/International	No
BellSouth	DS0, DS1, DS3	South USA	No
Bell Atlantic	DS0, DS1		No
Bell Canada	OS0, DS1	Canada	No
British Telecom (BT)	DS0, DS1	USA/International	No
Cable & Wireless	DS0, DS1	USA/International	No
EMI (ICI)	DS0, DS1	USA	Yes
GTE Comm. Corp	DS0, DS1	USA	No
LDDS Worldcom	DS0, DS1		No
MCI	DS0, DS1	USA/International	No
MFS Datanet	DS0, DS1	USA/International	Yes
Pacific Bell	DS0, DS1	West Coast	No
Southwestern Bell	DS0, DS1		No
Sprint	DS0, DS1	USA/International	No
US West	DS0, DS1		No

Of those carriers that offer support for VOF (see Exhibit 1), they are typically discussing tariffing data link connection identifiers (DLCIs) for voice to ensure acceptable delay. This would enable voice to travel alone on a dedicated virtual circuit, minimizing or eliminating many of the problems. (Note: The majority of carriers, as of this writing, do not provide voice over frame relay as a service offering. Many of the carriers listed in Exhibit 1 have announced plans for voice over frame relay service, but do not have definitive service offerings.)

Many leading switch vendors offer the ability to support different levels of QOS for voice using different DLCIs. As these devices become more prevalent and intelligent, the carriers will be able to provide higher-quality service, and users will gain more network options.

One challenge for end-user companies that have many sites is the interoperability between the carriers. The network-to-network interface (NNI) agreement covers the very basics and does not address voice issues and some network management issues.

Today, few carrier-based frame relay offerings support all the traditional voice applications, including interconnecting private branch exchanges (PBXs), use of off-premises extensions (OPX), and private line auto ring-down (PLAR). When available, such offerings can make frame relay networks an attractive option for everything from tying together telecommuters into a virtual office to linking the branch office and regional office locations. In this implementation, the home or small branch office can be connected with a single pipe that provides voice communications integrated with the office PBX and voice mail, as well as integrated data communications with the office network and host computers.

This configuration often creates an easier frame relay design and implementation because the end stations are typically homes back to a central office location. This means advanced functionality requirements of frame relay, such as switched virtual circuit (SVC) support for voice, are not required, as all voice calls need to be first routed to the office PBX.

ANTICIPATED COST AND MANAGEMENT ISSUES

By being able to send more information through compressed VOF (from 3:1 to 9:1 voice compression) and data circuitries, businesses can avoid upgrading to expensive T1 lines for another year or two. In many cases users would be able to eliminate current voice circuits. In the case where a point-to-point data network is replaced by frame relay and voice is combined into the circuit, overall costs could be lowered significantly.

Decision Criteria for Analyzing VOF

Three important implementation issues that must be addressed if voice is to be a practical application on a frame relay network:

- Voice quality.
- Transmission quality.
- Congestion control and prioritization.

Voice communication, unlike data, is very time sensitive and must be perceived to be performed in real time in order for users to accept it. Any delays need to be smaller than the human ear and brain can detect. Only recently have compression algorithms, combined with new architectures for identifying and prioritizing data, made this quality criteria a practical reality.

Mean Opinion Score as a Metric. Although perceptions of voice quality vary by individual, the mean opinion score (MOS) is a widely accepted measure of voice quality. MOS is derived from the absolute category rating (ACR) method that estimates the overall acceptability or quality of voice communications systems by requiring the listener to judge the overall quality of speech samples for telephone communications.

MOS ratings provide a subjective quality score averaged over a large number of speakers, utterances, and listeners. The value of MOS is expressed as follows:

Score	Quality
4.1 to 5.0	Excellent (e.g., toll quality)
3.1 to 4.0	Good (e.g., communication quality)
2.1 to 3.0	Fair (e.g., synthetic quality)
<2.1	Poor

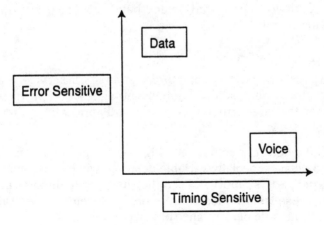

Exhibit 2. Difference between Data and Voice

TECHNICAL SPEAKING: REQUIREMENTS FOR EFFICIENT SERVICE

In order to understand why voice-over-frame relay technology and product offerings are not more widespread, it is important to realize there is a fundamental difference in priorities between voice and data.

Difference Between Voice and Data

Voice and data have differing and often contradictory requirements for successful transmission (see Exhibit 2). For example, although voice is very sensitive to jitter and time delays, LAN-based data traffic typically is not. And while it is perfectly acceptable for voice traffic to experience occasional bit errors and dropped packets (producing at most a static pop in the earpiece) data traffic must be completely error free.

Voice traffic prioritizes for consistent fast throughput, with no requirements for error recovery procedures — which saves tremendously on processor cycles and WAN bandwidth. Yet data prioritizes on error-free transmission, with a much larger acceptability for timing variances.

Therefore, the integration of both voice and data on the same circuit has the following requirements:

1. High speed.
2. Low delay.
3. Port sharing.
4. Bandwidth sharing.

Traditional voice transmission technology of time division multiplexing (TDM) meets the first two characteristics — high speed and low delay. X.25

meets the last two — port sharing and bandwidth sharing. Frame relay offers all four characteristics.

Handling Large File Transfers

Frame relay was designed first and foremost as a data service. Frame relay is most effective when used with intelligent higher-level protocols, transmission lines that are virtually error free, and applications that can support variable delay.

Voice traffic does not contain any higher-level protocols, and it is very sensitive to delay, especially variable delay. So whenever a manufacturer develops a device to support voice traffic, there has to be some method for addressing these issues. Most vendors have developed several ways of providing predictable performance of voice traffic.

Initially, most manufacturers simply fronted their existing data router with a voice port for bridging DS0s, creating a kind of multiplexer over the frame network. To provide more consistent voice quality, prioritization schemes were put in place based on input circuit. Voice and fax traffic, just like time-sensitive SNA traffic, was bumped to the top of the queue for transmission, thereby ensuring that time-sensitive traffic was being given a higher priority. However, this prioritization did not address the variable-delay nature of queuing multiple circuits onto a single transmission line.

Take, for example, the transmission of a large file transfer during a voice call. This scenario leads to the most difficult aspects of integrating voice and data over frame relay — that of jitter and delay.

Jitter. Once a packet is inside the network, it will have to transverse several intermediate switching/routing devices. If the frame arrives while the switch is busy with another packet, there may be moments of delay introduced in the transmission. Because these frames can be variable in length, the actual delay time is not predictable. This is referred to as *jitter.*

Most devices employ buffering techniques that compensate for this jitter effect. However, if the variability exceeds the end device's ability to compensate for this problem, then continuity and overall quality of the conversation is diminished. Typically, intermediate devices provide for at least 125 milliseconds of buffering to smooth out the conversation.

Transient Delay. Although employing frame relay technology introduces additional delay through the network, this delay can be engineered to be well within the acceptable limits required for voice communication (less that 400 milliseconds).

Total network delay for a complex frame network might, for example, allow 24 milliseconds for input buffer, 20 milliseconds for compression algorithm, 24 milliseconds for queuing, 25 milliseconds for latency through five network switches (five milliseconds each), 24 milliseconds for queuing at the far end, jitter buffering that takes 72 milliseconds, 7 milliseconds for compression — for a total of 196 milliseconds, which is well within the acceptable range of 400 milliseconds.

When compared to the network latency used in POTS lines, where values range from 20 to 30 milliseconds for terrestrial lines and 250 milliseconds plus for satellite, it is evident that frame relay networks are capable of providing network transmission in line with other technologies in use today.

Congestion Control and Prioritization. The network needs to be set up so that a large file transfer does not arbitrarily consume all available bandwidth. A priority mechanism needs to be in place that provides for consistent performance to time-sensitive traffic such as voice and SNA.

Other data traffic can make use of whatever bandwidth is available, normally without any associated problems or difficulties. The network administrator should be able to assign individual priorities to selected channels, as well as a prioritization scheme within DLCIs. This includes being able to manually determine the discard eligibility status of individual channels.

Segmentation. Another factor involved in avoiding transient delay is segmentation. Segmentation breaks up larger blocks of data into smaller frames similar in concept to asynchronous transfer mode (ATM), thus making the data less delay sensitive, since the data is being sent on a more continuous basis than waiting for a single large transfer. A 4K-byte (32,000 bit) frame can take more than a half second to transfer on a 64K-bps line. This makes it difficult to ensure consistent voice quality. Segmentation is, in fact, becoming a common approach for predictably supporting voice over frame relay — which is another reason many view frame relay as an interim step to ATM.

DESCRIPTION OF COMPRESSION TECHNIQUES AND EQUIPMENT

Background on Voice Digitization

The digitization of voice is an old concept typically employing the pulse code modulation (PCM) standard running at 64K bps, which equates to a single DS0. Two factors can affect the quality of a digitized voice call:

- Jitter.
- Dropped packets.

Jitter is a variation in the delay of one voice packet over the other. To compensate, additional buffer space can be used to store voice packets.

Once the packets are received they are smoothed prior to conversion to an analog signal, reducing the jitter effect.

Dropping packets is another matter. When a single packet is dropped the end user may not notice. However, when several packets are dropped for whatever reason (usually congestion of the network), then the connection is no longer acceptable.

To ensure reliable voice packet delivery, end-user equipment must be designed to minimize congestion. Some manufacturers use fragmenting data packets to allow voice packets to traverse the network within acceptable delay parameters. Configuring network buffers to reasonably small depths permits rapid transmission of voice across many network-level queues.

Voice Compression Algorithms

In the past 10 years, significant advances in the design of digital signal processors (DSPs) has occurred. A DSP is a microprocessor that is designed specifically to process digitized signals such as those found in voice and video applications. DSP development has allowed manufacturers to bring to market high-quality digitization algorithms that consume very little bandwidth.

Voice compression algorithms make it possible to provide high-quality audio while making efficient use of bandwidth. The most commonly used voice compression algorithms are:

- Pulse code modulation/adaptive differential pulse code modulation (PCM /ADPCM).
- Adaptive transform coding/improved multi-band excitation (ATC/IMBE).
- Code excited linear predication/algebraic code excited linear predication (CELP/ACELP).

PCM/ADPCM. PCM and ADPCM — the traditional algorithms used worldwide by the Public Switched Telephone Network (PSTN) and Europe's PTTs (Postal, Telegraph, and Telephone services) — receive high (e.g., toll quality) mean opinion scores. Mean opinion scores of 4.4 for PCM and 4.1 for ADPCM are achieved by consuming 64K-bps bandwidth and 32K-bps bandwidth, respectively.

ATC/IMBE. The adaptive transform coding (ATC) algorithm is actually a combination of time domain harmonic scaling (TDHS), linear predictive coding (LPC), and vector quantization (VQ). The key features of the ATC algorithm are low complexity and variable digitization rate. ATC has an MOS score of 2.0 to 3.8, depending on the voice digitization rate.

The IMBE (improved multiband excitation) algorithm is also a hybrid coder. The underlying theory of IMBE coding is that various frequency bands in the speech spectrum behave differently with respect to a voiced/unvoiced classification. ATC consumes 8K-bps to 16K-bps bandwidth, and IMBE consumes 2.4K-bps to 8K-bps bandwidth, with mean opinion scores of good (e.g., communication quality).

CELP/ACELP. Algebraic code excited linear prediction (ACELP) grew out of years of study at various research institutions using CELP and CELP-like coders. The three main elements of ACELP are:

- LPC modeling of the vocal track.
- Sophisticated pitch extraction and coding.
- Innovative excitation modeling and coding.

Independent tests indicate that the perceived quality of ACELP voice is equal to or better than the industry-standard 32K-bps ADPCM (G.721 standard). ACELP is rated with a mean opinion score of approximately 4.2.

The recent introduction of ACELP allows "toll quality" voice transmissions over frame relay networks. A variation of the ACELP algorithm is currently being reviewed by the International Telecommunications Union (ITU) for recommended G.729 at 8K bps.

One of the new methods used to achieve this compression is the actual analysis of the voice data. Instead of trying to simply compress information into fewer bits, it is possible to remove nonessential information from the bit stream and achieve greater efficiencies. Speech actually tends to have a substantial amount of pauses and repetitive elements that, while necessary for human communication, can be left out of the digital transmission. It is estimated that only 22% of our conversation contains essential speech components needed for communication.

Additional Options for Ensuring Quality of Sound

Typical digital encoding samples the analog waveform at 8,000 times per second, using 8 bits per sample. This generates the fundamental 64K-bps channel rate. For acceptable voice quality, the total round-trip delay should be less than 400 milliseconds. To minimize delay, voice compression algorithms are employed.

The PCM algorithm, which consumes 64K bps of bandwidth, is optimized for speech quality. Other voice compression algorithms try to send as much voice information with fewer bits.

For example, 16K CVSELP (codex vector sum excited linear prediction) and 8K CVSELP are algorithms developed by Motorola that consume much lower bandwidths. 16K CVSELP and 8K CVSELP also support digital speech interpolation (DSI), a compression technique that relies on the pauses between speech bursts to provide additional compression.

Echo Cancellation. One issue that can emerge when placing voice over frame relay is echo, a phenomenon in which the transmitted voice is reflected back to the point from which it was transmitted.

Depending on its severity, echo can be very annoying. In fact, if the delay time between speech and the echo return is significant — 45 milliseconds or more — the echo can bring the conversation to a halt.

The most sophisticated method of eliminating echo is with an echo canceler, which builds a mathematical model of a speech pattern and subtracts it from the transmit path. Both 16K and 8K CVSELP have built-in echo cancelers that filter out any near-end echo (up to a near-end delay of 32 milliseconds). This eliminates the requirement for expensive external echo cancellers.

FRAME RELAY DESIGN AND ARCHITECTURE

For frame relay service to provide on-demand any-to-any connectivity that makes these services efficient and cost-effective, they will need to be based on switched virtual circuits (SVCs). Unfortunately, it is estimated that SVCs will not be generally available until at least 1997 or 1998.

Switching in Frame Relay

A frame relay connection is based on a virtual circuit called a data link connection (DLC). Today DLCs are typically permanent virtual circuits (PVCs) predefined on both sides of the connection. Each DLC has an identifying number called a data link connection identifier (DLCI).

Switched virtual circuits are different in that they are an any-to-any connection initiated by the user and then torn down when the transmission is completed. With SVCs, calls are established over the frame relay network by requesting a destination based on either the X.121 or E.164 number schemes.

Although part of the original frame relay specification, SVCs are not commonly deployed in public networks today, though many carriers are expected to offer the service within the next 24 months. One of the delays from the carriers' perspective is the complex billing systems required to support the dynamic nature of SVC calls.

Unlike data connections, where the end points are easy to plan for and remain fairly static, voice calls have a broader, more dynamic connectivity requirement. Support for voice traffic outside of a private corporate network would dictate support for a larger number of locations. Some of these locations would be called as infrequently as once a month or less and others as often as several times a day.

Because SVCs are not readily available, the alternative is to implement PVCs for all locations. Having to set up PVC DLCIs for each possible location is simply impractical in today's public frame relay networks. Trying to establish PVC DLCIs to each possible location for voice support would consume massive resources and involve huge management nightmares dealing with DLCI tables. However, if scaled-down sufficiently, it may be possible and cost-effective to support a few branch office locations with PVCs.

VENDOR PERSPECTIVES

At present, leading voice-over-frame relay products are available from:

- ACT Networks Inc. (805) 388-2474.
- FastComm Communications (703) 318-7750.
- Memotec (514) 738-4781.
- Micom Communications Corp. (805) 583-8600.
- Motorola Information Systems Group (508) 261-4000.
- Netrix (703) 793-2088.
- Northern Telecom (214) 684-5930.
- Scitec (508) 821-4600.
- StrataCom Inc. (408) 294-7600.

Have you made your first call over the Net yet? You will. There have been several eye-catching liaisons and mergers in the past year that will push the envelope when it comes to multimedia, especially voice, over the Internet.

Many leading-edge technology companies are looking to make a name for themselves and gather market share with an early product offering of voice over the Internet. The changes in the marketplace are evident in recent partnerships such as Netscape Communications Corp. buying equity stakes in both Voxware Inc. and InSoft Inc., which supply Internet telephony software and develop voice, video, and data applications for the Internet, respectively. Look for the next version of Netscape Navigator to have Internet voice features.

In addition, Microsoft Corp. plans to include Internet telephony software and other multimedia applications with its next release of Internet Explorer. CompuServe is currently offering Internet Phone from VolcaTec Ltd.

Other mergers such as the $2 billion merger of UUNet Technologies and MFS Communications Co., Inc., in April 1996, outline plans to pursue Internet multimedia with an emphasis on voice over the Net. Offering an international flavor to voice over the Internet is especially attractive because of long-distance rates. Tele Danmark A/S is one of the first traditional telephone companies to announce a trial of Internet telephony.

There are expected to be many other examples of mergers and partnerships that will continue the onslaught of voice over the Internet and that will push the carriers to explore not only voice over the Net but to add voice support to current service offerings such as frame relay.

EMERGING REQUESTS FOR COMMENT AND STANDARDS

The advent of standards such as the Internet Engineering Task Force's resource reservation protocol (RSVP), which is intended to establish different levels of quality of service standards, will bring about huge changes. This protocol will make voice over the Internet much more readily available, bypassing the carriers' switched networks. One wonders what becomes of the carriers if they cannot at the very least support voice over frame relay.

Exhibit 3 lists the assorted user groups and standards bodies and their standards and recommendations — especially the Frame Relay Forum, ANSI, and ITU — for frame relay.

Migrating from Frame Relay to ATM

With voice over frame relay starting to mature, the business case can be made that frame relay is a good interim step to ATM, which will carry voice, data, and multimedia-driven traffic. Taking the plunge with voice over frame relay can give a customer invaluable insights into preparing for the ATM environment, as well as potentially saving an organization money.

Multimedia and other high-bandwidth applications are better suited to ATM, where a higher level of service is required. With frame relay to ATM interworking, users can deploy both frame relay and ATM as necessary to suit their particular enterprise's networking needs. Side by side, frame relay and ATM networks compare as follows:

	Frame Relay	*ATM*
Packet Delay	Variable	Deterministic
Packet Jitter	Variable	Deterministic
Overhead	Low	High
Typical Access Speeds	DS0, DS1, some DS3	OC1, OC3

Frame relay to ATM interworking provides a way to seamlessly integrate frame relay and ATM networks. Two implementation agreements (IAs) have been developed specifically for frame relay users and have been ratified by both the Frame Relay Forum and the ATM Forum:

• Network interworking (FRF.5).

The following is a list of non-RFC standards related to frame relay: *Frame Relay Forum Implementation Agreements (IAs)*

FRF.1 User-to-Network (UNI) IA
FRF.2 Network-to-Network (NNI) Phase 1 IA
FRF.3 Multiprotocol Encapsulation IA
FRF.4 Switched Virtual Circuit (SVC) IA
FRF.5 Frame Relay/ATM Network Interworking IA
FRF.6 Frame Relay Service Customer Network Management IA (MIB)
FRF.7 Frame Relay PVC Multicast Service and Protocol Description
FRF.8 Frame Relay/ATM PVC Service Interworking IA
FRF.9 Data Compression over Frame Relay IA
ANSI Standards
T1.606, ISDN Architectural Framework and Service Description for Frame Relay Bearer
   Service
T1.606 Addendum Frame Relay Bearer Service: Architectural Framework and Service
   Description
T1.617, ISDN:DSS1 Signaling Specification for Frame Relay Bearer Service
T1.617, Annex D Additional Procedures for PVCs Using Unnumbered
Information Frames
T1.618,ISDN Core Aspects of Frame Protocol for Use with Frame Relay Bearer Service
ITU Recommendations
I.122 Frame Relay Framework
I.233.1 Frame Relay Bearer Services
I.370 Congestion Management in Frame Relay Networks
I.555 Frame Relay Bearer Service Interworking
Q.933 DSS1 Signaling Specification for Frame Mode Bearer Service
Q.933, Annex A Additional Procedures for PVCs Using Unnumbered Information Frames
0.922, Annex A Core Aspects of Q.922 for Use with Frame Relaying Bearer Service
X.76 NNI Between Public Data Networks Providing the Frame Relay Data
Internet Requests for Comment (RFCs) and Drafts Related to Frame Relay
1604 PS T. Brown, "Definitions of Managed Objects for Frame Relay Service" (March 17,
   1994).
1586 I O. deSouza and M. Rodrigues, "Guidelines for Running OSPF over Frame Relay
   Networks" (March 24, 1994).
1490 DS T. Bradley, C. Brown, and A. Malis, "Multiprotocol Interconnect over Frame
   Relay" (July 20, 1993).
1483 PS J. Heinanen, "Multiprotocol Encapsulation over ATM Adaptation Layer 5" (July
   20, 1993).
1315 PS C. Brown, F. Baker, and C. Carvalho, "Management Information Base for Frame
   Relay DTEs" (April 9,1992).
1294 PS T. Bradley, C. Brown, and A. Malis, "Multiprotocol Interconnect over Frame
   Relay" (January 17, 1992).

Exhibit 3.   Standards Related to Frame Relay

• Service interworking (FRF.8).

Both of these implementation agreements describe how vendors map
frame relay addresses and logical connections to ATM, as well as other
internetworking functions.

Network internetworking (FRF.5) allows connections of two frame relay end nodes such as frame relay access devices (FRADs) or routers, which are attached to a frame relay network over an ATM backbone. FRADs have no knowledge of the ATM backbone because the network equipment (i.e., the ATM WAN switches) provides the interworking function. Several frame relay networks can be supported by an ATM backbone providing users with a scalable, high-speed option.

Service interworking (FRF.8) connects a frame relay network to the ATM network, allowing frame relay devices to send data to the ATM devices. Service interworking allows bidirectional permanent virtual connection management and protocol conversion functions.

FRF.8-compliant telecommunications companies allow ATM end user devices to receive data from frame relay and ATM services at speeds that range from 56K bps to 155M bps. Carriers that support FRF.8 today include Sprint, AT&T, MCI, and LDDS WorldCom.

Chapter 7
Voice Compression and Silence Suppression

Daniel A. Kosek

This chapter looks at several schemes for performing voice compression over communications links. Voice compression over new networks, such as asynchronous transfer mode (ATM), is compared with older time division multiplexing (TDM) links, such as conventional T1. Although some limited compression has been possible on a TDM link, these schemes were rigid and restricted traffic types. Silence suppression is a method of saving bandwidth.

ADVANCES IN NEW NETWORKS

New telecommunications service platforms such as ATM networks test, moment by moment, whether or not active speech is occurring. Traffic is only generated during active speech. Although TDM could suppress silence, no bandwidth saving occurred because the free bandwidth could not be reassigned.

During a voice conversation, silence represents more than 50% of all voice traffic, so the importance of preventing this wasteful bandwidth consumption is evident. ATM can deliver high-quality voice using much less bandwidth. Active silence suppression schemes deliver a full 2:1 compression over the voice encoding techniques offered on TDM platforms.

This return of bandwidth to the network allows companies to reduce operating costs or add new services to their network. The full spectrum of multimedia services can be mixed at the multimedia workstation to and throughout the network. This important advance will make it possible to merge all traffic types onto one common network architecture.

0-8493-9949-1/99/$0.00+$.50
© 1999 by CRC Press LLC

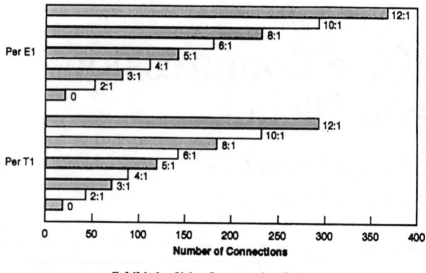

Exhibit 1. Voice Compression Ratios

ASSESSING DIFFERENT VOICE COMPRESSION SCHEMES

Voice compression technology is outstanding in its high-connection capacity, but several complications are usually encountered when implementing compression within a network. The remainder of this chapter describes current compression schemes and some that are soon to be available. They are evaluated in terms of:

- Their quality and ability to suppress bandwidth consumption during periods of silence.
- The use of faxes and high-speed modems.

The question is not whether voice compression should be used, but how much to use and how much it will cost or save the company.

The economic advantages are great, and voice quality is maintained. Currently, a T1 trunk between the U.K. and the U.S. can cost almost $70,000 a month. Which is more economical — 24, 96, or even 192 voice connections on that link, or 96 voice ports and a 768K-bps LAN connection, which would also be possible? Exhibit 1 shows connection capacity on T1s and E1s at compression rates from 0 to 12:1.

PCM — THE BENCHMARK FOR VOICE QUALITY

With the advent of pulse code modulation (PCM) little more than a decade ago, voice telecommunications made a major technological advance.

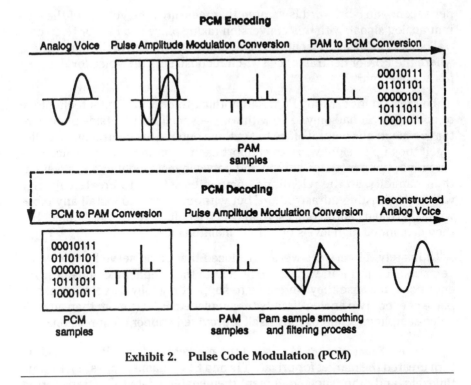

Exhibit 2. Pulse Code Modulation (PCM)

Today, PCM voice quality is the standard by which all other compression techniques are tested.

PCM can support voice, data, fax, and proprietary forms of interdevice communication (i.e., over a signaling channel). The PCM encoding and decoding processes for an analog voice waveform are illustrated in Exhibit 2.

How PCM Works

With PCM, the delay imposed by sample creation is low and is governed by the 8-KHz sample rate (one sample every 125 microseconds). It functions well, but telecommunications users may wonder how the PCM scheme was designed. Why 8-bit samples? Why an 8-KHz sampling? Why "mu" law and not "A" law encoding?

Analog voice communication by telephone was designed as a bandpass filter, allowing a frequency range from 300 Hz to 3,000 Hz. A basic law of 8-bit PCM states that the sample rate must be at least two times the highest frequency allowed — this means the minimum allowable sample rate is 6 KHz.

More Capacity without More Wires. The engineers may have chosen 8 KHz to ensure the delivery of excellent quality voice. Therefore 8,000 times per second, an 8-bit word is created that measures the voltage of the current analog signal, with this conversion taking place in a PBX or telco central office. The measurements are sent to the distant end of the connection, where the PBX or central office switch reconstructs the voice for delivery to the called party.

The reason for creating PCM had nothing to do with digital technology or computers. It had only to do with wire — specifically, outside plant wire that connects the central office to anything outside the central office building. It took up to eight wires to support each interoffice tie line voice conversation. Copper routes around and between metropolitan areas were at their capacity, so the telephone companies set out to create capacity within the existing infrastructure but without having to install any more wiring between central offices. Analog carriers like "N" carrier helped, but they demanded high levels of routine maintenance.

Ultimately, T1 services were introduced that could serve 24 voice conversations on just four wires. The benefit to the telephone companies was enormous, because they were able to support digitally 24 voice trunks in place of every two analog circuits they replaced. PCM is more than an 8-bit voice-sampling technology; by itself it provided copper compression.

Changing Economics. PCM created the market for digital PBXs, which in turn created the market for private T1s and E1s. Channel banks, T1/E1 multiplexers, and other such equipment then enabled data to be transported on those voice lines. Voice typically consumed 70% of the network's capacity while paying for it all, hence the data could ride for free.

In today's private networks, the trend has reversed itself and voice now rides for free, thanks to the growth of data applications. On a large wide area network (WAN), however, pure PCM will almost never be used.

Although it is a benchmark for voice quality, to assign 64K bps of capacity to one voice conversation wastes bandwidth, which is not acceptable on international WAN connections where costs are high and voice quality is usually sacrificed through the use of high-compression rates. In Mexico, an E1 from Mexico City to Monterey currently costs approximately $22,000 per month. This 450-mile circuit is equivalent to a T1 between Washington DC and Detroit, which typically costs less than $6,500 per month. In Brazil a 150-mile E1 from Sao Paulo to Rio de Janeiro currently costs $42,000 per month. A T1 from New York City to Baltimore costs less than $3,200 per month.

ADPCM

An engineering study that investigated ways to add compression to individual T1 trunk facilities without degrading voice quality discovered that more than half of all PCM samples were silence (this issue is covered in more detail later in this chapter in the section on "Voice Activity Detection"). The study also found that the rate of change from one PCM sample to the next stayed within a 16-bit range, either 8 bits higher or 8 bits lower.

A count of 16 can be expressed in binary in a 4-bit "nibble" instead of an 8-bit "word." This discovery allowed only half the bandwidth to be consumed with nearly the same quality voice transmission, using a scheme called adaptive pulse code modulation (ADPCM). (Modem and fax machines, however, have limited operating speeds when forced to operate across ADPCM services. Fax machines are throttled to 4.8K-bps throughput and modems to 2.4K bps.)

ADPCM has a unique feature in that it can be used as a conversion point between "mu" law and "A" law PCM. This feature is helpful for international networks.

ADPCM has matured. Currently, ANSI T1Y1 compatibility is the standard for 4-bit (32K bps) ADPCM. A version of ADPCM using a 3-bit sample (24K bps) has also been standardized, and a new 2-bit (16K bps) version is close to being standardized.

The 3-bit ADPCM delivers accurate and acceptable voice quality. The 2-bit ADPCM is less than acceptable, except for "order wire" quality connections. The frequency spectrum of the female voice is high enough that the 2-bit scheme degrades quality substantially. The lower frequency spectrum of the typical male voice performs more acceptably with the 2-bit scheme.

CVSD

Continuously variable slope delay (CVSD) voice compression is an aging technology that is still found in many legacy products, such as TDM multiplexers. CVSD technology requires the comparison of the current sample to the previous one. This comparison delivers a binary choice to issue an increase-value (1) or decrease-value (0) bit.

As an example, if the current voltage sample is 2.13 volts and the previous sample was 2.01 volts, an increase-value bit is issued from the encoding end of the connection. This constant ramping upward or downward of the digital samples causes the basic noise floor to be higher than with other compression techniques.

Limitations of CVSD

The volume of the incoming voice signal is extremely important in CVSD voice quality. Low volume causes high noise-to-voice ratios and can produce a raspy voice quality. Overdriving the input will certainly cause raspy, garbled, or even unintelligible voice.

Although CVSD has many limitations, it can deliver acceptable voice quality. The unique property of CVSD compression is that it supports bit rates as low as 8K bps and as high as 32K bps, all with one chip set. CVSD encoding is highly resistant to bit-error-induced noise. Because of its simplicity, encoding delay is minimal.

The only true hardware limitation is CVSD's inability to support fax or modem speeds above 1,200 bps. These types of traffic suffer severe bit errors that can render the user's data unusable or unrecoverable.

Voice compression in vendor equipment using CVSD typically produces a signal at either 32K bps or 16K bps. The less bandwidth consumed, the thinner the voice sounds. Small-bandwidth CVSD connections are especially damaging to female voices, whereas male voices seem to transmit more acceptably with low-bit-rate connections. If fax or modems are used at 9.6K bps and 14.4K bps, a different compression technique has to be selected.

CVSD as a technology platform has basically been abandoned and new features will not be added as with some other compression techniques.

CELP

Code excited linear predictive (CELP) encoding comes in a variety of versions, including:

- Variable slope excited linear predictive (VSELP).
- Linear predictive coding 10e (LPC10e).
- ITU-TS G.728.

CELP provides high-quality voice compression. Its only real limitation is the time required to perform the compression and decompression. Single-direction end-to-end delays can be as long as 135 to 160 milliseconds, though this delay allows voice to be carried in as little as 2.4K bps. CELP offers real compression at rates as high as 18:1, with 12:1 being typical of the best telecommunications products.

How CELP Works

CELP's compression is achieved by mapping the incoming speech onto a mathematical model of human voice. Whereas PCM sends quantized voice samples, CELP algorithms send only the model parameters as they change.

This technique of compression is called a *vocoder* (voice coder); PCM is defined as a waveform coder. This "lossy" compression technique lets the user of the algorithm define the trade off between quality and compression. The higher the compression, the lower the quality, and vice versa.

CELP is unique in that it is a compression algorithm that is not necessarily associated with a particular piece of hardware. This algorithm can be applied to a variety of digital signal processor (DSP) chips.

CELP is slowly making its way into communications products. It is now found in a wide variety of FRADs (frame relay access device) supporting voice services. CELP does not directly support fax or high-speed modems; engineering this support is up to the vendor.

Several of the software companies that offer CELP algorithm products also offer fax and modem software. A DSP-based voice compression product could, for example, have all three compression techniques available in memory. Upon detection of fax or modem traffic, it could instantly switch to the appropriate firmware. Voice compression could take place in an 8:1 to 12:1 range, and upon detection of a fax call, the hardware switches to fax mode using a data stream of either 4.8K, 9.6K, or 14.4K bps. Such products are available now.

The real benefits and challenges of using CELP come when the transport system uses an ATM switching architecture, because the ability to stop sending ATM cells to represent silence adds another 2:1 multiplier on top of CELP's already strong compression ratio. Thus, instead of 8:1 compression, the same quality could be achieved at 16:1 if the silence is removed.

This ability to start and stop sending information between CELP-based devices requires testing to prove the algorithms have the necessary retraining processes in place. Such a feature could potentially be added to products fairly easily.

TECHNIQUES AND GUIDELINES FOR VOICE COMPRESSION THROUGH SILENCE SUPPRESSION

Voice Activity Detection

Voice activity detection (VAD) combines new and old technologies. Digital speech interpolation — a process that can detect active speech as compared to silence or background noise — was introduced during the early 1980s. The result was a product that gave a 4:1 compression ratio over point-to-point links. The process is illustrated in Exhibit 3.

Voice quality was acceptable until traffic loads became heavy; when top performance was most needed, however, the process degraded. This degradation of quality occurred because of the TDM switching architecture used to support the application.

DSI and Cell Switching. The designers of digital speech interpolation (DSI), knowing that voice is active only about 32% of the time, tried to recover the unused bandwidth. But because bandwidth has to be assigned

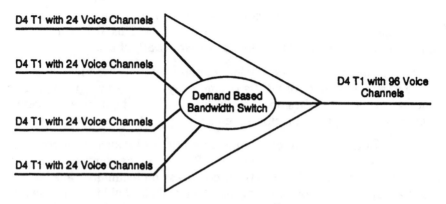

Exhibit 3. Digital Speech Interpolation (DSI) 4:1 Encoding on TDM

and reassigned moment by moment when TDM is used, the control change was discovered to consume a full 64K-bps channel and the timeslot map applied to both ends simultaneously. The control channel became congested with high use, and fax traffic caused a loss equivalent to four voice calls. A switching architecture was required that would allow the user ports to ship traffic only when they needed to and return unused bandwidth for use by others. ATM has all those features.

ATM with DSI represents true voice activity detection. DSI algorithms have always worked and have been improved since they were first introduced. Available DSP chips now perform in the 20 to 30+ MIPS range instead of the original 0.5 MIPS rate.

In addition, ATM does not use timeslot maps; instead, each cell is addressed to the correct destination. ATM also supports a wide variety of network topologies as opposed to the point-to-point TDM implementation; intermediate points in the network simply pass the traffic not terminating within that device through to the next device.

Because voice activity detection marries the benefits of DSI with a switching architecture that can support the starting and stopping of bandwidth consumption, voice activity detection can deliver an additional 2:1 compression on top of the voice compression scheme used. ADPOM at 32K bps becomes a 4:1 technology, for example, instead of a 2:1 compression technique. Low-delay CELP, which offers 4:1 compression, becomes an 8:1 compression technique.

To support voice activity detection, it is necessary to maintain the noise floor for an individual call while no information is being sent. This technique of maintaining the noise floor of the call masks whether active voice samples are being sent or not. However, the compression technique must be able to measure this parameter in some way and have the ability to re-create it at the distant party's end. If done with minimal use of bandwidth, this technique is helpful in ensuring the overall quality of the voice service.

Quality of Voice Service. One area of concern in cell switched services is how vendors of ATM products and services control the quality of service (QOS) for voice services. The current ATM Forum specifications only require four classes of service, though more are needed.

Voice is considered a constant bit rate (CBR) service. With variable bit rate (VBR) and available bit rate (ABR) services such as frame relay getting the lion's share of attention in the trade press, changes in voice technology will be less noticed but still vital for a true ATM or cell switched network. In addition to reserving bandwidth and guaranteeing traffic capacity, guaranteeing fairness has become one of the benchmarks of acceptability for goods and services in the ATM world.

CURRENT IMPLEMENTATIONS

True Speech

True Speech is an implementation of CELP — specifically, multipulse maximum likelihood quantization (MP-MLQ) and linear predictive coding (LPC) — designed for telephony technology products. This compression algorithm software can be placed on a variety of DSP products. Its compression process yields a signal from 8.5K bps down to 4.8K bps with acceptable quality.

True Speech is being integrated into products from Microsoft Corp., Compaq Computer, AT&T, and France Telecom, and its benefits will soon be available for a wide selection of applications. In addition, Northern Telecom now places voice services on its Magellen product; time (and customers) will test these brand-new services.

Narrowband ATM Compression Techniques

StrataCom, Inc.'s narrowband ATM implementation of voice services breathes new life into existing technology. By adding voice activity detection capabilities to standard PCM and all three modes of ADPCM, the company can offer no compression up to 8:1 (2-bit ADPCM with VAD).

High-quality voice is available with no compression through 5:1 (3-bit ADPCM with VAD). A compression rate can be selected on an individual DS-0 basis, allowing customers a great deal of flexibility. Most customers use the 4:1 (4-bit ADPCM with VAD) mechanism, which meets their performance requirements. All customers use digital echo cancelers to improve the echo return loss (ERL) performance of their PBXs and other voice products.

The fact that this voice traffic is mixed with other data, LAN, and video traffic demonstrates the true multimedia capabilities of ATM. Above Strata-Com's compression rates of 5:1, however, voice is strictly of "order wire" quality. The IPX product was the first product to offer these voice services. The new IGX switch also has these same services and can interoperate with IPX.

The BPX service node switch, which is StrataCom's largest ATM services platform, does not directly support voice services. Customers must have an IPX or IGX colocated with BPX to terminate voice services properly.

Internet Voice

The recent flurry of activity surrounding voice over the Internet cannot be ignored. While Internet telephony is a novel service, the Internet infrastructure is not designed to support it. Just try to download a large file several different times during the day. You will get different results each time.

The reason is because the Internet's switching architecture is based on routers, which are frame switches. Consequently, the switch cannot guarantee any performance or service to anyone. It is a datagram free-for-all controlled only by whoever got there first. Internet voice will be unacceptable in the long run unless the Internet service providers (ISPs) agree to change the switching architecture, which is unlikely.

SUMMARY

A comparatively small group of engineers, scientists, and technical gurus understand voice processing, and they rarely share that knowledge (although most of them appreciate answering sincere questions about what they do and why). The information in this chapter is intended to help users understand some of the advancements occurring in voice compression techniques — that is, what voice compression does and why it is important.

Hardware and software technologies have changed *significantly* in the past few years, much to the benefit of telecommunications (telecommunications companies, after all, funded much of the development of these new products and processes). Although TDM and PCM have endured for more than 20 years, with almost every organization having benefited greatly from these technologies, new demands are once again outpacing the capabilities of these older technologies. Voice compression schemes capable of surpassing an 8:1 ratio, and the flexibility of an ATM switching fabric, will make available to telecommunications users multimedia capabilities that require less, and hence more economical, bandwidth on the network.

Section III
Constant-Bit-Rate Data Services over Multimedia Networks

Two types of data applications are transported over multimedia networks. One type is "bursty," characterized by the random nature of computer work station data transmission. The other type requires a constant bit rate (CBR), as with synchronous data transmission or the digitized packets of voice and video applications. This section covers aspects of CBR data services.

One very effective means of providing a CBR is to reserve a portion of the transmission bandwidth for a virtual circuit. Asynchronous transfer mode (ATM) offers this as its "CBR" service. Fully implementing CBR-type applications over ATM requires that the behavior of the replaced voice or data circuit be emulated. ATM, with its inherent large bandwidth, still needs to respect the utilization of bandwidth. As most audio transmission, for example, consists of transient voice calls, ATM can use vacant bandwidth for the transmission of other less demanding data traffic.

Switching-oriented technologies, such as ATM, also need to provide methods to set up and tear down virtual circuits. These methods are standardized among equipment vendors such that one can expect a good level of interoperability.

Another area of connectivity for broadband circuit delivery is cell relay transport. A chapter is provided which covers the basics of interswitch cell relay for the carrier-class ATM switch environment. Because ATM was inherently designed for the transport of application-independent communications, including multimedia, it is necessarily a large part of the road map to the multimedia networking future.

Chapter 8
ATM Circuit Emulation Services

G. Thomas Des Jardins

Asynchronous transfer mode, or ATM, is a term in which the word asynchronous literally means "not synchronous," or "not having the same period between occurrences." In contrast, traditional POTS (plain old telephone service) circuits are designed with the assumption that they will always be used with a reference timing source and are therefore synchronous.

In order to adapt the existing equipment base of circuit-oriented equipment to ATM, it is desirable to define some method for carrying the data normally encoded by a circuit over an ATM virtual circuit. The ATM Forum has written an interoperability specification to address emulating circuits using ATM virtual circuit (VC) technology.

This document, the "Circuit Emulation Service Interoperability Specification" (CES-IS), specifies two types of constant bit rate (CBR) service:

- Structured DS1 /E1 N*64 (Fractional S1/E1) service.
- Unstructured DS1/E1 (1.544M bps/2.048M bps) service.

Both services are geared toward solving different types of problems.

STRUCTURED VERSUS UNSTRUCTURED, IN BRIEF

Structured service is designed to use an ATM network to provide low-rate voice traffic at many different points and is an "edge of the cloud"-oriented technology. Unstructured service is oriented toward the interior of the network cloud and allows the user to relay traffic straight through the network, but only between two points. This circuit emulation service is distinct from using circuits to carry ATM data, which is specified by other documents. Exhibit 1 compares structured versus unstructured service.

The next sections describe in more detail the circuit emulation services offered, how they are implemented, and how they are used. For purposes of illustrating their implementation and use, let's assume that a company

Exhibit 1   Structured versus Unstructured Circuit Emulation Service

Feature	Structured	Unstructured
Bandwidth used	Uses bandwidth in cost-effective N*64 increments	Full DS1/E1 link rate
Timing	Supplied by network	Supplied by equipment
Facility data link	Terminates	Passes through
Configuration	Somewhat complex	Simple
Framing	ESF,SF	Useful for nonstandard types of framing since it does not require framing (see note)

Note: Although framing is not required in unstructured service, an optional feature allows for performance monitoring when the unstructured service uses superframe (SF), extended superframe (ESF), or G.107 framing; however when this feature is offered, it must be designed such that it can be disabled if desired.

desires to connect circuits across an ATM cloud. These may be either DS1 or E1. Therefore let's begin with a review of the characteristics of these circuits.

DISTINGUISHING CHARACTERISTICS OF CIRCUITS

Circuits are discussed in the context of three basic characteristics: how much, when, and what. More specifically:

- "How much" refers to bandwidth, or how much of the circuit is actually in use.
- "When" refers to timing. A signal is used to maintain clocking so that the bits are decoded correctly.
- "What" refers to a framing scheme used to decode the bits, and for determining what all the bits are for. In addition, signaling information can be transmitted as well.

How Much Bandwidth. Constant bit rate circuits consist of some amount of bandwidth, which is usually either broken into 64K-bps blocks or utilized in its entirety. With regard to the two different types of circuit emulation service — structured and unstructured — a primary difference is whether the user is transmitting the circuits with "visibility" — that is, knowing how much of the circuit is in use (structured) — or as an opaque data stream (unstructured).

Briefly, a comparison of bandwidth ranges for structured versus unstructured service is as follows:

Service	El Bandwidth Range	DS1 Bandwidth Range
Structured	N = 1 to 24 × 64K bps	N = 1 to 31 × 64K bps
Unstructured	1.544	2.048

Timing. A timing source traceable to a primary reference source (PRS) must be supplied to the CBR circuit in order to keep it synchronized with the public network.

In the case of structured service, there are several means by which this timing source may be supplied. Structured timing options include:

- ATM link-derived timing (the ATM link must in turn receive its timing from a PRS-traceable source).
- An externally supplied source.
- A single clock source. For an entirely private network it may be possible to synchronize the entire network to a single clock source that is not PRS-traceable. Since there would be no interface to the public network, no timing slips would occur between the public and private networks.

Framing. Information used to align blocks of data, or frames, is also recovered from or imposed on the circuit. The framing specified in the CES-IS is the extended superframe (ESF) format. Two forms of signaling are supported, in-band using channel-associated signaling, and out-of-band, using basic service.

CIRCUIT EMULATION SPECIFICATIONS

In addition to the ATM Forum "Circuit Emulation Service Interoperability Specification" (CES-IS), circuit emulation is specified by the following documents:

- I-363, which specifies the various ATM adaptation layers (AALs).
- Request for Comment (RFC) 1573 "Evolution of the Interfaces Group of MIB-II."
- RFC 1406 "Definitions of Managed Objects for DS1 and E1 Interfaces."

There are many other standards and interoperability specifications as well. However, this chapter elucidates the operations of devices and services specified by the CES-IS.

Circuit Services: Theory and Description

With ATM, which is "not synchronous," rate adaptation is free. Circuits assume a reference timing source and are therefore synchronous. To adapt circuit-oriented equipment to ATM, a method is needed for carrying the data normally encoded by a circuit over an ATM virtual circuit.

Structured circuit services have extensive visibility into the data being carried across the network and can carry lesser amounts. Unstructured circuit service is provided with limited visibility into the data being carried, and only the full rate of the emulated technology can be transported.

Structured DS1 /E1 service is a transparent implementation useful for fractional circuits and backhauls, where knowledge of the layout of the data is important. It is, however, more complex; by allowing portions of a circuit to be mapped to different VCs, "fractions" of bandwidth can be assigned to different locations or equipment.

Unstructured DS1 /E1 service is an opaque implementation. No knowledge of the structure of the data being transmitted is presumed. This has the advantage of being simple, but it requires a whole circuit to be mapped to a single VC.

Structured DS1/E1 N*64 Service Description. The bandwidth is divided into N*64 portions and emulates a Fractional DS1 or E1 circuit. The service multiplexes N time slots, where each slot uses 64K bps. For DS1 (1.544M bps), $1 <= N <= 24$, and for E1 (2.048M bps) $1 <= N <= 31$.

The order is not required to be the same at both ends. Multiple fractional circuits can use the same CBR I/F and would receive separate VCs and might go to separate destinations.

Framing describes how data and signaling bits are packed. For DS1 equipment, extended superframe (ESF) is required to be supported and SF is optional. For E1, G.704 is required to be supported. Structured data transfer mode (SDT) is required to be used.

Structured AAL1 Requirements. Structured service may perform partial cell fill to reduce payload assembly delay. It must perform controlled frame slips. In the case of extended starvation (approximately 2.5 seconds, plus or minus .5 second), it must trigger trunk conditioning (i.e., a "red" alarm). It must provide common timing to the CBR side. This could be derived from an ATM-side primary reference source, an external source, other DS1 /E1 circuits, or an internal nonstratum 1 oscillator.

DS1/E1 Unstructured Service Description. Unstructured circuit emulation service emulates a complete DS1 or E1 circuit. It is opaque as far as data is concerned. It has a 1:1 VC-to-circuit mapping. It can optionally decode framing for SF, ESF, or G.704 framing standards (thereby permitting better maintenance). It uses unstructured data transfer (UDT) and has well-defined timing requirements. It requires full cell fill.

Unstructured AAL1 Requirements. Unstructured service must provide appropriate timing traceable to PRS to the CBR side, and this timing has specific jitter and wander requirements. Because of the requirements for recovering timing, some schemes that derive timing from information contained within the cells may place derived requirements upon the cell delay variation of the connection used to connect the line.

For DS1 /ESF, it is a requirement that the device terminate bit-oriented messages for yellow alarms and loopback. In general the device should work with facility data link by passing on performance report messages each second with cyclical redundancy checks and framing errors.

Configuration and Operation

Management of circuit emulation service (CES) interworking devices, and the services provided by them, is divided into two categories:

- Management of the ATM link.
- Management of the circuit side of the link.

Essentially a single task is accomplished: communicating how CBR data is mapped on and off a VC.

Management

Management of CES devices is performed through the use of the CES management information base (MIB) to define the VC to fractional mapping (according to the ATM Forum's CES-IS, as well as RFC 1442 "Structure of Management Information for SNMPv2" and RFC 1406 "Definitions of Managed Objects for DS1 and E1 Interfaces").

CES ATM Requirements

The first requirement is that sufficient bandwidth be provided for the connection. This is indicated by setting the peak cell rate (PCR) for the connection appropriately; also cell delay variation (CDV) must account for F4/F5 OAM cells, though these are limited to 1% of line rate. The ATM virtual circuit payload type and cell loss priority should be 0, and the connection type must be a CBR. The VC can convey timing from a primary reference source to the CES interworking facility.

Playout Buffer and Cell Fill. If there is underflow — that is, not enough bits to fill a frame before it must be transmitted, the playout buffer has been starved. If there is overflow — that is, too many bits — the playout buffer has been consumed.

Playout latency refers to the average amount of time that the play-out buffer contributes to the latency. Cell fill means that cells are not required to be completely used. Partially filled cells may be transmitted more quickly, thereby lowering latency but wasting bandwidth. Both sides must agree on how full a cell should be.

Role of CDV and PCR. When designing a box to emit cells at a given rate, an algorithm called a scheduler is constructed to control the cell emission. This algorithm, which is frequently implemented as a custom integrated circuit, must consider the possible rates that may be scheduled in various combinations and must emit cells to meet each connection's rate.

Some combinations of rates do not allow precise scheduling; for instance, two rates of 1/2 and 1/3 (of link rate) will conflict. Thus the scheduler must attempt to ensure that the average service a connection receives meets the constraints of the connection — the average rate, usually described as a peak cell rate (PCR), and the cell delay variation (CDV).

The amount of variance from the ideal position of a cell is known as CDV, which is defined as the difference between the cell's reference arrival time and the actual arrival time. Each device along a path contributes a certain amount of CDV to the connection, which is accumulated and added to the total CDV of the connection from end to end.

Essentially, all devices contribute a nonzero amount of CDV to a connection. The amount of variance that can be tolerated by a given connection is dependent on several factors, ranging from the amount of buffering built into the equipment to the nature of the traffic being transported.

Cell Delay Variation Tolerance. The maximum amount of CDV a device contributes is not defined by a specification. In fact, the ATM Forum CES-IS specifically states that the "CDV tolerance [CDVT] is considered a network option and is currently not subject to standardization." However, Bellcore documents have proposed an accumulated CDV level of 750 μs for a whole connection.

The maximum CDVT that can be tolerated, however, depends on two factors:

- How much memory the device has to buffer cells while waiting to assemble a complete frame.
- The temporal value of the data to be lost when a cell arrives at a different cell slot from the desired one.

If a connection is established with a certain CDVT, the connection is expressing to the network the bounds on the delay that can be tolerated by either of these two constraining factors.

Thus, when the network sets up the switched virtual circuit (SVC) or permanent virtual circuit (PVC), the path that the connection will be routed through will consider the CDV accumulated along that path and refuse to set up a connection that does not meet the required accumulate CDV (e.g., CDV < = CDVT).

Example: Adding Up CDVs. To fully define a CBR VC's traffic contract, the peak cell rate and the cell delay variation tolerance need to be specified. For example, suppose each device adds 10 μs CDV to the CDV on the connection (ATM Forum UNI version 3.1, page 322). If there are five devices in the path of the connection, the total CDV is 125 μs. Thus, if the contract specifies 150 as the CDVT, the connection would be permitted to be established.

Using FORE Systems' equipment, the CDVT defaults to 1,000 μs, and therefore the contract would indeed pass the traffic of the cell path 300. If the CDVT is set to 250 (the stated design parameter of the cell path 300) or even to 180 (the observed value), the traffic passes without cell loss. Just to prove that the switch would police correctly, if the CDVT is set to 50 you would observe the concomitant loss of cells.

The CDVs are simply added for the purposes of this example. Because the CDV describes the displacement of the cell from the ideal position in absolute terms, there is a nonzero chance that the first switch might delay, while the next switch might actually send a cell early. Thus the two CDVs might cancel each other out. Although this possibility exists, it would be poor engineering practice to count on this occurring, and therefore the CDVs are conservatively added up.

Tip for Customers. CDV is a part of any ATM network. When a company is requesting service, the service provider will want to know the maximum, allowable cell delay variation tolerance.

Cell delay variation is applicable to any connection with a PCR or SCR, such as a variable bit rate (VBR) or CBR connection, and is a parameter the customer will need to configure when setting up the PVC or SVC.

In the reassembly function, a buffer is used in which the stream is stored before it is transmitted. The buffer must be large enough to accommodate expected CDV and small enough so that excessive delays are not occurring in the circuit. The value is the maximum cell interarrival jitter that the reassembly process will tolerate without producing errors on the CBR interface.

Chapter 9
ATM Cell Relay Transport for Broadband Services

David H. Axner

Bandwidth has always been a precious commodity in the communications realm. Since the early days of data communications, users have demanded and vendors have provided products with increased performance, driving up line rates and requiring faster carrier services. With the emergence of distributed processing and local area network (LAN) internetworking, networks have become vital to the distribution of information. T1/E1 bandwidth once satisfied users' application needs and allowed the integration of data and voice channels. But T1/E1 speeds are not adequate for such bandwidth-intensive applications as file transfers and the transmission of graphic information, much less communications between 100M-bps fiber distributed data interface (FDDI), and rings, brought on by LAN internetworking. Other applications, such as computer-aided design (CAD), videoconferencing, and medical imaging, also require large amounts of bandwidth. The communications carriers have had to respond to increasing bandwidth requirements by offering T3/E3 services. Architects of private networks have also had to develop and introduce multiplexers and switches with more capacity to satisfy their customers' needs.

The emerging broadband transport mechanisms (e.g., synchronous optical network [SONET] and synchronous digital hierarchy [SDH]) and broadband services (switched multimegabit data services [SMDS] and broadband integrated services digital network [ISDN]) are targeted to existing and future bandwidth-intensive applications. SONET and its International Telephone and Telegraph Consultative Committee (CCITT) equivalent, SDH, are now under development by the carriers and will provide an extensive range of multimegabit bandwidths: SONET from 51.84M bps (OC-1) to 2.488G bps (OC-48), with provision to climb to 13G bps, and SDH from 155.52M bps (STM-1) to 2.488G bps (STM-16).

THE DEMAND FOR BROADBAND SERVICE

A trend away from centralized processing toward distributed processing began during the early 1980s with the emergence of microcomputers and LANS. Users within large corporate enterprises are interconnected over enterprisewide networks that incorporate numerous LANS. These users require access to network resources that support client–server computing for the access of files and applications and peer-to-peer networking for electronic mail and other applications.

The proliferation of LAN internetworking has become a leading force driving the development of broadband services. LAN traffic over wide area networks (WANs) is on the upswing and continues to rise. In a LAN internetworking environment, LAN resources (e.g., applications, files, and data bases) may reside on multiple servers throughout a global network. These resources are regularly accessed by users to conduct corporate business. WAN backbones that interconnect LANs must be able to support the bandwidth demands of rising LAN traffic. T1 backbones, once sufficient to support LAN internetwork traffic, are being upgraded to T3. Future bandwidth demands by backbone traffic, such as FDDI, will exceed even this capacity.

LAN traffic is bursty in comparison with other forms of data communications traffic, which requires bandwidth for a prolonged period. LAN traffic requires bandwidth only for the duration of a frame transmission. The available network bandwidth can then be applied to other LAN traffic. Therefore, bandwidth can be shared by multiple users. Besides bandwidth sharing, bandwidth demands are dynamic. Network bandwidth must be available on demand to support immediate bandwidth requirements. Delay is still another key factor that must be considered for LAN internetworking. Network delay affects response time at LAN work stations. Increased delay results in slower response time, causing work station users to wait longer for requested files or applications.

Multimedia applications at the desktop, another driving force for broadband services, are on the way. Future work station users will be able to view full-motion video presentations, communicate by audio and video transmission, send and receive CAD or medical images, download files, and transfer graphic information. These applications will require hefty amounts of bandwidth to handle the large amounts of information within a reasonable response time. For example, bit-mapped graphic images are composed of 75K to 100K bytes, while files can consist of multiple megabytes. In a LAN environment, a 100K-byte graphic image can be transmitted in 0.08 seconds over an Ethernet LAN and in 0.05 seconds over a 16M-bps Token Ring. But if the same image must be accessed from a remote LAN and transmitted over a WAN link at 56K bps, it would take at least 14.3 seconds, which is far too slow to satisfy user needs. At a T1 rate, the time is reduced to about one-half second. Large file transfers, medical images, and full-motion video all demand high WAN transmission rates for low response time and to prevent these applications from dominating the network.

Vendors are now discussing bandwidths of 100M bps or more at the desktop, using FDDI to support these bandwidth-intensive multimedia applications. Should this become a reality, current WAN rates will become a crippling bottleneck.

Such large-scale networks will generate heavy network traffic, which must be handled with minimum delay and rapid delivery. Broadband networks using SONET, SDH, or another broadband service promise to provide large bandwidth with minimum delay to satisfy heavy LAN traffic conditions. They will be analogous to information superhighways.

CELL RELAY AND ATM SWITCHING

Bandwidth on demand to support bursty LAN traffic is the criterion for fast packet technology, which is a general term applied to a variety of packet mode concepts that offer vast performance improvements of several orders of magnitude over conventional X.25 packet switching.

Cell relay is a form of fast packet switching not to be confused with frame relay. The distinguishing factors between frame relay and cell relay involve frame size, media support, and implementation. Cell relay technology dictates a fixed-length packet, is well suited to handling any form of information, and employs a fast packet switching technique called asynchronous transfer mode (ATM). By contrast, the frame relay standard employs a variable-length packet, is well suited to handling data but not voice, and can be implemented as an interface to a multiplexer or switch similar to the old X.25 specification.

The term *asynchronous* in ATM means that cells are transported through a network without regard to frame alignment, such as that required for T1 frames. Although the individual bits within a cell are synchronized, the timing between cells can vary.

The ATM cell relay concept offers a solution to the requirements for high bandwidth and multimedia transmission. It is adaptable to high switching speeds to support huge amounts of bandwidth and it accommodates traffic of any medium. Therefore, in 1988, the CCITT selected ATM as a target solution for future broadband services.

The fixed cell format and small cell size of ATM are ideal characteristics for low delay (latency) and predictable throughput. Minimum latency is essential for the transmission of video and voice, which require guaranteed bandwidth and a fixed delivery rate with constant delay. It is also amenable to the construction of larger networks. The small, fixed-size cell can be transported through a network faster than larger, variable-length frames or packets. The constant cell size is predictable and can be processed by faster switching algorithms than those for variable-length frames. Processing can be performed even faster by incorporating the algorithms in silicon chips, eliminating delays caused by software analysis. Cell switches can exploit the advantage of very large scale integration (VLSI), which can support very high speeds at a very low price per unit.

Bandwidth can be made available on demand because (as with statistical multiplexing) bandwidth is available only to active channels, but on a first-come, first-served basis. Bandwidth can be guaranteed using a priority-assignment concept called cell slotting, in which each cell occupies a slot of bandwidth. A cell stream that requires considerable bandwidth may be allocated every fourth slot of bandwidth; a lighter stream may need only one slot in 20. The cell-slotting scheme is conducive to handling bursty traffic, but an application that requires fixed transmission delay is equally accommodated, because cell slotting enables traffic to be scheduled to satisfy the delivery requirements of an application. This technique provides better use of network bandwidth.

The standards for ATM switching have been under development by the American National Standards Institute (ANSI) and CCITT standards committees. ATM responds to traffic bursts by providing bandwidth on demand for the duration of the burst. Traffic bursts are packetized in fixed-length cells, which are transported through the network to their destination where they are then depacketized and exit the network. The ATM cell consists of a header that provides routing information and is followed by an information field. The routing information identifies the channel sending the information and the overall path through the network to the destination point.

Cell size was heavily debated by North American and European standards organizations before the present standard was established. The European carriers leaned toward a small cell size (about 16 octets) to minimize latency on slower voice circuits, optimizing ATM for voice transmission. Voice dominates European communications traffic and circuit costs are eight times higher than the costs of U.S. circuits. U.S. carriers favored a large cell size (about 200 octets) to improve the performance of file transfers by reducing the number of headers to be processed. In the end, the compromise result is the current ATM cell.

The Components of an ATM Cell. The cell as defined by ANSI and the CCITT is 53 bytes in length and consists of a header and an information field. Its structure is shown in Exhibit 1. The first five bytes, referred to as octets, form the cell header, and the remaining 48 bytes form the information

Exhibit 1. ATM Cell Structure

ATM Cell Format

GFC 4	VPI 4		VPI/VCI	VCI		VCI	PT 2	R 2		HEC	
Octet 1			Octet 2	Octet 3		Octet 4				Octet 5	

Notes:

GFC   Generic flow control field. The initial field of the cell format, a 4-bit field within octet 1. It regulates the flow of traffic from the customer premises equipment into the network for different services.

HEC   Header error control. Octet 5 is used for multiple-bit error detection and single-bit error correction. Cells with multiple-bit errors are simply discarded.

PT   Payload type indicator. A cell can contain transport or signaling information. The cell type is identified by the PT indicator, which distinguishes between information and signaling cells. It consists of bits 5 and 6 octet 4. The remaining two bits in octet 4 are reserved for future use.

VPI/VCI   Virtual path identifier/virtual channel identifier. Cell routing is defined by a 24-bit field within octets 1-4. The VPI is a 12- or 16-bit field used to define a logical path through the network. The VCI is an 8- or 12-bit field that identifies a logical channel within the associated logical path.

field. The cell header contains fields that control traffic flow, cell routing, cell identification, and error correction.

BROADBAND MARKET SEGMENTS

Broadband requirements encompass three market segments: customer premises, private WANS, and public networks. Broadband support for customer premises focuses on the desktop and locally interconnected LANS. To support multimegabit speeds (e.g., with FDDI) at the desktop requires high-performance network interface cards to connect a work station with a multimegabit network. High-performance hubs that incorporate broadband routers are needed to interconnect LANs with broadband WAN facilities. These requirements fall into the domain of the network interface card and hub suppliers.

Private networks interconnect customer premises and use private high-speed backbone links to connect with public networks. Data communications customer premises equipment suppliers (of multiplexers and switches) that are currently developing ATM switches for backbone network support in the private domain include Adaptive Corporation (a majority-owned subsidiary of Network Equipment Technologies, Inc., Redwood City CA), BBN Communications (Cambridge MA), IBM, Newbridge Networks, Inc. (Herndon VA), and StrataCom, Inc. (Atlanta GA). Besides these suppliers, Alcatel Network Systems (Richardson TX) and AT&T Network Systems (Murray Hill NJ) have indicated that they will also offer switches for private broadband networks.

Adaptive Corporation's switch is targeted to the private networking environment for LAN internetworking applications. It connects desktops through adapter cards and subnetworks and metropolitan area networks (MANs) through routers, initially providing full-duplex interface rates of 100M bps.

BBN's ATM switch is targeted to the private sector as a broadband backbone node for private networks but will also support some public network applications. The target application is LAN internetworking with support for Transmission Control Protocol and Internet Protocol (TCP/IP) and open systems interconnection (OSI) when FDDI and Ethernet interfaces are introduced.

Newbridge Networks' ATM switch (to be introduced during the second quarter of 1993) will be targeted to both private and public network applications. Newbridge supports LAN interconnectivity through its existing Ethernet and Token Ring interfaces. Newbridge plans to provide FDDI interfaces and ATM interfaces to connect desktops. The switch is designed to support OC-3 at the desktop.

StrataCom's BIPX is in development and is expected to be available during the 1993–1994 time frame. It is targeted to both the private and public sectors. StrataCom has targeted LAN internetworking and plans to support frame relay and desktop applications.

Private networks are expected to eventually contain resource-rich FDDI backbone LANs and switches connecting multiple servers that range from microcomputers to mainframes. These servers will service requests from work stations and microcomputers on geographically dispersed LANs within an enterprise/wide network. High-speed routers will interconnect the LANs or groups of LANs with FDDI backbone LANs and switches at multimegabit rates over a broadband network.

Public networks are the domain of the local exchange and interexchange carriers, the providers of broadband public services that will interconnect customer premises and private networks. Broadband carrier facilities will be supported by ATM switches produced by communications vendors (i.e., central office switch manufacturers). ATM switches directed to the local exchange and interexchange carrier market will support central office switching for the emerging broadband transports (i.e., SONET, SDH, and MANs) and services (i.e., SMDS and broadband ISDN).

Alcatel, AT&T, and Fujitsu are developing switches for this market. Alcatel plans to complete its ATM switch in the third quarter of 1993 and make it generally available the following quarter. Alcatel has targeted multiple broadband applications that include LAN and MAN internetworking, cross-connecting T1/E1 channels, and videoconferencing.

AT&T announced the availability of its BNS-2000 for the third quarter of 1992. Early versions of the switch served on a test and trial basis at GTE and several regional Bell operating companies, including Ameritec, NYNEX, Pacific Telesis, Bell South, Southwestern Bell, and U.S. West. The BNS-2000 architecture is evolutionary and is intended for incorporation in a future multigigabit broadband switch for broadband ISDN.

Fujitsu has installed early models of its switches at central offices and test labs for testing. It expects to begin shipping production models during 1993. The FETEX 150, a combined narrowband/broadband switch, has been installed for testing in some U.S. LECs and IECS.

Telephone company local exchange carriers are responding to the need for LAN internetworking through MANS, which will be supported by cell relay ATM switches based on the IEEE 802.6 standard. These central office resident switches will provide bandwidth and connectivity for LAN internetworking within metropolitan areas, allowing users at LAN work stations and microcomputers to access resources on servers supported by the MAN or attached to LANs serviced by the MAN. These ATM switches will serve the business community as well as the university environment, providing MAN connections within one or more floors of a building and throughout a university campus.

Several data communications equipment suppliers have announced that they will also supply their switches to the public sector. These suppliers include BBN Communications, Newbridge Networks, and StrataCom.

BUS VS. BUSLESS ARCHITECTURE

The design trend for developers of ATM switches is a busless architecture to interface the switch to lines and trunks. Busless switch architecture is suited to broadband switching speeds. By contrast, bus architecture is common in the industry for all sorts of devices, from bridges and routers to communications processors, computers, and network switches that run at subbroadband rates.

Bus architecture employs a high-speed bus that links line cards that connect to external lines and devices and support the transfer of data between the device and card. The bus acts as a common highway to support all data transfer between the line cards. Because the bus is shared by all attached line cards, its bandwidth must equal the aggregate data rate of the attached cards. As more cards are added, the bus bandwidth must be high enough to accommodate the added cards that share the bus.

Bus architecture is adequate for applications that operate at speeds below broadband, but as line speeds increase to gigabit rates, this architecture exhibits severe limitations. Higher bus rates increase the cost of the cards. A number of designs have been created to solve this problem, such as high-density cards that support several devices and cascaded or hierarchical buses. These designs work to an extent, but they have their limits.

Other critical limitations of bus design are its single point of failure and nonscalability. In the event of a bus failure, all data flow is interrupted. This can be remedied by using a second bus to provide redundancy, but at extra cost.

Busless architecture directly interconnects attached devices and lines, eliminating common element sharing. Busless architecture also satisfies economies of scale. Switches can be designed that are modular and easily expanded by adding switching fabric to provide scalability. The same line cards can be used for all switch connections, eliminating the need for different line card parameters.

Parallel switching is applicable to cell relay technology and enables virtually unlimited performance, supporting switch bandwidths of 100G bps or more. With large switch capacity, access rates can be substantially improved and a broad range of access rates can be supported. For example, the switch could accommodate low-speed lines, such as 9.6K and 19.2K bps; high-speed fractional T1 and T1 links; and such broadband links as T3 and above, once they become available.

ATM PRODUCT PROFILES

The basic architectural profile and characteristics of ATM switches currently under development and testing are presented for several vendors. Much of the switch design activity is in its early stages; therefore, the profiles are presented to provide a basic understanding of switch configuration, performance, and customer interface support. They are not meant to be analytical evaluations of each product, because the information provided by the vendors is insufficient for critical evaluation.

Overview of Switches for Public Networks

ATM switches for public networks exhibit modular construction and fault tolerance. The Alcatel and Fujitsu switches employ a busless architecture and a scalable switching fabric, while AT&T's BNS-2000 uses a bus architecture. Both Alcatel's and Fujitsu's switches exhibit an extensive range of bandwidth scalability, from as low as 10G bps to as high as 160G bps, while AT&T's initial release of its BNS-2000 tops out at 200M bps. Characteristics of the switches are summarized in Exhibit 2.

Exhibit 2.   ATM Central Office Switch Characteristics

Supplier	Alcatel	AT&T	Fujitsu
Product	1 01 0 VPSS	BNS-2000	FETEX 150
Availability	4Q93	3Q92	1993
Switch architecture	Busless	Bus	Busless
Capacity	100G-159G bps	Release 1: 200M bps	9.6G–160G bps
		Release 2: 20G bps	
		(1993-1995)	
		Release 3: 80G bps	
		(1995–2000)	
Ports	128 bidirectional	N/A	256 bidirectional
Maximum port rate	155M/622M bps	T3/E3	155M/622M bps
Interface modules	SMDS; SONET; Broadband ISDN; Frame Relay	SMDS; Frame Relay; X.25; asynchronous; SDLC; HDLC	SONET Broadband; ISDN
Network management	Proprietary; SNMP and CMIP agent	Proprietary (StarKeeper); Accumaster and IBM NetView alarms; SNMP agent; CMIP (future)	Proprietary

Notes:

CMIP	Common management information protocol
HDLC	High-level data link control
ISDN	Integrated services digital network
SDLC	Synchronous data link control
SMDS	Switched multimegabit data services
SNMP	Simple network management protocol
SONET	Synchronous optical network

Alcatel Network Systems. The Model 1010 VPSS ATM switch is designed around a busless architecture. Access lines and trunks directly interface the switch through interface cards. The switch is modular and scalable. Each of up to a maximum of 16 switching modules contains 16 ports for a total of 128 bidirectional ports. Each port operates at a rate of 155M bps (OC-3) or 622M bps (OC- 12). Switched capacity is increased by adding switching matrix modules, which scale the switch capacity from 10G bps to 159G bps (5G to 79G bps bidirectional).

The VPSS consists of an ATM switch and virtual path (VP) multiplexer. The ATM switch is interfaced with the VP multiplexer to accommodate user and network access to the switch. The multiplexer can be located locally or remotely at access nodes for network configuration flexibility. It can be configured with a variety of user and network interface modules that support links operating at T1/E1, T3/E3, 140M bps, and 155M bps.

Alcatel's VP multiplexer provides 16 ports, three of which are used — two for bidirectional switch connections and one for control signals. A maximum of 64 VP multiplexers is supported, for a total of 838 user ports.

Alcatel also provides a multiplexer for customer premises, which multiplexes user data and converts the user data stream into ATM cells for delivery to the VPSS.

The VPSS is managed and configured from a network management center. Network management and configuration is performed in-band using Q3 protocol, which delivers management information to each network element. Alcatel plans to provide compliance with the simple network management protocol and common management information protocol; however, it does not support links to IBM's NetView, AT&T's Accumaster, or Digital Equipment Corp.'s EMA.

AT&T Network Systems. The BNS-2000 is designed to comply with CCITT cell relay standards and IEEE 802.6 and features an ATM-based architecture. The BNS-2000 complies with Bellcore SMDS specifications and can support MANs. In the private sector, the BNS-2000 serves as a backbone network switch to interconnect LANs, FDDI, and MANs.

The BNS-2000 features modular construction for configuration flexibility and is scalable to accommodate demands for expanded bandwidth. The BNS-2000 incorporates a bus-oriented architecture. A 200M-bps backplane transports information between the ATM switch and link and trunk interfaces. The backplane rate is independent of the link and trunk rates, which allows them to correspond to the type of service that they support. The BNS-2000 currently supports T1/E1 and T3/E3 trunks and eventually will support broadband SONET OC-3 (155M bps) trunks when the service becomes available.

Link and trunk interfaces use modular construction for system configuration flexibility. These interfaces support a wide range of user applications, including frame relay at 64K bps to 1.5M bps, X.25 at 56K and 64K bps, asynchronous communications at rates up to 19.2K bps, and synchronous communications up to 1.544M bps. The BNS-2000 is also equipped with SMDS service interface modules for T1/E1 links and for SMDS class 1 through 5 service at 4M, 10M, 16M, 25M, or 34M bps.

Internodal BNS-2000 connections are supported by trunks operating at T3. Routing is either connectionless or connection-oriented to provide connection flexibility. Additional bandwidth is provided through the use of multiple trunks. Fiber cable running at 8M bps can be used as an alternative to interconnect nodes up to distances of a few kilometers.

Fault tolerance is supported through standby power supplies and equipment redundancy. An optional redundant switch feature prevents the disruption of existing data sessions by a primary switch failure. Alternate rerouting prevents session disruptions over internodal trunks. Sessions from a failed facility are rerouted over spare capacity on other trunks.

AT&T provides network management for the BNS-2000 through its Star-Keeper 11 Network Management System (NMS), which enables users to configure and perform network management functions through a local or remote console for user flexibility. The NMS employs a graphical user interface, called the Open Look graphical interface, for ease of use. Network management compliance with the simple network management protocol is supported and is planned for the common management information protocol. The NMS exports alarms to IBM's NetView but has no additional NetView functions. It fully supports AT&T's Accumaster; however, AT&T has no plans to support DEC's Enterprise Management Architecture (EMA) on its StarKeeper NMS.

The BNS-2000 will enable local exchange carriers to offer users a MAN service that will provide interconnection among widely dispersed LANs. It will provide users with an alternative to private WANs and the flexibility to support a broad range of user applications. AT&T plans to offer a family of LAN bridges and routers as well as interfaces to support a number of high-speed transmission applications, such as file transfer between host processors, CAD/CAM, high-resolution graphics, and video system transmission.

Fujitsu. The FETEX-150 system uses a modular and scalable architecture to accommodate future enhancements and changing service and functional needs, thereby extending its life. The design of the FETEX-150 is based on three discrete subsystems: signal path, processing, and maintenance and operational subsystem. The signal path subsystem encompasses the switching fabric and the subscriber, network, and signaling interfaces. The original narrowband signal path subsystem supports the public switched network and switches up to 128 DS-0 channels, providing 8M-bps bandwidth.

The new broadband signal path subsystem, which complements the narrowband signal path subsystem, supports broadband applications, including high-speed LAN internetworking, imaging, and video. It consists of ATM and STM switching fabrics and broadband subscriber and network interfaces. Scalable bidirectional switch capacities from 9.6G to 160G bps are supported by a total of 16 16-port modules at 622M bps per port.

The initial switch supports subscriber rates from 64K bps to 155M bps; future plans are for rates to 622M bps. Subscriber and network fiber-optic connections terminate at a broadband signal path subsystem module called the broadband remote switching unit, which shortens fiber loop lengths and provides access to all switching fabrics, including ATM, STM, and narrowband. Network interfaces will support emerging carrier transports and services, including SONET, SMDS, and broadband ISDN.

Overview of Switches for Private Networks

These ATM switches, developed for private network applications, exhibit common characteristics. Their architecture is busless, except for Newbridge Network's 36150, which uses a star/bus architecture. They are scalable, modular switches and are also fault tolerant. Scalability allows broad expansion of switch capacity to accommodate growth, higher transmission rates, and the availability of extended broadband carrier services. Modularity provides flexible switch configuration using a variety of customer access interfaces and trunks. Fault tolerance prevents outages from component and power-supply failures, eliminating the interruption of services.

These switches plan interfaces for Ethernet, Token Ring, and FDDI to provide direct interconnection between LANs and backbone networks. Frame relay and SMDS interfaces are also slated for initial release in some cases. Initial releases support T1/E1 and T3/E3 trunks and internodal links, with future releases targeted for broadband services.

In all cases, network management is supported by the vendor's network management systems. The switches also support the simple network management protocol and can be managed through such a management system. Newbridge Network's 36150 is the only switch that will link with IBM's NetView or AT&T's Accumaster. It also supports management of the common management information protocol. Characteristics of these switches are summarized in Exhibit 3.

Adaptive Corp. Adaptive's ATM switch design is busless; access and network interface cards connect directly to the switch, eliminating the limitations of bus architecture. Modularity and scalability are inherent features of the switch, enabling expansion to accommodate growth and the flexibility to satisfy different application requirements. Switch bandwidth extends from 240M bps to 1.2G bps, while switch architecture enables extensibility to 10G bps. Internodal switch traffic is scalable in full-duplex increments of 100M bps.

Switch configuration is performed out-of-band through an Ethernet port, although in-band management is planned for a future release. Configuration commands are entered at a Sun work station using Adaptive's network management application, which is equipped with a graphical interface (OSF Motif) for user ease. The network management application includes diagnostic and maintenance facilities. The switch supports the simple network management protocol as an agent, allowing it to be managed from a simple network management protocol network console.

BBN Communications. BBN's Emerald is modular, scalable, and fault tolerant and is designed around a busless architecture, eliminating the constraints

Exhibit 3. ATM Private Network Switch Characteristics

Supplier	Adaptive	BBN	Newbridge	StrataCom
Product	ATMX	Emerald	36150	BIPX
Availability	1992	1993	Release 1: 1993 Release 2: 994	1993-94
Switch architecture	Busless	Busless	Star/bus	Busless
Capacity	240M–1.2G bps	160G bps	Release 1: 620M bps Release 2: 5G bps Future: 40G bps	4.60G bps
Total ports	90	72	128	36
Maximum port rate	100M bps	Release 1: 2 M bps	Release 1: 155 M bps Release 2: 622M bps	T3/E3
Interface modules	FDDI PMD	SMDS; SONET; Broadband ISDN; SDH; Frame Relay Future: Ethernet; FDDI	T1/E1; T3/E3/STM-1; Frame Relay; Ethernet; Token Ring; FDDI Ring; FDDI Release 2: STS-12/STM-4	T1/E1; T3/E3; SONET; SMDS; Broadband ISDN
Network management	Proprietary; SNMP agent	Proprietary; SNMP; CMIP future; Digital Equipment Corp.	Proprietary (4602 Network-Station); SNMP and CMIP agent	Proprietary SNMP agent; NetView Accumaster, Digital Equipment Corp. EMA support

Notes:

CMIP	Common management information protocol
EMA	Enterprise management architecture
FDDI	Fiber distributed data interface
ISDN	Integrated services digital network
PMD	Physical medium dependent
SDH	Synchronous digital hierarchy
SMDS	Switched multimegabit data services
SNMP	Simple network management protocol
SONET	Synchronous optical network
STS	Synchronous transport signal

of bus architecture. Line cards connect directly to the switch matrix over a 160M bps path. The maximum full-duplex switch capacity is 1.6G bps. The busless architecture is amenable to scalability through added switch matrices. Switch clustering will enable the switch to accommodate the demands for increased bandwidth that are expected to surface over the decade as bandwidth-intensive applications surface and become more prevalent. It will also enable higher switch speeds to accommodate higher speed broadband services.

Fault tolerance is implemented through redundant power supplies; line, trunk, and switch cards; disks; and network processors. The dual backplane provides two independent paths for connections between line and trunk cards and switch cards. In the event of a failure of one path, all information is routed over the remaining path. Cooling system redundancy is also provided.

The switch supports T1/E1 and T3/E3 trunks in its initial release. BBN plans to support broadband services, including SMDS, broadband ISDN, SDH, and SONET OC-1 (50M bps) and OC-3 (150M bps) in future releases as these carrier services become widely available. Emerald will support 20 broadband trunks.

Internodal trunks will accommodate T1/E1 or T3/E3 services for the initial release. OC-1, OC-3, and SMDS are planned for internodal trunk support in future releases. The entire switching capacity can be allocated for internodal trunks in tandem switch configurations. No single trunk can exceed OC-3. A total of 1,000 switching nodes is supported; however, the routing algorithm in the initial release is optimized for networks consisting of a maximum of 200 nodes.

The initial release of Emerald supports 72 user access ports with rates of 56K to 2M bps (DS-0, fractional T1, T1, and E1). A data communications equipment frame relay interface is provided, and frame forwarding is supported. Frame forwarding passes frames transparently within proprietary protocols, FDDI, and Ethernet. Support for TCP/IP routing is planned once FDDI and Ethernet interfaces are added. According to BBN, it will develop user interfaces for Emerald that are based on business needs and the evolution of the marketplace.

Switch configuration is performed locally through a terminal connected to an Ethernet port or centrally through a network management system. Management options include BBN's management system, which is based on DEC's EMA, or through management systems that support simple network management protocol, because it is supported in the initial release. Links with IBM's NetView or AT&T's Accumaster are currently not planned.

Newbridge Networks. The Newbridge 36150 is a modular and scalable totally nonblocking switch that employs a star/bus architecture. Multiple independent buses interconnect line cards to the switch fabric. Newbridge plans to introduce the 36150 with a 620M-bps switching module. A 5G-bps switch module is planned for the second release, and a 40G-bps switch module is planned for a future release.

Newbridge plans to make the 36150 upgradable from the low-capacity switch to a large capacity without replacing line and trunk cards or power supplies. All 36150 components are redundant, including 1/0 cards, power supplies, and buses. In addition, 1/0 cards can be configured for both path and module redundancy.

Planned port interfaces for the initial release include T1/E1, T3/E3, FDDI, and STS-3/STM-1 (155M bps). Newbridge plans to provide support for frame relay, Ethernet (10BASE2 and 10BASE5), and Token Ring (4M and 16M bps) using existing interfaces, plus all the existing data and voice interfaces from its 36XX family. The second release is expected to also support STS-12/STM-4 (622M-bps) port interfaces.

Newbridge plans to support switch configuration and network management with its 4602 Mainstreet NetworkStation. The 4602 currently supports simple network management and common information management protocols and provides full bidirectional NetView interfaces and an Accumaster interface. No decision has been made as yet for an EMA interface.

Newbridge Networks plans to support SMDS service interfaces; however, an IEEE 802.6 interface is not planned at this writing.

StrataCom. StrataCom pioneered fast packet switching. Its FastPacket IPX, in production since 1986, was originally based on proprietary technology, because it predated broadband standards. It was designed for transmission over T1 links; therefore, an IPX packet or cell was based on 24 bytes to conform with a T1 frame. StrataCom has since moved toward standards adopted by the ANSI and CCITT committees. It developed a trunk interface that converts between 24- and 53-byte cells on the fly. The interface (the ATM trunk module) connects an IPX node to a T3 or E3 trunk operating in a cell relay environment. The IPX can be configured to concurrently support 24-byte T1 trunks. An IPX node can consist of as many as four ATM trunk modules. User IPX installations are easily upgraded to ATM cell compliance by swapping the existing trunk interface card with the ATM version.

The StrataCom IPX is based on bus architecture. It contains a dual redundant backplane that runs at 32M bps and can operate in both packet and time-slot interchange modes. Fault tolerance is provided through a redundant backplane, power supplies, trunk and line cards, and ports. Internodal trunks are supported as fiber or copper cable at rates ranging from narrowband (64K bps) to broadband (45M bps). The IPX supports up to 20 trunks per node, four of which can be broadband trunks (T3/E3). Cross-connect and grooming functions are supported at the DS-0 level.

StrataCom's Broadband IPX (BIPX) switch architecture is busless, with line and trunk cards directly interfaced to the switch. Modularity, scalability, and fault tolerance are switch attributes. The switch bandwidth for the initial release is planned for 4.6G bps. StrataCom plans double the switch capacity in future releases. StrataCom plans to use the same fault tolerance strategy as is provided for its IPX.

A total of 36 ports is planned for user access lines and trunks. The initial release will support T1/E1 and T3/E3 trunks, which will also support internode connections. StrataCom plans to support grooming and cross-connection to provide application flexibility. Configuration and network management will be provided through StataCom's StrataView Plus network management system.

IBM. IBM announced its own version of a fast packet switch in 1990. Developed at IBM's Thomas J. Watson Research Center in Yorktown Heights NY, the original Packetized Automatic Routing Integrated System (PARIS) switch, a laboratory prototype, supports 100M-bps fiber-optic links and has a nodal throughput of 1.2G bps, which is more than one million packets per second.

IBM is now developing a second-generation switch. It is designed to support links rated at SONET OC-12 (622M bps) — equivalent to sending 14,000 single-spaced text pages per second — and to provide a nodal throughput of about six times that of the original switch.

PARIS is a multimedia switch that integrates data, imaging, video, and voice. It integrates LAN and WAN components to operate as a single homogeneous network and is designed to accommodate emerging high-bandwidth carrier services, such as SMDS, SONET, and broadband ISDN. However, PARIS differs from fast packet models that use the ATM fixed-cell size backed by the CCITT and IEEE standards committees. The PARIS approach to fast packet switching employs the packet transfer mode (PTM), which accommodates variable-length packets that can range in size from a few bytes to several thousand bytes. The advantage of PTM is that it can transport user packets in integral form with minimal adaptation layer processing and reduced overhead compared with the ATM technique, which must convert user traffic to a sequence of fixed-byte packets.

The PARIS architecture handles routing in layer 3 just as X.25 does, precluding the necessity of layer 2 use. PARIS's protocol implementation is logically a two-layer protocol that includes the physical layer and the routing layer. The PARIS routing technique, called automatic network routing (ANR), attaches a link-identifier field (ANR field) to each packet at the source node. The ANR field contains a sequence of link identifiers, each of which identifies an intermediate link in the route that the packet must travel from source to destination node. As the packet is routed to its destination over the source-identified links, each intermediate node strips off its own link identifier from the header and switches the packet to the next link in the route.

The advantage of this routing technique is that it minimizes internodal delay, because it does not require table lookup or processing at each intermediate node, eliminating lookup and processing delays that can cause bottlenecks. It also eliminates the need to update routing tables at call setup time, substantially improving call setup and teardown delay. However, the length of the ANR field, which varies according to the number of internode hops, adds to the overhead of using additional bandwidth. Because link identifiers are stripped off by each node, however, the average field length is reduced to half the number of link identifiers.

Network control functions are performed by the network control unit. These functions include source routing using ANR and call setup. Source routing is performed dynamically through an algorithm based on the open-shortest-path-first routing technique. Packets are automatically routed around link or node failures during call setup time, but not on transit. Packets in transit are discarded when a link or node failure occurs that is part of their route.

Packet construction and error detection and correction are handled at end-point nodes only. Packets with errors are discarded by intermediate nodes. End-point nodes also control traffic congestion and flow control.

The PARIS switch uses bus architecture to interconnect the switch and network link adapters. A link adapter handles the send and receive VO functions between the switch and a network link. Each link adapter within a node contains input and output first-in first-out buffers to handle packets arriving from a network link and packets departing to a network link. Link identifiers can be handled on the fly, but buffering is needed to support link traffic where several packets are queued for link departure or arrival.

IBM is also developing a very high-speed LAN to serve as an access loop for PARIS. It will connect work stations and other devices to the switch in its native operating mode. The LAN, called MetaRing, will operate at a gigabit-per-second rate and eliminates the need for gateways or bridging to the switch because it uses the same protocols as the wide area backbone.

The PARIS switch is committed to the support of evolving broadband ISDN standards. It will transport ATM cells without repackaging them for transport within the PARIS network.

IBM plans to use the latest version of PARIS, when it is completed, in several field trials. In 1991, IBM announced a joint study of broadband multimedia networking with Bell South using the PARIS switch. This three-year project will seek to address customers' requirements for information transmission. PARIS will probably not be available to prospective customers until broadband services supported by SONET are tariffed.

THE AVAILABILITY OF BROADBAND SERVICES

ATM cell relay technology promises to be the broadband WAN technology that will dynamically deliver vast amounts of bandwidth on demand to satisfy current and future broadband applications. It also provides a common method of handling all forms of information by integrating them within the transport mechanism.

Broadband switch development precedes the deployment and availability of the broadband transport mechanisms and services (i.e., SONET, SDH, SMDS, and broadband ISDN) that will begin to become available by the mid to late 1990s, once the ATM switches are deployed and tested. ATM switches delivered to customer premises before the availability of broadband services promise to meet the large bandwidth requirements of the private sector through multiple T3/E3 trunks or privately owned cable.

The capacity of the early ATM switches, such as AT&T Network Systems' BNS-2000, is small. This small bandwidth capacity is expected to satisfy the early needs of users when broadband services are still limited. However, these switch vendors will undoubtedly begin to increase the capacity of their switches to offer larger trunk bandwidths as broadband services escalate and user demand for higher broadband rates intensifies.

ATM-based products from different suppliers must be able to interoperate for the successful development of broadband networks employing ATM switches, hubs, routers, and other products from industry vendors. Industry developers have jointly formed an organization, called the ATM Forum, to achieve ATM interoperability. Founded in 1991, the ATM Forum's mission is to develop a common user interface specification for ATM to achieve interoperability among products from different vendors. The specification will be based on ANSI and CCITT ATM standards and on other international standards to ensure global interoperability.

SUMMARY

The success of broadband technology really lies with the service providers, who must introduce tariffed services and make them readily available to users. Private broadband networks can be created without the support of the service providers; however, many of these networks ultimately need to interconnect with tariffed services to satisfy user networking requirements.

Section IV

Bursty Data Communications Over Multimedia Networks

We have used the term "bursty" to describe a type of data transmission which can vary immensely in timing, duration, and volume. Picture for a moment a large local network connected via a T1 line to a moderate remote network. This network includes many computer work stations, some with multimedia (voice and video) capabilities, and a number of servers, shared printers, and image servers. At any point in time, each work station and server is performing some task at random (which may include idle time). How does one predict the instantaneous network load? The answer is that the average load may be predicted, as can a peak load, although the latter number may be more an indication of the capacity limit of the network. However, one cannot know the instantaneous load, because the individual network actions of the component devices are a random process. They are bursty.

Networks may handle bursty communications in several ways. If network traffic is low, the native throughput of the network may be sufficient to handle those times when several network elements are bursting data. As networks become larger, or as usage increases, additional stopgap measures such as segmentation through routers, network switched hubs, and bandwidth increases may help. However, even these methods may have limitations. Another way to handle the traffic is simply to block access at a certain point in the throughput curve. One could assign priorities to different types of traffic, or the throughput could simply be allocated evenly, such that everyone is slowed somewhat.

Whatever the method, multimedia applications provide severe demands to a network architecture that must allow for rapidly varying peaks in transport load. In this section, three approaches for bursty data transport are presented: LAN emulation over ATM, frame relay transport, and broadband ISDN dynamic bandwidth allocation.

ATM has, at its core, a suite of networking protocols to implement the establishment of connections between two points and the transport of data cells between the connection points. ATM technology is independent of physical transport media, although standards for each medium must be developed, and many already have. ATM can be used at every physical media level, from copper to fiber, and can use the underlying bandwidth "pipes" of T-carrier and SONET for WAN transmission. This strength of ATM has also produced much of the confusion and controversy that has surrounded the technology.

In order for ATM to inhabit both the local and wide area domains, it must coexist with dominant technologies in each. For the local area, this melding of technology requires that ATM transport be made available for "legacy" networking methods, such as Ethernet and Token Ring.

The transport of LAN traffic over ATM is surprisingly complex. The first chapter in this section explains the interactions and power of LAN emulation (LANE) services for ATM transport. LANE provides an effective means of handling the typical bursty nature of connectionless LAN transport protocols over a connection-oriented ATM network. The combination of centralized ATM switches and LAN-emulating ATM edge devices allows both campus and wide area installation of ATM transport services with little or no impact on traditional LAN configurations. This capability is very important in advancing the implementation of ATM across the enterprise.

Frame relay provides an innate mechanism for dealing with a certain level of bursty communication over the WAN. Typical frame relay access circuits allow two levels of data throughput, a maximum level and a guaranteed level. The user can then accommodate an additional burst of data above the steady-state maximum. If the frame relay provider's facilities are not overloaded, the additional burst bandwidth is available. The second chapter in this section pays special attention to the issues of flow control, congestion management, sequencing, and recovery in frame relay transport.

Broadband ISDN (B-IDSN) is the new paradigm to replace the older web of T-carrier networking. At the very highest level of communication transport is the SONET structure on which virtually all of the other lesser high-speed services reside. This third chapter touts the features of ATM to handle the bursty nature of certain types of communication traffic within the B-ISDN network.

This chapter is particularly timely in introducing us to the foibles of "the cloud." For many networking technologists, the public network is represented by a cloud, whether that cloud represents a switched, dedicated, or virtual network. The practical side of the matter is that the cloud has "innards." The cloud is, in actuality, a complex interconnection of an inter-city carrier's access nodes, internodal transport, switching nodes, and network management facilities. It almost never is a real cloud.

This nodal transport network must deal with congestion, facility availability, periodic and unexpected maintenance downtime, rerouting, and network control issues. Intercity bandwidth is an expensive and limited resource, and the level of success with which a carrier manages that resource and the connecting components will have a significant impact on the overall service quality its customers receive.

Chapter 10
ATM LAN Emulation

G. Thomas Des Jardins and
Gopala Krishna Tumuluri

This chapter describes one service used to provide interworking between asynchronous transfer mode (ATM) networks and the installed base of 802.3 (Ethernet) and 802.5 (Token Ring) network equipment — LAN emulation, or LANE.

LAN emulation allows users of an ATM network to run any higher-layer protocol in its existing state without requiring any changes. LANE is a method of performing basic bridging functionality between a host on an ATM-attached bridge and an ATM-attached host, or between two ATM-attached hosts. Because LANE masks much of the complexity from users while allowing them to benefit from ATM, it has become the standard of choice for transporting data traffic across heterogeneous networks.

TRANSPARENT AND SEAMLESS BRIDGING AND OTHER GOALS OF LANE

The overarching goal for LANE is to provide seamless and transparent bridging between an arbitrary number of hosts, where the hosts may be ATM native or connected to the ATM cloud via an interworking device. Therefore, many of the features of the emulated technology are specifically replicated, as are some of the design constraints posed by bridging.

To support the goal of transparent operation, the connection-oriented nature of ATM is concealed. To allow seamless operation, features found in the shared-medium domain such as broadcast are emulated.

Ease of use is addressed at the outset by designing in support for services, including automatic configuration and address registration, that allow true plug-and-play operation. A secondary goal is simplicity of design.

DESIGN

Packets on 802.3 or 802.5 networks typically can be grouped into two broad categories — unicast and multicast.

0-8493-9949-1/99/$0.00+$.50
© 1999 by CRC Press LLC

Unicast and Multicast. A unicast packet has a single intended destination and frequently is only one of several packets for that destination. By contrast, a multicast or broadcast packet has multiple destinations and is typically intended for the whole broadcast domain.

Once established, a virtual circuit between two end points, the source and the destination, would enable them to have point-to-point bidirectional communication, thereby emulating the 802 network for unicast packets. What is more difficult to imagine is how multicast might be replicated in a point-to-point connection-oriented technology such as ATM.

For that matter, the mechanisms of actually creating even a single point-to-point connection might give the reader pause. In fact, much of the complexity of LANE resides in simply preparing to exchange unicast and multicast data; the actual transfers themselves are relatively straightforward and not much different from any bridging technology.

Connections

ATM networks are connection-oriented by design. This design has the desired benefit of allowing ATM hardware to rapidly perform forwarding based on routing decisions determined when the call was set up. Because this function is not processor-intensive as routers are, very high throughput rates can be easily achieved.

Broadcast

The types of network technologies meant to be supplanted or augmented by ATM networks run LANE-provided connectionless service as a by-product of their design. ATM does not offer a similar feature, although there are ways it could be implemented. LANE specifies a simple and straightforward method for providing a broadcast facility using multicast support.

Emulated LANs

An emulated LAN is a group of ATM-attached stations that are logically grouped. This logical group is equivalent to a LAN segment on a traditional shared-media network.

This group of ATM stations belongs to the same broadcast domain. Of course, this broadcast domain is completely logical and does not have anything to do with the physical hardware connections. Later in this chapter we will discuss how to implement multiple emulated LANs on a single physical ATM network and also how a single ATM station can be part of multiple emulated LANs.

MAC Driver

LAN emulation is intended to provide an interface to the network-layer protocols that is identical to the one provided by traditional IEEE 802 LANs. The higher-layer protocols must function as though they are running on a traditional network. This virtual interface must be provided by the LANE implementation.

Interworking with Existing LANs

As mentioned previously, LAN emulation can be used to achieve interworking between devices attached to ATM networks and devices on traditional networks. Interworking devices (typically called *ATM access bridges*) must be used that can understand both the ATM and IEEE 802 networks. These devices implement the bridging functionality on the IEEE 802 interfaces, as is done in traditional networks.

On the ATM interface, however, they make use of LANE to implement bridging. (How such devices transparently bridge 802 stations and ATM stations by acting as proxies is discussed in more detail later in this chapter.)

Protocol Layering

In an IEEE 802 network there is the physical layer, media access control (MAC) layer, and the logical link control (LLC) layer. In an ATM network there is a physical layer, ATM layer, and the ATM adaptation layer (AAL). Any application needs to be implemented on top of the AAL layer. LAN emulation is just another application as far as the ATM network is concerned, thus it is implemented over the AAL layer. In particular, LAN emulation makes use of the AAL 5 layer.

LAN emulation also makes use of the signaling mechanism provided by the underlying ATM network to establish the switched virtual circuit (SVC) connections. LAN emulation in turn provides the functionality of the MAC layer and the logical link layer to the network layer.

Exhibit 1 illustrates how LAN emulation, ATM layers, and signaling all work in comparison with the Open Systems Interconnection (OSI) protocol stack.

COMPONENTS OF LANE

Now let's turn our attention to the implementation of the LAN emulation protocol. First, we describe the components that constitute an emulated LAN, then we explain how these components fit together and how the entire LAN emulation works.

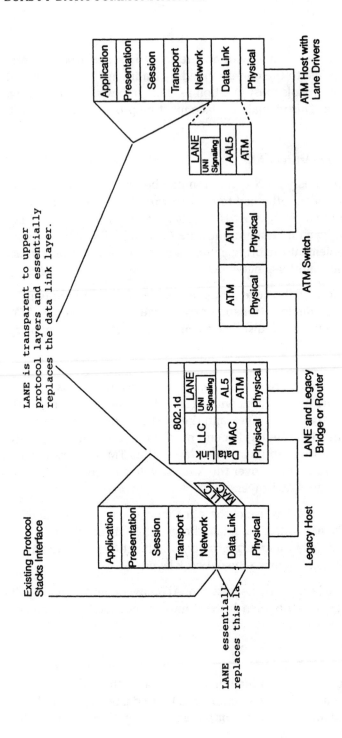

Exhibit 1. Open System Interconnection (OSI) and LANE Protocol Stacks

Notes:
Routing occurs at the network layer, is protocol independent, and is complex to administer. Some protocols, like SNA, are not routable.
Bridging occurs at the data link layer, is independent of protocols, and is simple to administer.
Hubs and routers operate at the physical layer.

LANE has the following components:

- LAN emulation client (LEC).
- LAN emulation server (LES).
- Broadcast and unknown server (BUS).
- LAN emulation configuration server (LECS).

The last three components — the LES, LEGS, and BUS — are often thought of as the LE services, since together they support the client's data exchange.

There are three steps to the process of exchanging data: LANE registration, address resolution, and data exchange. This process is explained further in a later section of this chapter titled "LAN Emulation in Action."

For now, however, a complete examination of the components, beginning with the client, is called for.

LAN Emulation Client (LEC)

- An LEC is the interface between the ATM world and the legacy world.

For any meaningful network communication to take place, there must be nodes that need to communicate. These nodes must be willing to participate in an emulated LAN that is a single broadcast domain. These entities are called LAN emulation clients, or simply LE clients.

Since an emulated LAN has meaning only in an ATM environment, the LE clients must be ATM-attached hosts or proxies for hosts that are sending data across an ATM network. These nodes can be host work stations or other interworking devices, such as bridges or routers with ATM interfaces that are acting as proxies for the MAC addresses in the non-ATM environment.

Data transfer takes place between two clients participating in an emulated LAN. Before exchanging data, the clients make use of the address resolution mechanism and the underlying signaling mechanism (discussed in greater detail in the section "LAN Emulation in Action").

Each LE client has a registered MAC address it represents. This address is an IEEE 802 network address that the LAN is emulating. For example, for emulated Ethernet LANs, this address would be a 6-byte hardware MAC address.

Each client is also equipped with an ATM address for it to be able to communicate with other clients that are ATM stations. Proxy clients, such as routers and bridges, extend this concept somewhat and will be addressed later.

LAN Emulation Server (LES)

- The LES tracks emulated LAN membership.
- The LES provides address resolution.
- The LES supplies the LEC with the address of the BUS.

In traditional networks, membership in a LAN is directly tied to a physical network topology. Membership is achieved by connecting the nodes using some sort of physical medium, which repeats signals throughout the medium, forming a broadcast domain.

In an ATM network, however, membership in a LAN has an explicitly defined relationship. Complexity arises because an emulated LAN is not a group of physically connected machines but a mesh of virtual circuits. An emulated LAN is completely virtual.

Network topology and emulated LAN membership are disjointed. This concept may be confusing at first; what is important to remember is that ATM networks define data paths using a concept of a virtual circuit and allocate resources according to defined policies of quality of service.

In this virtual environment, it becomes necessary for some entity to keep track of the membership of LE clients in an emulated LAN. This entity is called the LAN emulation server (LES), or the LE server.

This server is responsible for registering LE clients that would like to be part of a single emulated LAN. However, the LES has additional responsibilities to fulfill apart from maintaining the membership in an emulated LAN.

In an emulated LAN environment, for two LE clients to communicate with each other they need to establish an ATM virtual circuit, which requires the clients to know their ATM addresses. However, LAN emulation clients use IEEE 802 MAC addresses in the data frames they send to each other. So it becomes necessary that a client resolve a MAC address to an ATM address before any data transfer can take place.

This ATM address is then used to establish the necessary virtual circuit over which the IEEE 802 frames with source and destination MAC addresses can be sent. The LES provides a mechanism for the clients to resolve the MAC addresses to ATM addresses using the LAN emulation address resolution protocol (LEARP).

The LES also provides the LE clients with the ATM address of the broadcast and unknown server, which is the second-most important entity in an emulated LAN.

Broadcast and Unknown Server (BUS)

- BUS is used for unknown unicast traffic.
- BUS provides broadcast or multicast.
- BUS can be a bottleneck.

In traditional shared-media networks such as Ethernet, no "connections" exist. Rather, broadcast is achieved by all stations on the network listening to all traffic.

ATM networks, however, are point-to-point or connection-oriented networks that require an explicitly defined connection for traffic through a network, as well as a defined quality of service that this virtual connection should receive.

To emulate a traditional connectionless shared-media LAN on an ATM network, we need to define how the ATM layer will emulate a broadcast mechanism. This is extremely important because most of the network-layer protocols used today rely heavily on broadcasts. For example, IP uses the address resolution protocol (ARP) to resolve IP addresses to MAC address, and ARP uses broadcasts. In addition, bridges and other interworking devices use the same broadcast mechanism to send unknown unicast frames for which the address-to-port mappings are not resolved.

The entity that provides this mechanism is called a broadcast and unknown server (BUS). This entity makes use of the point-to-multipoint virtual connections provided by ATM networks to provide the broadcast mechanism to all LAN emulation clients.

A point-to-multipoint VC is a VC that replicates the traffic on one incoming VC to many outgoing VCs. This capability is standard in most ATM switch equipment. The clients send all the broadcast or unknown unicast frames to the BUS, which in turn sends the frame to all the clients over the point-to-multipoint VC.

LE Configuration Server (LECS)

- The LECS maps emulated LAN names to LES addresses.
- The LECS provides information about how an emulated LAN is configured.
- The LECS is reached via a well-known default address.

In an ATM network, every single entity needs to have its own ATM address for it to be uniquely identified. Therefore the LE clients, the LES, and the BUS all have their own unique ATM addresses that are obtained during the configuration phase when a client joins the emulated LAN.

The LE clients need to know the ATM addresses of the LES and the BUS. As discussed previously, the LES provides the clients with the ATM address information of the BUS. However, the clients need to be initially configured with the LES address if they are to successfully take part in an emulated LAN.

It would be difficult to configure each client with the 20-byte ATM address of the LES for each emulated LAN the client wishes to join. Therefore, LAN emulation specifies a service that provides a mapping of emulated LAN names to the LES ATM addresses. This entity is called the LAN emulation configuration server, or the LECS.

The LECS can respond at either a specified ATM address for security reasons (in which case all the clients need to be configured with this information), or the LECS can be configured to respond at a well-known ATM address, allowing all the clients to use this globally known LECS ATM address for simple plug-and-play operation.

LAN emulation provides both mechanisms for clients to communicate with the LECS. The LECS maintains a data base that has a name of the emulated LAN and the ATM address of the LES that is serving that emulated LAN, and responds to client queries by providing this information.

LAN emulation also provides flexibility because it directly configures the LE clients with the ATM addresses of the LES. The function of the LECS is similar to an IP network's name server. It is easier to address something by name rather than a number.

The LECS can also be optionally used to provide additional information about the characteristics of a particular emulated LAN. For example, one can query the LECS to find out what type of IEEE 802 LAN is being emulated by a particular LES.

ATM ADDRESSES

Each of the LAN emulation components — the LE clients, LE server, BUS, and LEGS — needs a unique ATM address. This section explains how these addresses are partly obtained and partly formed.

In the 20-byte ATM address, the last byte is called the *selector byte* and is reserved for use by different entities implemented on the same network interface. This selector byte can be given a different value, which gives users the choice of having 255 unique ATM addresses on the same physical interface.

By using a different selector byte, all of the LAN emulation components can be present on the same physical interface and yet have unique ATM addresses. In fact, multiple instances of the same LANE component can be implemented on the same physical interface.

VIRTUAL CONNECTIONS

Virtual connections form the basic component in LAN emulation and in any ATM implementation. Without VCs, no communication is possible. Exhibit 2 shows LANE components and their virtual connections.

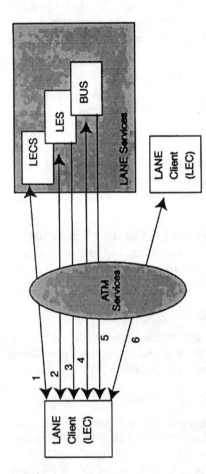

#	PP	PMP	Name	From	To	Phase	Purpose
1	X		Configuration direct	LEC	LECS	Initialization	LEC uses to give ELAN name get LES addr
2	X		Control direct	LEC	LES	Join	LEC uses to register with ELAN, get BUS addr
3		X	Control distribute	LES	LEC	Join	LES uses to send ARP requests to all clients
4	X		Multicast send	LEC	BUS	Bus Connect	LEC uses to send data to BUS for redistribution to all clients (see next)
5		X	Multicast forward	BUS	LEC	Bus Connect	BUS uses to send data to all clients
6	X		Data Direct	LEC	LEC	Data Exchange	LECs (clients) use to send data between each other

Keys:
ARP   address resolution protocol
BUS   broadcast and unknown server
LEC   LAN emulation client
LECS LAN emulation configuration server
LES   LAN emulation server
PP   point-to-point
PMP   point-to-multipoint

Exhibit 2.   LANE Components and Their Virtual Connections

LANE communication occurs between the LE clients and one of the other entities (possibly another LE client). Collectively the LECS/LES/BUS can be considered the LAN emulation services because their sole purpose is to serve the LE clients in one form or the other.

Connection 1: The Configuration Direct VC

The LE clients initially communicate with the LECS to retrieve the address of the LES of an emulated LAN that the client wishes to join. This emulated LAN name can be null in case the client wishes to join any emulated LAN. This communication with the LECS is a point-to-point communication between one client and the LECS and takes place on a virtual connection called the configuration direct VC.

Once the client retrieves the required information and the necessary characteristics of a particular emulated LAN, it does not need to communicate with the LECS further until there is a change in configuration.

Connection 2: The Control Direct VC

The LE client then needs to become a member of an emulated LAN by registering with the LES. This registration and other one-to-one communications between the LE client and the LES takes place over another VG called the control direct VG.

The name of this virtual connection derives from the fact that all of this communication involves purely control messages and not any useful data transfer. In addition, this VC is a direct point-to-point VC between the LES and the LEC and is therefore called a control direct VC.

Connection 3: The Control Distribute VC

The LES uses a point-to-multipoint VC to communicate with all the clients in an emulated LAN. This virtual connection is called the control distribute VC. (The use of this VC is described in more detail later.)

Connection 4: The Multicast Forward VC

LE clients that wish to send broadcast frames to all the clients in the emulated LAN need to first forward them to the BUS. To do this, the clients use a point-to-point VC to the BUS called the multicast send VC. The BUS then uses a point-to-multipoint VC called the multicast forward VC to forward these frames to all the clients. All the clients would be part of this multicast VC.

Connection 5: The Data Direct VC

So far we have only talked about how control frames and broadcast frames make it through the ATM network. The ultimate use of the emulated LAN is for two clients to exchange data directly between them. This exchange is carried over another virtual connection called the data direct VC, which is established once the MAC addresses are resolved to ATM addresses.

LAN EMULATION IN ACTION

Now that we have some understanding of the reasons for using LAN emulation and what components are required to implement LAN emulation, let's turn our attention to how all this works together and finally to how two ATM stations transfer data between them as if they are attached to an IEEE 802 LAN. Exhibit 2 also shows how LANE components and their virtual connections fit in the phases of data exchange.

Phase 1: LANE Registration

Step 1: Initialization. The LE clients are the final beneficiaries of LAN emulation, and they need to pass through several phases before they can actually communicate with each other.

First comes the initialization phase, during which the LEC establishes a configuration direct VC to the LECS and obtains the ATM address of the LES. If the LES address is manually provided to the LEC, then this initialization phase will be null and will not be executed. At the end of the initialization phase the LEC is supposed to know the ATM address of the LES to which it needs to connect and join the emulated LAN.

Step 2: Joining Emulated LANs. The second phase is the join phase. In this phase the LEC connects to the LES and expresses its interest in being part of the LAN being emulated by this LES.

Upon connecting to the LES, the LEC registers two addresses. One is the 6-byte MAC address that LEC represents in the emulated LAN; the second is the client ATM address at which the servers and other clients can connect in order to send data frames to the given MAC address.

The LES completes the join phase by saving this information in its data base and establishing a point-to-multipoint VC (i.e., the control distribute VC) to the client. If any of the connections fail or if the address registration does not take place correctly, the join phase is aborted and restarted.

Step 3: Connecting to the BUS. Once the LE client joins the emulated LAN successfully, it needs to connect to the BUS in order to be able to send or receive broadcast multicast and unknown unicast frames.

This phase is called the BUS connect phase. During this phase the LE client queries the LES for the BUS address using the LAN emulation ARP protocol (described later). The LES responds to the LE clients with the ATM address of the BUS, which it knows right from configuration time.

LE clients, after obtaining the BUS ATM address, establish a point-to-point VC (i.e., the multicast send VC) to the BUS. The BUS then establishes a point-to-multipoint VC (i.e., multicast forward VC).

Once all these connections are successfully established the emulated LAN is declared to be operational according to the LE clients. When any of these control connections to the LES or the BUS get dropped, the join phase is restarted. Until a successful join occurs, no communication can take place between any pair of clients.

Phase 2: Address Resolution

In any network, address resolution is the key for successful communication. This address resolution is required because of different types of addresses used by different protocol layers. MAC layers use MAC addresses, network layers use network-layer address (e.g., IP), and transport layers use ports. No matter what layer it is, each layer has its own addressing mechanism to distinguish itself from its peer.

In LAN emulation, there are two layers between the network layer and the physical layer. One is the MAC layer that is being emulated; the other is the LAN emulation layer, which is actually on top of an ATM network.

Since the MAC layer addressing and ATM network addressing are different, two levels of address resolution are needed. One is a network-layer-to-MAC-address resolution, which is done in a manner identical to the traditional networks by the network layer. The other is the MAC-address-to-ATM-address resolution, which is done by the LAN emulation layer. This second form of address resolution is called the LAN emulation address resolution protocol (LEARP).

This level of address resolution is completely transparent to the network layers. The network layers only see the MAC layer being emulated and therefore only see the traditional ARP.

How Two Levels of Address Resolution Work Together

Suppose one host is running some network protocol and wants to communicate with its peer. This host will first resolve the network address to MAC address just as if it were running on a traditional IEEE 802 network. Then the network layer uses the virtual MAC interface provided by LANE (which is identical to the traditional MAC interface) to send the data in the form of a MAC frame. This MAC frame is received by the LEC (running LANE).

Now the LEC needs to transmit this frame to its peer LEC, for which it needs to establish a connection. Establishing this connection requires an ATM address.

The transmitting client uses the services provided by the LES to resolve the MAC address to a unique ATM address. Once this resolution is done in a completely transparent way, the client establishes a virtual connection and delivers the original MAC frame intact to the other end as if nothing happened in the middle.

Thus, each MAC address must be resolved into a unique ATM address. This ATM address must be the address of the client that represents the MAC address.

It is possible and perfectly legal for many MAC addresses to map to a single ATM address, but not vice versa. Interworking devices may act, however, as proxy LE clients and represent more MAC addresses per each ATM address.

LEARP Requests and Responses.

We described the reason and mechanism for using LEARP — or LAN emulation address resolution protocol — in the previous section. Now let's explain exactly how it works.

Each LEC that wants to resolve a MAC address to an ATM address sends out a LEARP request to the LES. This request contains the following information:

- MAC address the requesting client represents.
- ATM address the requesting client represents.
- MAC address the client is trying to resolve.

The LE client uses the control direct virtual connection to send the LEARP requests. The LES, after getting the LEARP request, looks it up in the data base.

If the MAC address is registered and there is an ATM address associated with it, the LES responds to the LE client with positive information. If the LES fails to find the requested information in its data base, then it forwards the LEARP request to all the clients in the emulated LAN (using the control distribute VC).

If all clients are supposed to register the MAC address they represent with the LES, then how is it possible for the LES to fail in its search? That question will be answered in the section on "Proxy LE Clients." Some LE client would respond to the LES for the LEARP request that was flooded to all the clients. The LES now uses that information to respond to the original client that requested the information.

Phase 3: Data Exchange

LANE Data Frames. Each client sends IEEE 802 frames to the other client. These IEEE 802 frames need to be encapsulated in what is called a LANE data frame.

The LANE data frame has a 2-byte header with one field in it; the rest is the MAC frame. This 2-byte field is called the LEC-ID, which is a unique number assigned by the LES when the LE client registers in the emulated LAN.

In traditional networks, physical ports give a unique identity; however, in a virtual environment like LANE, there needs to be a way to identify and differentiate between LE clients. This LEC-ID is useful for the clients in recognizing the frames sent by them in case the response comes back to them through the BUS.

Data Transfer. There are three kinds of data frames that could be transmitted in the IEEE 802 LAN.

One is the unicast frame that a station wants to send directly to another station after the address resolution is done. The second is the unknown unicast frames that are destined for a particular client and are still awaiting address resolution. The third type is the broadcast and multicast frames; these are destined to all or a group of stations in the LAN. (Remember, we are not discussing address resolution at the network layer. We are only concerned with the LE address resolution, which involves resolving the MAC addresses to ATM addresses.)

Broadcast Frames. The broadcast frames received by the virtual MAC driver are encapsulated in LANE frames and are sent to the BUS for broadcast to all the clients in the emulated LAN. This is the most simple form of transferring the frames. If all the frames could be sent in this way, life would be simple, but at the same time it would be very inefficient.

Unknown Unicast Frames. These are the frames for which there is no ATM address that has been resolved for the destination MAC address in the MAC frame. For these frames the LE clients send a LEARP request to the LES and forward the frame to the BUS to be broadcast to all the clients.

To keep the performance of the BUS from degrading there is a limit imposed on the LEARP requests and the number of unknown unicast frames that can be forwarded to the BUS for broadcast. This limit is typically one frame per second for each unresolved destination MAC address.

Directed Unicast Frames. All the unknown frames would become directed unicast frames once the LE client gets a response to its LEARP request. At this point the MAC address is resolved and direct communication between the clients can start. At this point the transmitting client establishes a data direct virtual connection to the destination client and the unicast frames are sent over it.

LEARP Cache and Virtual Connection Cache. By now we know that LE clients resolve MAC addresses to ATM addresses using the services of the LES and then establish a virtual connection to the peer clients to transfer the actual data. It would be too inefficient for the LE clients to do LEARP requests and VC establishment for each unicast frame they get from the virtual MAC driver.

To be more efficient, the LE clients cache the LEARP entries and also the VCs associated with each MAC address. These cache entries are subject to aging based on a time-out period, which is a configurable parameter. The sizes of the caches can vary, depending on the implementation.

Flush Message Protocol. The unknown unicasts are forwarded to the BUS at a very slow rate until the LE address resolution completes. Once this LEARP is completed, the rest of the frames go through a direct virtual connection between the LE clients.

Since the BUS is a different entity running elsewhere in the ATM network, it is quite possible that the unknown unicast frames sent to the BUS would reach the destination client more slowly, and in some cases after the unicast frames sent on the direct VC reach it. If this happens then the frame ordering is not maintained; this situation could lead to unnecessary retransmissions.

To avoid this potential problem, each LE client implements a flush message protocol. After resolving an address and before transmitting data on the direct VC, each LE client sends a flush request to the BUS. The BUS, upon getting this request, transmits any frames pending for this client on the multicast send VC and sends a flush response to the client. The LE client, upon receiving this response, starts transmitting the unicast frames on the direct VC.

COMMON QUESTIONS ABOUT LAN EMULATION

How Many Emulated LANs?

Not only is it possible for multiple clients to be part of a single emulated LAN, but it is also possible for a single client to be part of multiple emulated LANs. Imagine an end station with two IEEE 802 network interface cards connected to two disjointed LAN segments. This station can in fact belong to multiple networks. However, in traditional networks the end station would require two physical interfaces and should be part of two physically disjointed LAN segments.

In LAN emulation, however, because the network is a virtual one and is purely a mesh of VCs over a physical ATM network, it is not difficult to imagine two or more virtual emulated networks. In this case the mesh of VCs needs to be disjointed and not the physical ATM network.

How Many Clients per Emulated LAN?

How many LE clients can be part of a single emulated LAN? As mentioned earlier, the LE frames have a 2-byte header that carries the unique LEC-ID in it. This limits the number of clients per emulated LAN to 216-1.

How Many MAC Addresses per Client?

Proxy LE Clients. The single most important goal of LAN emulation is to have seamless and transparent interoperability between legacy networks and ATM networks. We know that LAN emulation can be used to emulate an IEEE 802 LAN on top of a connection-oriented point-to-point ATM network.

How can this emulated LAN operate seamlessly with a legacy network? This is a tricky question because legacy networks do not understand LAN emulation.

A proxy LEC can solve this problem. A proxy LEC is a LAN emulation client that represents all the MAC addresses on the legacy network and does the bridging conversion from legacy network to LANE network. The proxy LEC incorporates some intelligence to do this.

There are few differences in the way proxy LE clients operate in comparison with their non-proxy counterparts. During the LE join phase, each LE client registers a MAC address it represents and the ATM address that other clients can connect at. If a proxy LEC has to register the MAC addresses it represents, then the data base of the LES can be huge (depending on the number of such clients and the number of addresses they represent).

There is another problem with registering all the addresses with the LES. Imagine transparent bridges that would like to act as proxy LECs. These bridges learn the MAC addresses on different ports slowly, as they see frames from different sources. When these proxy clients want to join the emulated LAN at the beginning, they do not know all the MAC addresses they would like to represent.

LAN emulation provides for all these problems. Any proxy LEC is only allowed to register one MAC address during the join phase just as any other LE client. However, the proxy LEC should register itself as a proxy with the LES. The proxy LEC should never register any more MAC addresses at any time. The LES forwards unresolvable LEARP requests to all the proxy LE clients and the proxy clients respond to these requests dynamically, as and when needed. Other than these differences, all the other functions and operations are the same.

How Can LE Clients Participate in Multiple Emulated LANs?

The LE clients need to obtain as many unique ATM addresses and MAC addresses as the number of emulated LANs they would like to be part of. Remember, an LEC can only represent one MAC address, and each MAC address should map to a unique ATM address.

The magic of LAN emulation lies in the fact that neither the ATM address nor the MAC address needs to have physical relevance. This makes the life of an LE client simple. It can use the selector byte in the ATM address to form more unique ATM addresses and generate multiple unique MAC addresses from their hardware address by following a deterministic algorithm.

Once these addresses are formed or generated, the LE client needs to locate a LES/BUS pair for each emulated LAN it would like to be part of and establish the necessary connections. Then the client needs to maintain the list of VCs and addresses associated with each emulated LAN and should make sure complete isolation of all traffic among emulated LANs is maintained.

What is the limit on the number of emulated LANs that a single client can be part of? The theoretical limit is 255, since the selector byte can be used to generate 255 unique ATM addresses.

However, a more practical limit would depend on the realistic number of network interfaces an end station or an interworking device would like to have. In most current implementations this limit is 16.

SUMMARY

LAN emulation, like most protocol implementations, is standards based. Standards ensure proper interoperability between the implementations by different vendors. Just as the IEEE standardizes most of the IEEE 802 networks and their implementation, the ATM Forum has standardized the implementation of LAN emulation.

The ATM Forum has released a document that contains every single detail on how LAN emulation must be implemented. This document is called the "LAN Emulation over ATM, version 1.0." This specification can be ordered directly from the ATM Forum (phone: [415] 578-6860; e-mail:info@ atmforum.com).

The ATM Forum LANE specification provides a mechanism to emulate only IEEE 802.3 (Ethernet) and IEEE 802.5 (Token Ring) networks. There is no specification yet to emulate fiber distributed data interface (FDDI) net-works on top of ATM, though this does not preclude vendors from having proprietary implementations.

Chapter 11
Transport Over Frame Relay: Issues and Considerations

Tim Kelly

The users of network services (e.g., frame relay) are concerned with the end-to-end integrity of data transfer. Ensuring this integrity is the function of the transport layer. This chapter examines transport issues as they relate to the quality of the underlying service.

WHAT IS FRAME RELAY?

Frame relay and X.25 are connection-oriented services (as opposed to the Internet Protocol [IP], which is a connectionless service). Frame relay is a development of integrated services digital network (ISDN), prompted by the need to handle the standard 2 *n* by 75-bps data rates over a 64K-bps standard digital telephone channel. The general problem goes by the name of rate adaption. Several adaption schemes have been standardized. International Telegraph and Telephone Consultative Committee (CCITT) standards V.110 and X.31 are examples, but these are unwieldy schemes and require special hardware and software in the terminal or terminal adapter. Another idea was to use the ISDN D channel, which already has a link layer protocol (link access procedure D [LAP-D]) that is built into any ISDN terminal. The D channel is used for call setup of the 64K-bps B channels and for access to the packet switching function (X.25) on the basic rate interface. By modifying the LAP-D frame format slightly, a switched virtual circuit service and permanent virtual circuit service could be provided. Switched virtual service is possible because signaling packets that are sent over the D channel to set up the B channel can be used to define another type of connection (i.e., frame relay).

The idea is to take the basic LAP-D link layer frame and replace the 13-bit service access point identifier and terminal end point identifier with a value that provides the same function as the logical channel address in the

X.25 world. A 10-bit field, called the data link connection identifier (DLCI), is used. With this approach, packet switching functions no longer need to unpack the link layer frame to find the network layer address. They can route (relay) the link layer frame directly based on the DLCI. The relationship of the DLCI to the source and destination address is established when the connection is established. In ISDN, a signaling packet that contains the end point addresses is sent to the network to set up the virtual circuit connection. Currently, only permanent virtual circuit service is available over frame relay offerings, and therefore the association between end points is set up as subscription time.

The interest in frame relay stems from the frame relay switch being able to relay the frame in as little as 4 milliseconds. This is much shorter than the 30 to 100 milliseconds required by a typical X.25 packet switch. For transfer of a large file, reduced network latency is not very important, but for a transaction-oriented application (typical of local area network [LAN] applications), reducing network latency contributes directly to reduced network response time.

THE OSI REFERENCE MODEL

To set the stage for this discussion of transport issues, a review of the open systems interconnection (OSI) model is in order. Only the lower four layers are considered, because they are application independent and as a whole provide the reliable transportation mechanism generally required by applications.

The physical layer is responsible for bit transmission and, if needed, synchronization. The link layer is responsible for a series of functions that includes basic character phasing, sequencing, and acknowledgment. The list, in order of ascending value, might be as follows: character synchronization, block framing, error detection, device addressing, block sequencing, block acknowledgment, automatic retransmission (in the case of errors or out-of-sequence conditions).

How many of these link layer functions are used depends on the application. X.25 employs all these functions to provide reliable link layer transmission between users and the network and between switching nodes within the network. The data or contents of the link layer frame are fully protected from errors during transport on the telephone lines interconnecting these network nodes.

On LANS, the link layer contains a new sublayer, called the media access control (MAC), that performs frame synchronization and error detection. This MAC layer is unique to each type of LAN (i.e., token passing bus, token passing ring, contention bus). Frame relay is a link layer function. All that is needed to connect a LAN to a frame relay service is a bridge that functions at the MAC layer.

The network layer is responsible for routing and switching. To do routing or switching, an address plan is needed that is consistent (and unique) across the network. Each addressable node has a network level address. This address is quite separate from the link layer address. The link layer address is analogous to a street address; two houses in different towns could have the same street address (e.g., 540 W. Main). Because more than one individual may be living at each address, a network layer address, which is the address of the individual, is also needed. The structure of these addresses, how they are known to the routing nodes in the network, and how they are updated when people move are topics that are beyond the scope of this chapter.

CONNECTIONLESS AND CONNECTION-ORIENTED SERVICES

There are two basic types of network layer services: connection oriented and connectionless. A connection-oriented network (e.g., the dial-up telephone network) provides the users of the network layer service with a dedicated electrical connection that is set up when the called party acknowledges the call. Data sent across the network is acknowledged by the receiving party and the connection is terminated with a call termination sequence. Both X.25 and frame relay are connection-oriented network services.

A connectionless network (such as that provided by the IP) works like the mail. A letter (i.e., data) is sent, but the sender does not receive acknowledgment of its arrival.

The transport layer is responsible for the end-to-end delivery of information. It uses the network layer for a delivery mechanism that spans the network just as the network layer uses the link layer to get the data across each link and the link layer uses the physical layer to accomplish bit transmission. Like the network layer services, those of the transport layer may be connection oriented or connectionless. If the layers associated with the user (the session, presentation, and application layers will be considered here as an undivided user layer) are involved in supporting a transaction-oriented application such as credit authorization, a failure in the underlying layers (including transport) is not critical because the user can always reenter the request. For this application, a connectionless transport layer is sufficient.

For users desiring high-integrity data transfer, a connection-oriented transport layer is needed so that delivery assurance can be provided to the user layers. The obvious question is where this connection-oriented service should be offered. The candidates are the link, network, and transport layers, either all or one. The X.25 community believes that the network layer should be responsible for the connection. The Transmission Control Protocol (TCP) and IP community believe it should be accomplished at the transport layer. The goal of this chapter is not to take sides but to point out the implications of implementations at the transport layer, given that the services provided by the underlying layer are reliable.

Perspective can be gained on the variety of opinions on this matter by looking at the OSI transport layer protocols. There are five of them, from TP0 to TP4. TP4 is a full-function, connection-oriented protocol.

THE NATURE OF TRAFFIC

All traffic through the network is bursty, meaning technically that it follows a Poisson distribution. The only apparently nonbursty traffic is that which, for lack of bandwidth, takes a long time to send. For example, a large file transfer sent over the wide area network (WAN) that takes several hours at 9,600 bps is not, for the sake of this discussion, bursty. The only reason data is sent this way is that bandwidth costs are so high that it is cost effective to send the traffic for several hours rather than pay for the cost of a high-bandwidth circuit. Another kind of nonstochastic traffic is encrypted military communications. The underlying information is in fact bursty, but the system also sends constant nonsense data to mask the transfer of actual information.

The argument can be made that video communications are continuous. This is true for current implementations because the receiving devices have no substantial storage capacity. Frame information is repeated because the receiver cannot store and display the nonchanging information. In terms of the actual information content, the signal is stochastic. Here, information is defined as changes to the signal. A constant, non-changing signal, as far as the need for bandwidth goes, contains no information. A test pattern transmitted from a television transmitter contains all the information in the first frame transmitted; the subsequent frames contain no new information.

The point being made here is that the lack of new information means that the user at the receiving station, if the initial test pattern can be stored, needs zero bandwidth after the initial burst. Therefore, the information content of broadcast television is indeed bursty. Videoconferencing systems make use of this fact; they transmit only the changes from the previous frame. Because the information content is bursty (stochastic), the information can be sent effectively over a bandwidth-on-demand system such as frame relay.

Voice traffic at first appears to require continuous bandwidth, but if examined over short enough periods, speech is bursty; approximately 40%

of the time when we are speaking, no sounds are being made. This fact is made use of in low bit-rate voice technology.

Dedicated bandwidth is available in fixed increments and there is a cost associated with each increment. This cost per increment is typically non-linear. The major cost is the initial cost of procuring the right of way and route construction; the incremental cost of additional fiber waveguides is small. Once the facility exists, its real cost is therefore its initial installation cost plus continuing maintenance cost.

The fact that bandwidth in this sense is fixed and that the traffic is bursty poses the classic problem of providing sufficient bandwidth for the burst peaks while maintaining efficiency. After all is said and done, there is no satisfactory solution to this problem. Traffic can be queued and sent later to distribute peak traffic over time. This improves efficiency (efficiency is measured as bandwidth used divided by bandwidth available). The parties waiting for their turn on the network may, however, be unhappy. An alternative is to build more bandwidth, but this will be partly (i.e., inefficiently) used most of the time.

Frame relay offers the possibility of effective solutions to the problems of bursty traffic, not in the technology per se but in its ability to differentiate between types of traffic. The goal is to identify small chunks of the types of data to be transmitted, then assign them priorities based on their need for timely delivery. They can then be interleaved on the same transmission facility. For example, voice and video data could be given transmission priority over transaction data or file transfer data. This, in effect, provides a leveling of demand on the facility. In the limit, of course, the file transfer takes longer and the response time for the transaction is extended, but these inconveniences may be acceptable if the greater overall efficiency yields lower costs.

In practice, it may turn out that this solution to peak traffic demands is ineffective. Traffic is, on the whole, stochastic, and bandwidth cost is still fixed. If users expect to receive or providers expect to offer bandwidth on demand, they will require bandwidth capacity sufficient to accommodate peak rush hour traffic. From a carrier's point of view, there may be some benefits. To the extent that the traffic's peaks for the entire range of traffic to be handled are distributed more or less evenly throughout the day, bandwidth on demand allows the carrier to more efficiently use this bandwidth throughout the day. The carrier can only add bandwidth in fixed increments (e.g., DS-0, DS-1, or DS-3), but the carrier has (theoretically at least) the ability to add bandwidth to the frame relay switches during anticipated traffic peaks and at other times to allocate that bandwidth to other kinds of traffic. Unfortunately, the demand for practically all types of traffic in the network peaks at around 10:00 a.m. and 2:00 p.m.; in the middle of the night, there is little traffic of any kind. The carriers can level demand to some extent by lowering the cost of frame relay service during off-peak times, as is done with switched telephone rates.

TRANSPORT ISSUES

Although frame relay has the potential for providing faster, more efficient delivery across the network, it presents some interesting problems to the user in its lack of flow control and congestion management. X.25 networks offer error-free, sequenced, acknowledged, connection-oriented service. Frame relay leaves the implementation of such functions to the user, but eliminates considerable overhead. Frame relay is a connectionless service, but users can implement connection-oriented services at higher layers. Frame relay is well suited to TCP/IP users, who desire maximum speed and minimum service from the underlying layers.

Nearly tenfold increases in frame routing speed are claimed for frame relay switches in comparison with conventional X.25 packet switches. These comparisons may be suspect, unless it is certain that the tests were conducted on the same hardware platform, that the code was optimized for that platform, and that other, similar adjustments were made. Also, comparing new frame relay hardware with a 5-year-old X.25 packet switch is an invidious comparison.

For users not concerned that the network supply all the functions of X.25, frame relay offers the ideal link layer transportation mechanism. The only service provided is unacknowledged rapid routing with error detection. The frame itself makes provision for the frame relay switch to route it through the permanent virtual circuit and contains a cyclic redundancy check to detect errors. Thus, at least the frames received are known to be without detected error even if no mechanism is implemented (at the link layer) to request retransmission. This leaves the complete responsibility for flow control and congestion management to the upper layers. In keeping with this philosophy, the network layer is also a minimum service entity. Thus, the responsibility for all error handling falls to the transport layer.

SEQUENCE NUMBERING

Both high-level data link control (HDLC) and X.25 provide sequence numbering capability; frame relay and the IP do not. Therefore, over a frame relay network, if the user layer requires sequencing services, it is up to the transport layer to provide them. In this general case, the transport layer may make no assumptions about the underlying layers, or it must make the worst-case assumptions (i.e., segments will not be delivered in order, segments may become lost, and segments may be delayed). Because most frame relay connections are permanent virtual circuits and possess short delays, the extended sequence numbering capability of, for example, TCP is not needed.

ACKNOWLEDGMENTS

The X.25 protocols provide acknowledgments at the link layer, on a link-by-link basis, and at the network layer. Because no such acknowledgments are provided by frame relay, this task, for the same reasons given for sequencing, must be handled by the transport layer. The acknowledgment number field is the same size as the sequence number field. This allows the receiver to provide the next expected segment number. The next expected segment number is the inclusive acknowledgment for all previously received segments.

FLOW CONTROL

Flow control in an X.25 network is provided on a link-by-link basis and across the network by the network layer. Here again, the underlying layers of a frame relay implementation provide no flow control. Flow control is performed at the transport layer, using a credit window mechanism. The receiver sends a credit to the transmitter for the maximum number of segments it is willing to accept. The transmitter may send until it has exhausted the credit. This value must be chosen with great care because the underlying network may store (i.e., delay) many segments. The receiver cannot offer the transmitter too much credit because it must be prepared to receive all of the segments outstanding in the network should they be delivered all at once; it must offer enough credit so that the transmitter does not frequently exhaust its credit and have to stop and wait for more (which reduces efficiency). This is not a severe problem on an end-to-end frame relay network because the network delays are quite small. On the other hand, if the frame relay connection is one component of a greater network (i.e., the frame relay is a subnetwork concatenated with several other subnetworks), the credit value must be carefully considered. The transport layer's responsibility is end to end and transcends any underlying services.

ERROR RECOVERY

Any underlying network or subnetwork will on occasion make an unrecoverable error such that a frame or packet is lost. For this reason, transport must provide some sequencing capability. Errors manifest themselves to transport as missing segments, because an error detected by the cyclic redundancy check (CRC) at the link layer will simply cause the link layer to not deliver that frame. This is true of frame relay and HDLC, but it happens much less often with a full HDLC implementation because the link layer can request retransmission of the missing frame. This feature slows the delivery at the link layer (on an error-prone link); this additional overhead is deemed unnecessary on modern links, which are based on digital transmission technology and therefore are less error prone.

If the digital links never made errors, there would be no need for error checking or the ability to automatically retransmit frames in which errors are detected. In an HDLC frame, removing both the control field (assuming the address field is still needed) and the CRC saves three octets of overhead per frame. The reality is that errors do occur, and so the CRC is needed. Thus, the sole savings is one octet per frame. An error-free link would also not require the use of retransmission software. But errors do occur and retransmission is required, and this task ultimately falls to the transport layer, which must have these capabilities anyway.

CONGESTION MANAGEMENT

Congestion management is the heart of the transport problem. As previously discussed, all connectionless services tend to suffer from congestion, because traffic is bursty and bandwidth is fixed. To the extent that the bandwidth exceeds use, congestion is not a problem, but efficiency suffers. Networks must balance the cost of bandwidth against use; in other words, they must trade off efficiency against lower response time.

There are three possible ways to address this problem. For want of better names they could be called the smart link, the smart network, and the smart transport approaches.

The smart link approach implements flow control only at the link layer. This is acceptable for small networks. It works, for example, for a node receiving, over a single input link, traffic destined for multiple outbound links. If one of the output links is congested, the node exercises flow control on the inbound link to keep from being overrun by data it cannot deliver. The unwanted side effect is to cut off the traffic to all the outbound links.

In X.25 networks, the flow control at both link and network layers effectively provides congestion management. Should a node or link suffer from congestion, flow control can be used on that link or on some or all of the virtual circuits passing through that node to minimize congestion. Of course, response time across the network for that logical channel suffers accordingly. Other logical channels passing through that node, however, continue to operate. This is the smart network approach to congestion management.

In connectionless networks, congestion is typically handled at the network layer by discarding packets. This is acceptable because transport protocols used with unreliable connectionless networks do not have high expectations of the network layer and are capable of retransmitting these missing packets. Unfortunately, this exacerbates the congestion problem. (The IP now has a mechanism for sending a source quench packet to the source when a node is overrun by packets.) It is by no means assured that the IP will be used over a frame relay network, where the same condition exists. Work is being done to address this issue. Some of the issues and potential solutions are discussed here. The actual solution, at least in the short term, will depend on the exigencies of the network design.

With the smart transport approach, the transport layer is informed of the congestion status of the underlying network sublayers. This is comparable to noticing that United Parcel Service (UPS) acknowledgments (i.e., network layer packets) that normally flow between offices in New York and Los Angeles are not returning in the expected one day. If the UPS van is stuck in traffic on the New York end or the Los Angeles end, that is comparable to link layer congestion. If the air traffic control system is delaying flights, or if one or more of the UPS package-handling depots is overflowing with packages, that is comparable to network layer congestion. If the assumption is made that packages (i.e., packets) are lost and copies are resent, this congests the network further. One dilemma is the length of time it is appropriate to wait for acknowledgments to arrive. In a stable network with relatively uniform traffic flow, this is not a problem. But network traffic is bursty and the network is subject to sudden overloads (in the UPS example, this might be the Christmas rush). One approach (used in TCP) is to monitor the response time and store the average. But sudden increases in network delay can cause retransmissions and delays. The goal of the transport layer is to balance response time (minimum delay across the network) with maximum efficiency (high throughput).

There are two ways the transport layer can achieve these goals. One is to calculate and monitor the existing round trip propagation delay. The trick is to avoid making the system too sensitive. The retransmission timer should not respond for congestion of short duration but should be sensitive enough to identify the real network propagation delay if a serious case of congestion does occur. By implementing a congestion control scheme (e.g., Karn's algorithm), transport can dynamically adapt to changes in delay on the underlying network.

The other approach is for the underlying (i.e., the frame relay) network to supply enough buffers to temporarily store the large volume of packets. This approach works as long as the network can determine what the peak traffic is going to be and provide enough buffers. In addition, users must be willing to tolerate the attendant transit delay caused by buffering the traffic while waiting for bandwidth to become available. With buffering, frames (or packets) are not discarded during congestion, but the transit delay of the subnet varies with the load. If the transport has not properly implemented Karn's algorithm or a similar mechanism, inefficiencies are introduced as the transport layer responds to these sudden increases (and decreases) in subnet delay.

SUMMARY

Although frame relay provides low delay and efficient bandwidth on demand, bandwidth still is available only in fixed sized increments. Because traffic is bursty, network users need to plan strategies for those temporary peak traffic conditions when the traffic exceeds the bandwidth.

There are four ways to handle the problem:

- *Provide more bandwidth than needed so that traffic requiring network access never exceeds the bandwidth allocated.* This is the approach being taken with current frame relay offerings through the committed information rate.
- *Limit the traffic.* This is implemented in the transport layer by having it show restraint. Restraint implies that the transport mechanism, as previously discussed, can detect congestion by sensing temporary increases in subnetwork delay. Because the transport layer has no control over subnetwork delay, it has to choose responses that will not inadvertently add to congestion.
- *Temporarily store traffic overload in buffers.* This must be implemented in the underlying frame relay or other subnetwork.
- *Implement flow control either at the frame relay or the network layers.* It could be argued that this problem of congestion should be handled at the lowest layer of the architecture possible (i.e., at the frame relay layer) and not at the transport layer, which is two layers removed from the problem. To this end, the frame relay standard has defined two bits for congestion management. These are called the forward explicit congestion notification and backward explicit congestion notification bits. Exactly what course of action the frame relay switches should take in response to these bits is still the subject of discussion.

Buffering data within the subnetwork runs counter to the philosophy of a low-delay fast transportation mechanism. Implementation of flow control is not just a subnetwork problem but affects the whole frame relay layer. The use of the congestion notification bits ripples back through all of the attached frame relay networks to the customer's attachment point. This implies the need for much coordination (i.e., standards activity) to provide easily interconnected frame relay services and equipment. Rather than go through the protracted process of establishing a standard, the more likely scenario is that vendors will simply let users apply the functions of the transport layer to the problem. Therefore, whatever transport layer protocol is used over frame relay (e.g., TCP or OSI TP4), it must be capable of implementing the adaptive behavior described above. Because transport layer functions are several layers removed from the problem, it is hard to make delicate adjustments. On the other hand, as long as frame relay provides the fast, low-delay delivery mechanism, it is quite usable by any robust transport layer application.

Chapter 12
Dynamic Bandwidth Allocation in Broadband ISDN

Johnny S. K. Wong, Prerana Vaidya, and Armin R. Mikler

The broadband integrated services digital network (B-ISDN) is to provide voice, high-speed data, and video services. It must therefore offer high throughput and sufficient flexibility to support the traffic's different peak and average bit rates, as well as varying statistical distribution of cell inter-arrival times. The asynchronous transfer mode (ATM) will provide the desired flexibility by applying the concept of high-speed packet switching networks at the level of bandwidth allocation. Due to its inherent flexibility, simplicity, service independence, and high performance, ATM offers many advantages as the transport multiplexing technique across the user network interface of the B-ISDN.

Congestion controls are required to allocate the shared bandwidth in a fair manner that satisfies the performance requirements of each service type. These congestion control mechanisms should be simple, effective, fair, and not optimized for any particular service type.

Besides having to deal with a wide range of traffic characteristics, the control algorithm needs to be effective in yielding predictable network behavior. Moreover, any control algorithm in a broadband network should also be simple in terms of the required processing resources. A real-time adaptability to changes in the offered traffic characteristics and to additional requests for new services is required for an effective control.

DYNAMIC BANDWIDTH ALLOCATION

In a multimedia environment, the bandwidth requirements vary with the connections and types of services. In the case of static allocation, in which a virtual path's allocated bandwidth is equal to the connection's peak

0-8493-9949-1/99/$0.00+$.50
© 1999 by CRC Press LLC

bandwidth requirement, no cell loss occurs due to buffer overflow. The stringent requirements can be met in a simple manner with minimal cell delay. The disadvantage of this approach is a potential low bandwidth use. Due to its static nature, it cannot cope with bursty traffic, and hence network resources are not optimally exploited.

Thus, dynamic bandwidth allocation with statistical multiplexing is used. Appropriate bandwidth is allocated to each call, with the bandwidth varying between the peak rate and the average bit rate declared by the source. Cell multiplexing offers high use gains if the traffic profile is bursty.

Congestion Control

An overview of the concepts involved in congestion control in broadband networks is presented and the various approaches used to solve the problem are discussed in the following sections.

Reactive Control vs. Preventive Control. Reactive controls respond to congestion by sending an immediate throttle message to the source node, which then controls the influx of traffic in the network. The major drawbacks of this scheme are high lead time in reacting to the throttle feedback, sensitivity to transient traffic conditions leading to oscillations and overreactions in a bursty environment, and high propagation delays in sending throttle messages.

Preventive controls involve preventing congestion rather than trying to resolve it. This can be done by monitoring the flow into the network at the access nodes, keeping the bandwidth within the bounds established during call setup, and smoothing out bursty traffic by throttling the traffic flow into the network.

Connection Oriented vs. Connectionless. The transport protocol type has an important effect on how well the access control mechanisms operate. In a connection-oriented protocol, the packets belonging to the same connection follow the same route. With a connectionless protocol, the packets belonging to the same connection can take different routes through the network, as determined by the destination address in their headers and bandwidth availability.

Access control is most effective in a connection-oriented approach. The status of the connection's path can be obtained because it is already fixed. Thus, the decision to serve the request can be based on this knowledge. Also, because connections support various service types, fair bandwidth allocation can be done by differentiating and flow-controlling the traffic of individual connections. ATM, a connection-oriented protocol, can achieve this effectively.

It appears, however, that some capacity to dynamically change the paths is necessary in order to avoid local congestion in parts of the network. Based on the probability of performance improvement, alternative routes can be searched and dynamic path splitting may be incorporated in the connection-oriented protocol.

Traffic Management Approach. A traffic management approach is necessary to meet the performance needs of different traffic types. In a single grade of service (GoS) approach, there is no differentiation between cells at the transport layer irrespective of their associated service requirements. Performance parameters must therefore be set up such that they satisfy the most stringent requirements. A multiple GoS approach involves grouping various services into multiple performance classes. Interclass interactions could be managed using a priority scheme or bandwidth segregation.

Incoming traffic can be divided into multiple classes to follow a single GoS approach within a class. This dynamically assigns priorities to a class of traffic and minimizes processing overhead within a class.

TRADITIONAL APPROACHES

Traditionally, a connection is refused by the network when the service requirements cannot be guaranteed. ATM is connection oriented and a particular path is established through the network when the connection is set up. Network nodes along this path are expected to provide sufficient resources for the duration of such a connection.

In reality, however, the traffic is subject to variations (i.e., traffic levels may exceed the average in parts of the network and at the same time be below the average level in other parts of the network). Due to uncertainty about traffic behavior and network loads along a particular path, the network cannot easily reconfigure to incorporate a newly arriving connection. These conditions have led to the development of nonadaptive approaches.

A static nonadaptive approach suffers from the following shortcomings:

- In a multimedia environment, as a connection proceeds along a path in the network, its traffic characteristics may change due to interference at the intermediate buffers. Traffic patterns indicate the interdependencies (i.e., whether there is interference) between different traffic sources. Accounting for this interdependency could produce an optimizing effect on the network use or a negative effect on the traffic flow, increasing the cell loss and cell delay beyond acceptable limits. It is difficult to estimate the positive or negative nature of this effect, and no previous approach has tried to quantify it. The commonly made assumption that the various traffic sources are statistically independent no longer holds if these interactions are taken into account.

- The responsiveness of congestion control schemes, because they may be difficult to quantify, has generally been ignored. The available bandwidth is a constantly changing quantity, and as traffic through the nodes goes up or down, the available bandwidth increases or decreases. When the links on a particular route have exhausted their quota of available bandwidth, alternative paths might be searched. If the optimal path is congested, path splitting can be used to generate a nonoptimal path (i.e., the traffic will be split along several paths of different capacities).

- The equivalent bandwidth associated with a connection, which is derived from the set of traffic descriptors and declared at the virtual call setup, is assumed to be independent of the particular traffic load on each link composing the connection route through the network. This may not lead to an accurate measure, as it is difficult to define such an equivalent bandwidth without considering the mix of the stream and the bursty traffic multiplexed on each link.

- Giving higher priority to voice traffic (a commonly proposed nonadaptive approach) might not be suitable in all environments.

- Cell transmission delays and the cell loss probabilities are applied as the decision criteria in admission control because they accurately reflect the degree of network congestion. Usually their long-term values, averaged over a period, are used to make a decision. However, this might lead to a temporary congestion if the network traffic is bursty and changing relatively fast. It is possible for a large number of cells to be lost during such a period of congestion even though the long-term time-averaged loss rate is kept small. In voice communications, a loss of a burst of cells may cause a loss of a complete phrase.

A NEW APPROACH

An adaptive scheme takes into consideration the changes in the network with respect to the load, the availability of bandwidth, and traffic characteristics. Hence, this approach adapts to the changes in the dynamics of the network and bases all decisions on the current knowledge of the network. It is connection oriented in a loose sense as the packets may follow alternate links or the bandwidth may be split between paths. Unlike conventional dynamic bandwidth allocation schemes, the constraints are not just met in order to satisfy the performance requirements; they are exploited to gain additional performance. Loss-sensitive traffic might be delayed at a node in order to achieve better network performance, if this delay does not violate any traffic requirements. A certain threshold of load condition stability needs to be maintained in order to distinguish the overall changes in load conditions or network traffic requirements from transient fluctuations or spurious noises.

Network Dynamics

Network dynamics can be examined with respect to two different time scales:

- *Short-term changes,* in which load changes at network nodes are caused by data packets introduced by the set of current connections.
- *Long-term changes,* in which the overall network load changes with respect to source–destination pairs and traffic types.

While fluctuations introduced by the first type of network dynamics appear in a much shorter time, it is generally assumed that fluctuations due to the second type of network dynamics appear over a much larger time scale.

For a bandwidth allocation function to guarantee that traffic requirements are met and at the same time to manage network use such that the probability of congestion is minimized, it has to take the overall network dynamics (i.e., long-term changes) into consideration.

This requires that each node have the following capabilities, in order to update itself about each of the two types of dynamics:

- *A direct feedback mechanism.* This monitors immediate load changes that are due to data packets of current connections.
- *A decision function.* This considers such factors as bandwidth availability, predicted performance along the path, and change in the network conditions after the acceptance of the new connection. This function is based on the information acquired by the feedback mechanism as well as traffic parameters attached to each packet. This function requires explicit control messages in order to respond to the long-term network changes.

Concepts and Definitions

The following sections describe the different traffic classes used and formally characterize various traffic sources by associating traffic descriptors and performance criteria with them.

Traffic Characterization. The various traffic sources are placed in three different categories:

- Bursty sources.
- Constant-bit-rate or stream sources.
- Variable-bit-rate sources.

The bursty source has active and idle states; the active state generates a stream of cells at a uniform rate. A stream source is modeled as a continuous flow of cells at a uniform predictable rate. The variable bit rate sources are characterized by a complex traffic pattern and hence are not considered. A bursty source is characterized by:

- B_p, the peak rate, in megabits per second.
- B_m, the mean rate, in megabits per second.
- $P(T_b, T_c)$, the periodicity, where, T_b is the burst width and T_c is the burst spacing.

The periodicity is defined as the distribution of burst widths over the holding time for a particular connection. The parameters T_b and T_c indicate the level of predictability and the level of certainty with which the network might predict the traffic pattern of a particular service. Thus, periodicity gives an accurate prediction for the burstiness of a traffic type. Hence, a traffic descriptor is characterized by (B_p, B_m, P).

The performance parameters taken into account are the instantaneous cell loss probability, p, due to buffer overflow and the maximum queuing delay (proportional to the buffer length, k). Thus a grade of service constraint is specified by (δ, p), where δ denotes the delay requirement in terms of cell transmission time and p denotes the tolerable instantaneous cell loss probability.

Traffic Classes. All the traffic entering the system is assigned among three basic traffic classes. For making decisions for allocating bandwidth, a queue is allocated for each traffic class. (The number of classes can be extended to include traffic types that do not satisfy the criteria of these basic classes.) The three basic traffic classes are:

- A nonpreemptive exhaustive priority class for signaling and control.
- A low-delay service priority class for voice and delay-sensitive traffic.
- A low-priority class with potentially higher network delay for delay-tolerant and bursty traffic.

Priority Algorithm. To support these multiple classes of traffic, priorities are used. Priorities can be assigned by marking special bits in the packet header. A static priority scheme, which would always schedule the highest priority traffic, might degrade the performance for the low-priority traffic. Another possibility is a dynamic priority scheme, in which the priority changes with time. Two different priority mechanisms are used — one as a general scheduling scheme and the other as a local congestion control scheme.

Priority for Scheduling. Giving a static high priority to delay-sensitive traffic can produce relatively high losses for loss-sensitive traffic or block this traffic indefinitely. Thus, the following scheme is adopted:

- A cell remains in the queue until it is transmitted, or while it is being delayed, as a multiple number of slots, until its deadline expires. The cell is discarded when its deadline expires.
- Highest priority is given to the signaling and controlling traffic class which contains control messages.
- Among the delay-sensitive and loss-sensitive traffic classes, priority is given to the delay-sensitive traffic (i.e., delay-sensitive cells in queue that have some multiple of slots remaining) before its deadlines expire; otherwise priority is given to the loss-sensitive traffic.
- When the queue length of the loss-sensitive class exceeds threshold, the contents of the queue become delay sensitive and receive higher priority.

A desired performance level for each of the high- and the low-priority classes could be achieved by choosing a proper value for the changeover threshold. By simulation, a changeover threshold value can be found to give satisfactory performance, achieving cell losses and delays within specified bounds for the admitted traffic classes.

Priority for Congestion Control. When the load conditions in a network change and the nodes start getting congested, it might be necessary to change the priority scheme dynamically. The idea is to control the congestion without seriously degrading the network's performance. Thus the priority scheme now works as follows:

- Priority is given to loss-sensitive cells over the delay-sensitive traffic.
- Low-priority cells are discarded first. By discarding the voice cells during congestion periods, the mean waiting time for loss-sensitive services can be greatly improved.

LAYERED CONGESTION CONTROL

In an integrated network, congestion can occur at the call level, the burst or packet level, or the cell level. Congestion in such a network is measured by the probability of call blocking, packet or burst blocking, and cell blocking. A multilevel traffic characterization is shown in Exhibit 1.

Blocking is defined as the failure to allocate the bandwidth demanded. A call is blocked when the initiation is denied. A packet or burst is blocked when a completed call fails to deliver the burst. A cell is blocked in a packet when the cell is missing upon delivery.

An arriving call may cause blocking at any of the three levels. If a packet-level blocking occurs in the nodes corresponding to a preestablished route, it might result in a call blocking for that route. This call blocking might be avoided for the incoming call if an alternative route may be tried at the packet level, or the packet-level blocking can be reduced by splitting

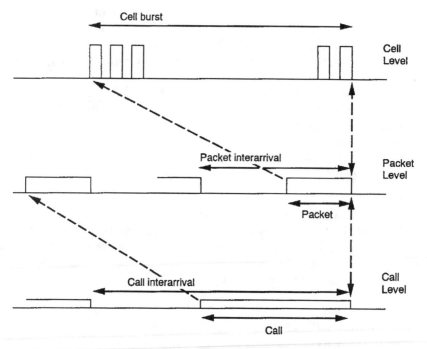

Exhibit 1. Characterization of Multilevel Traffic

the bandwidth among multiple routes for the same destination. Similarly, alternate routing and path splitting at the cell level may reduce the burst-level blocking.

The central idea is to come up with strategies for each service type that will maintain an admissible level of cell blocking. This admissible region will correspond to a cluster of nodes along a path where, in response to the incoming request, there is acceptable burst-level blocking. These admissible regions of call combinations would then allow the call-blocking probability to be predicted for the corresponding paths.

The approach does not lead to a closed-loop congestion control policy, as the feedback from the destination or intermediate nodes is not used directly to decide whether to admit new packets to the network. The short-term feedback from immediate neighbors is used as control messages; these help a node to update itself with information about relatively recent network conditions.

This would ensure congestion-free communication with a guaranteed level of throughput and a constant end-to-end delay per connection. The constant end-to-end delay is achieved by setting an upper bound on the number of slots a packet is delayed at an intermediate node before being forwarded. This is possible because queuing delays are less significant at broadband speeds.

PROSPECTS FOR OBJECT-ORIENTED STRATEGIES

The complex and uncertain traffic that characterizes a broadband environment asks for a modular and flexible design approach. One difficulty is the uncertainty involved in modeling the statistical behavior of many types of traffic sources. But more importantly, the broadband traffic environment is characterized by connections that have different bandwidth requirements, connections with changing service quality requirements, changing relationships between a connection and the class it belongs to, and interactions between the different traffic classes. Thus, object-oriented design frameworks for adaptive, multilevel congestion control for bandwidth allocation are currently being investigated.

A multilevel control is desired because traffic congestion in broadband networks occurs at three different levels: call level, burst level, and cell level. The control at one level may depend on another control decision at a low level. In addition, a control decision at a higher layer may influence the decision at a lower layer. This is well supported by the object-oriented approach in which the dynamic binding of objects to a class allows the decision parameters and decision-making entities to change dynamically. In addition, the function at a level can be inherited by all the lower levels and thus provide an abstraction by avoiding any duplication of functions at any level. Also, each level is shielded from others in terms of the implementation details at the other level. This information hiding allows a scheduler working at a global level not to be bothered by the details at the local level. This provides the required modularity and flexibility for the design.

SUMMARY

Different approaches to bandwidth allocation have been considered. Because different traffic types generally impose different requirements on the network, how bandwidth is allocated to different traffic types significantly affects the degree of network use. Bandwidth allocation and routing mechanisms are responsible for meeting these requirements of network traffic.

Dynamic bandwidth allocation strategies appear to be most useful in B-ISDN, as they can accommodate diverse traffic types and the dynamics of the network. They can provide reactive congestion control by changing the amounts of bandwidth allocated for a set of concurrent connections. This way, traffic may be throttled to respond to congested conditions.

BURSTY DATA COMMUNICATIONS

As multimedia traffic has been introduced, different traffic types in different connections may become dependent on each other. New bandwidth allocation mechanisms are needed that can account for traffic dependencies. These mechanisms must be designed to maximize bandwidth use while guaranteeing the stringent requirements of different traffic types. At the same time, mechanisms must be flexible enough to provide for responsive congestion and flow control mechanisms. The design of new responsive bandwidth allocation strategies is extremely complex as the network's dynamic behavior generally cannot be predicted.

Section V
Video Communications Over Multimedia Networks

The inclusion of video communication on a network is one of the most technically challenging feats that has been accomplished since the advent of computers. The maxim "a picture is worth a thousand words" never envisioned the complexity of the video image. The thousand is just the down payment. Whereas the audio content of a voice connection can be digitized and transported without compression in a mere 64k bps, it requires on the order of 10M bps to transport a rather low-quality uncompressed video signal, such as that on our television sets.

Fortunately, we can compress the heck out of a video signal, once it has been properly digitized. Unfortunately, it will still require a considerable amount of bandwidth on our current LAN and WAN networks. This sort of good news/bad news trade-off is the topic of this section on video and the multimedia network.

The possibility of adding video transport to a mature corporate network is enough to bring terror and outrage to the most stoic of IT managers. Unless the network was just installed, with all of the future expansions provided for, the capacity for a significant amount of additional video traffic simply does not exist. The manager thinks, "It is not yet in the budget; we will never get approval for a budget variance, and some of the users want it right now, anyway." Fortunately, the first chapter in this section details all these issues in such a manner that they can be used both for planning and defense.

Next, we approach the subject of providing bidirectional video for conferencing over Internet protocol (IP). This area has applications both within the internal corporate intranet and in the wider area of the Internet. The presence of the IP protocol stack, with accompanying facilities for routing, switching, and encapsulation, is quite pervasive. This chapter touches the issues of perceived service quality, facility utilization, image parameters, and enabling technologies. It also provides useful insight into bandwidth reservation, prioritization, point-to-point streaming, and multi-casting.

Finally, an excellent overview of the compression issues and techniques now used for video and image transmission is presented. The reason that video images may be easily compressed is that there is a high degree of redundancy, both in the two-dimensional image frame and in the temporal sequence of frames.

This technique has actually been used to compress images for longer than one might think. Walt Disney used a manual version of the technique to compress the amount of illustration his cartoonists required to produce animated classics such as *Snow White* and *Fantasia*. Disney noted that a great deal of redundant content existed between animated frames. The background of a scene rarely changed, other than through side-to-side motion. Rather than paint the background repetitively for each frame, along with the foreground action, Disney's artists prepared detailed back-grounds and then placed a sequence of transparent gels, painted with the character actions, onto the background as each frame was photographed. The same type of compression may be used in motion video.

The still-image compression of JPEG has been incorporated into motion standards of MPEG-I and -II to greatly decrease the amount of network bandwidth needed to transport multimedia imagery. This is the enabling technology that makes video transport practical.

Chapter 13
Placing Images and Multimedia on the Corporate Network

Gilbert Held

Until recently, it was rare for a corporate network to transport images, and multimedia was more talked about than actually available. The primary use of images was for incorporation into word processing or desktop publishing applications, and most images remained local to the personal computer they were stored on.

The use of images has moved off the individual PC workstation and onto network servers and mainframes, making images available for retrieval by virtually any employee with a PC connected to a local area network or to the corporate network. In addition, the recent standardization of multimedia data storage has increased the ability of organizations to purchase or develop applications that merge audio, video, and data.

This chapter discusses methods of restructuring an existing network to accommodate the transportation of images and multimedia cost-effectively. The chapter also reviews techniques that enhance the transmission of images while minimizing their effect on the network.

IMAGE UTILIZATION

In spite of the vast increase in the amount of data that must be transported to support image applications, the use of imaging is rapidly increasing. The old adage "a picture is worth a thousand words" is especially true when considering many computer applications.

Today, several network-compliant data base programs support the attachment of image files to data base records. Using a Canon digital camera or similar product, real estate agents can photograph the exterior and interior of homes and transfer the digitized images to the network server upon their return to the office. When a potential client comes into the

0-8493-9949-1/99/$0.00+$.50
© 1999 by CRC Press LLC

office, an agent can enter the client's home criteria, such as the number of bedrooms, baths, price range, school district, and similar information, and have textual information as well as photographs of the suitable homes meeting the client's criteria displayed on their screen. This capability significantly reduces the time required to develop a list of homes that the client may wish to physically view.

AUDIO UTILIZATION

The primary use of audio is to supplement images and text with sound. Unlike a conventional PC, which can display any image supported by the resolution of the computer's monitor, the use of audio requires specialized equipment. First, the computer must have a sound board or specialized adapter card that supports the method used to digitize audio. Second, each computer must have one or more speakers connected to the sound board or speech adapter card to broadcast the resulting reconverted analog signal.

MULTIMEDIA STORAGE REQUIREMENTS

The term *multimedia* is a catchall phrase that refers to the use of two or more methods for conveying information. Thus, multimedia can include voice or sound (both collectively referred to as audio), still images, moving images, and fax images, as well as text documents. This means that multimedia can be considered an extension of image storage. To understand how multimedia data storage requirements differ from conventional data storage requirements; these requirements are especially evident when considering the storage of images.

Image Data — Scanners versus Digital Cameras

Images are converted into a series of pixels or picture elements by a scanner or a digital camera. Software used to control a scanner places the resulting pixels into a particular order according to the file format selected from the scanning software menu. Digital cameras store images directly in the form of a matrix of pixels that can be downloaded to a personal computer or workstation for storage or for incorporation into an application, such as an employee picture data base.

Some file storage formats require the use of compression before the image can be stored. Compression typically reduces data storage requirements by 50% or more.

Text and image data storage requirements are significantly different. A full page of text, such as a one-page letter, might contain approximately 300 words, with an average of five characters per word. Thus, a typical one-page text document would require 1500 characters of data storage. Adding formatting characters used by a word processor, a one-page text document might require up to 2,000 characters, or 16,000 bits of data storage.

When an image is scanned, the data storage requirements of the resulting file depend on four factors:

- The size of the image.
- The scan resolution used during the scanning process.
- The type of image being scanned — color or black-and-white.
- Whether or not the selected file format results in the compression of pixels before their storage.

When an image is captured with a digital camera, the resulting data storage required to represent the image is based on similar factors. However, instead of the scan resolution, image density or the camera's horizontal and vertical resolution determine the data storage requirements.

To illustrate the data storage requirements of different types of images, one example focuses on a 3" × 5" photograph. That photograph contains a total of 15 square inches that must be scanned.

A low-resolution black-and-white scan normally occurs using 150 lines per inch and 150 pixels per line per inch, where a pixel with a zero value represents white and a pixel whose value is one represents black. Thus, the total number of bits required to store a 3" × 5" black-and-white photograph using a low-resolution scan without first compressing the data would be 337,500 bits, which would result in a requirement to store 42,188 bytes of data. Thus, a 3" × 5" black-and-white photograph would require 42,188/2,000, or approximately 21 times the amount of storage required by a one-page document.

Most scanners now consider 300 lines per inch, with 300 pixels per line, per inch, to represent a high-resolution scan. However, some newly introduced scanning products now consider 300 lines per inch with 300 pixels per line to represent a medium- or high-resolution scan.

Regardless of the pixel density considered to represent a medium- or high-resolution scan, the computation of the resulting data storage requirement is performed in the same manner. That is, storing the photograph would entail multiplying the number of square inches of the document — in this example, 15 — by the pixel density squared.

The data storage requirements of a one-page text document can be compared to the data storage required to store a 3" × 5" black-and-white photograph at different scan resolutions. The requirements are as follows:

Type of Document/Image	Data Storage (Bytes)
300-word text document	2,000
3" × 5" B&W photo scanned at 150 pixels/inch	42,188
3" × 5" B&W photo scanned at 300 pixels/inch	84,375
3" × 5" B&W photo scanned at 450 pixels/inch	126,563
3" × 5" B&W photo scanned at 600 pixels/inch	168,750

To store an image in color, data storage requirements would increase significantly. For example, if a scanner supports color, each pixel would require one byte to represent each possible color of the pixel. Thus, a color image would require eight times the data storage of a black-and-white image when a scanner supports up to 256 colors per pixel. This means that the 3" × 5" photograph scanned at 300 pixels per inch would require 675,000 bytes of storage. Similarly, a 3" × 5" color photograph scanned at a resolution of 600 pixels per inch would require 1.35M bytes of storage, or 675 times the amount of storage required for a 300-word, one-page document.

Without considering the effect of data compression, the transmission of images on a network can require from 20 to more than 600 times the amount of time required to transmit a one-page standard text document. Thus, it is obvious that the transmission of images by themselves or as a part of a multimedia application can adversely affect the capability of a network to support other users in an efficient manner unless proper planning precedes the support of the multimedia data transfer.

Minimizing Image Storage

It is possible to reduce the transmission time of the image on a network, since that time is directly related to the number of bytes required to represent an image. One method is obtained through the selection of an appropriate image format.

For example, consider an image that is part of an on-line document. When stored using the tagged image file (TIF) format with LZW compression, the image requires 7,039 bytes of storage. If a TIF format was selected without specifying the use of LZW compression, the storage requirements for that same image would increase to 24,726 bytes. If the CompuServe graphics interchange format (GIF) file format was used to store the image, 11,196 bytes of storage would be required.

GIF also uses a version of the LZW compression method, but it is slightly less efficient than LZW compression used in TIF. Thus the use of a TIF file format with compression is almost 50% more efficient than GIF and approximately three times more efficient than using TIF without compression.

Audio Storage

The most popular method of voice digitization is known as pulse code modulation (PCM), in which analog speech is digitized at a rate of 64K bps. Thus, one minute of speech would require 480,000 bytes of data storage. At this digitization rate, data storage of digitized speech can easily expand to require a significant portion of a hard disk for just 10 to 20 minutes of audio.

Multimedia applications developers do not store audio using PCM. Instead, they store audio using a standardized audio compression technique that results in a lower level of audio fidelity but significantly lowers the data storage requirement of digitized audio.

Today, several competing multimedia voice digitization standards permit speech to be digitized at 8K bps. Although this is a significant improvement over PCM used by telephone companies to digitize voice, it still requires a substantial amount of disk space to store a meaningful amount of voice.

For example, one hour of voice would require 2.8M bytes of data storage. Thus, data storage of audio is similar to video, in that a meaningful data base of images and sound must either be placed on a CD-ROM or on the hard disk of a network server or mainframe computer that usually has a larger data storage capacity than individual personal computers.

STORING IMAGES ON A LAN SERVER OR MAINFRAME

There are three methods for storing images on a LAN server or mainframe. First, images can be transferred to a computer's hard disk using either a personal computer and scanner, or by connecting the PC to a digital camera. Another method for storing images involves forwarding each image after it is scanned or transferred from a digital camera or similar device. A third method for placing images on a file server or mainframe is based on premastering a CD-ROM or another type of optical disk.

Transferring a large number of images at one time can adversely affect network users. To minimize the effect, images can be transferred from a computer to a server or mainframe after normal work hours. As an alternative, a removable hard disk can be used, permitting movement of the disk to a similarly equipped network server to transfer images without affecting network users.

Forwarding Images After Scanning

This method of storing images on the LAN has the greatest potential for negative impact on network users. Some document scanners are capable of scanning several pages per minute. If a large number of images were scanned, transferring the digitized images through a local or wide area network connection could saturate a network during the scanning and transferring process.

This happens because, as other network users are transferring a few thousand bytes, transferring images containing 20 to 600 times more data would consume most of the network bandwidth for relatively long periods of time. Thus, the effect of image transfer can be compared to the addition of 20 to 600 network users transferring one-page documents, with the actual addition based on the resolution of the images and whether or not they are in black-and-white or color.

Premastering

Premastering a CD-ROM or other type of optical disk permits images to become accessible by other network users without adversely affecting network operations. However, cost and ease of image modification or replacement must be weighed against the advantage of this method.

From a cost perspective, equipment required to master images on a CD-ROM will cost between $3,000 and $5,000. In comparison, the use of conventional magnetic storage on the server or mainframe can avoid that equipment cost as well as the cost of a CD-ROM drive connected to a file server.

Concerning ease of image modification or replacement, CD-ROM data cannot be modified once a disk is mastered. This means that a new CD-ROM disk must be mastered each time previously stored images or data must be modified or replaced.

If real-time or daily updates are not required, this method of image placement on a network server or mainframe should be considered. The time required to master a CD-ROM disk has been reduced to a few hours, when mastering occurs on a 486-based personal computer.

In addition, write-once CD-ROM disks now cost under $20. Thus, a weekly update of an image data base could be performed for a one-time cost of between $3,000 and $5,000, and $20 per week for each write-once CD-ROM disk used. Since this method would have no negative impact on network operations, its cost would be minor in comparison to the cost of modifying a network.

The next section focuses on methods used to provide access to images stored in a central repository. Use of both LAN and WAN transmission facilities are examined, with several strategies for minimizing the effect of image transfers on network users.

ACCESSING IMAGES ON THE NETWORK

Once a decision is made to add images to a data base or other application, the potential effect of the retrieval of images by network users against the current organizational network infrastructure must be examined. Doing so provides the information necessary to determine if an existing network should be modified to support the transfer of images, as well as data.

To illustrate the factors that must be considered, this example assumes that images are to be added to a 50-node LAN server. The network server is attached to a 10M-bps Ethernet network as illustrated in Exhibit 1a, with images placed on a CD-ROM jukebox connected to the server.

Based on an analysis of the expected use of the LAN, 15 stations were identified that are expected to primarily use the images stored on the

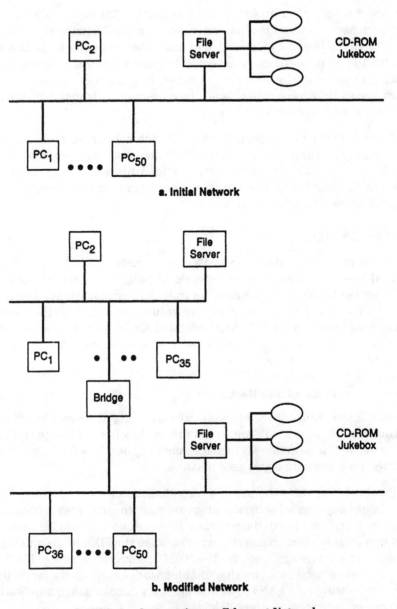

a. Initial Network

b. Modified Network

Exhibit 1.   Segmenting an Ethernet Network

CD-ROM jukebox. The other 35 network users are expected to casually use the CD-ROM jukebox, primarily using the LAN to access other applications on the server, such as workgroup software and other application programs, including a conventional text-based data base and electronic mail.

One method of minimizing the contention for network resources between network users is obtained by segmenting the network. Exhibit 1b illustrates the use of a local bridge to link separate networks. In this illustration the 35 network users expected to have a minimal requirement for image transfers are located on one network, while the remaining 15 network users that have a significant requirement to transfer images are placed on a second network.

The use of the bridge permits users of each network to access applications stored on the file server on the other network. However, this new network structure segments network stations by their expected usage, minimizing the adverse effect of heavy image transfer by 15 users on what was a total network of 50 users.

INTERNETWORKING

The segmentation of an Ethernet LAN into two networks linked together by a local bridge created an internetwork. Although the network structure was created to minimize the effect of transporting images on a larger network, this method of increasing the volume of image traffic through bridges that directly interconnect separate LANs can produce a bottleneck and inhibit the flow of other traffic, such as client/server queues, e-mail, and other network applications.

Image Servers on a Fiber Backbone

When constructing a local internetwork consisting of several linked LANs within a building, one method to minimize the effect of image traffic on other network applications is to place image applications on image servers located on a separate high-speed network.

Exhibit 2 illustrates the use of a fiber distributed data interface (FDDI) backbone ring consisting of two image servers whose access is obtainable from workstations located on several Ethernet and token ring networks through local bridges linking those networks to the FDDI ring. By using the FDDI ring for image applications, the 100M-bps operating rate of FDDI provides a delivery mechanism that enables workstation users on multiple lower operating rate LANs to simultaneously access image applications without experiencing network delays.

For example, one network user on each LAN illustrated in Exhibit 2 accesses the same image application on an image server connected to the FDDI backbone LAN. If each token ring network operates at 16M bps, and each Ethernet operates at 10M bps, the composite transfer rate from the FDDI network to each of the lower operating rate LANs bridged to that network is 52M bps. Because the FDDI network operates at 100M bps, it can

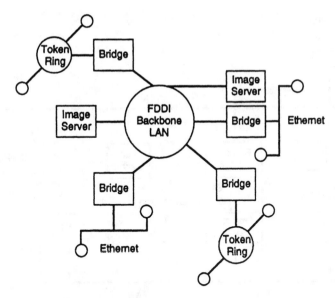

Exhibit 2.   Using a High-Speed FDDI Backbone

simultaneously present images to network users on each of the four LANs without any internetwork bottlenecks occurring.

Another advantage associated with using an FDDI backbone restricted to supporting image servers and bridges is economics. This configuration minimizes the requirement for using more expensive FDDI adapter cards to one card per image server and one card per bridge. In comparison, upgrading an existing network to FDDI would require replacing each workstation's existing network adapter card with a more expensive FDDI adapter card.

To illustrate the potential cost savings, assume each Ethernet and token ring network has 100 workstations, resulting in a total of 400 adapter cards, including two image servers that would require replacement if each existing LAN was replaced by a common FDDI network. Because FDDI adapter cards cost approximately $800, this replacement would result in the expenditure of $320,000. In comparison, the acquisition of four bridges and six FDDI adapter cards would cost less than $20,000.

TRANSFERRING IMAGES THROUGH WIDE AREA NETWORKS

In the next example, a group of PC users requires the use of a WAN to access images on a data base at a remote location. Images are placed on a CD-ROM jukebox connected to a server on LAN A, which in turn is connected to LAN B through a pair of remote bridges operating at 64K bps. This network configuration is illustrated in Exhibit 3.

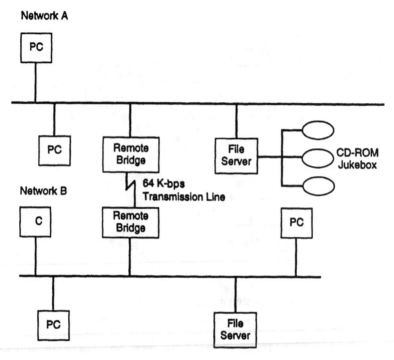

Exhibit 3. Image Transfers Using a WAN Link

If users on network A access several applications on network B and vice versa, in addition to accessing the images stored on the CD-ROM jukebox on network A, what happens when a user on network B attempts to access text data on network A during an image transfer? If another network B user requested an image transfer, the user requesting a text transfer is now contending for network resources with the user performing the image transfer. This means that alternate frames of data flow over the 64K-bps transmission facility — first a frame containing a portion of an image, then a frame containing a portion of the text transfer. This alternate frame transmission continues until one transfer is completed, prior to all network resources becoming devoted to the remaining transfer.

Not only is the 64K-bps transmission rate a significant bottleneck to the transfer of images, but WAN users must contend for access to that resource. A 640K-byte image would require 80 seconds to transfer between remotely located LANs on a digital circuit operating at 64K bps and devoted to a single remote user. If that remote user had to share the use of the WAN link with another user performing another image transfer, each transfer would require 160 seconds. Thus, transferring images through a WAN connection can result in a relatively long waiting time.

Although the WAN connection could be upgraded to a T1 or a fractional T1 circuit, the monthly incremental cost of a 500-mile 64K-bps digital circuit is approximately $300. In comparison, the monthly cost of a 500-mile 1.544M-bps digital circuit would exceed $1,500.

Localizing Images

One alternative to problems associated with the transfer of images through a WAN can be obtained by localizing images to each LAN to remove or substantially reduce the necessity to transfer images through a WAN. To do so with respect to the network configuration illustrated in Exhibit 3 would require the installation of either a single CD-ROM drive or a CD-ROM jukebox onto network B's file server.

This method would enable network users on each LAN to obtain the majority of the images they require through a LAN transmission facility that normally operates at 10 to 100 times the operating rate of most WAN transmission facilities. The placement of additional image storage facilities on each LAN can substantially reduce potential WAN bottlenecks by reducing the need to transfer images via the WAN.

Bandwidth-on-Demand Inverse Multiplexers

A second method of reducing WAN bottlenecks caused by the transfer of images is obtained by the use of bandwidth-on-demand inverse multiplexers. Several vendors market bandwidth-on-demand inverse multiplexers that can monitor the utilization of a leased line and initiate a switched network call when a predefined lease line utilization threshold is reached.

Exhibit 4 illustrates the use of a bandwidth-on-demand inverse multiplexer at the network B location shown in Exhibit 3. Under normal operating conditions, a 64K-bps leased line connects network A to network B. When the transfer of images begins to saturate the use of the leased line, one inverse multiplexer will automatically initiate a call over the switched network to the other multiplexer. That call can be a switched digital call at 56/64K bps or a call over the public switched telephone network, in which the data transfer operating rate depends on the type of modems used with each inverse multiplexer.

Because a switched digital or analog call costs between 10 and 25 cents per minute, the use of inverse multiplexers can represent an economical alternative to the use of additional or higher-speed leased lines when image transfers only occur periodically during the work day.

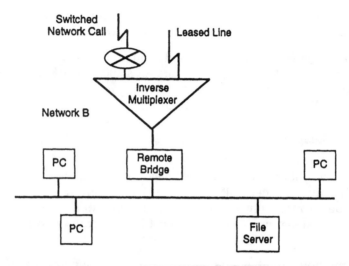

Exhibit 4.   Using a Bandwidth-on-Demand Inverse Multiplexer

SUMMARY

Because multimedia includes either digitized images, digitized speech, or both, all of these methods and techniques for handling images are applicable for multimedia:

- The segmentation of a local area network.
- The use of a high-speed backbone network for providing access to image servers.
- The addition of multimedia storage facilities on individual LANs to reduce WAN traffic are all applicable to the transfer of multimedia information.

Placing images and multimedia on the corporate network can be considered equivalent to the addition of a very large number of network users. When planning to add access to image and multimedia data bases, network managers should use the same planning process required to support conventional access to file servers and mainframe data bases.

When data transfer requirements begin to adversely affect network performance, managers should consider transferring multimedia data to storage repositories and accessing it through the methods suggested in this chapter. The goal at all times is to avoid burdening network users while remaining able to support an organization's image and multimedia data base access requirements in an efficient and cost-effective manner.

Chapter 14
Videoconferencing over IP Networks

Christine Perey and Matthew Feldman

According to Larry Irving, assistant secretary for communications and information, in a May 8, 1996 letter to Reed Hundt, chairman of the Federal Communications Commission, "The Internet now connects more than 10 million computers, tens of millions of users, and is growing at a rate of 10% to 15% a month. This growth has created opportunities for entrepreneurs to develop new services and applications such as videoconferencing, multicasting, electronic payments, networked virtual reality, and intelligent agents. Perhaps more important, it creates a growing number of opportunities for users to identify new communication and information needs and to meet those needs."

Most engineers designing networks today recall that the world's largest system of interconnected networks had ambitious roots: to define how transmission would take place over networks connecting dissimilar computers. Chances are that few of those who developed internetworking protocols in the Department of Defense 25 years ago foresaw the variety and vast number of applications their protocols would be called on to support. Today, the protocols that together are the basis of the Internet continue to evolve to accommodate the demands of new media types.

This chapter reviews the underlying principles of Internet protocols in the context of one of the most demanding application sets to date: real-time videoconferencing and visual collaboration. It discusses the advantages and disadvantages of choosing Internet protocol (IP) networks for real-time multimedia communications and how real-time videoconferencing is achieved on IP networks — today and in the near future.

BASIC INTERNET PROTOCOL CONVENTIONS

Protocols that together manage packets on the Internet build on several widely accepted conventions/foundations. The principal components of the network are data connecting equipment (DCE), such as routers, and data terminating equipment (DTE), such as desktop computers (also called "hosts").

Without any special adjustments for the unique requirements of different media types, the network layers work in concert to transmit packets of user information. In its simplest implementation, the flow of the data from and to end points over an IP network is monitored or verified by a simple layer 3 communications protocol (e.g., Transmission Control Protocol, or TCP).

The advantage is that there is very little communications overhead associated with components in IP networks "talking" to one another. TCP running over IP in effect takes care of this. Each packet allocates the maximum number of bits to the user's information.

Together, protocols ratified by the Institute of Electrical and Electronics Engineers (IEEE) and the Internet Engineering Task Force (IETF) ensure that packets of data are reliably transmitted under any condition, as quickly as possible (e.g., bandwidth or network load on the segments of the networks tying together two or more points).

Several protocols have been developed to manage the unique requirements of real-time streaming data. To understand the importance of these developments, this chapter begins with a high-level discussion of videoconferencing and visual collaboration using networked multimedia desktop computers.

PRINCIPLES OF VIDEOCONFERENCING AND MULTIMEDIA COMMUNICATIONS

When a video camera and microphone pick up real-life events, the imagery and sound can be turned into digital formats for communications between properly enabled end points over local or wide area networks. For the user to perceive the moving images and intelligible sounds, the digital information moves from transmitter to receiver (transmitters are simultaneously receiving in the case of two-way videoconferencing) in a highly consistent fashion. Compressed in real time, the data streams over a network in such a way that frames of video can be reconstructed and synchronized with audio with the least end-to-end delay.

Quantitative Quality of Service Parameters

End-to-end quality of service (QOS) in videoconferencing and visual collaboration is defined as the level of satisfaction a user has with a given session. It is a function of many independent and interdependent factors (e.g., window size, processor speed, network bandwidth), which together influence frame rate, bit depth, image clarity and resolution, audio clarity, lip synchronization, and latency.

In contrast to conventional data applications in which data transmission is bursty, digital video and audio applications require continuous data transmission. In IP environments, precise bit rates during the transmission vary. In the following list, the factors influencing bit rates (bandwidth) during videoconferencing and collaborative computing are presented as a function of the media (i.e., video, audio, and data):

Video factors include:

- Bit depth (number of colors).
- Resolution (size of the image being captured, compressed, transmitted, and decompressed). Resolution is contrasted with window size, which is the size of the image that is displayed for viewing. If the window size is different from resolution, then interpolation is used to generate a new image that fits the window.
- Q factor (sharpness of edges in any given frame).
- Smoothing (this is a result of — and dependent on — motion estimation algorithms and content changes from one frame to the next).
- Frame rate (frames per second). For example, NTSC video, the U.S. standard, is 30 fps; PAL, the European standard, is 25 fps.

Audio factors include:

- Sampling rate (the number of audio samples captured, compressed, and transmitted, expressed in KHz cycles per second). For example, telephony is 6.3 KHz, FM radio is 36 KHz, music CDs 44.1 KHz (See Exhibit 1).
- Bit rate (the number of bits the system has in order to accurately represent different tones; for example, 8-bit or 16-bit).
- Mono and stereo sound.

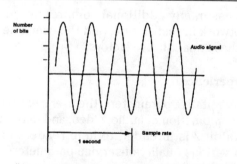

Note:
Frequency response is how high and low the audio signal can go. Clipping occurs if the actual audio signal becomes higher or lower than the signal the analog-to-digital or other chips can handle. Sample rate refers to how many audio samples are taken in a 1-second interval. Numbers of bits (usually 8 or 16) represents the accuracy of each audio sample.

Exhibit 1. Audio Sampling

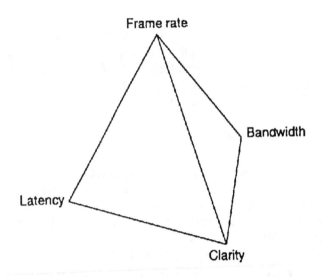

Frame rate

Bandwidth

Latency

Clarity

Note:
The four-sided pyramid represents quality of service (QOS) for videoconferencing. By choosing a single plane (triangle) of the pyramid, one corner remains constant. The remaining three corners are closely dependent; if any one corner changes, the others are affected. Usually systems can be optimized for any two of the three.

Exhibit 2. Interdependence of Quality of Service Parameters in Time-Dependent Streaming Media

Data factors include:

- Quantity of data.
- Frequency of transmissions.
- Latency of transmission (how long it takes to send at a given bit rate).

The central processor, any additional compression/decompression (codec) circuits, network infrastructure, and the user's network connection directly affect these quantitative factors.

Qualitative QOS Experience

Depending on the quantitative parameters, the user's experience with multimedia (which is a combination of audio, video, and data) may be qualitatively different. Exhibit 2 is intended to help readers understand the interdependence of various quality-of-service parameters in time-dependent streaming media.

The user's experience with bidirectional live video and visual collaboration over any network can be expressed quantitatively and qualitatively; in general, though, the objective is to reproduce a live meeting or conversa-

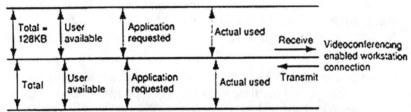

ISBN basic rate Interface (BRI) bandwidth allocation using H.320-compliant application – measured in each direction, therefore two times the bandwidth for each connection dedicated to a single user

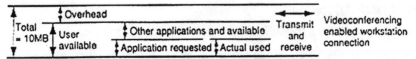

Ethernet-based bandwidth allocation using TCP/IP-compliant application – measured in both directions; connection shared between multiple users and applications

Exhibit 3. Examples of Bandwidth Allocation

---

tion. For the interaction to be as close to natural as possible, it is especially important that both (or all) users in a videoconference experience a uniformly low latency (minimum delay). Any variation in the frame rate between points is perceived as jitter. Poor synchronization between lips and audio is also distracting.

Thus, the most important factors in the user's qualitative experience of a videoconferencing system are:

- Synchronization of audio, video, and data.
- End-to-end latency.
- Window size.
- Jitter.
- Richness and clarity of audio.
- Image clarity (bit depth, sharpness, smoothing, and resolution).

All these quality-of-service concepts are critical to the reader's overall understanding of the pros and cons of selecting IP networks for videoconferencing.

PROS AND CONS OF VIDEOCONFERENCING OVER IP NETWORKS

Founders of the Internet were academics driven by four guiding principles:

- Reliability (guaranteed delivery of packets), not efficiency.
- End systems' interoperability, and information or packet loss recovery.

- Variable quality of service, not guaranteed bandwidth, so that any network bandwidth can be accommodated by a single protocol.
- No support for charging mechanisms, since commercial traffic was not envisioned.

Internet protocols have withstood the test of multiple applications at the user interface, new operating systems in end points, and ever-changing transport media in the physical layers (e.g., SONET, ATM). For videoconferencing and visual collaboration, there are fundamental principles that determine bandwidth use in any session.

Bandwidth Allocation

Exhibit 3 illustrates the following types of bandwidth allocation:

- *Total bandwidth.* This is the maximum bandwidth available for user data and network management overhead.
- *User-available bandwidth.* This is the total bandwidth minus the network management overhead.
- *Application-specific bandwidth.* This is the bandwidth requested by the application.
- *Actual used bandwidth.* This is the minimum bandwidth of either what the application requested or what is available over the end-to-end network during a particular session (whichever is lower).
- *Allocated bandwidth.* This is the portion of the total user-available bandwidth that can be reserved; it only applies when a reservation mechanism is in place, requested, and granted.

IP Network Advantages

Compared with other wide area network communications protocols, IP has four principal advantages for videoconferencing:

- Low management architecture overhead and high carrying capacity make IP cost effective.
- No guaranteed quality of service and low overhead make IP bandwidth scalable (64K bps to 100M bps and beyond).
- IP architecture provides for many simultaneous virtual circuits, thereby enabling multiple services and multiple connections (through well-recognized sockets) at the same time.
- Packet structure and network design make it possible for both broadcasting and multicasting to occur in the same network, without requiring packet redundancy.

Using extensions of IP to modify the payload format and reduce overhead associated with packet acknowledgment between end points, the communications between end points dedicated to user information is high. In some cases as much as 95% of the bandwidth can be assigned to user traffic. The actual bandwidth a data stream uses is a function of the bit rate the end points have agreed to send upon call establishment.

When two end points have only very low bit rate capacity, owing to the local bus architecture or modem technologies over a POTS (plain old telephone service) line, the IP-based videoconference session operates within this constraint. On the other hand, when the same software (e.g., user application) is used over a high-bandwidth connection, a videoconference can take advantage of the increased capacity without any change in the application or communications protocol stack.

Networks without support for Internet Protocol Independent Multicasting (PIM) must recreate a data stream for each of the desktops to which the user wishes to communicate simultaneously. This puts extra pressure on the source (i.e., the host has to create, manage, and transmit the same packets more than once) and on the shared resources connecting all users, whether they are multimedia communications enabled or using traditional transactional functions between clients and servers. Multicasting on IP enables multiple participants (so-called multipoints) to experience the same real-time conference at the same time. The importance of this feature cannot be underestimated.

IP Network Disadvantages

Many practitioners believe that connectionless communications and best-effort delivery of packets is inappropriate for isochronous network traffic (e.g., where data needs to be sent sequentially and arrive at its destination at specific intervals), such as that generated by digital video and audio. The principal disadvantages of IP network for videoconferencing are basically:

- Lack of guaranteed bandwidth, unless all the network components are controlled by a central manager that has chosen to implement network-wide bandwidth reservation schemes.
- Lack of international standards that would support interoperability of products from different vendors for intra- and intercompany communications.

The most common wide area network solution for videoconferencing has been integrated services digital network (ISDN). With a dedicated connection (i.e., a communications circuit) between two end points, bandwidth is guaranteed and, consequently, the quality of service remains consistent throughout a session.

The next most common wide area network for point-to-point desktop videoconferencing has been POTS, which despite its low bandwidth, ensures, like ISDN, a dedicated circuit for a conference between two end points.

Users find that they prefer running business applications over networks in which the bandwidth allocated, requested, and used are all the same (i.e., the circuit-switched environment). And there are many competitive, standards-compliant offerings for desktop videoconferencing over basic rate ISDN.

The natural consequence of a large — and especially a standards-compliant — installed base is that there are more people with which a system can interoperate without modification of any software or hardware. Until more vendors deliver standards-compliant, interoperable solutions for videoconferencing, the installed base will be confined to pockets of proprietary products that interoperate among themselves, but do not permit end-point application independence.

Though specifications for session setup, management, and compression were under development (e.g., IETF Audio/Visual Transport Working Group and the International Telecommunications Union's [ITU] H.323), they were not expected in commercial products until early or mid-1997. Standards and interoperability are essential for vendor independence, but they may be sacrificed for exceptional functionality and quality until such time that vendor independence is possible.

Compared to other protocols on the local area network for managing desktop videoconferencing (e.g., IsoEthernet or the specialized multimedia operating system, such as MOS, by First Virtual Corp., for 25M-bps ATM to the desktop), IP communications over 10BaseT Ethernets are prone to suffering from network contention and congestion. The relatively low bandwidth available for each user on a 10BaseT network has, to date, been unsuitable for business-quality videoconferencing using inexpensive software codecs.

GETTING STARTED WITH IP-BASED VIDEOCONFERENCING

Disadvantages and drawbacks aside, it is clear that many organizations will choose IP-based videoconferencing for its:

- Low cost of entry (e.g., integration into existing infrastructure).
- Low cost of ownership (e.g., low maintenance and no telecommunications charges).
- Ease of use (e.g., accessibility of the global IP network compared to ISDN provisioning).

For many years, real-time packetized audio and video over IP networks were tested and used on an isolated portion of the Internet: the multicast backbone (Mbone). The Mbone is operating, expanding, and improving.

Some of the protocols used on the Mbone (developed by the Audio/Visual Working Group of IETF) are being ratified by the IETF and have migrated from this relatively exclusive academic and industrial environment into commercial routers for Internet and intranet deployment. Over the next 12 to 18 months, IETF protocols for managing video and audio packets will be widely incorporated in enterprises and on the Internet in general.

This section examines the components users need to add to their desktops for videoconferencing on IP. Local (LAN), metropolitan (MAN), virtual (VAN), wide area (WAN), and global network managers need to modify and prepare their networks to support the types of traffic generated by video-enabled desktops. The scope of these networking component changes and alternatives is discussed in more detail later in the chapter.

Desktop-Enabling Technologies

To experience desktop videoconferencing on the Internet (or intranet) firsthand, the user needs only a camera for video input, a microphone for audio input, speakers (presuming the user wants to hear what others say), software to give the user access to connection initiation and answering, session management, compression algorithms, a video display board, an IP network interface, and a premium CPU.

CU-SeeMe and Other Software Supporting Multicasting. The most unique and proprietary of these desktop components is the user application and interface software. The first, and consequently the most widely deployed, application designed for videoconferencing on the Internet-CU-SeeMe, originated at Cornell University. Distributed as freeware/shareware for the first several years, the application satisfied the needs of many Macintosh users in academic and nonprofit institutions for distance learning and research applications.

In 1995 Cornell University issued an exclusive license for commercial distribution of CU-SeeMe to White Pine Software. Since then, White Pine Software has ported the application to other platforms and greatly enhanced the functionality (e.g., adding color video, password security, and whiteboard capabilities).

CU-SeeMe, like three or more competing user applications currently offered on the Internet — for example, VDOnet's VDOphone, CineCom's CineVideo/Direct, Apple Computer's QuickTime Conferencing, and Intelligence at Large's Being There — provides a directory management system, call initiation, answering and management software, and some utilities for controlling video and audio quality during a session.

The Desktop's Connected to the Mbone. Precept Software has developed multicast audio/video server and viewer products for Windows 3.1.1, Windows 95, and Windows NT to help enable the PC/Windows world to join the Mbone community. The viewer, called FlashWare Client, can receive Mbone sessions transmitted with Livermore Berkeley Laboratory's vat 4.0 in real-time transport protocol (RTP) mode (selected via the -r option) using PCM, DVI, or GSM audio-encoding algorithms and vic 2.7 using its default H.261 video codec.

On the Precept Web site is a program guide that lists Mbone sessions using these protocols; users can launch the client automatically from there. The client is built as a media control interface (MCI) device driver so it can be invoked through Microsoft's Media Player, a Netscape plug-in, or other applications using the MCI A-PI. Playback of audio and video is synchronized using the time-stamping mechanisms in RTP and real-time transport control protocol (RTCP).

The IETF Audio/Visual Transport Working Group's RTP and RTCP protocols have been developed to facilitate the smooth transmission, arrival, and display of streaming data types. When end-point applications support RTP, packets leave the sender's desktop with a time stamp and content identification label. Using this information, and through congestion-monitoring facilities at either end, the proper sequences of frames can be more reliably recreated at the receiving station, using a specified delay buffer (generally less than 100 milliseconds). Netscape's Cooltalk is another example of an architecture for streaming video and audio with RTP-ready end points.

Compressing Audio and Video Streams. In all but the most exceptional conditions (e.g., broadcast-quality production requirements), digital video and audio need to be compressed for superior management. Subsequently, the information must be decompressed (decoded) upon arrival so that it can be displayed on its destination screen.

A comprehensive discussion of compression technology and the ensuing debates over the virtues of different algorithms are not within the scope of this chapter; however, it must be noted that digital video compression has a marked impact on the quality of the experience users can expect when videoconferencing over an IP network.

All freeware applications for IP-based videoconferencing bundle a software codec for encoding and decoding the audio and video streams at the appropriate bandwidth for the station. Software codecs deliver lower quality audio and video than hardware in which there are optimized digital signal processors (DSPs) for these functions. Currently, there are no standard compression algorithms for use on the IP-based networks, so users receive the codec specified by the desktop application.

In the case of freeware developed by Livermore Berkeley Laboratory, as well as Apple's QuickTime Conferencing, the architecture can accommodate any number of compression algorithms, including H.261, which is the basis of all H.320 systems. The products will comply with a new specification — H.323 — for videoconferencing over IP networks and use H.261 as a codec; however, a new and more efficient version (H.263) is less bandwidth consumptive and will quickly replace H.261 on IP networks.

Hardware Implementations for Business-Quality Videoconferencing. In general, videoconferencing on IP networks is like any other commodity: the customer gets what he or she pays for. The software packages mentioned so far are considered suitable for academic, nonprofit, and perhaps "personal" applications. For now, customers who seek "business-quality" video and audio will need to evaluate and select desktop videoconferencing systems that have been implemented in hardware.

Video and audio compression hardware for IP-based conferencing is available for Industry Standard Architecture (ISA) as well as Peripheral Component Interconnect (PCI), Sbus interfaces, and all major operating systems. Examples include those offered in Intellect Visual Communications Corp.'s TeamVision family of products (using very large scale integration [VLSI] chips and Mosaic's own design) and Netscape's Communique line of products (using an Osprey Technology board and Lucent Technologies' AVP chips for DSP-assisted compression and decompression of audio and video).

Network Interface Hardware. All videoconferencing systems require a network interface adapter for LAN or WAN access. Most institutions with intranets or T1 access to the Internet provide an Ethernet adapter at each desktop. The bandwidth and suitability for video depend on whether this interface adapter is 10BaseT, IsoEthernet, or 100BaseT and an assortment of network design issues. IP-based videoconferencing can also run locally over Token Ring networks with routers providing connectivity to and from the wide area networks.

For those who do not have a dedicated connection to an IP network, dial-up access to the Internet is accomplished with a point-to-point protocol (PPP) or serial line IP (SLIP) connection via a modem or an ISDN terminal adapter through an Internet services provider (ISP). In general, dial-up IP network interfaces accommodate consumer applications adequately, but are not suitable for business-quality video and audio supported with specialized hardware.

VIDEO-READY NETWORKS

In the previous connectivity scenarios, an Internet communications protocol stack in the host operating system negotiates and monitors connections. This section, however, focuses on the steps needed to address bandwidth, as well as the IP facilities and the internetworking software commonly used and currently being proposed for desktop videoconferencing in IP environments.

Network Upgrade and Management Issues

Preparing a network for any new application, including multimedia, requires careful analysis of existing components and user requirements. As far as network upgrades for videoconferencing are concerned, an intranet is quite different from the public Internet.

In the private network (e.g., intranets over LANs, MANs, VANs, and WANs), technologies can be more consistently deployed, more effectively maintained by a central IT group, and are often more economical to purchase when large site licenses are negotiated. This said, jurisdictional (i.e., work group) management of LANs is increasingly popular.

In contrast to the situation with LANs and private WANS, new protocols and architectures take much longer to deploy in the public/commercial IP environment. There is an inherent lack of control in this progress, especially if new management challenges are associated with upgrades. Video-enabling upgrades clearly fall in this category.

One way for LAN administrators and managers to approach the design of a video-ready network is by working from the end points toward the common infrastructure (e.g., the Internet).

End-Point Performance. Initially, users and planners should evaluate the end-point CPU performance. If the CPU is involved in any general data application management and compression or decompression tasks (which is almost always the case in the desktop videoconferencing applications distributed as freeware, and less the case when add-on compression hardware is necessary), then low performance at the desktop will translate to poor quality of service and less efficient bandwidth usage patterns. When end points are enhanced and capable of compressing video frames, bandwidth will be more efficiently utilized between desktops.

Network bandwidth requirements for desktop videoconferencing vary with applications as well. Some applications — especially precision medical or surgical applications or high-quality entertainment and advertisement production — require many megabits per second to transmit lossless (i.e., compressed without any loss of information) or nearly lossless video between points.

In most business scenarios, however, the combination of efficient compression algorithms, network management software, and user tolerance of less than TV quality video keeps the bandwidth requirement (per bidirectional session) between 28.8K and 768K bps.

Because, in general, users' lowest level of tolerance is the highest performance they have had the privilege of using, it is safe to assume that IP networks in place today need modification to deliver acceptable business-quality video in real time. On a shared network, such as an Ethernet, Token Ring, or fiber distributed data interface (FDDI) network, or the commercial Internet today, all stations have equal opportunity to send and receive data. This is known as "time division multiplexing."

Several options exist for changing network designs to accommodate the demands of streaming data types. One of these is to supplant or augment best-effort protocols in order to prioritize video and audio streams in such a way that end points receive consistently low latency. This approach is discussed in greater depth a little later in this chapter.

If, prior to changing the data management, an enterprise decides to deploy high-speed LAN technologies (e.g., 100BaseT, 100VG-AnyLAN, ATM), there also needs to be upgrades to WAN infrastructures. Options and issues in this arena are the focus of many books and current articles and outside the scope of the present chapter.

Evolving Bandwidth Management Protocols. From an integration perspective, however, one of the most important advantages of planning the network using IP is that IP is well adapted to LAN as WAN environments.

DVMRP. At the network architecture level, prioritization schemes in the IP specifications issued by IETF working groups hold the greatest promise for improved management and distribution of video over IP networks. In the late 1980s, the IETF ratified the distance vector multicast routing protocol (DVMRP) to transport live video feeds in IP multicast mode over the Mbone. DVMRP works by essentially "flooding" all available routes with a broadcast message, something which could be tolerated more easily before the Internet grew in popularity.

IPv5 or Streaming II Protocol. About the same time DVMRP was introduced, the Streaming II (ST-II) protocol was proposed by Bolt Beranek and Newman (BBN). A connection-oriented routing protocol, ST11, is used in end-point and router software and offers a call setup facility that lets the originator control bandwidth in a video and audio session by allocating bandwidth through the router upon request. Virtual links are established for the duration of the session and resources are allocated along the virtual links.

ST-II, also known as IPv5 and sometimes called ST-II+, is evolving to address connection setup delays and options for allowing both receivers and senders to open sockets without a conference administrator's approval. Today's version of ST-II+ is not backward-compatible with ST-II.

Protocol Independent Multicasting (PIM). To address the inherently "unscalable nature of DVMRP," the PIM system was proposed. This protocol designates so-called rendezvous points for registration of both senders and receivers of multimedia multicasts.

Because the protocol (implemented in routers such as those shipping from Cisco Systems) is not restrictive, it also works with any unicast routing protocol (as in the case in a private videoconference over an IP WAN). Dense mode PIM, which applies where the volume of multicast traffic is high and senders and receivers are in close geographic proximity to one another, uses reverse path forwarding and operates much like DVMRP.

RSVP. The bandwidth management protocol with the most enthusiastic following to date is known as the reservation protocol (RSVP). Implemented in end-point and router software on the Mbone and currently under review for IETF ratification, RSVP guarantees bandwidth allocation in connectionless networks according to a receiver-driven model.

RSVP is fixed-bit-rate allocation, with routines to handle available bit rate in the future. It is also technology independent and can run on ISDN and private network connections such as Ethernet-based intranets.

Prototype support for RSVP has been demonstrated by several different router vendors and became available in many products in 1997. With these new products, RSVP will be quickly deployed throughout intranets, although it is unlikely that the same protocol will be deployed throughout the Internet until at least a year later.

Billing and Related Issues. In addition to the impediments cited so far — namely, complex management challenges associated with video — current Internet pricing models do not reflect guaranteed bandwidth allocation. As a result, most commercial Internet service providers will be reluctant to implement RSVP in their routers because, in using this protocol, a few users could potentially monopolize router resources without appropriately compensating the service provider. New research at BBN and in the IETF's Internet Services Working Group promises to address the problem with specific billing protocols built into end points and routers.

Researchers at the University of Illinois-Champaign are exploring a solution to circumvent the successive layers of management code over IP. The video datagram protocol (VDP) eliminates TCP and works at the IP level to move video, audio, and data simultaneously. The protocol itself addresses the delivery timing issues by dynamically using a best-effort adaptive flow control methodology.

HOW DESKTOP-TO-DESKTOP VIDEO AND AUDIO CONNECTIONS OPERATE IN IP NETWORKS

Given the large number of freeware and shareware solutions for videoconferencing on IP networks and proposed standards, and the rapidity of new developments on the IP landscape, it is difficult to make generalizations about the manner in which desktop-to-desktop connections are negotiated, maintained, and torn down in all user applications. This section explores some of the approaches different products use to enable videoconferencing and collaboration over IP networks.

Negotiating/Establishing Desktop Connections

Some applications have relied primarily on Internet (and later intranet) servers for negotiating desktop connections over LANs and WANS. White Pine Software's Reflector software, for example, supports unicast, broadcast, and multicast sessions.

Unicasting and multicasting are achieved by specifying a reflector as the destination and sharing (publishing) the appropriate IP address of the reflector in question with other conference participants. To control unwanted participants, the reflector lets network managers issue passwords for different conferences. In addition, a roster of conference participants (one for a unicast, more for multicasts) is published dynamically to all participating desktops.

Several freeware and shareware programs are available to initiate and administer on-line conferences over IP networks. Confman is one such tool for conference initiation and monitoring that employs certain Mbone tools: vat (for audio data), vic and nv (for video transmission), and wb (for whiteboarding) on the Internet.

Confman does not handle multimedia data, but helps the user to plan, set up, and control a conference by letting the network manager choose meeting participants (by IP address), the start time, and the tools (and codecs) the session members need to run on their end points. Conferences can be held in two different modes:

- *Closed mode.* Using this mode with more than two participants requires a server process to route the multimedia data. This process might be regarded as a conference room. All connections are unicast connections; no multicast features are required.
- *Multicast mode.* Multimedia data is sent via multicast. To restrict access, data has to be encrypted. A conference management tool distributes the encryption key to the selected participants in advance.

Microsoft's and Intel's Internet telephony products (and subsequent IP-based videoconferencing offerings) use the standard User Locator Service

(ULS) to negotiate/establish calls between desktop videoconferencing users on IP networks. In June 1996, ULS was submitted to the IETF for consideration to become a standard and incorporated with LDAP (lightweight directory addressing protocol).

Ideally, all intranet and Internet service providers will have standards-compliant directories. For users not on a corporate network, the ISP's directory will automatically associate the e-mail address with a person. Every time users connect to the Internet, the network service can then pick up the IP address and initiate a local call to the end point nearest the recipient.

In a corporate environment, where there is a Novell network with ULS and computer telephony integration, simply having a desktop computer turned on and connected to the network should suffice to identify the end point for any incoming video and audio (or audio-only) sessions.

Maintaining/Modulating a Videoconference Session

As long as the sockets between end points, or between the end point and server, are open, the IP session is maintained. Another way of expressing this is that within a conference, the virtual circuits are always present.

Some applications use a single circuit for all audio, video, and data; other applications use a separate circuit for each media type. Having a separate socket for each permits higher error recovery and, therefore, fewer chances for problems to occur during a live conference.

Multicasting

The focus of this chapter is bidirectional real-time video and audio between two or a few desktop systems, otherwise known as desktop videoconferencing or, in Internet terms, strictly a unicast transaction.

For most who participate in unicast or simple point-to-point sessions, there comes a time when applications, especially meetings, require more than two participants. To execute on a network limited to unicast sessions, applications must generate a unique copy of each packet and send those packets to each participant's desktop (by specifying the end points' IP address). This is inherently inefficient if there is an alternative.

With Internet multicast protocols, an application generates a single copy of each packet and sends it to a group address. End points (e.g., clients on the client/server network) can selectively choose to listen to the multicast address. Multicasting minimizes network traffic and gives all users on a network greater flexibility.

For an application to take advantage of multicasting, the IP stack in the network software on the host must support multicast and broadcast addressing. Multicast is implemented at both the data link layer (layer 2) and the network layer (layer 3). For multicast confined to a single LAN, the data link layer implementation is sufficient.

When a multicast application extends into different network media, such as frame relay, FDDI, or Ethernet, network layer implementations are recommended. Therefore, multipoint applications with both LAN and WAN participants must implement in both layers.

For all vendors of end-point applications and network components to interoperate in multicast IP networks, several parameters must be defined. The IETF has standards specifying the addressing (i.e., network-layer address mapping onto data link layer multicast addresses), dynamic registration (i.e., a mechanism for clients to inform the network that they wish to be a member of a specific multicast group), and multicast routing (e.g., DVMRP and PIM).

Monitoring and Managing a Videoconference Session

In general, reflectors, as the servers are sometimes called, provide network bandwidth control, video "pruning," audio prioritization, and a range of conference control software. Using network management utilities, the reflector/server can adjust transmission rates of specific individual users on-the-fly, if packet loss is running too high because of heavy network traffic.

If contention is too heavy for a reliable conference, the transmission remains at the lowest setting and only moves up when the network is less congested. This is an important tool for network managers and ISPs who have to be concerned with balancing the needs of their other nonvideoconferencing network users during peak load.

Network monitoring utilities allow network managers to control the maximum bandwidth allocated per videoconference and the maximum number of simultaneous videoconferences. In this way, sufficient bandwidth is reserved for other users who have conventional network applications.

One of the freeware network monitoring tools for videoconferencing is Rtpmon. Rtpmon is a tool for viewing RTCP feedback packets from a session using the real-time transport protocol. It presents loss rate and jitter information from RTCP receiver report (RR) packets in a tabular format. The table can be sorted by various parameters and the recent history of reports from a particular receiver can be viewed in a stripchart.

SUMMARY

There are advantages and disadvantages in any network selection for any set of applications. The popularity of the IP for enabling a vast number of applications for users, as well as the advantages inherent in this network protocol, are fostering the development of new tools and technologies for real-time data types. Simultaneously, videoconferencing is coming to the desktop in force, largely because computers in business leverage LANs extensively and their users are interested in adding videoconferencing applications.

As a result, network managers must become more familiar with the underlying real-time technologies for their IP networks. This chapter has introduced the basic terminology and concepts of videoconferencing, as well as the components that enable the desktop for real-time video and audio. The network must be prepared for maximum quality of service in videoconferencing without compromising other application users, as is a requirement in any high-bandwidth application.

In the future, enterprise network managers can anticipate the very rapid deployment of new technologies as a result of:

- Ratification of protocols by the IETF and ITU, and the subsequent implementation of standard protocols.
- Reduction in cost of all video network system components, including those for end points, LANs, gateway (internetworking), and WANs.

Those who manage enterprise resources, from the CFO to the IS director, will experience a profound shift in the way "best-of-class" companies do business in the near future. The reduced cycle times and increased creativity and productivity made possible with real-time conferencing locally, nationally, and globally will justify — to different degrees — the investments necessary to deploy technologies such as are described throughout this chapter.

Chapter 15
Video Compression Techniques and Bandwidth Utilization

Jeffrey Weiss

The desire of network users to have access to video of broadcast quality for their multimedia applications is tempered by the practical reality that internetworking bandwidth and local data storage are of limited through-put and size. The amount of data that has to be transmitted or stored in order to create even a minute of uncompressed video is staggering.

A single 640 × 480 pel (a pel is a minimum-size picture element) video image with 8-bit color, without compression, requires 300K byte of storage. One minute of video at 30 frames per second requires 550M byte of storage. If color resolution is increased from 8 bits per pel to 8 bits per color plane (i.e., RGB color), storage requirements increase to 1.7G byte per minute.

DIGITAL VIDEO AND IMAGE COMPRESSION TECHNIQUES

The economical distribution and storage of both digital photographs and digital video mandates the use of specialized compression techniques. To achieve practical transmission rates and storage requirements, compres-sion ratios in excess of 50:1 are required, and these ratios are not attainable using known lossless compression techniques.

Although existing lossless image compression algorithms allow 100% accurate reconstruction of the original image, they offer relatively low compression performance, typically in the order of 3:1. Lossy compression algorithms offer much higher compression ratios, but at the expense of some reconstruction accuracy. Therefore, lossless video compression algorithms are typically reserved for medical imaging applications and for transmission of images from satellites and planetary probes.

0-8493-9949-1/99/$0.00+$.50
© 1999 by CRC Press LLC

Through extensive research, the users of video compression algorithms have settled on Joint Photographic Experts Group (JPEG) and Moving Picture Experts Group (MPEG) compression standards for multimedia video applications. Other proprietary compression systems exist, as a means to reduce the CPU requirements of video decompression or to achieve higher compression ratios. Real-time MPEG and JPEG require specialized hardware; however, because of the projected volumes of use of these systems, the hardware is expected to become inexpensive.

This chapter explains the operation of JPEG, MPEG, and DigiCipher systems and provides insight into how and why the algorithms were selected.

JPEG, MPEG, and DigiCipher

JPEG was initially developed to compress still images and is often used in video teleconferencing systems where packet losses due to network congestion are high.

MPEG I and MPEG II were developed as extensions to JPEG and form the basis for most next-generation video services and storage. DigiCipher is a proprietary subset of MPEG II and will be used in most cable television set-top decoders.

Even in supposedly lossless compression systems, image reconstruction is not perfect. Each pel is a digital data point arrived at by sampling the signal for an analog picture, and the quality of a reconstructed image is a function of the resolution and rate at which sampling occurs. Resolution is measured in a number of dimensions — for example, the number of pels in both the horizontal and vertical directions, and the number of bits used to represent each color.

Another factor is how much motion occurred during the sampling interval. When referring to sampled data systems, the term *lossless* means that after the sampling process there are no additional losses due to the coding, storage, and retrieval processes.

TECHNICAL ISSUES IN MAKING IMAGES ACCEPTABLE TO THE HUMAN EYE

Substantial research has been conducted on the limitations of human vision. The resulting rules may be followed to reduce the information content in images without causing, for the viewer, an unacceptable degrading of the image's quality. The following paragraphs discuss some important properties of human vision that are taken advantage of by compression systems.

Visual Sensitivity

Visual sensitivity is known to be inversely proportional to average light intensity. This means that the human eye is very sensitive to changes in low-intensity areas of a picture and not very sensitive to comparable changes in high-intensity areas.

Visual sensitivity to changes in intensity and color is higher along both the horizontal axis and vertical axis than along the diagonals. Sensitivity to high-frequency (rapid) changes in either intensity or color is much lower than to low-frequency (less rapid) changes. Sensitivity to changes in overall (i.e., monochrome) light intensity is higher than to comparable changes in color.

Luminance and Chrominance

For image compression purposes, substantially less information about color needs to be retained than for monochrome intensity. To take advantage of this property, image data must be converted into separate metrics for brightness and color.

The primary colors are red, green, and blue. In many computer graphics applications, video cards use individual red, green, and blue intensity values for each pel on the screen. In other cases, a card may use a single value that is indexed to a color lookup table. The color lookup table holds the individual red, green, and blue (RGB) intensity values.

For compression purposes, RGB data is converted to separate values for luminance and chrominance properties of an image. Luminance is a measurement of monochrome intensity. Chrominance consists of two measurements of pel color that are based on a reference white pel at the specified luminance level. Only one luminance and two chrominance values are required because the third color can always be directly derived from them.

Two-Dimensional Spatial Frequency

To take advantage of visual limitations as they relate to spatial changes, it is convenient to convert pictures from their two-dimensional "time domain" representation, which is what a person normally sees, into a two-dimensional spatial frequency domain representation. One dimension represents horizontal spatial frequencies, and the other dimension represents vertical spatial frequencies. As an example of this concept, when an image is scanned, slow variations in intensity or color have low spatial frequency components, and rapid variations or abrupt transitions have high spatial frequency components.

Conversion to the frequency domain is particularly useful because the eye's sensitivity to high spatial frequency components is much lower than

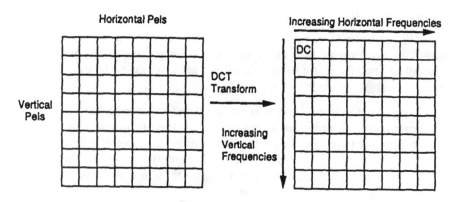

Exhibit 1. Discrete Cosine Transform (DCT)

for low spatial frequency components. Therefore high-frequency components below the threshold of normal human perception can be discarded. In addition, measurements of spatial frequency can be quantized or reduced in accuracy as a function of frequency. Low-frequency components are generally retained at a higher resolution than higher-frequency components.

Discrete Cosine Transform. JPEG and MPEG use a mathematical technique called the discrete cosine transform (DCT) to convert small blocks of 8×8 pels from the time domain into the frequency domain (see Exhibit 1). The transform is done in two dimensions, horizontal and vertical.

Initially, the individual planes of the picture are aggregated into blocks of 8×8 pels. Luminance and chrominance planes are transformed independently.

DCT uses a mathematical property that any discrete sequence of data may be represented by a sequence of orthogonal waveforms. (Orthogonal waveforms are waveforms that are independent of each other.) For a set of orthogonal waveforms, there is no way that one waveform can be represented by a linear combination of other waveforms of the same set.

The multipliers of each waveform used to represent the transformed sequence in the frequency domain are called "coefficients." Each coefficient may be thought of as the amplitude of a given frequency component. The DC coefficient is the average value across all of the pels in the block. All other coefficients are referred to as AC coefficients. When a block is of uniform intensity its AC coefficients are zero and its DC coefficient is nonzero.

Achieving high compression ratios requires that significant amounts of data be discarded. This is done by limiting the accuracy of each coefficient to a level of coarseness that can be perceived. The process of scaling DCT coefficients and truncating them to integer values is called quantization. For example, if humans can only perceive 10% changes at a particular spatial frequency, it is not necessary to retain 1% resolution for the associated coefficient.

During the development of the JPEG standard, experimental tests were made to determine the minimum coefficient value (i.e., amplitude) at each frequency that could be readily perceived by the human eye at a given distance from a video screen. These values were then used to establish recommended quantization values. Computed coefficients are scaled to the nearest integer multiple of their associated quantization value.

The desired outcome of quantization is that most of the high-frequency coefficients end up as zeros. By ordering the coefficients into the data stream such that the coefficients for low horizontal frequencies and low vertical frequencies come first, most of the later coefficients are zero.

In JPEG, AC coefficients are then statistically encoded using conventional Huffman or arithmetic coding, giving substantial compression gains. In MPEG, coefficients are transmitted as predefined variable-length bit strings. Most probable values only require a few bits; less probable values require more bits. While less efficient than adaptive Huffman or arithmetic coding, error extension does not occur. This becomes an important issue in transmission environments that are error prone.

During image reconstruction, the appropriate quantization values are multiplied by the scaled coefficients generated in the compression process. The new coefficients are approximately equal to their originally computed values, within the degree of accuracy imposed by the quantization value associated with each frequency. Depending on the quantization levels chosen, when blocks are reconstructed, discontinuities between blocks may become visible because of a loss of high-frequency information.

Differential Pulse Code Modulation

An additional compression technique used by JPEG and MPEG is differential pulse code modulation (DPCM). In pulse code modulation systems, the binary value of a characteristic such as the average luminance of a block is directly transmitted. When the expected changes from measurement to measurement are small, it is generally more efficient to retain the difference between the current and previous values (i.e., the delta) than the absolute value.

In JPEG and MPEG, DPCM is used to encode the DC coefficient in each 8 × 8 pel block. Once again, a DC coefficient is the average value of a luminance or chrominance component in a block. Except at severe boundaries,

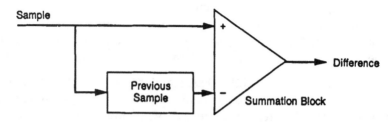

Note:
In DPCM, the last sample is used as a reference for the next sample. DPCM is effective when changes from sample to sample are small.

Exhibit 2. Differential Pulse Code Modulation (DPCM)

---

the DC coefficient tends to change slowly from block to block and may be efficiently coded differentially.

In MPEG systems, DPCM is also used to encode motion vectors. During still shots and video pans, the motion of one block tends to be very similar to the motion of adjacent ones. An example of DPCM is shown in Exhibit 2.

SUB-SAMPLING OF CHROMINANCE INFORMATION

Human vision is far more sensitive to changes in luminance than to changes in chrominance. Therefore JPEG allows and MPEG mandates that chrominance be sub-sampled relative to luminance.

Sub-sampling is a technique whereby the sampling process produces less data for one property (e.g., chrominance) than for the other (e.g., luminance). In MPEG systems, each 2×2 set of chrominance pels is averaged into a single data pel value. As a result, only one-fourth of the data for each chrominance class is retained relative to luminance. In JPEG, sampling rates may be established by the user.

Motion Compensation

In a short sequence of pictures of the same general scene, many objects remain in the same location, whereas others move only a short distance. By taking advantage of picture-to-picture similarities, MPEG systems achieve significant coding gains. This requires the ability to transmit several different types of pictures; some of these picture types consist only of information that changes from picture to picture.

To understand motion compensation, the different picture types supported in MPEG need to be explained. MPEG defines four pictures types — I, P, B, and D — as follows:

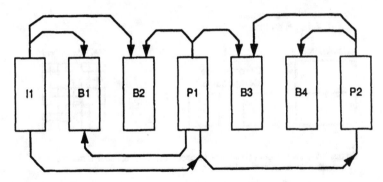

Exhibit 3. Typical Video Encoding Sequence for MPEG I or MPEG II

- Intracoded (I) pictures are encoded without reference to any other picture — that is, there is no motion compensation. Intracoded pictures require the most bits to represent, but they must be included in the signal or else arithmetic and transmission errors introduced in the reconstruction of the other picture types accumulate, degrading image quality. Intracoded pictures provide a fixed reference point for the creation of the other picture types.
- Predictive (P) coded pictures are coded using motion compensation from a previous I picture or P picture.
- Bidirectionally (B) predictive coded pictures use motion compensation from a previous I or P picture or from a future I or P picture. B pictures may not reference other B pictures.
- DC coefficient (D) coded pictures are designed for use in fast-forward applications. D pictures are similar to I pictures, with the exception that only DC coefficients are retained. Periodically interspersing D pictures into the data stream allows rapid fast-forward viewing without the overhead of decoding I, P, and B pictures at high speed. Given their limited applicability, D pictures are not supported in most existing MPEG I implementations and have been deleted from the MPEG II draft specification.

A typical video sequence consists of a mixture of I, P, and B pictures. A sample sequence is shown in Exhibit 3. In the sequence, I1 is independently coded and has no dependencies. P1 is derived from I1 and P2 is derived from P1. B1 and B2 are derived from an interpolation of both I1 and P1. B4 is derived from P1 and P2. B4 is derived only from P2.

The concept of picture prediction based on future pictures may seem improbable; however, during the encoding process pictures are placed in a buffer. The transmission sequence is reordered so that the decoder will receive the pictures in the sequence that allows decoding. The decoder is

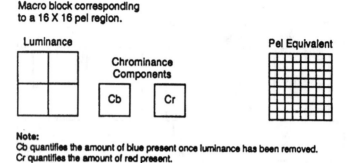

Exhibit 4.   Macro Blocks for Motion Prediction

then responsible for reordering the pictures as necessary to achieve proper sequencing for playback. In MPEG II applications, a history store of approximately 8 megabits is required.

In the example, the transmission sequence will be I1, P1, B1, B2, P2, B3, and B4. Although P1 is decoded before B1 and B2, P1 is not released for display until after B1 and B2 have been decoded and released. Similarly, P2 is decoded but not released for display until after B3 and B4 have been decoded and released. Therefore the display sequence will be I1, B1, B2, P1, B3, B4, and P2, as in Exhibit 3.

To perform motion compensation, each picture is further divided into macro blocks. A macro block consists of four DCT blocks for the luminance component, and one of each DCT block for the chrominance components. A macro block equates to a 16 × 16 pel region on the screen (see Exhibit 4).

Because I pictures do not reference other pictures, every macro block of an I picture is individually transmitted with its quantized DCT coefficients. DC coefficients are DPCM encoded.

Encoding of P pictures is a bit more difficult. The last I or P picture encoded is searched for a matching macro block. The search centers around the position of the macro block being encoded. The search width and search strategy is encoder dependent. If a close macro block match is found, a motion compensation vector is calculated. This vector provides a measurement of horizontal and vertical displacement for the new block in comparison to the matching macro block in the reference picture. If there are differences between the reference block and the block being encoded, then a residual error macro block is DCT encoded. The encoder now determines the most efficient representation of the macro block. The options are a conventional DCT macro block, a motion compensation vector, or a motion compensation vector and associated residual error block.

Encoding B pictures is the most technically challenging. The encoder tests the last I picture or P picture and the next I picture or P picture for macro block matches. The optimal result may reference either forward or backward, or may be an interpolation of macro blocks from both pictures. After a selection of the best match, a residual error block is generated if significant errors exist.

When choosing the optimal macro block to transmit, the encoder must make the following decisions:

- Is the motion vector transmitted or is it assumed to be zero (no movement)? This is a choice between motion compensation or no motion compensation.
- Is the block directly coded or predicted using the motion vector(s)?
- If predicted, is the residual error large enough to be encoded using a DCT transform?
- Is the quantizer scale appropriate? If not, it has to be adjusted.

Motion vectors within a localized region of a picture tend to be very similar. This is because scenes are often static or uniformly panned. Therefore, motion vectors are also predictively coded (i.e., using DPCM).

JPEG Encoders and Decoders

A block diagram of a typical JPEG encoder is shown in Exhibit 5. First, the RGB image is converted into a signal that consists of separate luminance and chrominance representations. The 8 × 8 blocks of pixels are converted into the frequency domain using the discrete cosine transform. The resulting coefficients are quantized and divided into AC and DC components. The DC components are then differentially encoded using DPCM. Finally, the result is statistically encoded using either a Huffman encoder or an arithmetic encoder. The resulting data stream is aggregated for storage or transmission.

A block diagram of a typical JPEG decoder is shown in Exhibit 6. To decompress a JPEG picture, the data stream is first demultiplexed into its individual components. The coefficients are then statistically decoded using a Huffman or arithmetic decoder. Subsequently, DC coefficients are differentially decoded. All of the coefficients are then scaled by their appropriate quantization factors and inverse-transformed into the time domain. Finally, the output is converted from the luminance/chrominance format into an RGB format for display.

MPEG Video Decoders

MPEG standards define video decoders but not encoders. In terms of processing, encoders do as much as 150 times the work of a decoder, doing searches to generate motion vectors, iterative evaluation of the best com-

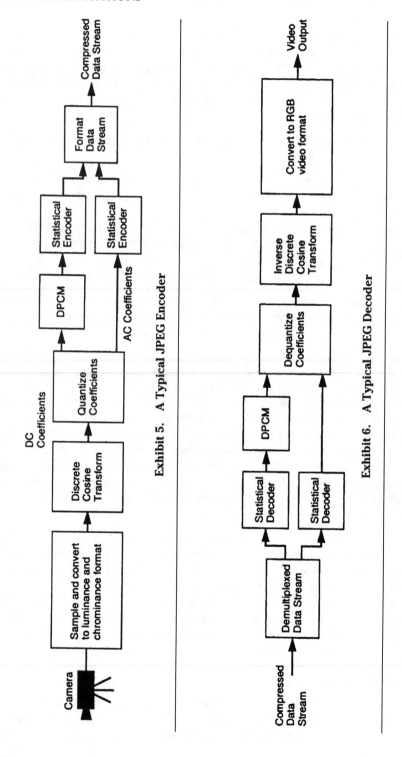

Exhibit 5.   A Typical JPEG Encoder

Exhibit 6.   A Typical JPEG Decoder

pression representation, and dynamically adjusting quantization levels to meet bandwidth targets.

A block diagram of a typical MPEG video decoder is shown in Exhibit 7. The compressed video stream is first demultiplexed and decoded. An I picture begins the decompression process. Its macro block coefficients are dequantized and inverse-transformed. The I picture is then stored in both the display buffer and the previous picture store.

Assuming the next picture is a P picture, it is derived from received forward-motion vectors referencing the I picture in the previous picture store. Received macro blocks are inverse-transformed and either directly retained (when a motion vector is not found) or summed into the predicted picture (when prediction errors are found). The P picture is then stored in the future picture store as a reference for future B pictures.

The next pictures are typically B pictures. Macro blocks from a B picture may be decoded from a number of formats. They may have been entirely defined using DCT coefficients. Alternatively, they may have been defined using forward-motion vectors, backward motion vectors, or both types of motion vectors.

When both types of vectors are used, a predicted macro block is the interpolation of referenced macro blocks from the previous picture store and the future pictures store. Compensation for prediction errors may be required if the predicted macro block is not identical to the original being encoded. Pictures may be released to the display buffer immediately after decompression. Once the next I picture or P picture is received, the future store buffer is copied into the previous buffer store and into the display buffer.

DigiCipher

General Instruments, the leading manufacturer of cable television set-top decoders, offers a slight variant of MPEG II called DigiCipher. The technology has also been licensed to Scientific Atlanta, the second-largest manufacturer, and will therefore appear in most digital set-top decoders. General Instruments has, with Motorola, developed a "dual mode" compression device that allows its boxes to receive either DigiCipher or MPEG II, if sufficient memory is available.

The use of B pictures requires that considerable storage be available in each decoder, so that frames can be reordered as required for correct time alignment. DigiCipher eliminates the use of B pictures. Because it uses only I and P pictures, DigiCipher requires 1 megabyte of RAM instead of the 2 megabytes of RAM for MPEG II. At a target price of $200 to $300 per cable box, the cost difference for the smaller memory requirement is important.

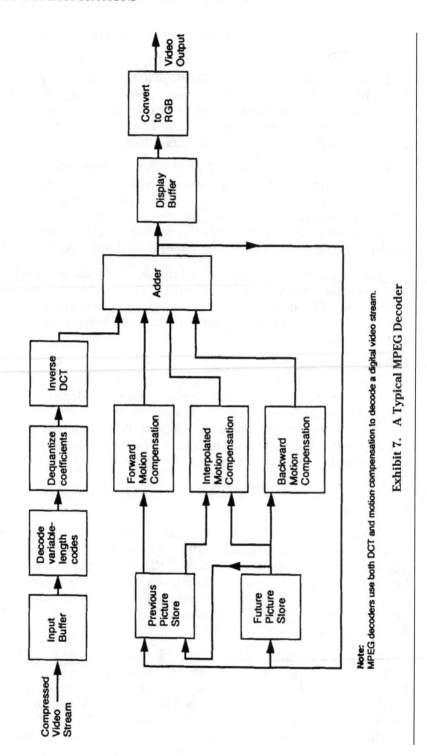

Note:
MPEG decoders use both DCT and motion compensation to decode a digital video stream.

Exhibit 7. A Typical MPEG Decoder

MPEG VERSUS MPEG II STANDARDS

The JPEG standard (formally known as ISO 10918-1) was created for the distribution of still images. JPEG is the foundation for MPEG I and MPEG II. MPEG I and MPEG II chips and systems are already in early production.

MPEG I (referred to formally as ISO/IEG 11172-2) was designed to support real-time video at data rates as high as 1.856M bps, although it is typically used at 1.5M bps. MPEG I typically supports a frame format of 352 horizontal pels × 240 vertical pels at 24 to 30 frames per second. The quality of an MPEG I image is equal to that displayed on a home VCR.

Some examples of the use of MPEG I are video-on-demand applications across 1.5M-bps links, multimedia on CD-ROM, and limited-resolution broadcast television. MPEG I does not support the interlaced frame formats typically used in broadcast television, so pictures must be converted from and to the interlaced format when MPEG I is used in this environment.

Although MPEG II is similar to MPEG I in technology, it offers a wider range of frame formats and data rates. MPEG II decoders are also backward-compatible to MPEG I. MPEG II fully supports interlaced video, as used in TV signals. MPEG II provides three basic modes of operation:

- Low profile, used for MPEG I-quality applications.
- Medium profile (702 × 480 pel), used for broadcast-video-quality applications. MPEG II medium profile requires from 3M to 20M bps. Most upcoming U.S.-based MPEG II applications will use the medium profile at 30 frames per second.
- High profile, to be used for upcoming high-definition television (HDTV) applications (i.e., 1,920 × 1,024 pel). High-profile HDTV applications will require as much as 40M bps.

Television Considerations

The network data rates required to support MPEG signals depends on the source material and the desired picture quality. Broadcast-quality television requires from 3M to 20M bps, depending on picture content. For example, a live broadcast of a rapidly moving subject requires many times the bandwidth of a movie.

In the U.S., standard NTSC (National TV Standards Committee) channels occupy 6 MHz of bandwidth for both broadcasts and cable distribution. Using digital coding technologies developed by Zenith Electronics and others, each 6-MHz television channel is capable of transporting between 37M bps and 43M bps.

A 37M-bps data rate accommodates as many as 24 MPEG I data streams, or typically between 6 and 10 MPEG II data streams, depending on how bandwidth is allocated. In a system developed by General Instruments, up to 10 channels statistically share bandwidth according to programming requirements. A 100-channel analog system can therefore handle 600 to 1,000 digital channels if fully converted.

SUMMARY

The leading standard for compressing images, JPEG, and its counterparts for full-motion video compression — MPEG, MPEG II, and an evolving technology known as DigiCipher — take advantage of what is known about the limitations of human vision. This chapter has explained how these systems accomplish compression and, just as importantly, how these video and image compression techniques make it both practical and economical to transmit and store digital photographs and digital video over multimedia networks without causing, for the viewer, an unacceptable degrading of the image's quality.

Section VI
Technologies for Multimedia Transport

The heart of our subject is multimedia transport technologies. How the multimedia content gets from source to destination depends upon where the destination is. We can transport over a local area network, over wide area services, and even over the airwaves. This section includes chapters on each method.

We have spent many pages talking about the individual types of multimedia content that are carried on a multimedia network. Each of these content types (video, voice, and the two types of data) has specific needs that must be met for successful network implementation. Some of these requirements are contradictory: time sensitive vs. time insensitive, bursty vs. continuous, periodic vs. random, uniform unit size vs. varying unit size. Now we propose to meet all these needs on a single network model. How shall we accomplish this goal?

As you might expect, there are several potential candidates for our network of multiple media content. Some were designed with a random traffic model in mind. Others were designed for constant-bit-rate transport of content that is predictable and stable. A few were created to overcome specific shortcomings of predecessor network models. All purport to meet our multimedia networking needs, through adaptation, modification, or raw power. What are the differences between them? What are the operating characteristics, strengths, and weaknesses of each?

To answer some of these important questions and to discuss other important networking issues, this section offers chapters on LAN and WAN network approaches. Additional chapters cover the multimedia transport aspects of the Internet and the transport of high-speed network signals to the customer premise. Finally, we will explore the extension of the network over cellular radio links … right to that laptop PC sitting on your lap at the beach. "Hello, New York, here is my chapter on multimedia transport."

Chapter 16
Networking Approaches for Multimedia LANs

Frederick W. Scholl and Gilbert Held

A variety of new network architectures are being proposed for use in multimedia applications. At stake is the next generation of LAN technology.

Although multimedia applications today are few in number, users need to see how the new LAN infrastructures can support tomorrow's needs for integrated voice, video, image, and data traffic. Applications include multimedia training, multimedia compound documents, and teleconferencing.

This chapter reviews the status of some technical approaches that are promising for multimedia use. There is no clear winner at this point because, simultaneously, technology is evolving, user tests are ongoing, and some standards are as yet incomplete. Significant efforts are also being expended to make maximum use of existing network standards including fiber distributed data interface (FDDI), 802.3 (Ethernet), and 802.5 (Token Ring).

Several new technical approaches lend themselves to multiuse applications involving images, data, and full motion video. The purpose of this chapter is to review these approaches and some of the trade-offs involved in deploying each. The architectures surveyed include the following: time division multiplexed LANs, Fibre Channel LANs (ANSI Standards Committee X3T9.3), and asynchronous transfer mode (ATM) LANs. The chapter also outlines approaches to multimedia that optimize the use of existing LANs.

TDM LANs

Time division multiplexed (TDM) LAN backbones are ideally suited for transporting a wide variety of applications information throughout an enterprise. The basic concept is to allocate a fixed bandwidth for each service — data, image, or video — and scale that bandwidth to meet the

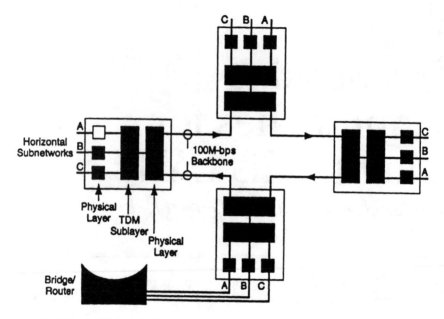

Exhibit 1. Network Backbone Based on Time Division Multiplexing

application needs. Exhibit 1 shows an example of a TDM backbone in which four wiring closets are interconnected through a 100M-bps fiber-optic backbone.

This backbone interconnects subnetworks labeled A, B, and C. Each of these subnetworks could run separate services such as digitized video, image, and data. The networks could be bridged together (as shown in Exhibit 1) in a central wiring closet. For more demanding video or image applications, separate servers might be employed for each subnetwork.

Several firms market backbone products based on this concept. Luxcom, Inc. (Fremont CA) and Fibermux Corp. (Chatsworth CA) are the product leaders at present.

Pros. The pros and cons of TDM technology may be summarized as follows:

- Hubs are reasonably priced; TDM systems are straightforward.
- No complex token-passing protocols.
- Allows for completely isolated subnetworks, with no adverse interference effects between LANs.
- Backbone carries widest variety of information formats.

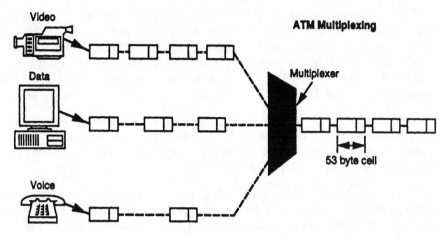

Exhibit 2. Multiplexing Several Traffic Types on an ATM Network

---

Cons. The disadvantages of TDM technology are that it:

- Is not represented by any international LAN standard.
- Does not allow flexible allocation of backbone bandwidth to adjust to instantaneous needs.

ATM LANs

A multiplexing alternative that overcomes some of the shortcomings of TDM is asynchronous transfer mode, a type of asynchronous time division multiplexing. This technology was originally developed for use in wide area network connections under the umbrella known as broadband integrated services digital network (B-ISDN). It was developed with two specific goals in mind: high throughput and network transport independent of the network application.

These goals were developed to allow efficient transport of voice, video, and data information of varying formats and data rates. These same objectives are being applied to the LAN environment. Hence, ATM is actively being considered for LAN backbones and for direct workstation connections.

ATM Basics

The basic ATM concept for multiple traffic types is illustrated in Exhibit 2, which shows multiplexing of three sources of information — video, data, and voice. Data is usually bursty in nature, video is variable rate depending on desired quality and application, and voice is fixed rate (usually 64K bps).

This information is chopped into 53-byte cells, with 48 bytes for information and 5 bytes for addressing. Cells are assigned as needed, depending on the required bandwidth, so one voice channel would consume 1 out of 2,400 cells in a 155M-bps stream. A 10M-bps Ethernet packet would use 1 out of 16 cells during the data burst. A video codec operating at 45M bps would use 1 out of 3 cells.

As developed for broadband ISDN, ATM cells would be transported over synchronous optical network, or SONET (known as synchronous digital hierarchy, or SDH, internationally) links. SONET rates are OC-3, 155M bps; OC-12, 622M bps; and OC48, 2.4G bps.

Over the WAN, ATM cell multiplexing would transport such services as ATM permanent and switched virtual circuits, frame relay, and switched multimegabit data services (SMDS). The ATM technique may be contrasted with TDM, where precise bandwidth allocations are made to each service, and to space division multiplexing, where separate wires are allocated to each information service.

ATM meets the goals of high throughput and independent network transport through the use of the cell structure described in the previous paragraphs. Required bandwidth is made available on a "fine-grain" basis to any information source. At OC-3 rates, the basic 53-byte cell has a duration of 2.7 s. A variable packet-length protocol such as FDDI may have a packet length as great as 0.3 ms. High network throughput is accomplished by locating cell routing information in layer two rather than layer three of the Open Systems Interconnection (OSI) model.

ATM Backbone

ATM's application to LANs is illustrated in Exhibit 3. This exhibit shows the interconnection of video and data servers to multimedia workstations using ATM LANs. ATM may be used as a backbone medium and as a direct pipe to each workstation. A router may be used to connect local Ethernet work groups to the backbone, for example.

Several groups are working to define interoperability interfaces for premises ATM and to promote ATM use. The ATM Forum is the largest such group, with approximately 100 members currently. It has developed draft standards for three premises-based ATM interfaces. They include a 100M-bps FDDI-like interface, a 155M-bps Fibre Channel-like interface, and a 155M-bps SONET compatible interface. The hope is that the ATM Forum will be able to define useful interoperability standards at a faster pace than other standards committees.

In parallel with work on interoperability standards, several vendors have introduced products or have announced ATM products for LAN application.

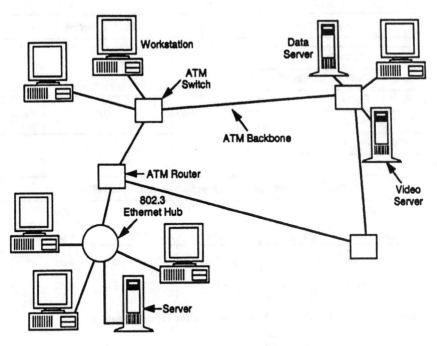

Exhibit 3. ATM Multimedia LANs

Fore Systems, Inc. (Warrendale PA) has hardware for ATM to the desktop applications, with network interface cards for SBus and Turbo Channel that operate at 140M bps. MPR Teltech Ltd. (Burnaby BC Canada) has Atm-Net, a system providing transport of IEEE 802 LANs, NTSC video (i.e., TV-standard video), and other multimedia connections. Another start-up firm committed to ATM technology is Multimedia Networks, Inc. (Lexington MA). ROUTEREXchange 7000 from Retix (Santa Monica CA) provides an interface between conventional work area LANs such as Ethernet and Token Ring, and ATM backbones.

Pros. The advantages of ATM technology are that it:

- Offers seamless connectivity with coming WAN transport systems.
- Has significant momentum in the commercial arena.
- Offers most flexible performance for multimedia information.

Cons. Among the disadvantages of ATM technology:

- Standards for ATM premises LANs are still evolving and fully operational systems are still rare.
- Cost/performance may be inadequate for ATM-to-workstation application.

Architecture	
FC-4	Application
FC-3	Common Services Protocol
FC-2	Framing
FC-1	Encoding (8B/10B)
FC-0	Physical Layer

Packet Format		
28 bytes	0 to 2112 bytes	8 bytes
Header	Data	Trailer

Physical Layer Specifications: 62.5-μm Multimode Fiber

Data Rate	Line Rate	Distance	Light Source	Flux Budget
12.5M byte	133M bps	0 – 2 km	1300-nm LED	6 dB
25M byte	266M bps	0 – 1 km	1300-nm LED	6 dB

Exhibit 4. Specifications for Fibre Channel

FIBRE CHANNEL LANs

A third approach for multimedia networking is represented by the Fibre Channel work proceeding in the ANSI standards committee X3T9.3. This work has focused on fiber-optic transport, high speed, and flexible data formats. Exhibits 4 and 5 illustrate the topology and summarize some of the key operating parameters of this approach.

The Fibre Channel standard under development defines point-to-point fiber-optic links and the necessary protocols to switch packets through a switching fabric. This fabric forms the hub of the network. A wide range of line rates and physical layer interfaces are defined, with line rates from 133M bps to 1.062G bps.

Both laser and LED (light emitting diode) sources are defined in the physical layer interface specification. For premises LAN application, most interest is associated with the LED-based applications operating at 12.5M bps and 25M bps.

Above the physical layer (known as FC-0 in the draft standard) are the FC-1 and FC-2 layers. These three layers are grouped together to form the PH layer, in X3T9.3 parlance. Above the PH layer resides a layer for common services protocol, followed by network applications.

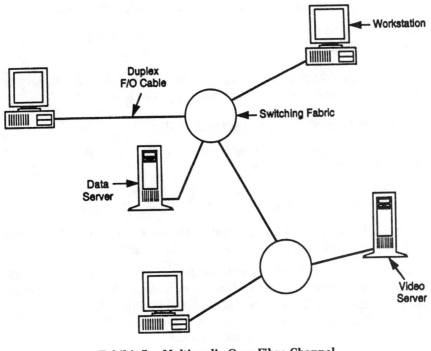

Exhibit 5. Multimedia Over Fibre Channel

Fibre Channel is interesting for certain multimedia applications because it implements a high-speed circuit-switched fabric. Referring to Exhibit 5, a node can dial up any server on the network; the requested information flows through the hub.

The hub is implemented as a nonblocking switch; with N ports, N/2 simultaneous transactions can be running. Each transaction can be running at 133M bps or 266M bps, depending on which implementation of Fibre Channel is used. Because any node is connected to the server through its own logical channel, the data could be a file transfer or real time video clip or any other information. Video compression is not needed because of Fibre Channel's speed. Interference from other channels does not take place. A user could view video information and later switch to running spreadsheets from another server.

This technology has been implemented as an end-user product by Ancor Communications, Inc. (Brea CA). The CXT 100/125 hub offers 4M bps or 12.5M bps per port speeds, with up to 64 ports per hub. The hub operates with NetWare LAN software and work station interface cards for AT bus, Extended Industry Standard Architecture (EISA), Microchannel, and YME-class machines.

Pros. The advantages of Fibre Channel technology are that it:

- Is supported by active standards effort.
- Has wide bandwidth per channel.

Cons. The primary disadvantages of Fibre Channel is that it does not offer certain conventional LAN functions, such as multicasting.

LEVERAGING EXISTING LAN TECHNOLOGIES

The decision to optimize existing LANs has great appeal. Among the benefits are that this approach:

- Makes good use of the installed base of hardware.
- Allows incremental improvements in technology deployment.

However, if a company decides to put multimedia on existing LANs, it must deal with limitations of LANs designed for data only.

There are two existing LAN technologies that deserve special attention because of their suitability to transport multimedia: isoEthernet and 100VG-AnyLAN. IsoEthernet is standardized by the Institute of Electrical and Electronic Engineers as IEEE standard 802.9a, while 100VG-AnyLAN is standardized by that body as standard 802.12.

IsoEthernet

IsoEthernet, or isochronous Ethernet (sometimes called isoENET), represents an extension to 10Base-T technology by adding time-sensitive multimedia support. This support is added through the addition of 6.144M bps of isochronous bandwidth to existing 10M-bps 10Base-T Ethernet.

Here, the term *isochronous* refers to a series of repetitive time slots used for the transmission of constant bit-rate services at the physical bit-transmission level. Since multimedia applications transporting audio or video are time-sensitive, an isochronous transmission scheme provides an ideal mechanism to support this type of application.

The 6.144M bps of additional bandwidth added by isoEthernet is designed to accommodate 96 ISDN B-channels, either individually or in multiple combinations of Nx64 K bps. For example, 12K bps of bandwidth would be assigned two 64K-bps channels, whereas digitized voice that requires 64K bps when pulse code modulation (PCM) is used for digitization would be assigned one channel.

IsoEthernet uses a different coding method than 10Base-T, requiring new adapters and hubs to obtain access to the 6.144 M bps of additional bandwidth. However, network users who do not require an isochronous communications capability can continue to use their existing 10Base-T adapter cards, and 802.3 traffic will not notice any change to the operation of a 10Base-T network.

One of the first applications to use isoEthernet was IBM's Person-to-Person videoconferencing software. Introduced in mid-1995, this application software integrates with desktop video cameras to provide personal conferencing at 15 frames per seconds.

100VG-AnyLAN

A second type of LAN well suited for supporting multimedia is 100VG-AnyLAN. Although this type of LAN is commonly considered to represent a version of high-speed Ethernet, in actuality it replaces the Ethernet CSMA/CD protocol with a demand-priority scheme. This scheme enables the transmission of time-sensitive voice and video associated with multimedia applications in preference to conventional data that is relatively time-insensitive.

100VG-AnyLAN uses a hub-centric network architecture. Under that architecture a central hub, known as a level-1 or root hub, functions as an inverted tree base in establishing a 100VG-AnyLAN network. From this hub, other hubs or modes form a star topology, fanning out underneath the root hub. Exhibit 6 illustrates the 100VG-AnyLAN topology.

In a 100VG-AnyLAN network, each hub has one uplink port and downlink ports. The uplink port is used for connecting lower-level hubs to an upper-level hub, while the downlink ports are used to connect an upper-level hub to work stations, bridges, and other network devices to include lower-level hubs. Up to three levels of cascading are supported on a 100VG-Any LAN network.

Under 100VG-AnyLAN, access to the network occurs by a mode issuing a request, referred to as a demand," to the hub it is connected to. Each request includes a priority label assigned by the upper layer application. The priority label is normal for normal data packets or high for packets carrying time-sensitive multimedia information.

Demand-Priority Access. A level-1 or root hub continuously scans its ports using a round-robin sequence for requests. Lower-level hubs connected as modes also perform a round-robin scanning process and forward mode requests to the root hub. The root hub determines which nodes are requesting permission to transmit a packet as well as the priority level associated with the packet. Each hub maintains a separate list for both normal- and high-priority requests.

Normal-priority requests are serviced in their port order until a higher-priority request is received. Upon receipt of a higher-priority request, the hub completes any packet transmission in progress and then services the high-priority packet before returning to service the normal-priority list. To prevent a long sequence of high-priority requests from abnormally delaying low-priority

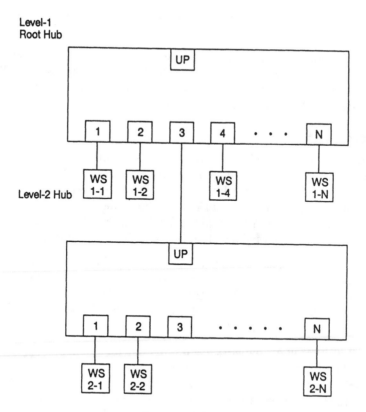

Level-1
Root Hub

Level-2 Hub

Key:
WS 1-N—workstation hub level/port number

Exhibit 6.   100VG-AnyLAN Topology

requests from being serviced, the hub also monitors request-to-send response times. If the delay exceeds a predefined time, the hub automatically raises the normal-priority level to a high-priority level.

The use of a demand-priority access scheme extends 100VG-AnyLAN beyond Ethernet, enabling this network to support Token Ring, FDDI, and other types of LANs. However, all hubs located in the same network segment must be configured to support the same frame format, such as IEEE 802.3 Ethernet or IEEE 802.5 Token Ring, so the user can use 100VG-AnyLAN as a mechanism to add multimedia capability to legacy 10Base-T or Token Ring networks.

Software Solutions

Software products are available that put multimedia on existing Ethernet and Token Ring LANs. For example, StarWare from Starlight Networks, Mountain View CA, is one such offering.

This approach makes use of software overlays to best handle simultaneous video and data files and to integrate data, video or image, and voice. For Ethernet, this number can be in the range of three to six simultaneous video transactions at CD-ROM video rates (150K bps).

Universal Software Platform. Nynex (White Plains NY) has announced trials of new software that integrates voice, video, and data into multimedia interactive applications. The software was developed in the Medial Broadband Services (MBS) group within Nynex Science & Technology. It allows interactive displays of data and image information as well as coordination with voice information.

Early trials have been in the medical field, where the system is being used to facilitate interactive sessions between several physicians. The MBS system facilitates exchange of patient records, including data and visual information.

Nynex's approach is to create a universal multimedia software platform with which applications developers can design a wide variety of multimedia applications. This platform rides on top of the network transport service and interfaces to the multimedia application. Exhibit 7 illustrates Nynex's MBS multimedia services with reference to OSI's seven-layer protocol stack.

The Nynex software, called MEDOS, resides at the presentation and session layer in OSI parlance. It operates independent of the underlying network transport protocol (e.g., TCP/IP or IPX ISPX). It is also transparent to underlying network access layers, whether FDDI or Ethernet in the LAN environment or SMDS, leased line, or ATM in the WAN arena.

The network architecture that MEDOS facilitates is shown in Exhibit 8. The starting points are the conventional data LAN hub and voice telephone service.

The LAN hub is now commonly based on some type of managed, intelligent hub; the voice telephone service is a passive distribution system with the private automatic brand exchange (PABX) as interface to the public switched telephone network (PSTN). For a multimedia application, voice and image/video servers are added as well as multimedia workstations. The functions of the image server and data server are obvious; the voice server records and archives voice records (e.g., medical diagnoses in the hospital applications).

The MEDOS software provides network access to image-based information, integration of image and data records, and interactive consultation making use of these records. Nynex envisions that numerous applications, ranging from the retail clothing business to oil exploration to advertising to

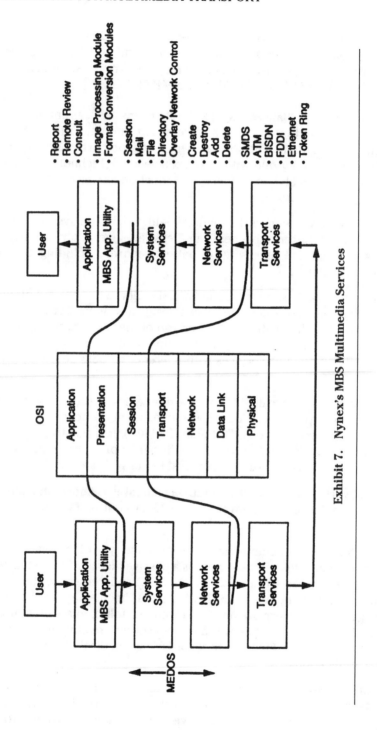

Exhibit 7.   Nynex's MBS Multimedia Services

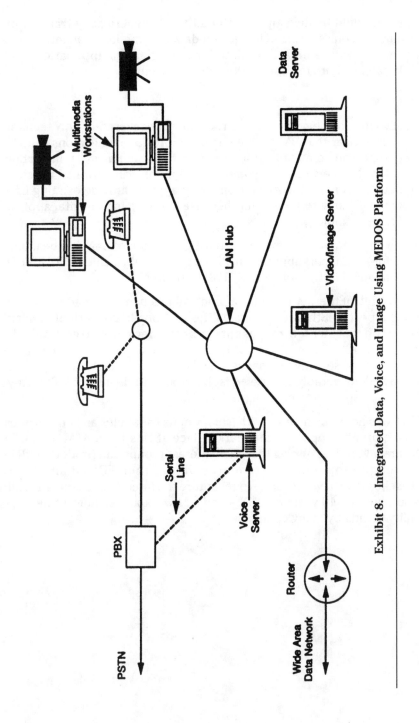

Exhibit 8.   Integrated Data, Voice, and Image Using MEDOS Platform

education, could be developed with MEDOS. In general, any transaction with simultaneous sharing of image and data information in an interactive environment would be a candidate for a multimedia application, and MEDOS can facilitate the applications development.

SUMMARY

No real winner has emerged in the race for next-generation LAN technology, but it is clear that LANs have become more communications centric. Person-to-person communication over LANs is emerging as an important application. The network is becoming much more than a wire on which to hang data servers and work stations. Any approach using existing LAN technology is likely to be popular because it allows incremental application of new technology.

In the next few years, however, a third generation of LAN will be implemented for multimedia application. Prime contestants include FDDI II, FDDI follow-on LAN (FFOL), isoEthernet, 100VG-AnyLAN, and ATM.

Although isoEthernet provides a practical mechanism for adding multimedia support to Ethernet, it retains the 10M bps bandwidth of conventional Ethernet, which represents a bottleneck for large LANs. In comparison, 100VG-AnyLAN provides a 100M-bps operating rate and the support of time-sensitive transmission. Thus, 100-VGAnyLAN equipment sales have considerably surpassed isoEthernet and the use of 100VG-AnyLAN can be expected to challenge ATM.

FDDI was not implemented with isochronous capability, and FDDI II does not have broad support in the marketplace at this time. ATM premises LANs are favored, assuming that ATM interest groups can produce widely accepted interoperability standards. If not, then FDDI II and FFOL approaches may have a chance to recapture the interest of users. After all, they are built on 10 years of FDDI standards work and significant interoperability testing by many companies.

Chapter 17
Integrated Services: The Multimedia Internet

John Galgay

As has already been mentioned in this book, the Internet as we know it today is a worldwide collection of networks providing sublayer-independent, end-to-end, connectionless packet services on a hop-by-hop, best-effort basis at the network layer of the OSI reference model. Let's begin by examining these key architecture elements in turn:

sub-layer independent The IP protocol stack is defined from layer 3 and above with each layer 2 (data link layer) protocol providing services to IP.

end-to-end Both host devices establishing communication and layer 3 internetworking devices must implement the IP protocol stack

connectionless The IP protocol stack defines a single layer 3 protocol which provides connectionless services only (compared with the OSI protocol stack which defines two layer 3 protocols — CLNS for Connectionless Network Services and CONS for Connection-Oriented Network Services).

packet Layer 3 protocol data units are termed packets.

hop-by-hop All packets are individual units with no dependence on preceding or subsequent packets. Each packet is routed from source to destination by forwarding the packet to the next internetworking device toward the destination. The next hop decision is performed independently on each internetworking device.

0-8493-9949-1/99/$0.00+$.50
© 1999 by CRC Press LLC

The above architectural elements all combine to provide a best-effort, nonreal-time service. Each packet is provided the same forwarding priority and provided the same access to internetworking resources (link bandwidth, internetworking device buffer space and processing capacity); however, no guarantee of delivery is provided. Any other services required by an end station application must be provided by protocols operating at higher layers of the OSI Reference Model.

Together these elements represent the paradigm and philosophy that have guided the Internet from the beginning as a DARPA research project to the explosive worldwide network for universities, government agencies, corporate intranets, intercorporate communication, electronic commerce, information dissemination, individual dial access, and an expanding list of other uses. This paradigm has allowed the Internet to provide the internetworking service for a wide range of applications and services, including remote login (TELNET), file transfer (FTP), electronic mail (SMTP), Web browsing (HTTP), network file system (NFS), network management (SNMP), and others. Each application is ultimately responsible for end-to-end data integrity and reliability and may utilize either IP transport protocol to do so:

- Connection-Oriented Transmission Control Protocol (TCP)
- Connectionless User Datagram Protocol (UDP).

Additionally, much of the success of the Internet can be attributed to the contribution of the (Internet Engineering Task Force (IETF, www.ietf.org) and the standards process which has established and sustained the framework of the Internet. The IETF is composed of all sectors of the Internet community, including application vendors, internetworking element vendors, service providers, and users. These parties meet regularly, work continuously, and effectively implement the Delphi process (i.e., debate all issues until a consensus is reached or until all parties agree on elements of disagreement) to meet the constantly evolving needs for standards-based, end-to-end service offerings.

The applications which have flourished on the Internet with the IP protocol suite are nonreal-time applications which can afford to wait for data to arrive without impacting the integrity of the application. These applications provide services across both lightly loaded and heavily loaded network segments. As the Internet has grown, individuals and businesses have constantly pushed to provide new applications and services over the existing Internet services model. Experiments with real-time applications and services, such as voice and video, have demonstrated that the existing Internet services model is not adequate to meet the quality-of-service needs required by these applications and services. The market for these new applications and services requires a service model that delivers the quality-of-service characteristics requested by the application. This new service model does not necessarily have to come from the Internet community; however, the history of the Internet demonstrates that the Internet community will take on the challenge.

NEXT INTERNET ARCHITECTURE PARADIGM

Full quality of service is an end-to-end issue that cannot be delivered through the efforts of a single organization, standards body, or company. Defining and deploying an integrated services Internet will require the cooperation among multiple standards bodies and industries. All layers of the OSI reference model must address integrated services issues. The IETF works primarily at layer 3 and above, based on the requirement for sub-layer independence. Other standards bodies work primarily at layers 1 and layers 2, providing the necessary standards for one or multiple sublayer functionality. Currently, only ATM has defined quality-of-service classes at layer 2; however, these quality-of-services classes were not developed in conjunction with the upper-layer IP service requirements. Some IEEE 802.x standards provide deterministic qualities and/or a priority mechanism, such as 802.4 (Token-Bus), 802.5 (Token-Ring), and 802.6 (DQDB); however, these qualities will have to be expanded to meet quality-of-service needs of real-time applications. The current cooperative environment among all of the standards bodies and working groups within the standards bodies shows promise for a well-defined end-to-end quality-of-service solution. The remainder of this chapter focuses on the efforts of the IETF.

Key IETF working groups supplying solutions for end-to-end quality of service are listed below:

- **INTSERV WG** Integrated Services Working Group
  - Co-chairs: Craig Partridge, John Wroclawski, David Clark
  - The charter is to specify an enhanced Internet service model which will integrate real-time and classical nonreal-time data traffic across a single network infrastructure. The group must define the service model and the standard interfaces required to implement the service model.
- **ISSLL WG** Integrated Services over Specific Link Layers Working Group
  - Co-chairs: Eric Crawley, John Wroclawski
  - The charter is to define the mapping of the extensions to the IP architecture defined by the Integrated Services and RSVP working groups onto specific subnetwork technologies, including service mappings, setup protocol mappings, and adaptation protocols. Additionally, the ISSLL working group must identify link-layer technologies which will not support integrated services.

- **QOSR WG** Quality of Service Routing Working Group
  — Co-chairs: Eric Crawley, Hal Sandick
  — The charter is to define a framework for selection and maintenance of packet-forwarding paths which meet the requested service class objectives, to address the extension and integration of routing and quality-of-service setup protocols, respectively, and possibly initiate the research of new quality-of-service routing protocols.
- **RSVP WG** Resource Reservation Setup Protocol Working Group
  — Co-chairs: Robert Braden, Lixia Zhang
  — The charter is to evolve a resource reservation setup protocol that meets the requirements defined by the Integrated Services Working Group in RFC 1633 (Integrated Services in the Internet Architecture: An Overview).

The goal of establishing an integrated services Internet is clearly a very large task, involving multiple standards bodies and impacting all layers of the OSI reference model. The remainder of this chapter focuses on the elements of an integrated services service model as defined by the IETF Integrated Services Working Group in RFC 1633.[3]

INTEGRATED SERVICES

The IETF formed the Integrated Services Working Group (Integrated Services WG) with a charter to specify an enhanced Internet service model and define the standard interfaces and requirements necessary to implement the new service model.

The Integrated Services WG has not simply addressed the need for a real-time quality-of-service model for the Internet, but has addressed three issues that must all be satisfied for the Internet to serve as the desired single infrastructure for multiple services. Integrated services defines a service model that includes nonreal-time services, real-time services, and controlled link sharing.[3] The addition of a real-time service model to the current best-effort service model without the inclusion of controlled link sharing would create an unmanageable, unpredictable, and unstable network infrastructure.

The current use of real-time applications in the Internet relies heavily on IP multicasting technologies, including advanced multimedia hardware and software components, the Mbone and IP multicast routing protocols, and adaptive applications. As the new integrated services model continues to move forward, all of these technologies will continue to be critically important.

REAL-TIME SERVICE CLASSES

The Integrated Services WG has defined two service classes of real-time quality of service: controlled load service and guaranteed service. Other classifications may be added to the extensible integrated services model in the future, but these two classifications will provide the necessary quality of service to the current set of applications requiring real-time service over the Internet. Each class of service must be defined through quantifiable traffic flow characteristics that may be requested through the reservation setup protocol. These traffic flow characteristics represent the commitment into which internetworking devices enter to deliver datagrams for the traffic flow. The primary element of both defined service classes is the minimum and maximum delay a packet will receive from an individual link.

The definition of the controlled load service class is defined in Reference 5 and describes the service as the quality of service a traffic flow receives on an unloaded network element (i.e., a network link operating below peak load conditions). The client must supply an estimate of the traffic it will generate in the RSVP traffic flow request. Controlled load service is intended to serve the large class of adaptive real-time applications, which normally work well on unloaded networks but suffer severe performance issues as the traffic load on the network increases. Each internetworking device accepting the request must ensure that adequate link capacity, buffer capacity, computational capacity, and forwarding capacity will be available for the flow. This flow should receive little or no average packet queuing delays or congestion loss in excess of the defined burst period. The burst period allows individual packets to suffer a delay or loss during the burst, however, the quality-of-service guarantees are average delay and average loss. The router implementation of controlled load service must ensure that a flow experiencing congestion during a burst does not impact other flows on the link.

The definition of the guaranteed service class is defined in Reference 8 and describes the service as a quality of service which provides firm bounds on end-to-end datagram queuing delays (assumes propagation delays are constant). Queuing delay is primarily a function of the requested token bucket size and data rate, providing applications considerable control over the upper delay bound. A larger requested token bucket may serve a higher data rate. Playback applications, a one-way video or audio data stream, are intolerant of late packets and may use guaranteed service to provide a constant data stream to the application from a variable internetwork packet receive rate. As long as packets arrive within the upper delay bound, the application will play back a smooth data stream without jitter. Interactive applications, such as two-way video and audio, must maintain a much lower upper delay bound for effective two-way communication. The guaranteed service is intended to approximate a "fluid model," such that the reserved data rate through all nodes between end points provides the same quality of service as a dedicated link between the end points themselves.

Exhibit 1.   Examples of Traffic Type Classifications

Organizational	Multiple organizations may share the expense of a high-bandwidth WAN link
Departmental	Multiple departments may share the expense of the link
Protocol multiple	Protocols may share the same link (i.e., IP, IPX, SNA, etc.)
Service type	Multiple service types may share the same link (i.e., controlled load real time, guaranteed real time, and nonreal time)

Exhibit 2.   Example Application: Corporate Campus Internetwork Backbone Link

Organization	Department	Protocol	Service Type	Application
ABC Co.	Finance	IP	Nonreal time	Network file system
	Finance	IP	Controlled load	Accounting system
	Finance	IP	Guaranteed service	Videoconference room
	Training	IP	Nonreal time	Network file system
	Training	IP	Controlled load	Video training
	Manufacturing	IP	Guaranteed service	Computer-controlled assembly
	Manufacturing	IP	Guaranteed service	Videoconference room

Neither of the integrated-services-defined quality-of-service classes allow for IP fragmentation of controlled load or guaranteed service data. Therefore, RSVP provides a mechanism for receivers to communicate and senders to determine the maximum transmission unit (MTU) along a multicast tree, as defined in Reference 1.

CONTROLLED LINK SHARING

Integrated services accomplishes the combination of differing traffic types on a single infrastructure through a mechanism called controlled link sharing. Controlled link sharing implies that the combination of traffic is understood, defined, managed, and must be authorized by a gatekeeper function. Every packet on the link falls into a defined class and possibly subclass. Unclassified packets are prevented from utilizing the link.

Examples of traffic type classifications are listed in Exhibit 1.

The classes may be combined in a hierarchical fashion on a single link to provide extremely efficient and defined use of the internetwork resources. Examples of controlled link sharing in three different environments appear in the following exhibits: a corporate campus internetwork backbone link (Exhibit 2), an intrabuilding infrastructure provider link (Exhibit 3), and a service provider backbone link (Exhibit 4).

Exhibit 3. Example Application — Intrabuilding Infrastructure Provider Link

Organization	Department	Protocol	Service Type	Application
ABC Co.	Finance	IP	Nonreal time	Network file system
	Finance	IP	Controlled load	Accounting system
	Finance	IP	Guaranteed service	Videoconference room
	Training	IP	Nonreal time	Network file system
	Training	IP	Controlled load	Video training
	Business Admin	IP	Nonreal time	Network file system
	Business Admin	IP	Guaranteed service	Videoconference room
	Info Systems	IP	Guaranteed service	Voice services
XYZ Co.	Finance	IP	Nonreal time	Network file system
	Finance	IP	Controlled load	Accounting system
	Finance	IP	Guaranteed service	Videoconference room
	Sales	IP	Controlled load	Stock market news/quote
	Info Systems	IP	Nonreal time	Internet access/web services
	Info Systems	IP	Guaranteed service	Voice services

Exhibit 4. Example Application—Service Provider Backbone Link

Organization	Department	Protocol	Service Type	Application
ABC Co., Boston	All	IP	Nonreal time	Web services, e-mail, file systems
	Customer Service	IP	Controlled load	Customer order system
	All	IP	Guaranteed service	Voice over IP, videoconferencing
ABC Co., New York	All	IP	Nonreal time	Web services, e-mail, file systems
	Customer Service	IP	Controlled load	Customer order system
	All	IP	Guaranteed service	Voice over IP, videoconferencing
GHI Co.	All	IP	Nonreal time	Web services, e-mail, etc.
	Operations	IP	Controlled load	Training services
	Info Services	IP	Guaranteed service	Videoconferencing services
XYZ Co.	All	IP	Nonreal time	Web services, e-mail, etc.
	Operations	IP	Controlled load	Entertainment content
	Info Services	IP	Guaranteed service	Videoconferencing services

THE INTEGRATED SERVICE FRAMEWORK

The Integrated Services WG began developing the integrated services model with two key assumptions:

1. Internetworking resources must be managed
2. A single internetworking infrastructure in preferable to multiple

The strongest argument against an integrated service Internet which implements resource guarantees in the Internet is that bandwidth will become an infinite resource; therefore, bandwidth management will become unnecessary. This argument has received attention in the press from George Gilder, who wrote in his 1992 *Forbes ASAP* article entitled "The Coming of the Fibersphere"[9] that bandwidth would be infinite in the world of the all optical network. However, even if bandwidth becomes infinite, managed bandwidth allows for the collection of management data, usage data, billing data, etc. Also, until the time of all-optical networks, the buffer and processing resources of internetworking devices will not be infinite and therefore must be managed to provide guaranteed quality of service.

The strongest impact a new integrated services Internet will have on the elements of the current Internet architecture paradigm discussed above will be a violation of the hop-by-hop element. The current architecture ensured that all state data for end-to-end data flows was only required in the end stations. The routers and intermediate internetworking devices would process each packet independently on a hop-by-hop basis with no packet-by-packet dependencies and would maintain no flow-oriented-state data.

The integrated service Internet model set forth in RFC 1633 clearly violates the hop-by-hop element with the requirement of traffic flow state maintenance in all internetworking devices in the end-to-end quality-of-service data path. The state maintenance required is referred to as soft-state, requiring the establishment and periodic maintenance of the traffic flow, but allowing the dynamic modification of the path and traffic flow characteristics, which may react to a failed link in the path without tearing down the reserved data flow and reestablishing a new path. Since soft-state is a connectionless state mechanism, this approach preserves many of the robust characteristics of the current Internet architecture. More about the soft-state mechanism will be discussed under RSVP.

One of the largest challenges of the Integrated Services WG is the heterogeneity of end-to-end integrated services. Along the end-to-end path, integrated services will encounter internetworking equipment from multiple vendors, different algorithms attempting to provide the same quality of service, possible replacement service offerings and partial deployment,[6] integrated services tunnels through nonintegrated services networks,[4] different methods of mapping a service class on to a link layer, and possibly different quality-of-service routing algorithms.

The road to a fully defined, implemented, and installed integrated services Internet will continue for the next 5 years. In fact, many of the critical components of an integrated services Internet are yet to be standardized. Although the integrated services architecture was defined in RFC 1633, the majority of the components are still in draft form within the IETF, awaiting implementation experience, feedback, and updating.

The reference framework put forth by the Integrated Services WG in RFC 1633 includes four components:

1. A packet scheduler module.
2. A packet classifier module.
3. An admission control module.
4. A reservation setup protocol module.

Together the packet scheduler, packet classifier, and admission control modules compose the elements of traffic control which must be implemented in a router. Undoubtedly, multiple algorithms will be defined to accomplish the traffic control requirements of a router, allowing vendors to deliver differing competitive implementations. In fact, individual routers along the traffic flow path may implement different algorithms for traffic control to serve the same traffic flow request; however, as long as the router delivers the defined service characteristics of the traffic flow request, the algorithm is acceptable. Two other working groups within the IETF define the acceptance tests and criteria for each class of service and adherence to proper controlled link sharing characteristics. The Benchmarking and Test Methodologies WG, co-chaired by Kevin Dubray and Guy Almes, focuses on the evaluation of a node in isolation, and the Real-Time Traffic Flow Measurement WG, co-chaired by Nevil Brownlee, Greg Ruth, and Sig Handelman, focuses on the evaluation of a flow traversing a series of nodes and issues regarding the interoperability of vendor implementations and multiple algorithms along a path. The reservation setup protocol is a method for establishing, maintaining, and forwarding authorized service requests end to end along the internetworking path and is currently the only module which must be standardized among all internetworking devices.

THE PACKET SCHEDULER

The packet scheduler module provides the necessary structure to manage the forwarding of different classes of packet streams onto an individual link, tasks that correspond to the data link layer of the OSI model. The packet scheduler must identify the correct class for each packet that must be sent over a specific link. All packets belonging to the same class must receive equal treatment, such as a class-oriented FIFO queue. The packet scheduling algorithm may be different for different types of link layers, such as Token Ring, PPP, ATM, and FDDI. The algorithm for a specific link layer type must accomplish the quality of service and controlled link sharing requirements of the integrated services framework and must adhere to the requirements of the specific link layer type, as specified by the Integrated Services over Specific Link Layers WG or other standards bodies, such as the IEEE and ITU.

Traffic policing is a function of the packet scheduler, since it involves the packet-by-packet enforcement of an established classification; however, the rules regarding when to perform traffic policing differ when servicing a controlled load data flow vs. a guaranteed service data flow. When servicing a controlled load data flow, no assumptions are made regarding the actions of upstream internetworking devices. Each node in the data flow must perform traffic policing of a controlled load data flow to ensure the flow conforms to the reserved traffic flow characteristics on the outbound link.

When servicing a guaranteed service data flow, traffic policing is only performed at the edge of the network to ensure that the source of a traffic flow does not violate the approved and reserved traffic flow characteristics. If a data flow must be policed, packets may be discarded at the edge of the network to bring the data flow into alignment with the data flow reservation. Packet scheduling inside the edge of the network for a specific data flow should not engage in traffic policing, since the data flow was policed at the edge of the network if necessary, and an approved reservation for the data flow has already been established. Traffic reshaping for a data flow may be performed by a packet scheduler, at nodes inside the edge of the network as necessary to restore the characteristics of a reservation. For example, the heterogeneity of a multicast distribution tree may have two sources sharing a reservation that branches at a node into a large and small outbound link reservation. The merging node may perform traffic reshaping on the outbound links to meet the traffic flow characteristics of each reservation.

Beyond traffic policing at the edge of the network, the issue of intelligent packet dropping when needed must be performed by the packet scheduler. During periods of resource scarcity, random packet dropping can have a negative effect on end-to-end performance and violate the bounded service parameters. Intelligent packet dropping can also be assisted by the multimedia application. For example, assume a B quality video session is a frame receive rate of 10 to 15 frames per second (FPS). An application may send the packets of every third frame as discardable if resource scarcity is encountered along the end-to-end path, thus increasing the chances that the minimum 10-FPS rate will be realized.

THE PACKET CLASSIFIER

The packet classifier is responsible for identifying the class of each inbound packet. All packets belonging to the same class will be provided equal service by the packet scheduler. It is important to realize that the packet classifier module, like the packet scheduler and admission control modules, functions as a unit only within a single router along the reservation path. Therefore, classification of traffic may vary per internetworking device along a reservation path. For example, a classification may be established for a video stream received at a router on the edge of an internetwork that corresponds to a single work station; however, the router on the internetwork backbone may establish a classification for all video stream packets transiting a backbone link, regardless of the source address.

Multiple methods are available for establishing packet classifications, each with its own benefits and drawbacks regarding scaling, impact on router performance, compatibility with existing protocols and applications, and integration into the current IP service model. Perhaps the most promising approach is the flow-id approach, already adopted by the IETF IPv6 WG, which should minimize packet classification latency.

ADMISSION CONTROL

The admission control module must determine if the received RSVP request for a new flow may be approved, based on the current subscription of the link and administratively defined policy. Administratively defined policy provides the necessary control and management of network resources. Integrated services without extensive policy controls would not provide the reliable and robust single internetwork infrastructure the Internet community requires. Lack of policy controls would lead to inappropriate reservations, idle reserved resources (bandwidth, buffers, and CPU), and large-scale denial of reservation requests. Administrative policies will allow the administrator of a link and associated internetworking devices to specify the user identity, application, scope of bandwidth request (token bucket size and quality of service), etc. An implementation of Internet drafts defining the extensions,[7] architecture,[10] and local policy management[11] to accomplish the admission control requirements will be discussed in the section on RSVP.

THE TRAFFIC ESTIMATOR

The interaction of the individual modules of traffic control within the router follows structured networking and programming guidelines, with each module performing specific services for the other modules and collectively accomplishing the overall service objective. Both the packet scheduler and admission control modules provide dynamic decisions on a continuous basis, regarding the proper queuing of outbound packets to meet all accepted service requests and the acceptance or denial of additional service requests, respectively. The source of the data required by these modules is not specifically defined in the integrated service framework document, although reference is made to the need for a traffic estimator function, slated to belong to the packet scheduling module. The traffic estimator will continually evaluate the success of the packet scheduling algorithm in servicing the accepted real-time traffic flows for all classes of service, the performance of nonreal-time traffic, and the proper allocation of excess bandwidth among all traffic according to the requirements of controlled link management. The output data from the traffic estimator would provide valuable input to multiple modules and network management requirements.

RSVP

The last element of the integrated services framework is the reservation setup protocol required to communicate and maintain traffic flow reservations. The RSVP protocol as defined in Reference 2 is designed to serve as the reservation setup protocol for the integrated services framework; however, RFC1633 defines the requirements for an integrated services setup protocol in general.[3] These requirements are listed below:

- Must serve a multicast environment.
- Must serve heterogeneous service requests.
- Must provide flexibility and control over the resource sharing among multicast branches.
- Must serve each sender/receiver independent of established multicast flows and vice versa.
- Must scale well to serve the needs of multicast group.
- Must provide advanced acceptance/rejection of reservation requests.

Resource Reservation Setup Protocol (RSVP), has been defined and is currently in draft form. The setup protocol is perhaps farther along the standards path than other elements of the integrated services model, with multiple vendors having implemented the draft and currently participating in interoperability tests. Since it does not appear that specific algorithms to serve the defined quality-of-services classes will be mandated, the setup protocol has been the most visible and end-to-end coordinated element of the integrated services framework.

The design elements implemented by RSVP to meet the defined setup protocol requirements are:

- All data streams or traffic flows are simplex, identified by the set (Destination IP Address, Protocol ID, Destination Port).
- Service of multicast and unicast traffic flows.
- Transport of flow specs containing the characteristics of the defined service classes.

- Definition of filter specs to classify packets which receive the services of a flow spec.
- Definition of reservation styles which may allow for the aggregation of flow specs within an internetworking device.
- A receiver initiated model.
- A soft-state, or connectionless, setup and maintenance reservation model.

Role of RSVP in the Framework

RSVP is a reservation signaling protocol which meets the framework requirements of the IETF Integrated Services WG. The purpose of RSVP is *not* to transport data, but only to establish and maintain administratively approved traffic flows. The protocol sits at the upper half of OSI layer 3, similar to ICMP, utilizing the services of IP and layer 3 routing protocols. RSVP sends raw IP datagrams as protocol ID 46. Additionally, RSVP does *not* provide quality of service; this function is performed by the elements of traffic control in an internetworking device, as discussed above.

RSVP does pass reservation requests (traffic flow descriptors generated by applications and end systems) and responses (determined by admission control modules) along an internetworking path (dictated by unicast/multicast routing protocols). The contents passed by RSVP are primarily opaque to the protocol, allowing additional quality-of-service classes, extensive administrative control options, and routing protocol enhancements to be implemented transparently to RSVP. RSVP may also operate transparently across a non-RSVP cloud, as RSVP packets are forwarded toward the destination IP address unchanged, until they reach the destination or another router which recognized the RSVP protocol ID (46). Additionally, RSVP may operate across tunnels established by an IP multicast routing protocol. For both cases, RSVP defines and utilizes a Logical Interface Handle (LIH) to identify the router and process packets received over the tunnel or on an unexpected interface.

FLOW DESCRIPTOR

RSVP messages carry the necessary information to establish a reservation between receivers and sources. The data which expresses the reservation parameters is called the flow descriptor, which is composed of two parts, the flow spec and the filter spec. The flow descriptor is opaque to RSVP, which means RSVP is not aware of or concerned with the contents of the flow descriptor. RSVP simply transports the data and hands the data to other modules within the internetworking device for processing. This property allows new and additional information to be added to the flow descriptor without having to update the RSVP protocol.

Flow Spec. This data generally serves the needs of the packet scheduler in the internetworking device, which must supply and enforce the quality-of-service parameters established for the data flow.

Filter Spec. This data generally serves the needs of the packet classifier in the internetworking device, describing how to identify to which packets the flow spec applies.

The next generation of IP, IPv6, has integrated the flow characteristic of the next Internet architecture paradigm into the protocol header. Most likely, the integrated services flow descriptor will be mapped into the IPv6 Flow Label for efficient forwarding of IPv6 flow-oriented datagrams.

RESERVATION STYLES

RSVP has defined three reservation styles that define the treatment of traffic flows with different senders for the same session. How are the reservations to be merged and bandwidth conserved where appropriate, yet still provide all receivers the requested quality of service? The three reservation styles are as follows:

Wildcard Filter. This filter allows a single reservation to be shared by the flows from all upstream senders. The reservation must meet the requirements of the largest set of resources required by all receivers.

Fixed Filter. This filter provides an individual reservation for a data flow from an individual sender. The filter may supply a specific list of IP source addresses which may use the established reservation. This filter serves applications that require multiple simultaneous senders, each requiring an individual, possibly varying, flow spec, such as a many-to-many videoconference.

Dynamic Filter (also referred to as Shared Explicit). This filter creates a single reservation which may be shared by a list of upstream senders. This filter is an extension of the Wildcard Filter, except the receiver may specify the set of senders that 'may utilize the single reservation. The Wildcard and Dynamic filters are appropriate for nonsimultaneous multicast applications, such as audio conferencing.

Each filter type is mutually exclusive and can only be merged with similar filter types as the flow descriptor is propagated upstream.

RSVP MESSAGES

The RSVP protocol has intentionally kept the protocol complexity to a minimum and has only defined seven packet types. These packets are described below, with the constraint that no packet may exceed a maximum size of 64K and may be fragmented by IP as needed.

The following object types are required in every RSVP message:

- **SESSION.** Contains the IP destination address, protocol ID, and destination port, which collectively define a specific session.
- **TIME_VALUES.** Contains the Refresh period used by the message creator and indicates to the receiver how often new messages should be expected. This value may differ for each sender on each link.

Other common object types are:

- **INTEGRITY.** Contains cryptographic data to identify the originating node and protect the contents of the RSVP message, described in Reference 14.
- **RSVP_HOP.** Contains the IP interface address (or LIH) of the RSVP-capable node which sent the message. NHOP refers to the next hop upstream device and PHOP refers to the next hop downstream device.
- **POLICY_DATA.** Contains data the local policy module may use to determine if the reservation is authorized.
- **SCOPE.** Contains an explicit list of senders to which this message must be forwarded.

MESSAGES GENERATED BY THE SENDER

- Path Message (Path)
  - Initiated periodically by senders to inform receivers of session availability and application data flow requirements.
  - Initiated by senders along multicast IP destination address along multicast tree or to unicast IP destination address along unicast routing path, both of which follow the same path as the data will follow to ensure the proper reservation path is established.
  - Must contain a SENDER_TEMPLATE object which provides the filter spec, passed unmodified to the destination.
  - Must contain a SENDER_TSPEC object which provides the flow spec required by the sending application, passed unmodified to the destination.
  - Must contain an RSVP_HOP object.
  - May optionally contain an AdSpec object which defines the true flow spec provided the receiver along the reservation path. This object, originally defined in Reference 16, implements the One-Pass With Advertisement (OPWA) reservation mechanism.
  - May optionally contain INTEGRITY and POLICY_DATA objects.

- Path Teardown Message (PathTear)
  - Initiated by sources or intermediate systems in the reservation path for a session.
  - Initiated in response to the expiration of a Lifetime Timer or closure of a source application.

— Must be sent with the Router Alert Option set, as defined in Reference 13.
— Must match the SESSION, SENDER_TEMPLATE, and RSVP_HOP objects of a previously received Path Message.
— May optionally contain an INTEGRITY object.
— Internetworking devices must make the proper adjustments to existing reservations and continue to meet existing service obligations.

- Path Error Message (PathErr)
  — Initiated by intermediate systems in the path, indicating an error in processing a Path message.
  — Messages are forwarded upstream toward the sender and do not impact any RSVP node through which it passes.
  — Must contain an RSVP_HOP object.
  — Must contain an ERROR_SPEC object, specifying the defined error and the IP address of the node declaring the error.
  — May optionally contain INTEGRITY and POLICY_DATA objects.

MESSAGES GENERATED BY THE RECEIVER

- Reservation Message (Resv)
  — Initiated by receivers in response to a received Path message (or out-of-band method), if the user desires to initiate the session.
  — Message flows upstream toward senders along the reverse multicast tree or unicast data flow path for the session, carrying the parameters of the reservation request.
  — Message will setup, modify, and maintain a reservation.
  — Must contain a STYLE object containing the flow spec and filter spec for the session.
  — May optionally contain the RESV_CONFIRM object which requests a reservation confirmation to the supplied IP address.
  — May optionally contain SCOPE and POLICY_DATA objects.

- Reservation Teardown Message (ResvTear)
  — Initiated by receivers or any intermediate system in the reservation path for a session.
  — Initiated in response to the expiration of a Lifetime Timer or closure of a receiving application.
  — Must match the SESSION, STYLE, FILTER_SPEC, and RSVP_HOP objects of a previously received Resv message.
  — Must contain STYLE and RSVP_HOP objects.
  — May optionally contain INTEGRITY and SCOPE objects.
  — Internetworking devices must make the proper adjustments to existing reservations and continue to meet existing service obligations.

- Reservation Error Message — ResvErr
  - Initiated by intermediate systems in the reservation path, indicating an error in processing a Resv message.
  - Messages are forwarded downstream toward a receiver and do not impact any RSVP node through which it passes.
  - Must contain an RSVP_HOP object.
  - Must contain an ERROR_SPEC object, specifying the defined error and the IP address of the node declaring the error.
  - May optionally contain INTEGRITY, SCOPE, STYLE, and POLICY_DATA objects.

- Reservation Confirmation Message (ResvConf)
  - Initiated by intermediate nodes in response to the presence of the RESV_CONFIRM object in an Resv message.
  - May optionally contain INTEGRITY, ERROR_SPEC, RESV_CONFIRM, and STYLE objects.
  - Message is sent to the unicast address of the receiver.
  - Must be sent with the Router Alert option set, as defined in Reference 13.

Receipt of this message by a receiver is not a guarantee of a successful end-to-end reservation. If the receiver's flowspec is merged with a larger flowspec upstream, the router performing the merge will initiate a Resv-Conf message, even if the reservation is still in the process of being established. A receiver must await the reception of a Path message with the AdSpec object to make positive determination regarding the existence and characteristics of the upstream path.

THE RESERVATION PROCESS

The reservation process includes a coordinated effort among the host multicast registration protocol IGMP, multicast or unicast IP routing protocols, and source applications. The steps in the reservation process are listed below, along with the details regarding each step in the process.

1. A receiver determines the need to establish an RSVP data flow

A sender sends RSVP Path messages for an application service.

The receiver may determine the need to establish an RSVP data flow either by:

- Joining a published, well-known, or agreed-upon multicast group (a 32-bit IP destination address in the range 224.0.0.0 to 239.255.255.255).
- Based on information received from the source, through a unicast message.

The sender may send RSVP Path messages to the multicast group over which it plans to deliver a service at any time, regardless of whether any receivers are available to receive the service. The mechanisms of IP multicast routing protocols ensure that packets destined for a multicast group with no listeners do not propagate any further in a network than necessary; all branches of an IP multicast tree with zero listeners will be pruned from the distribution tree. A multicast group with zero listeners will be dropped at the first router to which the sender is connected.

As Path messages flow downstream (either across a multicast tree or based on unicast routing to a destination), the router stores the flow identification parameters (IP destination address, protocol ID, port number) to match with future Resv messages.

2. A receiver receives RSVP Path messages

A receiver processes Path messages and presents the session and the sending application's suggested quality-of-service parameters to the user. The user may optionally decide to access the application with quality-of-service parameters less than the suggested parameters, understanding that the application may not perform as well.

3. A receiver sends an RSVP Resv message describing the desired flow

An Resv message traverses the data path in reverse, establishing the reservation as it travels upstream. Each router matches the flow identification parameters (IP destination address, protocol ID, port number) with the parameters saved in the router from Path messages which have flowed downstream.

At each internetworking device, the reservation request is submitted by RSVP to the Admission Control module, which must make two determinations:

- Is the requester authorized to make the reservation?
- Does the required upstream link layer (determined by the routing protocol) have the necessary capacity to provide the requested service without impacting existing reservations?

Traffic control may modify the flow description at this point and hand the modified data to RSVP for transmission upstream. The traffic control module may merge elements of the flow description according to the guidelines in Reference 1.

Traffic control must avoid approving traffic flows or merging flow descriptions that result in a "killer reservation." A new flow:

- Must allow existing reservations to remain in place (i.e., approval of Flow2 cannot displace existing Flow1).

- The constraining element of a merged flow (element preventing a successful reservation) must be dropped to allow less binding element to succeed (i.e., Flow1 must not be merged with Flow2, if Flow1 would succeed if not merged with Flow2, and Flow2 is preventing the combined flows from succeeding).

4. A sender receives the RSVP message and sends data

As soon as the sender receives the Resv message indicating at least one receiver with an established reservation is prepared to receive the data stream, the sender may begin transmitting data with the proper flow identification.

SOFT-STATE

End-to-end sessions may be established by either maintaining no-state, soft-state, or hard-state in the internetworking nodes. The current Internet architecture paradigm maintains no-state in routers regarding end-to-end data flows. Each packet is an individual unit, not a part of any group or unit. However, a new Internet architecture paradigm constructed to serve the quality needs of individual data flows will not be able to maintain no-state in the routers.

The soft-state, connectionless approach provides a list of benefits that maintain the original Internet architecture paradigm. Soft-state mechanisms may utilize unreliable datagrams for state construction and maintenance, with a timer to provide robustness. Reservation modifications, or updates, continue upstream only as far as an adjustment to the reservation is needed, providing conservation of process.

The alternative to soft-state is hard-state, in which an end-to-end connection-oriented overlay is created across the network infrastructure, similar to an end-to-end virtual circuit (VC). Two properties of a connection-oriented state mechanism which violate the original Internet architecture paradigm are that all communications must be reliable and an end-to-end keep-alive mechanism must utilized.

RSVP has adopted the soft-state approach which provides the necessary services to the new Internet architecture paradigm but minimizes divergence from the original architecture paradigm. The RSVP soft-state approach does include a timer mechanism for reservation refresh and link teardown. The use of a teardown timer can lead to a reservation blocking state, as resources are maintained in an internetworking device waiting for a reservation to expire, as described by D. Mitzel.[17] However, as recommended by Mitzel, RSVP does include an explicit reservation teardown message to avoid this common cause of a reservation blocking state. The only time a teardown timer should expire is due to the failure of a link or internetworking device along the reservation path.

The two timers established by the RSVP WG are the Refresh timer and the Lifetime timer. The current Internet draft recommends a refresh timer of 30 seconds, implemented as a bounded, randomized timer value of 0.5×30 s to 1.5×30 seconds, for an effective timer range between 15 and 45 seconds. The recommended value for the Lifetime timer is three times the Refresh timer, or 90 seconds.

RESERVATION MECHANISMS

There are two primary approaches for end-to-end session establishment, one-pass and two-pass. One-pass mechanisms generally lend themselves well to soft-state protocols, work well for multicasting (generally seen as necessary for distribution of scaleable multimedia applications), and provide the reservation protocol idempotent qualities. An idempotent protocol mechanism is one in which the router reacts the same when processing new and updated messages. A drawback to a one-pass reservation mechanism is that the application is never provided feedback information regarding the true service being provided the data flow; therefore, the true end-to-end quality of service is never determined.

Two-pass mechanisms have different characteristics than one-pass mechanisms. Although the receiver has no information regarding the quality of service that can be provided by the internetwork prior to session establishment, an indication of how the reservation path was modified and the true end-to-end quality of service provided by the internetwork is provided by the reply. Two-pass mechanisms, however, are not idempotent (i.e., compatible with soft-state) and do not merge traffic specifications well or dynamically, both key elements of the integrated services framework.

Early versions of the RSVP framework implemented a one-pass reservation mechanism which constructed a link-by-link reservation with no end-to-end performance feedback; however, based on research papers, such as Reference 16, the RSVP WG adopted a mechanism known as one-pass with advertisement. As the name implies, this is an extension of the one-pass mechanism, where the receiver is provided feedback data regarding the end-to-end performance of the reservation path. This quality is implemented via the optional AdSpec object of the Path message. The sender generates the AdSpec object and sends the Path message. At each router, the AdSpec is passed to the traffic control module, which modifies the AdSpec based on the characteristics of the reservation for this session and returns the updated AdSpec to RSVP for propagation downstream, as described in Reference 1. This information allows the receiving application to determine end-to-end quality of service received for a specific quality-of-service request (as a function of the sum of the quality of service provided by each link in the reservation path). The receiving application can then make cost-performance decisions, possibly from multiple quality-of-service options offered by the routing protocol or source application.

RSVP ADMINISTRATIVE POLICY AND SECURITY

The RSVP WG realized that without well-established, flexible, and enforceable administrative policy regarding the use of internetwork resources, RSVP could quickly become more of a hindrance than an asset for meeting the growing internetwork demands. Based on the Internet drafts defining the extensions,[7] architecture,[10] and local policy management,[11] a functional protocol has been defined to meet the administrative policy needs of RSVP. Open Outsourcing Policy Service (OOPS)[15] defines a transaction protocol supporting a wide range of router configurations, RSVP implementations, local policy approaches, and administrative control needs.

OOPS allows a broad range of administrative control options regarding preferential access to network resources. The protocol exchanges policy information via a TCP connection and allows distributed decision authority between RSVP-capable routers and policy servers. OOPS uses an asymmetric client/server architecture which allows new policy elements to be added to the policy server without modification to the router platform and vice versa. OOPS allows for a flexible division of administrative responsibilities between the router and policy server. For example, some POLICY_DATA elements recognized by the router may be processed locally on the router, while unrecognized and other POLICY_DATA elements are sent to the policy server for processing. The determination regarding which POLICY_DATA elements will be handled by each is determined during TCP connection establishment.

The security needs of the RSVP protocol and reserved data flows have been identified by the RSVP WG as follows:

Need for Message Integrity and Node Identification. RSVP uses the INTEGRITY object, which may optionally appear in any RSVP message and uses a keyed cryptographic digest approach, requiring RSVP neighbors to share a secret key.[14] This approach further drives the need for a network infrastructure key distribution and management protocol.

Need for User Authentication. Provided by the POLICY_DATA object described above.

Need for Secure Data Streams. Once the reservation has been securely established and authorized utilizing the services of the two items listed above, the data stream itself needs to be addressed. Although the datagrams are IP packets, IP Security (IPSEC) encrypts the header of the transport layer,

Exhibit 5. IP Multicast Routing Protocols

DVMRP	Distance Vector Multicast Routing Protocol (RFC 1075)
MOSPF	Multicast Open Shortest Path First (RFC 1584)
PIM	Protocol Independent Multicasting (RFC 2117) <draft-ietf-idmr-pim-dm-spec-05.txt>
CBT	Core Based Tree < draft-ietf-idmr-cbt-spec-09.txt>

which therefore hides the port number used by RSVP to identify unique data flow sessions. In this case, the IP Security Association Identifier[18] may be used as a substitute for the port number.

ROUTING AND MULTICASTING

Integrated services is primarily driven by applications which distribute information in a one-to-many or many-to-many fashion. In order to distribute this information, routing protocols which serve this distribution need must be used; these protocols are referred to as IP multicast routing protocols. The IETF has defined a number of IP multicast routing protocols, as listed in Exhibit 5.

The Mbone was constructed utilizing DVMRP and is the most widely deployed IP multicast routing protocol. However, MOSPF is the only IP multicast routing protocol which is an extension of an IP unicast routing protocol and may provide better scaling properties for internetworking devices. Additionally, the OSPF WG has already seen a draft for providing quality-of-service extensions to the protocol.[12]

RSVP is intentionally independent of the IP routing protocol and requires the routing protocol provide the following services:

- Determine a path with RSVP capable routers.
- Determine a path with available resource to meet the reservation request.
- Adapt to a network link or node failure.
- Adapt to a network change resulting in a different path for an established reservation.

An additional service the RSVP WG has identified which the RSVP protocol should receive from the routing protocol is notification to RSVP by the routing protocol of a path change in the network. This service is termed local repair and allows RSVP to quickly attempt to establish the required reservation across the new path, before the timers have expired along the existing path.

Members of the IETF have recognized the fact that none of the current protocol efforts addresses the needs of RSVP and the integrated services model. An initial Internet draft has been compiled[19] which identifies the issues that need to be addressed for quality-of-service-based routing and defines a framework for the process of addressing the issues.

The draft identifies quality-of-service routing as the ability to route reservations based on knowledge of internetwork resource availability and application quality-of-service requirements. Such routing services need to dynamically determine one or multiple feasible paths, within policy constraints, which optimize internetwork resource usage for efficient network engineering and may provide graceful degradation of internetwork performance. In order to accomplish such adaptive, network-state-dependent routing, the routing protocol must be able to measure and gather network state information, and compute routes based on this information and administrative policy requirements. The process of establishing quality-of-service routing must address a whole new set of questions, including:

- How do routers dynamically and periodically determine and report the quality-of-service capability of each outbound link?
- What set of routing metrics are needed to serve the existing and future defined quality-of-service classes?
- How will quality-of-service paths compute multicast flow that serve multiple reservation styles and the heterogeneity of receivers?
- How will such a quality-of-service multicast routing protocol scale?
- How will the internetwork be managed to provide stable, controlled, and verified integrated services?

CONCLUSION

Current Research on RSVP

Although the core documents for RSVP have been ratified as Internet RFCs,[1-4] there are still many areas of ongoing research regarding all the components needed for full-scale deployment of RSVP and the integration of RSVP with current and developing protocols (such as RSVP over ATM[20] and MPLS[21]).

Differentiated Services

During the development of RSVP, many groups in the Internet community began to feel that an end-to-end resource reservation protocol which tracks, maintains, and enforces the flow specifications of individual application flows would not scale when deployed in the global Internet. Although RSVP may be deployed incrementally, RSVP requires changes to almost all internetworking components, end systems, and the provider billing infrastructure before it may be utilized. In an effort to address these technical, delivery, and business issues, the IETF has chartered the Differentiated Services WG. At the time of this writing, the charter of the Differentiated Services WG is still being defined. The objective of the group is to identify and standardize a packet marking and drop preference mechanism which may be quickly deployed in a subset of internetworking devices and allow Internet service providers to offer various grades of best-effort service to their customers which may be communicated and reconciled across service provider boundaries.

Differentiated services will clearly play a large role in the delivery of service quality in the Internet. The direction of the Internet community will mature over the next few months to such a level that they may be covered in the next edition of this publication.

Moving to an Integrated Services Internet

The migration of the current Internet architecture to the integrated services model, including the completion and implementation of specific link layer standards, should be accomplished within the next 5 years. The architecture of RSVP allows for a partial and incremental deployment of RSVP into the current Internet, an approach successfully demonstrated by the growth of the Mbone and IP multicasting routing protocols. RSVP allows for data to traverse non-RSVP clouds or establish tunnels between RSVP clouds.

The road for upgrading the Internet to the integrated services model involves formalizing the extension of the Internet service model, modifying the services provided by internetworking devices and service providers, and establishing an end-to-end reservation protocol, integrated with quality-of-service-capable unicast and multicast routing protocols. The effort to define the needed standards, algorithms, and performance requirements will be the continuing effort of many working groups within the IETF and other standards bodies.

References

1. A. Mankin et al., Internet Draft, March 1997, <draft-ietf- intserv-rsvp-use-02.txt>.
2. B. Braden et al., Internet Draft, June 1997, <draft-ietf-rsvp-spec-16.ps>.
3. B. Braden, D. Clark, S. Shenker, RFC 1633 Integrated Services in the Internet Architecture: An Overview, June 1994.
4. J. Krawczyk, Internet Draft, March 1997, <draft-ietf-rsvp-tunnels-interop-00.txt>.
5. J. Wroclawski, Internet Draft, May 1997, <draft-ietf-intserv-ctrl-load-svc-05.txt>.
6. L. Breslau, S. Shenker, Internet Draft, April 1997, <draft-ietf-rsvp-partial-service-00.txt>.
7. S. Herzog, Internet Draft, April 1997, <draft-ietf-rsvp-policy-ext-02.txt>.
8. S. Shenker, C. Partridge, R. Guerin, Internet Draft, February 1997, <draft-ietf-intserv-guaranteed-svc-07.txt>.
9. G. Gilder, "The Coming of the Fibersphere," *Forbes ASAP,* December 7, 1992.
10. S. Herzog, Internet Draft, November 1996, <draft-ietf-rsvp-policy-arch-01.txt>.
11. S. Herzog, Internet Draft, April 1997, <draft-ietf-rsvp-policy-lpm-01.txt>.
12. Z. Zhang et al., Internet Draft, June 1996, <draft-zhang-qos-ospf-00.txt>.
13. D. Katz, RFC 2113 IP Router Alert Option, February 1997.
14. F. Baker, Internet Draft, June 1996, <draft-ietf-rsvp-md5-02.txt>.
15. S. Herzog et al., Internet Draft, April 1997, <draft-ietf-rsvp-policy-oops-00.ps>.

16. S. Shenker, L. Breslau, "Two Issues in Reservation Establishment," Xerox Corporation.
17. D. Mitzel et al., "A Study of Reservation Dynamics in Integrated Services Packet Networks."
18. L. Berger, T. O'Malley, Internet Draft, March 1997, <draft-ietf-rsvp-ext-07.txt>.
19. E. Crawley et al., Internet Draft, March 1996, <draft-ietf-qosr-framework-00.txt>.
20. E. Crawley et al., Internet Draft, <draft-crawley-rsvp-over-atm-00.txt>.
21. B. Davie et al., Internet Draft, <draft-ietf-mpls-rsvp-00.txt>.

Chapter 18
T1, T3, and SONET Networks

Roohollah Hajbandeh

Broadband networks are configured through the use of several types of digital communications links. The most common of these, which have been in use by communications carriers for approximately 20 years and available to users for approximately a decade, are T1 and T3 links. These will be superseded eventually by the synchronous optical network (SONET), a set of standards for broadband networks that operate over fiber-optic links and that will provide more versatile bandwidth to both carriers and users.

T1 NETWORKS

T1 is a digital communications system for simultaneously transmitting 24 voice, data, and video signals over the same circuit. The original users of T1 were telephone companies and government agencies. Because each T1 is equivalent to 24 voicegrade circuits, the telephone companies' savings from using T1 were substantial. At first the cost of T1 to end users was prohibitive; since T1 services were tariffed during the 1980s, however, competition among major carriers has brought the prices down significantly. In addition, at first the need for higher bandwidth and additional services and capabilities increased the demand for T1 circuits such that the waiting time for installation was several months.

Advantages of T1

Each T1 is equivalent to 24 separate circuits between two sites, an advantage for T1 because multiple lines and multiple-site networks are expensive and hard to manage. The end-user equipment at each site can be PBXs, videoconferencing systems, imaging systems, or host computers. T1s connecting two PBXs are called tie trunks. For some old PBXs that cannot directly receive a T1 signal, a T1 line must first be terminated at a channel bank.

0-8493-9949-1/99/$0.00+$.50
© 1999 by CRC Press LLC

Analog lines are subject to noise and signal deterioration, and equipment that is used for reconstructing the analog signal cannot make them suitable for data transmission, because analog lines amplify both original signal and noise. T1 circuits are more immune to noise and distortion than multiple lines. T1 signals can also be corrupted, but because they are digital, processing will regenerate the original signal without amplifying the noise.

User-to-Network Access

Because T1s are dedicated point-to-point circuits, each customer pays a fixed rate for that service. The T1 charges depend on the distance between the two locations and each location's distance to the carrier's closest point of presence or local central office. However, the closest connection may not be the least expensive one. Recently, interexchange carriers have started offering switched T1 services. With switched T1, customers pay for the portion of bandwidth they use. In either case, the connection between the customer's site and the closest central office is a dedicated circuit and has a fixed cost. U.S. telephone serving areas are divided into about 200 local access and transport areas (LATAs). A LATA can include part or all of one state. The transmission between LATAs is done by long-distance or interexchange carriers even if both LATAs are part of the same local exchange carrier's serving area, so a T1 circuit may involve more than the local exchange carrier.

T1 Functional Elements

Channel Service Unit. The channel service unit is the first interface between the user and the network and the last regeneration point for the incoming signal before it is delivered to customer premises equipment. (In the past, channel service units were part of the network, but now they also are considered as customer premises equipment.) The channel service unit is responsible for general line monitoring functions, discussed later in this chapter. If a T1 multiplexer or piece of customer premises equipment fails, the channel service unit sends streams of 1s to the network to keep the connection alive until the customer premises equipment recovers. Some T1 multiplexers and PBXs have built-in channel service units.

Current intelligent channel service units provide, by supporting the extended superframe format, sophisticated line monitoring and diagnostic capabilities. Basic channel service units have limited diagnostic and monitoring capabilities. If the long-distance carrier provides T1 service in the extended superframe format, the channel service unit should also support it. FCC Part 68 local tariffs require that each T1 be terminated on a channel service unit. Channel service units are also responsible for:

- Protecting the network from the surge of a long stream of 0s.
- Signal monitoring.
- Interfacing with remote network testing equipment.
- The loop back to the network, which is also used for testing and monitoring.

Digital Service Unit. Digital service units are for digital circuits what modems are for analog circuits. The analog line transmission rate is limited to 19.2K bps, but digital service units can accept a full T1 rate (i.e., 1.544M bps). Channel service units and digital service units functions may be combined into a single unit or both can be built into terminal equipment. The physical interface between carrier and user equipment is through an RJ-48C or a DB-15 connector.

Channel Banks. Channel banks are a special kind of T1 multiplexer. The main function of channel banks is to convert analog voice signals into digital signals and combine the digital signals from 24 channels into a single channel. A basic channel bank multiplexes voice and data, but it is not software driven, and to reconfigure it the unit must be physically rewired. An intelligent channel bank is software driven and can be reconfigured through a local or remote terminal. Not all channel banks are compatible with all long-distance carriers, nor are all PBXs compatible with the T1 services of all carriers. Some channel banks can interface only with standard services and not with such advanced services as MEGACOM and MEGA-COM 800.

Digital Access and Cross Connect System. The digital access and cross connect system (DACS) is used for multiplexing and routing T1s at the central office switch. The routing is done at both full T1 and individual circuit levels. Newer DACS route services such as MEGACOM, MEGACOM 800, Accunet, ISDN H channels, fractional T1, and T1. The more advanced DACSs are software driven and can be accessed and controlled by customers. Usually, they are designed to accommodate at least 64 incoming and 64 outgoing T1s.

Regenerators/Repeaters. Voice traffic signals are converted into 0- and 1-bit streams and are formatted in a specific order. During transmission the original data mixes with line noise (which depends on wire material and environmental factors such as temperature and electromagnetic fields), but because the noise signal does not follow any particular format it is distinguishable from the original data. Regenerators/repeaters retrieve data and discard the noise. Usually, one regenerator/repeater is required for every 6,000 feet of cable.

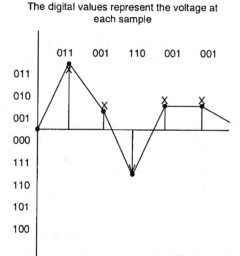

Exhibit 1.   Analog-to-Digital Conversion

T1 Integration of Voice and Data

The main advantage of T1 is that voice and data can be simultaneously transmitted over the same line. This is done by digitizing the voice signals using a digitizing process called pulse code modulation (PCM) (see Exhibit 1). For a human speaking voice to be audible the upper frequency is about 3,500 Hz. To maintain the integrity of an analog signal after digitizing it must be scanned at at least twice its upper frequency. Therefore, a voice signal is scanned 8,000 times per second. Each scanned segment is called a pulse.

Based on the amplitude or the height of each pulse, it is assigned an equivalent 8-bit binary value. In the absence of a signal, a value of 0 is assigned. The total rate of each channel on a T1 link is derived by multiplying samples per second by the number of bits in each sample (i.e., 8,000 samples × 8 bits per sample = 64,000 bps).

Voice frequencies that are substantially above 3,500 Hz are filtered out; otherwise, they create noise on the line. Filtering adversely affects the adjacent frequencies. As a result the effective frequencies scanned are between 300 and 3,300 Hz.

Variations of PCM

Vector Quantizing Code. Vector quantizing code reduces the bandwidth required for a voice channel from 64K bps to 16K bps. Voice transmission quality is lowered but is acceptable in some applications. After the voice signal is scanned, 0s and 1s are grouped together and form strings, or vectors. A vector is compared with a set of vectors stored in the system's lookup table. When the closest match to its bit pattern is found, a shorter code signifying that vector is transmitted. At the receiving side, the shorter code is replaced with the string of 0s and 1s it represents.

Differential Pulse Code Modulation. Differential pulse code modulation (DPCM) uses 4 bits per sample, instead of 8. This technique requires less bandwidth for transmitting voice signals. DPCM is suitable when there is not much variation in volume from one sample to another. Otherwise, it cannot accurately reproduce the original voice signal.

Adaptive Differential Pulse Code Modulation. Several proprietary adaptive differential pulse code modulation (ADPCM) techniques and the standard CCITT G.721 version are in use. ADPCM's scanning rate is 8,000 times per second, but there are 4 bits per sample. By assigning a different significance to each of the 4 bits, ADPCM can produce as true a representation of voice signals as PCM does.

Continuously Variable Slope Delta Modulation. Continuously variable slope delta modulation (CVSD) uses a 1-bit word per sample. A 1 bit indicates the presence of a signal but gives no indication of the signal's strength. The sample represents the slope or variation in slope of the curve. (The slope is the rate of change in height divided by the rate of change in run.) Before transmission, slopes are compared with the reference values in a lookup table. If the slope is greater than the reference value, a 1 is transmitted. If the slope is less than the reference value, a 0 is transmitted. A rising curve is presented by a series of 1s. The receiver functions in reverse and reconstructs an approximation of the original curve. CVSD reduces the bandwidth required for a voice channel to 32K bps.

The availability of several PCM techniques has created many incompatibility problems, and the T1 equipment using the ADPCM technique cannot be directly connected to a central office that only uses PCM.

AMI and Bipolar with 8-Zero Substitution. In a binary format, a 1 value (i.e., a pulse) is represented by a square wave and a 0 value (i.e., the absence of a pulse) by a straight line (see Exhibit 2). To change from +1 to −1 the wave must take the value of zero first. In a proper T1 signal, the value of two consecutive pulses alternate between positive and negative, a scheme known as alternate mark inversion (AMI) (see Exhibit 2). Two or more consecutive pulses of the same polarity (known as a bipolar violation) is an indication that the incoming data is corrupted or that there is noise on the line. The timing for scanning the voice signal is derived from pulses received by the end user equipment. A long stream of 0s causes the scanning process to lose its synchronization. Different applications have

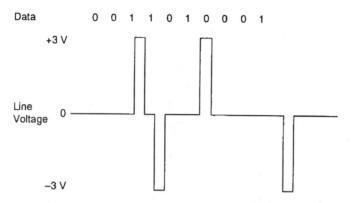

Exhibit 2. Alternate Mark Inversion and Bipolar Signal Format on a T1 Line

different tolerances for violations of the 1s density rule. Generally, if the number of consecutive 0s exceeds seven, the time-keeping and operation of regenerators/repeaters is disrupted. To allow a legitimate long stream of 0 bits (i.e., a stream that represents valid data), the bipolar eight-zero substitution (B8ZS) technique is used. B8ZS inserts additional 1s into the data stream at the eighth bit and bipolar variation indicators. At the receiving end the additional 1s are discarded and the original data is regenerated.

Time Division Multiplexing

PCM is for voice traffic only. To transmit over a single T1 link, the combined bit streams generated from PCM and other sources of data are multiplexed (i.e., combined). Multiplexing is done by sequentially accepting data from each of the 24 time slots on the T1 link, allowing the transmission of 8 bits of data onto each time slot. If a channel is idle and has no data to transmit, the time slot will be wasted. By definition, one frame of data consists of 24 8-bit words, or 192 bits. At the end of every 192 bits, a 1 bit is inserted to separate one frame from the other.

The T1 bandwidth works out as follows:

(24×8) information bits per frame + 1 framing bit = 193 bits per frame. 193 bits per frame $\times$ 8000 samples per second = 1,544,000 bps.

Because of variations in scanning rate, the 1,544,000 bps rate varies by ±50 bps.

D4 Framing

Each of the 24 T1 channels is assigned an 8-bit time slot, and the channels are numbered in the same sequence that their data appears on the bit stream. To separate one frame from the next, one bit (called the F bit) is inserted at the end of each frame. The values given to the F bits for the first 12 frames are 100011011100, and the same sequence is repeated for the next 12 frames. Separation of frames with the 193rd bit is called frame level synchronization, or D4 framing. To identify the start of each T1 frame, the receiver postulates the beginning of a frame to be at point X. If after 192 bits another framing bit is found and the above sequence is repeated, the receiver knows that point X is the beginning of the frame. If not, the system tries $X + 1$ as the beginning of the frame. This process is repeated until the beginning of the frame is located. This method, which is the simplest form of T1 service, uses 8,000 bps of the available bandwidth and has limited monitoring and network management capabilities. To test or monitor a T1 with D4 framing, the network should be temporarily taken out of service.

To use some of the overhead bits for network management capabilities, 12 individual frames can share the same signaling information bit. For 12 frames to share the same signaling bit, D4 framing uses a process called robbed bit signaling, and the summation of 12 frames is also called superframe. In a superframe, the sequence 10001 1 01 1 100 is repeated in the first 12 frames. The overhead bits freed by this process can be used for test and monitoring, allowing out-of-band signaling and monitoring of a T1 circuit without bringing the circuit down. To allow more network management capabilities, extended superframe is created. With extended superframe only every fourth frame (frame 4, 8, ... ,24) carries the synchronization bit and the 001011 sequence is used. This reduces the overhead from 8,000 bps to 2,000 bps. Of the remaining 6,000 bps, 2,000 bps is used for error checking and 4,000 bps for monitoring the line condition. The channel used for monitoring and testing is called the facility data link. The facility data link also provides the following information:

- *Errored seconds.* The number of seconds that contain one error.
- *Bursty seconds.* The number of seconds that contain 2 to 319 errors.
- *Severely errored seconds.* The number of seconds that contain 320 or more errors. That is equivalent to 96% of frames having at least one error.
- *Failed seconds.* The number of seconds in which the error rate was so high that the link had to be taken down.

Compatibility Issues

For a T1 circuit to be compatible with a public network, its bit stream must have the following characteristics:

- If the channel service unit and central office use different PCM techniques, a conversion must be made between them.

- A framing bit is inserted after every 192 bits. If the public network uses the extended superframe format, the customer premises equipment (i.e., the channel service unit, channel bank) should also support it.
- The 24 channels are numbered sequentially, 1 to 24.
- B8ZS and alternate mark inversion techniques are used.

Means of Transmission

Transmission of T1 signals can be by copper wire, microwave, satellite, or fiber-optic networks. Because transmission is handled by the telephone companies, users might not have a choice, but they should be aware that each medium has its advantages and limitations. Terrestrial networks have shorter delays than satellite channels, but they are subject to service interruption. Generally, for distances longer than 500 miles, satellite rates are lower than other alternatives, but each round trip introduces an additional 0.5-second delay. If the transmitting and receiving devices are not configured to accommodate the delay, data transmission is disrupted. Terrestrial wiring can be twisted-pair or coaxial cable. Over copper wire, repeaters/regenerators are placed at each mile interval. Error rates on fiber networks are much lower, and transmission of data over distances to 25 miles without repeaters is possible. Microwave networks are more immune to noise and do not have cable breaks (e.g., by backhoes) and do not need as many repeaters as terrestrial cables, but they are less secure.

Fractional T1

When the cost of a full T1 circuit is not justified, customers can subscribe to fractional T1 or to as many DS-0 channels as they need. Once a fractional T1 is terminated on customer premises it can be broken down into smaller subrates. But there is a limit on how the bandwidth can be subdivided. If the rates required are 9.6K, 4.8K, 2.4K, and 1.2K bps, the DS-0 is divided into multiples of the highest rate, 9.6K bps in this case; the bandwidth assigned to lower rate devices is not fully used. Generally, if customers need more than five or six DS-0s between two points, it is more cost effective to subscribe to a full T1. Usually, the DS-0s of a fractional T1 circuit are channelized and not contiguous. For example, by subscribing to two DS-0 channels, customers have access to two separate channels of 64K bps each and not a single 128K-bps channel. To bundle a number of DS-0s together, a customer has to subscribe to the ISDN primary rate interface (PRI) and have an ISDN-compatible device on the customer premises. Fractional T1 is available with 56K and 64K-bps channels. Some carriers charge extra for providing clear 64K-bps channels.

Cost-Justifying a T1 Circuit

The following factors should be considered in justifying a dedicated T1 link vs. switched access:

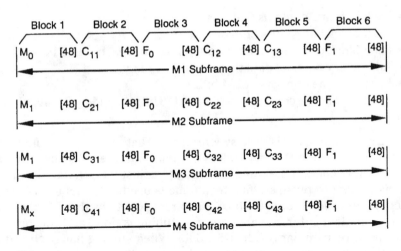

Notes:
$M_0 M_1 M_1 M_x$ is the multiframe alignment signal. $M_0 = 0$, $M_1 = 1$, and M_x may be a 0 or a 1.
$C_{11} C_{12} C_{13}$ = stuffing indicators for DS-1 input 1.
$C_{21} C_{22} C_{23}$ = stuffing indicators for DS-1 input 2.
$C_{31} C_{32} C_{33}$ = stuffing indicators for DS-1 input 3.
$C_{41} C_{42} C_{43}$ = stuffing indicators for DS-1 input 4.
$F_0 F_1$ is the frame alignment signal. $F_0 = 0$ and $F_1 = 1$.
[48] represents 48 information bits from each DS-1.

Exhibit 3. DS-2 Frame Format

- The bandwidth required during peak hours.
- The use of bandwidth during each day.
- The cost of dedicated circuits including the connection to the local central office at both ends.
- The cost of customer premises equipment for terminating the T1.
- The cost and availability of other services such as ISDN PRI and switched T1.

T3 NETWORKS

The next level above T1 in the digital service hierarchy is T3. Each T3 link is the equivalent of 28 T1s. The multiplexing of T1s to form a T3 signal is done in two steps.

Step 1. Four DS-1s are multiplexed to form a DS-2 signal (see Exhibit 3). Each DS-2 consists of four subframes (also called M frames), numbered M1 through M4. The four M frames do not represent each DS-1 on a one-to-one basis. This is just a way of interleaving the bit streams from four DS-1s into a single bit stream. The DS-2 frame format is as follows:

- Each M frame contains 6 blocks.
- Each block has 48 bits of data.
- Each block contains 12 information bits from each four T1s.
- After every block of data there is one bit of overhead.
- Each M frame consists of 294 bits.
- Each DS-2 frame contains $4 \times 294 = 1,176$ bits, including 24 bits of overhead.

DS-2 service to each DS-1 is synchronous. That means equal time slots are assigned to each DS-1 regardless of their data rates. Because the four DS-1s do not generate the same data rate, to adjust for different data rates the bit stuffing or pulse stuffing technique is used. The bits used for this function are called C bits. Each DS-2 subframe contains three C bits. If all three C bits in a subframe are zero, no stuffing is done and the zeros in those positions are part of the DS-1 data. When stuffing has occurred all three C bits in a subframe are set to 1.

The normal output rate for each DS-1 is 1.544M bps, and four DS-1s amount to 6.176M bps. The output rate selected for a DS-2 is 6.312M bps. Because there are 1,176 bits per frame, the number of frames per second is:

6.312M bps ÷ 1,176 bits per frame = 5,367.35 frames per second
5,367.35 frames per second × 24 overhead bits per frame
    = 128,816 bits of overhead

The available space for stuffing is:

Total DS-2 bandwidth	6,312,000 bps	
Overhead bits	−128,816 bps	
Four DS-1s (4 × 1,544,000)	−6,176,000 bps	
Stuffing Bits	7,184 bps	(1,796 bits per DS-1)

If no stuffing has occurred, the maximum available rate is:

6,312,000 − 128,816 = 6,183,184 bps per DS-2 or 1,545,796 bps per DS-1.

Step 2. Seven DS-2s are multiplexed to form one DS-3 signal (Exhibit 4). To form a DS-3 from seven DS-2s two standards are available: the M13 format (Exhibit 5) and C-bit parity format (Exhibit 6). M13 is similar to D4 framing for T1 and has limited monitoring and error correction capabilities. It uses all 21 C bits for bit-stuffing. Each DS-3 frame using M13 standards is structured as follows:

- Each DS-3 frame contains seven subframes.
- Each subframe consists of eight blocks.
- Each block consists of 84 bits of data (12 from each 7 DS-2s).
- After every 84 bits of information, there is 1 bit of overhead.
- Each DS-3 frame consists of $8 \times 85 \times 7 = 4760$ bits.

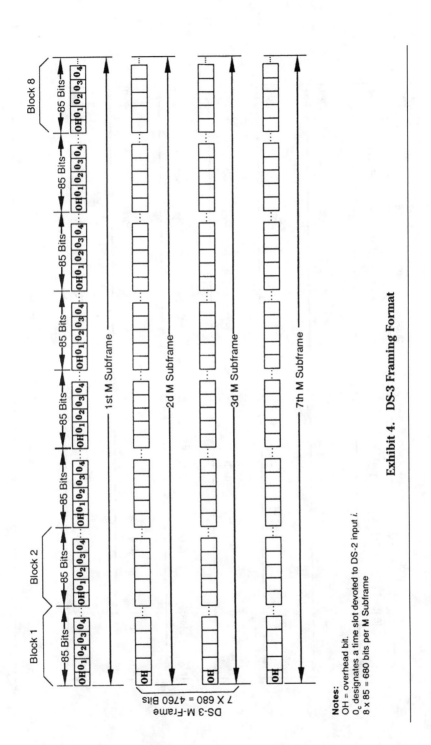

Exhibit 4. DS-3 Framing Format

Notes:
OH = overhead bit.
O_c designates a time slot devoted to DS-2 input i.
$8 \times 85 = 680$ bits per M Subframe

DS-3 M-Frame
$7 \times 680 = 4760$ Bits

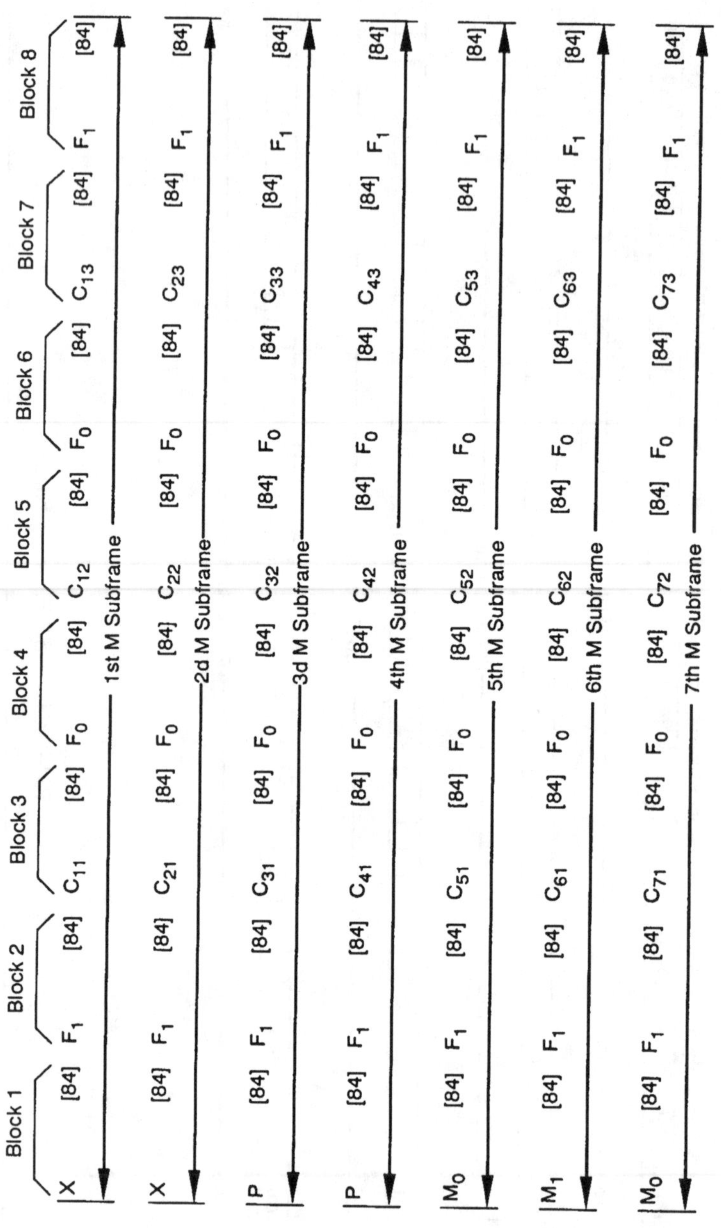

Exhibit 5. M13 Signaling Format

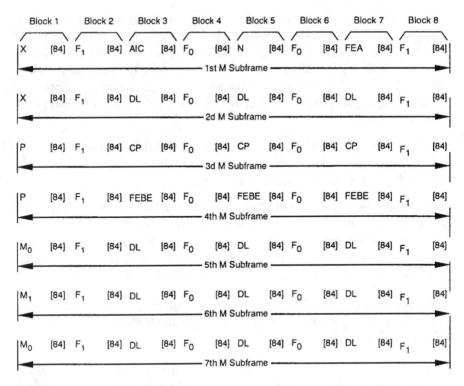

Notes:
The X bits transmit a "degraded second" indicator from the far end to the near end.
$M_0M_1M_0$ is the multiframe alignment signal. $M_0 = 0$, $M_1 = 1$.
$F_1F_0F_0F_1$ is the frame alignment signal. $F_0 = 0$ and $F_1 = 1$.
C-bit definitions:
    AIC = Application identification channel = 1.
    NA   = Reserved network application bit.
    FEA = Far-end alarm channel.
    DL   = Data link.
    CP   = C-bit parity.
    FEBE = Far-end block error
P is the parity information bit.
[84] represents 84 bits from every DS-2 frame.

Exhibit 6. DS-3 Signal Using C-Bit Parity Format

The seven subframes do not represent the seven DS-2s on a one-to-one basis. Because each DS-3 consists of seven DS-2s, its transmission rate should be: 6.312M bps per DS-2 × 7 DS-2s = 44.182M bps. But the assigned rate is 44.736M bps. The additional capacity is used for bit stuffing and overhead. Each DS-2 in a DS-3 is treated synchronously. That means equal time slots are assigned to each DS-2 whether it has data to transmit or not. Since not all DS-2s have the same bit rates, to adjust for varied transmission rates among DS-2s the bit stuffing technique is used. The three C bits in a subframe are used as bit-stuffing indicators. For example, if all C bits in the fourth subframe are 0, no stuffing is done for the fourth DS-2. But if all C-bits in the fourth subframe are 1, bit stuffing is performed in the fourth DS-2. By using three C bits as bit-stuffing indicators, the possibility of misidentifying the DS-2s that are bit-stuffed will be significantly reduced. The amount of bandwidth used for this function is 526,306 bps, as shown by the following calculation:

44,736,000 bps ÷ 4,760 bits per frame = 9,398.32 frames per second

56 overhead bits per frame × 9,398 frames per second

= 526,306 bits of overhead per second

The C-bit parity format redefines the C bits and X bits (the message bits) to be used for additional monitoring capabilities. The C-bit parity format is for DS-3 what extended superframe is for T1. M bits are located at the first position of subframes 5 (value = 0), 6 (value = 1), and 7 (value = 0). Signaling in a C-bit parity format is described in the following sections.

Message Bits (X Bits). The X bits are at the beginning of subframes 1 and 2. They both have the same value (either 1 or 0) and their function is to carry in-band messages.

Parity Bits (P Bits). P bits are located at the first positions of subframe 2 and 4. Their function is to provide an in-band parity check for the data. If the data in the DS-3 contains an odd number of bits, P is set to 0; otherwise, P is set to 1. All P bits have identical functions.

Framing Bits (F Bits). Each DS-3 frame contains 28 F bits, 4 per subframe. The sequence of their respective value is 1001. F bits are also used by the receiving equipment to locate the boundary of a DS-3 frame.

The C bits and X bits can also be defined to perform the following functions.

Application Identification Channel. This field is used for identifying the framing standard that is used. For the M1 3 standard, the application identification channel is set to 0, and for the C-bit parity format it is set to 1.

X Bit. The value of this bit is usually 1. If the receiving device detects any signal degradation for longer than one second, it sets the X bits to 0 and sends them back to the transmitter.

Far-End Alarm Control Bits. These bits are used for loopbacks and testing. If an alarm condition is detected at the receiving device, these bits are used to send a status signal to the transmitting device.

T3 Users

DS-3 circuits have been less than successful as a commercial communications service. Primary users have been a few major corporations. The reasons are the high cost and lack of a commonly accepted standard among manufacturers of equipment, network providers, and other broadband networks. Other broadband technologies will eventually take the place of T3 service.

SYNCHRONOUS OPTICAL NETWORK

Although the principle of using light waves for communications is an old one, the use of fiber optics for transmitting communications signals became technically acceptable and economically feasible only after the development of laser technology. An optical fiber is a fine wirelike structure made of a glass or plastic dielectric. It consists of the core, which reflects the light waves; the cladding, which protects the core; and the primary and secondary coatings, for more strength and protection.

Fibers used in communications are of two kinds: single mode and multimode. Single-mode fiber is used in public networks, and the multimode fibers are used in private networks and LANs. These two types of networks are based on two different standards and use different transmission rates. The fiber distributed data interface (FDDI), which uses multimode fiber, is the basis for private backbone networks and is limited to 100M bps and a maximum diameter of 60 miles. The SONET uses single-mode technology; its transmission rate can be as high as 13G bps, and its maximum network size is almost unlimited.

Fiber-optic-based networks have the following advantages:

- Fiber-optic signals are immune to and do not cause electrical and environmental interference.
- Fiber-optic communications are secure because an attempt to tap the signal causes the error rate to climb and can be easily detected.
- Fiber-optic bandwidth is wide, starting at 51.84M bps and climbing to 13G bps. The first phase of SONET will provide 2.488G bps, the equivalent of 32,000 telephone circuits.
- Optical cables do not corrode and are strong; optical fiber has the same tensile strength as steel wire of the same gauge. Cables are reinforced with protective shields to withstand severe conditions.
- The error rate of fiber-optics is less than IO - 1', approximately 100 times lower than that of a typical copper wire. Such a low error rate reduces the number of retransmissions and transmission overhead, and simplifies error checking.

- Optical signals can travel 25 to 54 miles without needing to be regenerated or repeated. T1 signals transmitted on copper wire should be regenerated after every mile.
- Optical fiber becomes increasingly cost effective with the development of new technologies. As the demand for higher bandwidth increases, there will be no technical or economical alternatives to optical fiber.
- Fiber-optic interfaces are being standardized. Because there is no standard DS-3 interface, connections to other broadband networks are made over proprietary interfaces. This limits equipment choice. In addition, DS-3 networks do not provide enough bandwidth for network management.

SONET is a North American standard. Its first phase is specified in American National Standards Institute (ANSI) documents T1-105 and T1.106. SONET circuits are software defined and can be assigned and provisioned quickly and without the need for physical rewiring. Only SONET can accommodate future high-bandwidth services (e.g., high-definition TV, broadband ISDN, and interactive videoconferencing).

SONET Applications

SONET is a transmission medium with many applications. Local exchange carriers use SONET for connecting their central offices, interexchange carriers use it for their trunks, and private corporations use SONET for connecting high-speed work stations.

SONET Transmission Rates

SONET is designed to multiplex T1, T3, and higher rates. Lower rates can also be transmitted, but they should be multiplexed to higher rates before being connected to SONET. The SONET optical carrier (OC) line rates defined so far are:

- OC-1: 51.840 M bps (equivalent to 810 DS-0s).
- OC-3: 155.520M bps.
- OC-9: 466.560M bps.
- OC-12: 622.080M bps.
- OC-18: 933.120M bps.
- OC-24: 1.244G bps.
- OC-36: 1.866G bps.
- OC-48: 2.488G bps.

Provisions are being made for the transmission rate to reach 13G bps in the future.

SONET Definitions

SONET is a transport system that can be compared to a system for moving physical objects. It breaks the load into smaller pieces, palletizes, labels, transmits, unloads, and reassembles the shipment at its destination. The following sections define some SONET characteristics.

OC. This is the applicable SONET data rate.

Synchronous Transport System (STS). This is the frame structure. STS has 51.84M-bps (STS-1) and 155.520M-bps (STS-3) formats, or it can achieve higher capacity by interleaving several STS-1s. Each STS-1 frame consists of 90 rows and 9 columns of data with 8 bits in each cell. Each frame is repeated 8,000 times per second. The data rate for STS-1 is derived as follows:

90 rows × 9 columns × 8 bits per cell × 8,000 frames per second = 51.84M bps

Synchronous Payload Envelope (SPE). This is an area within the STS frame. STS consists of two parts: the payload, or capacity, part and the overhead part. Three columns or 27 bytes of each STS are set aside for transport overhead and one column or 9 bytes for path overhead. The remaining 86 columns by 9 rows or 774 bytes are the payload part of the STS frame. SPE is the payload part of the STS, so the useful data rate is derived as follows:

86 columns × 9 rows × 8 bits per cell × 8,000 frames per second = 49.536M bps

Virtual Tributary (VT). An area within the SPE that is allocated based on the data rate or services assigned. The standard transmission rates for VT are as follows:

- VT-1.5: 1.728M bps.
- VT-2: 2.304M bps.
- VT-3: 3.456M bps.
- VT-6: 6.912M bps.
- VT6-N: $N \times$ 6.912M bps.
- Asynch DS-3: 44.736M bps.

Building Blocks of SONETs

The major functional components of a SONET, as defined by Bellcore or ANSI standards, are:

- Digital loop carrier.
- Terminal multiplexer.
- Regenerator.
- Digital cross connect system.
- Add/drop multiplexer.

Exhibit 7. Bellcore SONET Specifications

SONET digital loop carrier	Bellcore TR-TSY-000303
Add/drop multiplexers	Bellcore TR-TSY-000496
Regenerators, terminal multiplexers	Bellcore TA-TSY-000917 and TR-TSY-000253
Digital cross connect system	Bellcore TR-TSY-000499

The references to published standards for these components are given in Exhibit 7.

Digital Loop Carrier System. The digital loop carrier concentrates low-speed traffic before it enters the SONET or a central office switch. This technique is also called optical remote switching. If the remote users are connected to the central office without their data streams being concentrated, the capacity of the central office would be limited by its total number of ports. For the interface between digital loop carrier and end users, from 1 to 2,016 DS-0s are used, while the interface between the digital loop carrier and the central office is at OC-3 (155M bps), equivalent to 2,430 DS-0s. The main application of the digital loop carrier is for telephone companies to connect remote switches to their host switches. This capability allows customers at remote sites to be served as effectively as customers on the main switches. The digital loop carrier reduces cabling costs substantially, increases service choices, makes more bandwidth available, and increases switch capacities.

Terminal Multiplexer. The terminal multiplexer is for multiplexing T1, E1, T3, broadband ISDN, and their subrates onto a SONET channel. The transmission rate for a terminal multiplexer is usually OC-12 (622M bps) and higher. As the terminal multiplexer performs both the multiplexing and switching functions, it accepts a wide range of bandwidth and can assign alternative routes to each incoming channel. Because of its high capacity, it is considered part of the network.

Add/Drop Multiplexer. The add/drop multiplexer is capable of adding and dropping DS-1, DS-3, and OC-n signals onto other OC-n circuits. An add/drop multiplexer is a combination of terminal multiplexer and digital cross connect system. Multiplexing of interfaces at DS-0 rates is not part of the current add/drop multiplexer requirements.

Regenerators. After conversion and multiplexing, a signal can travel 25 to 54 miles without being degraded. Beyond those distances, regenerators are used. They convert the incoming optical signal to an electrical signal. They also measure amplitude, shape, density of zeros and ones, and timing. Distorted signals are corrected, then converted from electrical to optical, and retransmitted onto the SONET. The distance signals travel before they need regeneration depends on the wavelength and the kind of fiber being used. It is expected that as new materials and amplifiers come into use the distance between repeaters will substantially increase. Repeaters also have network management, monitoring, and alarm capabilities.

Digital Cross-Connects. The digital cross-connect system is part of the carriers' networks and is the first point of deployment of SONET. It operates at the OC-12 level (622M bps), and its function is to separate voice, data, switched, and nonswitched signals. The multiplexing and demultiplexing schemes are not the same as for combining T1s to T2s and then to T3s and do not consume as much overhead.

SONET Customer Premises Equipment. Essential to deployment of SONET is an intelligent T1 multiplexer that can interface the customer's DS-0, fractional T1, T1, ISDN PRI, and subrate equipment with OC-1 or higher channels on the public network side of the interface. The equipment connected to this multiplexer can be PBXs, LAN bridges, or similar facilities.

SONET Switch. The SONET switch is the last element in the hierarchy of the SONET network. Its function is to multiplex rates from DS-0 to OC-48. These functions are performed in the digital interface unit, which is an adjunct processor to the switch. The use of the digital interface unit eliminates the need for M13 multiplexers and their associated space and wiring.

SUMMARY

Currently, there are few devices that can consume all the bandwidth SONET can provide. Until such devices become available, demand for T1 service and T1 multiplexers will rise. As carriers install more fiber and create more transmission capacity, T1 prices are bound to fall, which leads to more demand. In addition, for many applications T1 is quite sufficient. Availability of ISDN will not diminish the demand for T1, fractional T1, and their related equipment. As carriers continue to offer ISDN H channels (which are 6, 12, and 23 contiguous B channels), the use of T1 will be stimulated.

Chapter 19

Customer Premises Equipment (CPE) for Broadband Network Access

Nathan J. Muller

Global communications is undergoing a sweeping transformation as it migrates from analog systems to digital-based technologies capable of supporting such broadband applications as local area network (LAN) interconnection, image processing, multimedia computing, and video. Underlying the migration to broadband networks is the revolutionary increase in the processing power of all types of computers, which makes such applications not only possible but economical and easy to implement.

T3 SERVICE

Perhaps the most popular broadband service is T3, which is offered at the DS-3 rate of 44.736M bps. Its applications include LAN interconnection, replacement of multiple T1 lines, and high-speed backbones on which voice, data, video, and image can be integrated.

Usually T3 is implemented over optical fiber, requiring an interface for electrical-to-optical signal conversion. The lack of optical standards for DS-3 has led to a proliferation of proprietary customer premises equipment as well as network equipment. This restricts the ability of users to mix and match different manufacturer's equipment end to end.

T3's proprietary optics also means that implementing the service entails special construction of access lines from the customer premises to the local exchange carrier's serving office. Construction costs at each end for that connection differ widely from region to region, from a low of about $8,000 to a high of about $150,000.

0-8493-9949-1/99/$0.00+$.50
© 1999 by CRC Press LLC

The majority of T3 devices sold today are M13 multiplexers. The M13 is a simple T1 concentrator that consolidates as many as 28 DS-1 signals into a single higher-speed DS-3 signal. The M13 lacks network management capabilities and support for such T1 features as binary eight zero substitution (B8ZS) (used for clear channel transmission) and the extended superframe format (ESF) (used for such link maintenance functions as performance monitoring, end-to-end diagnostics, and reporting). Consequently, DS-3 services generally do not provide the network management features T1 users have come to expect.

However, this situation is changing through the implementation of C-bit parity on T3 facilities. This alternative T3 framing format is roughly equivalent to T1's extended superframe format. C-bit parity can help ensure reliable service through end-to-end performance monitoring, remote maintenance and control, performance history, error detection, and trouble notification. Most new T3 equipment supports both C-bit parity and M13. Users of M13s must add new interface cards and reconfigure their software to work with the new framing format.

THE SYNCHRONOUS OPTICAL NETWORK

Synchronous optical network (SONET) standards will eventually allow the full communications potential of fiber optics to be realized. In addition to specifying a standard fiber-optic interface, current SONET standards specify transmission rates that start at 51.48M bps and reach to 2.488G bps. The long-term ramification is that throughout the 1990s SONET will gradually replace today's high-speed, T3-based proprietary networks.

Although SONET-based services are available now only from some alternative access carriers, organizations can implement private synchronous optical networks using waveguides, referred to as dark fiber, that are leased from local exchange carriers. Dark fiber refers to facilities for which the customer has control of transmission format and optical equipment at both ends of the link. This requires that the user provide all the necessary equipment and interfaces, because the carrier has no management responsibility.

Usually an entry-level private implementation of SONET employs terminal multiplexers, which consolidate multiple DS-1 signals for transmission over a point-to-point wide area network (WAN). The simplest deployment would involve two terminal multiplexers, one at each end of a WAN backbone (see Exhibit 1) that links corporate locations. Device provisioning, collection of performance statistics, and detection of alarms can be performed at one of the multiplexer's maintenance ports.

A multipoint network can be implemented by combining terminal multiplexers with a more advanced SONET multiplexer called an add–drop multiplexer (ADM). The ADM can be used in simple point-to-point

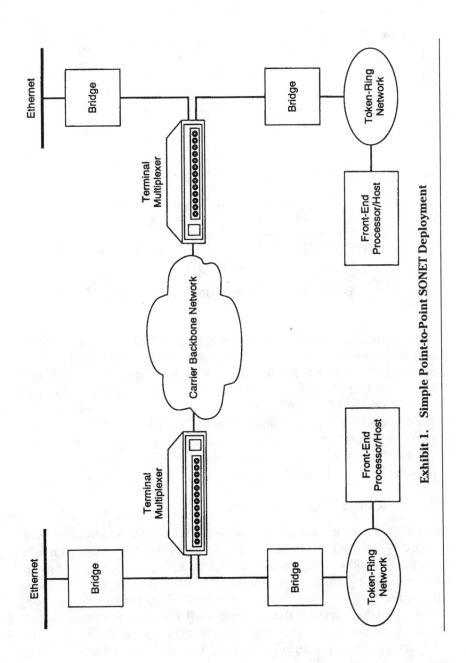

Exhibit 1. Simple Point-to-Point SONET Deployment

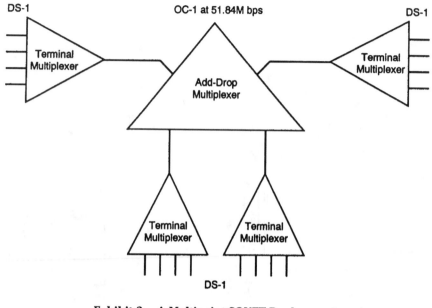

Exhibit 2. A Multipoint SONET Deployment

configurations, but its real value is in complex multipoint configurations. ADMs provide far more bandwidth management and network configuration flexibility than terminal multiplexers. They have an integral cross-connect capability and so can electronically patch DS-1 signals from one port to another. Multiple ADMs may be used to drop or add digital signals at intermediate locations along a transmission path. The ADMs can also be used to increase the fill of the high-capacity optical carrier signal to ensure optimal efficiency and cost savings. The terminal multiplexers in Exhibit 2 as well as the intermediate site ADM are manageable from any single site.

FIBER DISTRIBUTED DATA INTERFACE

While SONET is being deployed as a WAN backbone, another fiber standard — the fiber distributed data interface (FDDI) — is intended as a high-speed backbone for connecting LANs in large office buildings or between buildings in a campus environment. The FDDI specifications define three types of access devices. Single attached stations (SASs), concentrators (CONs), and dual attached stations (DASs) may be arranged in any of three topologies: dual ring, tree, and dual ring of trees (see Exhibit 3). In the dual-ring topology, DASs are linked to two physical loops; all the stations are connected to the rings through a dual attachment. In a tree topology, remote SASs are linked through a single connection to a concentrator, which is con-

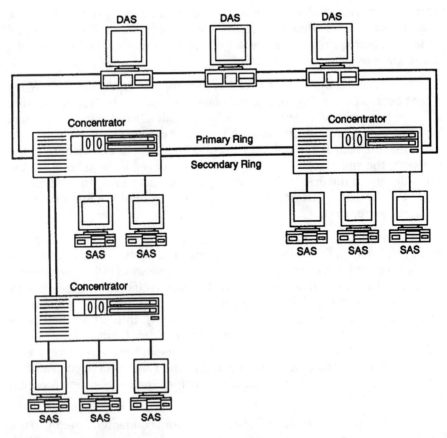

Notes:
DAS Dual attached station
SAS Single attached station

Exhibit 3. FDDI Ring with Interconnected Access Devices

nected to another concentrator on the main ring. Any DASs connected to a concentrator perform as SASs. Concentrators may be used to create a network hierarchy, which is known as a dual ring of trees.

Concentrators and dual attachment stations connect to the two physical fiber-optic rings so that instantaneous fault recovery can be performed. The primary function of the concentrator is to manage access to the fiber-optic backbone for the many non-FDDI devices attached to it and to isolate faulty devices that are not equipped with integral fault-recovery capabilities from the backbone.

Devices requiring highly reliable communications are attached to the main ring; those that are less critical can be attached to branches off the main ring.

Thus, SAS devices can communicate with the main ring but without the added cost of a dual-ring interface or a loop-around capability that would otherwise be required to ensure the reliability of the ring in the event of a station failure.

A failed node is bypassed optically, removing it from the network. When a fault occurs on the ring, the devices on either side of the fault detect that a failure has occurred. Each node then automatically reconfigures the data path, wrapping around the network fault. The network continues to operate until this fault is repaired. If a second fault occurs somewhere in the network, the same node-wrapping occurs. However, if the second fault is not adjacent to the first fault, the wrapping causes the ring to segment, so that two physically distinct networks are created until the first or second fault can be repaired.

As many as three nodes in sequence may be bypassed; enough optical power will remain to operate what remains of the network. In the event of a cable break, the dual counter-rotating ring topology of FDDI allows use of the redundant cable to handle normal 100M-bps traffic. If both the primary and secondary cables fail, the stations adjacent to the failures automatically loop the data between rings (see Exhibit 4), thus using the operational portions of the original two rings to form a new C-shaped ring. When the fault is healed, the network reconfigures itself. Fault tolerance is also provided for stations that are connected to the ring by a concentrator, in which case, it is the concentrator that provides the loop-around function for attached stations.

One of the advantages of having concentrators connected directly to the dual ring is that network managers can then define local rings, in addition to the primary and secondary rings. This allows nodes to be isolated from the rest of the network (for troubleshooting and testing) without having to bring down the entire network. When the faulty station is restored, it can be tested on a live local ring without disrupting the majority of users. Local rings can also be used to add new stations to the network and test them before bringing them onto the primary ring.

Local rings also provide security and enhance performance: User groups with stringent security requirements can be isolated and stations with heavy file transfer requirements can be connected directly so that other users do not experience performance problems.

FRAME RELAY

Although it is most often compared to X.25, frame relay is a fast packet technology rooted in ISDN. A streamlined packet protocol, frame relay's performance advantages over X.25 enable users to more easily interconnect high-speed LANs over a WAN. Frame relay achieves its higher throughput by

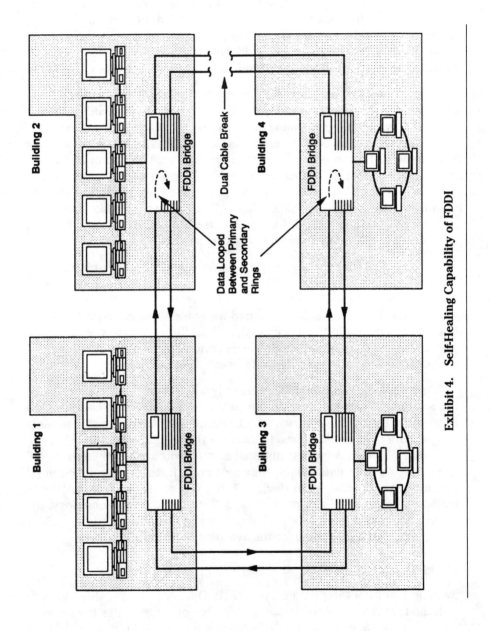

Exhibit 4. Self-Healing Capability of FDDI

eliminating error correction and many other X.25-associated overhead functions between the source and destination.

Frame relay is so appropriate for LAN interconnection because it supports sporadic bursts of data at high speeds without requiring users to dedicate large amounts of bandwidth. Connections between LANs can be established instantly, using bandwidth that is reallocated to other applications when the transmission is completed.

Any of several types of devices can be equipped with frame relay interfaces for access to a frame relay network (as depicted in Exhibit 5). The interfaces encapsulate incoming data into the frame relay format for transport through the network. Interconnection of LANs by means of a frame relay network requires a bridge, router, or intelligent hub equipped with a frame relay interface. Connecting individual terminals, work stations, or minicomputers to a remote host over frame relay would require either a stand-alone frame relay terminal adapter that can be shared like a server or a frame relay interface card that can be inserted into any network access device (e.g., a T1 multiplexer or fast packet switch).

Vendors of T1 multiplexers and fast packet switches support frame relay in different ways. For example, LAN-to-LAN data may be encapsulated in the frame relay format as it enters one channel of a properly equipped T1 multiplexer. There, it can be combined with video and voice for transport over a T1 network. In this scheme, the T1 multiplexer provides access to public voice switching and multiplexed services, while the internetworking traffic is transported over private T1 lines.

A fast packet switch sends packets only when there is information to be transmitted. This means many more channels can share the same physical connection than is possible with a T1 multiplexer. Voice and data packets can be statistically multiplexed to increase the channel capacity of a fixed-bandwidth T1 link. A more traditional circuit-switched multiplexer would waste capacity, because each time slot constitutes a specific channel assigned to a specific input device. If that device has no information to transmit, its assigned slot goes unused. With fast packet technology, the silent periods are immediately filled with packets from other data applications, which are contending for the available bandwidth.

SMDS

Switched multimegabit data service (SMDS) is a carrier-provided packet-switched service. LAN packets from a bridge or router enter the network over T1 or T3 access lines. Configured as a metropolitan area network (MAN), SMDS is essentially a public data backbone network and is shared by many users.

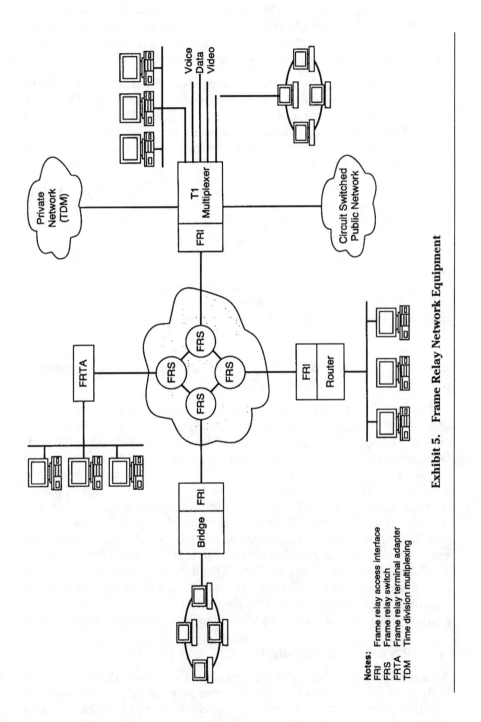

Exhibit 5. Frame Relay Network Equipment

Notes:
FRI   Frame relay access interface
FRS   Frame relay switch
FRTA   Frame relay terminal adapter
TDM   Time division multiplexing

SMDS employs a packet-switched, dual counter-rotating ring architecture. The two rings each transmit data in only one direction. If one ring fails, the other handles packet transmission. This protection mechanism safeguards users' data against loss due to a network fault.

SMDS is based in part on Bellcore standards finalized in late 1989. To the original standard was added the distributed-queue dual bus (DQDB) architecture for access control to create the IEEE 802.6 set of standards (Exhibit 6). Bellcore's standard specifies customer premises equipment access to an SMDS switch using twisted-pair wiring (at the T1 rate) or optical fiber (at the T3 rate).

Each customer has private DQDB access to an SMDS switch for as many as 16 devices per access link, with the devices connected in a bus arrangement. Access may be customized to suit the individual bandwidth needs of subscribers. For example, by means of access classes, limits can be enforced on the level of sustained information transfer and on the burstiness of the transfer. In the case of T3, the access classes are 4M, 10M, 16M, 25M, and 34M bps. For T3 access paths, an ingress access class may be applied to the information flow from the customer premises equipment to the MAN switching system, and an egress access class applied to information flowing from the MAN switching system to the customer premises equipment. Both types of access classes may be selected by the subscriber. For T1 access paths, the same 1.536M-bps access class is applied to both directions of information flow.

The SMDS interface in customer premises equipment consists of SMDS software, which can reside in any router or bridge, and a special channel service unit/data service unit (CSU/DSU), which is connected to a serial port. Depending on the interface used and the speed of the SMDS network, access can be provided at the T1 or T3 rate. The router or bridge works in concert with the CSU/DSU. The router handles the protocol processing and passes the information to the CSU/DSU for lower level protocol processing and transmission to the SMDS network. The interface uses the high-level data link control (HDLC) protocol for communications between the two devices. For example, the router-bridge takes the LAN frame and encapsulates it inside an SMDS level 3 protocol data unit (L3 PDU), the basis SMDS data block. Next the router encapsulates the L3 PDU into an HDLC frame and sends it to the CSU/DSU. The CSU/DSU receives the data, removes the HDLC envelope, and performs the conversions needed for transmission to the SMDS network.

The SMDS Data Exchange Interface

A potential problem with SMDS equipment is interoperatibility — a user typically cannot plug any vendor's router into just any other vendor's CSU/DSU. Several vendors have cooperatively developed an SMDS interface

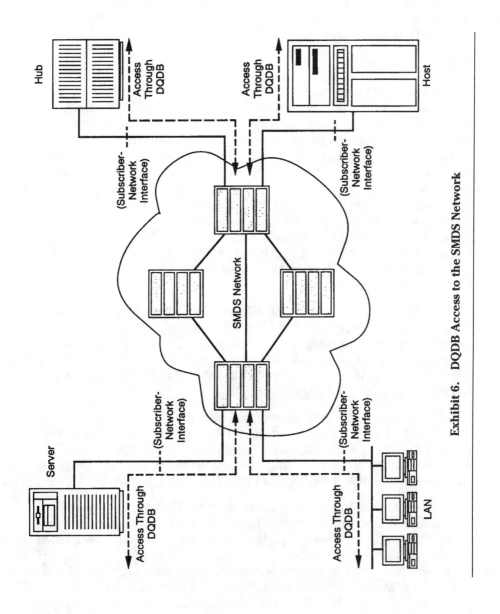

Exhibit 6. DQDB Access to the SMDS Network

specification, the SMDS data exchange interface, that they are promoting as a de facto industry standard. The specification is being considered for standardization by the SMDS Interest Group, an organization of users and vendors. The SMDS data exchange interface affords users a standard interface between router-bridges and CSUs/DSUs in an SMDS network, lowering costs and eliminating interoperatibility problems.

ATM

Asynchronous transfer mode (ATM) is a cell-relay transmission method. Under ATM, circuits are defined as paths through the ATM network. No bandwidth is actually assigned until it is needed. As soon as the transmission of fixed-length cells (a cell consists of 53 bytes) begins, the cells are assigned to one virtual circuit. The 5-byte address is included in each cell, so there is no need for a dedicated connection to ensure that the information gets to its intended destination. Thus, bandwidth is instantaneously allocated in whatever increments are needed to support the application. When an application is not sending any data, the ATM network's bandwidth is assigned to other virtual circuits. This process closely resembles traditional statistical multiplexing, except that ATM has much more traffic-handling capacity. Operating at the lower levels of the open systems interconnection (OSI) protocol stack, ATM is fast and simple.

Because it can operate at the SONET rate of 155M bps, ATM may be used in the future to interconnect 100M-bps FDDI networks. This is not simple, however. The two technologies are so dissimilar that a significant amount of translation must be done to make them work together. For example, frame sizes vary. ATM cells are fixed at 53 bytes, and FDDI frames vary in length and may exceed 4,000 bytes.

What is required are FDDI routers that have the capability to break the accepted FDDI frames into smaller ATM cells, attach the required addressing, and then feed the cells into an ATM network over high-speed fiber. This capability will be provided at the customer premises through intelligent hubs and routers that are equipped with ATM interfaces.

SMDS may be another solution to transporting FDDI over ATM. Exhibit 7 illustrates how such an interconnection might work. At the customer premises, FDDI traffic to be sent to a remote FDDI network is first broken down into fixed-length cells for transmission, by way of an SMDS link, to the local exchange carrier. The carrier transports the information to the switch providing the ATM service. There, the 48 bytes from the SMDS service become the payload for the ATM cells. (Addressing consumes an additional 5 bytes for a total of 53 bytes per cell.) At the receiving end, the process is reversed, with the ATM cells being unloaded into SMDS cells. When these cells reach the customer premises, they are repackaged into FDDI frames.

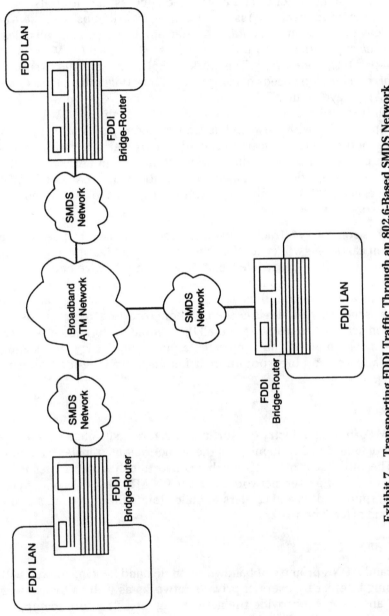

Exhibit 7. Transporting FDDI Traffic Through an 802.6-Based SMDS Network

ATM-based customer premises equipment does not yet exist, although several hub vendors have announced plans for hub architectures that use ATM. Synoptics Communications, Inc. (Santa Clara CA) has already built and installed ATM switches and conducted successful field trials. David Systems, Inc. (Sunnyvale CA) is developing network hubs that use ATM technology for voice, image, data, and video applications. This will deliver multimedia applications over LANs and WANs using plug-in ATM cards and twisted-pair telephone wiring. The hub's backplane is expected to support internal transmission speeds of more than 1G bps. Ungermann-Bass (Santa Clara CA) is developing ATM products for its Access/One hub. The products will transmit multimedia data at speeds as high as 100M bps over twisted-pair wiring with between-hub transmission speeds of 1G bps. The ATM products include a concentrator card and a router, along with desktop interface cards for microcomputers, work stations, and LAN servers that will provide voice, video, and data communications over LANs and WANS. A premises-based ATM switch will provide connections to ATM-based wide area network services.

ATM has some very attractive features. In addition to high-speed switching within carrier networks, it offers the prospect of high-speed switching in private network nodes, while facilitating the interchange of high-speed data between private and public network nodes. And unlike transport technologies in which bandwidth is fixed, ATM-based devices can continue to scale up as more bandwidth is needed, without resorting to ring or bus segmentation schemes to maintain overall throughput performance. Network managers contemplating hub implementations should ask vendors about their ATM plans and incorporate their findings into long-term network planning.

The ATM Forum

The ATM Forum, an industry consortium, was formed in late 1992 with the mission of finalizing development of the asynchronous transfer mode protocol. The initial focus of the 40-member consortium has been to define the specifications for a user–network interface for ATM networks and, in the process, spur vendors and carriers to build standardized products to link public and private networks.

BROADBAND ISDN

Broadband ISDN's promise of bandwidth on demand is being viewed with increasing interest by users of private networks as well as by carriers. SONET and ATM will provide the networking infrastructure to support broadband ISDN. SONET is already in its formative stages of deployment, and ATM network switches and customer premises equipment have already been announced by several vendors.

Broadband ISDN requires intelligent network elements that can respond to customer requests for bandwidth. So the broadband ISDN architecture embraces SONET terminal multiplexers, add-drop multiplexers, digital cross-connects, and optical switches. In the SONET environment, these devices can be configured as customer premises equipment as well as elements of carrier networks, allowing customers and carriers to share management responsibilities.

In addition to supporting SONET overhead functions, broadband ISDN standards will define such maintenance features as trouble indicators, fault locators, and performance monitors. These will work in conjunction with customer equipment (e.g., PBXs, LANs, T1 multiplexers) and provide transport to the central office, where a SONET cross-connect or switch will further concentrate or segment the information.

The first actual SONET/broadband ISDN switching systems will be large adjunct networks to existing ISDN switches. The adjunct approach, as opposed to entirely new switches, will help to mitigate the additional switching plant cost of SONET/broadband ISDN. As the demand for broadband services increases throughout the 1990s, new photonic switching systems will come into use in the network.

Broadband ISDN holds great promise, primarily because it can deliver enough bandwidth on demand to support virtually all existing services and the high-bandwidth applications of the future. Broadband ISDN will make the most efficient use of bandwidth, allow dynamic channel allocation and assignment through the use of intelligent control protocols, and support LAN interconnection and the transmission of voice, data, image, and video over common access and transmission resources.

Private networks using broadband ISDN technology would require only a small number of physical interfaces to any particular location. Users requiring 45M bps for high-quality videoconferencing, for example, could simply dial up a 45M-bps connection. Even FDDI, which provides a transmission rate of 100M bps for LAN interconnection, may be accommodated. Full-time dedicated facilities between corporate locations could be established in a matter of seconds from a predefined configuration stored in a network management terminal. Corporate LANs and supercomputers could be connected over access lines that are shared with all of the user's other applications. Virtually any bandwidth requirement between network locations could be set up and taken down on demand.

SUMMARY

Network managers would do well to monitor trends in broadband technology and customer premises equipment availability. By incorporating their findings into upgrade and expansion plans, their companies will be the first to reap the advantages of broadband services. With the appropriate equipment and standardized interfaces, users can access new and emerging carrier-provided broadband services to support bandwidth-intensive applications. In doing so, they can realize competitive advantages that come with the efficient and timely flow of mission-critical information.

Chapter 20
Cellular Digital Packet Data (CDPD): Extending the Reach of Data

Gerald L. Bahr

The dream of business travelers and employees who need to conduct business in the field is for a universal digital dial tone that they can use from anywhere in the world. Cellular digital packet data (CDPD) is one of the technologies that ultimately will help achieve what is now an elusive dream.

CDPD takes advantage of the existing cellular telephone infrastructure as well as other hardwire networks that are already in place, such as the telephone companies and the Internet. This chapter reviews cellular phone system technology and then describes CDPD technology and how it is implemented.

CELLULAR TELEPHONY

The cellular telephone system gets its name from the fact that an area to be serviced is divided into individual cells. Each cell has its own set of radio frequency (RF) channels. Each channel has two frequencies, one for transmission and one for reception, providing full-duplex (i.e., simultaneous transmit and receive) capability. The Federal Communications Commission (FCC) licenses 832 channels to a cellular market, with two licenses per market giving 416 channels per licensee.

One method of channel reuse is to divide the channels into seven groups (as shown in Exhibit 1) so that channels can be reused without having the same channel in an adjacent cell.

0-8493-9949-1/99/$0.00+$.50
© 1999 by CRC Press LLC

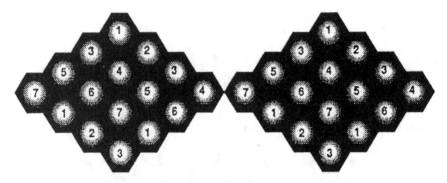

Exhibit 1.   Cellular Telephony: Channel Reuse

Depending on the number of users, a cell's size ranges from 1 to 20 miles in diameter. Each cell has its own set of frequencies, which alternate according to location. Each transmitter and receiver is connected to the mobile telephone switching office (MTSO). The MTSO then connects to the local access transport area and long-distance service providers.

The power of the cell structure is realized by the MTSO handing off the signal from one cell to another, generally without the user being aware of the handoff. The MTSO monitors the RF signal strength and adjusts its own transmitted power as well as the mobile radio's transmit power to maximize range without adjacent channel interference. As the use increases, the size of the cell shrinks in diameter, and cells are added to provide coverage. By reusing the frequencies in adjacent cells, a virtually unlimited number of users can be accommodated.

HOW CDPD WORKS

A consortium comprising McCaw Cellular, GTE Corp., and five regional Bell operating companies — Ameritech Corp., Bell Atlantic Corp., Nynex Corp., Pacific Telesis Group, and Southwestern Bell Corp — published its CDPD specification (release 1.0) in July 1993 and began deployment in 1994. The specification provides the ability for mobile data users to transmit digital information on the same channels used by cellular telephones.

CDPD breaks the data into packets and transmits them over the cellular voice channels during idle channel times. Using this technique, a baud rate of up to 19.2K bps over the Transmission Control Protocol/Internet protocol (TCP/IP) can be achieved.

Statistically, a voice channel is idle 30% or more of the time, even during very heavy traffic loads. By using a very fast "snooping algorithm" and channel hopping, CDPD technology fills this idle time with digital data, without excessive loading or interference to the voice traffic that is being carried on the channel. Using the snooping algorithm, CDPD detects voice traffic and switches to another channel so quickly that a voice user never knows that data was being transmitted on the channel. Although voice traffic has priority over CDPD traffic, the service provider may reserve some channels just for data traffic.

Some typical applications for CDPD use are:

- Remote data base access and mobile office functions (e.g., facsimile and e-mail).
- Credit card authorization machines (e.g., for use by taxi drivers).
- Home or remote-site monitoring through the use of telemetry.
- Filing health care insurance claims from on-site and the retrieval of patient data by medical personnel.
- Road traffic reports.
- Silent alarms that show the location, cause, and time of event.
- Field service for checking of sales calls by sales representatives.
- Information service, such as for taxi and truck dispatching.
- Internet access.
- Product, inventory levels, and pricing information.
- Monitoring vending machines.

CDPD network services are currently being implemented by GTE Mobilenet, Bell-Atlantic-NYNEX Mobile, AT&T Wireless, Vanguard Cellular, Ameritech, Comcast and Sprint Cellular.

The Benefits of CDPD

CDPD is often chosen for remote wireless service because of its reliability, protocol support, quick setup time, coverage, and competitive pricing. The benefits provided by CDPD are discussed briefly in the following paragraphs.

Reliability. CDPD employs the Reed-Solomon forward error-correcting algorithm. It is designed to be a robust, reliable protocol and uses digital modulation. It is connectionless oriented. A bit-error rate of nearly 3×10^8 or better can be expected.

Protocol Support. CDPD can be used in conjunction with most existing connectionless networking protocols and supports several of the leading open networking architectures. Specifically, CDPD supports the connectionless network services (CLNS) protocol, which routes each packet individually according to its destination.

The CLNS protocol is a centerpiece of the Open Systems Interconnection (OSI) architecture. The design of many CDPD systems uses another

OSI protocol, the X.400 messaging standard, to pass data to the accounting and billing applications. In addition, CDPD supports the Internet protocol (IP), which in turn supports many Internet-related applications and protocols, such as the World Wide Web, the simple mail transfer protocol, and the file transfer protocol.

Security. The user's identity is protected, as is user data from eavesdropping. Encryption and decryption use the RC4 encryption algorithm. The mobile data intermediate system (MD-IS) also verifies user authentication, thus preventing the use of stolen modems. Each card uses an equipment identifier (EUI-48) assigned by the Institute of Electrical and Electronics Engineers (IEEE), as defined in the CDPD system specification.

The EUI48 consists of the 24-bit company_id (assigned by the IEEE/RAC) and a 24-bit unique CDPD mobile end station (M-ES) number (assigned by the manufacturer). Only M-ESs that have a valid equipment identifier (i.e., EUI-48) are allowed to decode the received data.

User Support. Because CDPD uses existing cellular technology, the number of users it can support is virtually unlimited.

Leveraging the Existing Infrastructure. Because CDPD uses existing cellular technology, the cost to install the service is approximately $50,000 per cell, compared to nearly $1,000,000 if implemented separately.

Setup Time. A CDPD connection is typically established in less than 3 seconds versus 20 to 30 seconds for a typical analog setup.

Coverage. Once CDPD and the recently adopted CDPD/circuit-switched hybrid service have been fully deployed, they offer the same universal coverage that the cellular voice network does today.

Competitive Pricing. CDPD's use of existing cellular phone technology — which is provided by more than one provider in a given area — ensures a choice of providers for the service. The wider number of available providers keeps pricing and service offerings competitive.

Data Rate. CDPD supports data rates at 19,200 bps, with a realized throughput of approximately 9,600 bps.

Charges. Unlike the charges for cellular service, CDPD charges are for the actual amount of data transferred rather than for connection time.

The CDPD Architecture

CDPD is an open architecture that is designed to accommodate and support new technologies at various levels of interconnection. Examples include new OSI network layer standards, such as IPv6 and alternative air-link technologies.

The four basic network elements are shown in Exhibit 2 and described in the following paragraphs

The Mobile End Station (M-ES). The M-ES is actually a wireless modem that sends and receives data from the mobile data base station. It can be part of, or mounted in, a computer, a car, or a handheld unit.

The Mobile Data Base Station (MDBS). The MDBS is the part of the system that transmits and receives data from the M-ES. MDBS functions are:

- Managing the radio resource through the airlink interface, including management of:
  — Radio channel selection and configuration.
  — Forward-channel (i.e., M-ES) messaging, such as adjacent cell information, best hopping list, current cell information, and synchronization.
- Media access control through the data link relay, including control of the:
  — Forward channel (to the M-ES) through error detection and correction, frame recognition, frame delimiting, and Reed-Solomon encoding.
  — Reverse channel (to the MDBS) through data packetization, error checking, and Reed-Solomon decoding.
- Voice channel monitoring of channel hopping (i.e., both forced and planned hops) through the use of adaptive hopping, channel snooping, and predictive hopping.

The Mobile Data Intermediate System (MD-IS). The MD-IS is the heart of a CDPD system. It routes traffic between the MDBSs and other M-ES users either from the same MDBS or another one or to a fixed end system via a frame-relay network. It acts as an interface to administration and management modules for authenticating and locating subscribers, monitoring performance, and managing traffic connection between mobile users and landlines. It also provides directory functions, such as:

- Mobile home functions for maintaining a directory of registered subscribers' M-ESs and providing forwarding instructions when an M-ES transfers to another cell.
- Move serving functions for maintaining a registration directory, feeding usage information to an accounting application, and providing encryption for the wireless data link.

In addition, the MD-IS is a source of useful statistics regarding:

- The number of active, registered, and rejected users.
- Traffic count in bytes and packets.

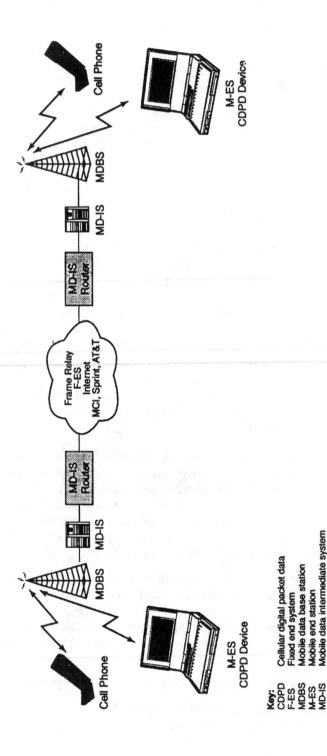

Exhibit 2. CDPD Network Elements

Key:
CDPD   Cellular digital packet data
F-ES   Fixed end system
MDBS   Mobile data base station
M-ES   Mobile end station
MD-IS   Mobile data intermediate system

- The number of retransmissions caused by errors.
- Performance of data transfers between the MDBS and the M-ES.

The Fixed End System (F-ES). The F-ES is any normal wireline network to which the CDPD provider wishes to connect. External F-ESs are those networks that are outside the control of the CDPD network operator (e.g., the Internet and typically MCI, Sprint, and AT&T). Internal F-ESs are value-added network services administered and provided by the CDPD network operator.

The Technology

CDPD sends packet data on unused voice channels on the cellular network. Data from the transmitting device (e.g., laptop computer) is segmented, encrypted, and formatted into frames by the CDPD M-ES device. These frames are sent over one of the 30 KHz channels in the cellular network using a protocol called digital-sense multiple access with collision detection (DSMA/CD), which is similar to the carrier-sense-multiple-access-with-collision-detection (CSMA/CD) protocol used with Ethernet devices.

The M-ES transmitting device monitors the forward channel for the state of the idle/busy flag. If the flag indicates that the channel is idle, it transmits the frame immediately; otherwise, it waits a random amount of time until a channel is free. The frames are picked up by the MDBS and passed to the network management system (i.e., MD-IS), where they are either sent to a wireline network or passed on to another mobile user. To ensure that the frames arrive in the correct order, CDPD calls for higher-level Internet or OSI protocols.

REED-SOLOMON FORWARD-CORRECTION ENCODING

CDPD uses the same type of forward error correction that is used with many satellite telemetry transmissions. It is used to correct problems at the receiver, when they are detected. This prevents more potential retransmissions than would a more typical error-correction scheme. Greater throughput is realized because it frees up bandwidth for new data rather than consuming bandwidth for retransmissions.

The forward error-correction algorithm pre-encodes the message with error-correction bits. Even if some data bits are corrupted, the receiver can execute a decoding algorithm that provides recovery of the original data, without the need for retransmission.

CDPD uses the Reed-Solomon (63,47) coding scheme as shown in Exhibit 3. This scheme provides for the data to be transmitted as 63 symbols of 6 bits in length. The 63 symbols are divided into 47 6-bit symbols that carry user data. The remaining 16 6-bit symbols carry the error-correction code and detection information. This scheme allows for the possi-

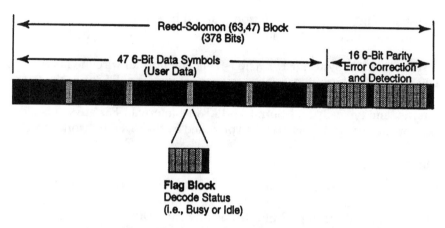

Exhibit 3. The Reed-Solomon Forward Error-Correction Code Block

bility to correct up to 8, 6-bit symbol errors, or up to 48 corrupted bits in each 378 bits transmitted.

The Reed-Solomon coding system is based on groups of bits (i.e., bytes) rather than individual 0s and 1s, allowing the handling of bursts of errors. However, the reliability that Reed-Solomon provides does come with a price: the overhead for the forward error correction reduces that throughput from a raw data rate of 19.2K bps to approximately 9.6K bps. Use of the Reed-Solomon (63,47) coding provides for an undetected error probability of better than 2.75×10^8.

Synchronization is extremely important in decoding the packets. To enhance synchronization, the information and parity bits in each block are exclusive-ORed with a pseudorandom sequence generator after Reed-Solomon encoding. An 8-bit color code is added to each block prior to each 274-bit data stream to detect cochannel interference from another MDBS cell site. (The frame packet format is illustrated in Exhibit 4)

The resultant 282-bit block is then encoded by the Reed-Solomon (63,47) code word over a 64-ary alphabet, using 6-bit symbols. This results in a 378-bit block of data. Each block is then combined with the flags and synchronization signals that are discussed later in this chapter.

Encryption and decryption are provided using the built-in RC4 encryption algorithm.

The Forward Channel

The forward channel (i.e., base-to-mobile channel) is considered to be continuous except for the interruption of the radio frequency channel hopping.

The Frame/Packet Format

| —————————— 420 Bits in 21.875 ms = 19.2K bps —————————— |

| 42 Control Bits | 378-Bit Reed-Solomon (63,47) Code Word |

| 8-Bit Color Code | 274-Bit Data |

Exhibit 4. The Frame/Packet Format

The forward channel is used to transmit flags, which are in turn used to synchronize the DSMA/CD microslot clock, determine forward error-correction control block boundaries, and acquire reverse-channel flags.

The forward channel is received by all mobile stations. This provides to the mobile station synchronization (using the 22-bit reverse channel synchronization word), a reverse-channel idle/busy status flag, decode failure flags, and the Reed-Solomon blocks for error correction. When data is detected from a mobile station (on the reverse channel), the idle/busy flag is set to busy on the forward channel, notifying all other M-ESs that the reverse channel is in use.

When the mobile end station decodes the Reed-Solomon code word successfully, the decode status flag is set on the reverse channel, notifying the mobile base that the data was received correctly and that it can send the next block of data.

A mobile end station wishing to transmit data, first checks the idle/busy flag from the forward channel. If the flag is set to idle, it begins to transmit. If the flag is set to the busy state, the mobile station initiates a random delay before trying to access the reverse channel again. The delay is based on the number of microslots delay. This provides for the random access that the mobile stations use, as provided by DSMA/CD.

The Reverse Channel

The reverse-channel data is encoded by the same Reed-Solomon code word that is used on the forward channel. Up to 64 encoded blocks may be transmitted in a single burst to the mobile base station. A 7-bit continuity indicator is interspersed into each code block. The last block contains all zeros to indicate that it is the last block in the transmission.

When the mobile station gains access to the reverse channel, it continues to transmit until it detects an error in its received data, as signaled by the decode status flag. If an error is indicated it immediately stops transmission and implements an exponential back-off before trying to retransmit the next packet.

What Is a Protocol?

A protocol is a standard or method by which two entities communicate or interface. For communications devices, a protocol covers everything from the physical connector and electrical properties (i.e., both voltage and current) to the various software layers used to hand off information from one defined layer to another.

Unfortunately, many have come to the conclusion that only the network layer or transport layer as referenced by the OSI model are protocols. It is true that IP and the internetwork packet exchange (IPX) are protocols, but they are not the only protocols used in networking. RS-232, RS-488, and X.25, along with all of their physical and electrical properties, are also communications protocols.

In an effort to help make data communications more open and universal, the International Standards Organization developed the seven-layer Open Systems Interconnection (OSI) model. Although many standards were developed before OSI and even a few since, today virtually all data communications protocols are at least compared to, if not developed around, this model.

The OSI Model

CDPD uses layers 1 through 3 of the seven-layer OSI model, as shown in Exhibit 5. (The ways in which CDPD uses these first three layers for communications are explored in the next section.) The full seven-layer model breaks down as follows:

- *Layer 1: Physical.* The first layer consists of the bit stream of data as sent to, and received from the network. The raw transmission rate and the electrical encoding scheme are part of this layer.
- *Layer 2: Data Link.* The second layer defines a basic packet structure and rules for establishing a link with another device on the network. The packet format, which layer 2 describes, is transmitted over the network using the services of layer 1. Layer 2 is also subdivided into the media access control and the logical link control layers.
- *Layer 3: Network.* This layer is responsible for the routing and switching of data throughout the network. It must recognize network addresses and route information (i.e., packets) to the appropriate networks.

Cellular Digital Packet Data (CDPD): Extending the Reach of Data

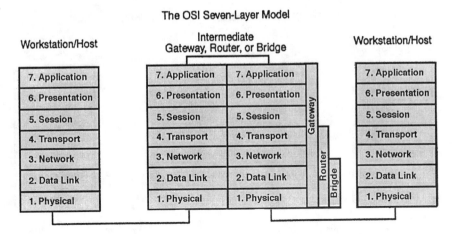

Exhibit 5.   The OSI Seven-Layer Model

- *Layer 4: Transport.* The fourth layer is responsible for the reliable transfer of end-to-end information between stations. It implements such features as acknowledgments, sequence numbers, and time-outs for resending unacknowledged packets.
- *Layer 5: Session.* This layer supports logical naming and establishes sessions, or logical links, between two logical names on the network.
- *Layer 6: Presentation.* The sixth layer negotiates the syntax that will be used when passing information to and from the application layer (i.e., layer 7). Included are character formats, such as EBCDIC or ASCII and other formats for number representation or file formats.
- *Layer 7: Application.* This layer presents services to the end user.

The CDPD Implementation of the OSI Model

CDPD design ensures that no impact is exerted on the transport and higher protocols. This design approach allows existing applications to continue to operate without change. The CDPD implementation of the OSI model, represented in Exhibit 6, is discussed in the following paragraphs.

Layer 1: Physical. To maintain channel bandwidth and avoid adjacent channel interference, a Gaussian pulse-shaping filter is used with a bandwidth-time product of BwT 0.5. Data transmission uses Gaussian-filtered minimum-shift-keying modulation at the transmitters. The received signal level is measured at both the M-ES and the MDBS to determine whether the M-ES is transmitting at the correct radio frequency power output.

The physical layer provides the following functions:

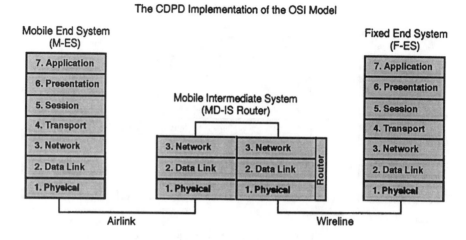

Exhibit 6.   The CDPD Implementation of the OSI Model

- Selection of the appropriate radio frequency channels between the M-ES and the MDBS.
- Modulation and demodulation of the data stream on the radio frequency channel.
- Setting of the power level for transmission between the M-ES and the MDBS.
- Measurement of the received radio frequency channel level at the M-ES and the MDBS.
- Suspension and restoration monitoring of radio frequency channels in the M-ES, to conserve battery life.

Layer 2: Data Link-Media Access Control Layer. The media access control (MAC) layer allows multiple M-ES units to share a common radio frequency channel. When an M-ES has data to send it checks for the idle/busy flag status as transmitted on the forward frequency. If the channel is not busy it begins transmission immediately. If the channel is busy, or a collision is detected after beginning a transmission, it backs off and waits for a random amount of time. The forward (i.e., base-to-mobile) channel is monitored by all M-ES units.

The MDBS supports full-duplex operation, whereas some M-ES units may not. The MDBS adjusts accordingly. Because the MDBS operates in a point-to-multipoint mode, the forward channel operates in a contentionless mode. The MDBS forms data frames by adding standard high-level data link control (HDLC) terminating flags and inserting zero bits and then segments the frame into blocks of 274 bits.

The reverse channel operates in a contention mode because many transmitters may be trying to access one receiver. Access and contention resolution of the reverse channel is maintained by each M-ES and assisted by the forward channel from the MDBS.

The MAC layer tries to deliver frames in sequence and in a timely manner. If it is unsuccessful, the frames are discarded and recovery from the error becomes the responsibility of the higher-layer protocols. The MAC layer performs two functions: encapsulation and management.

Encapsulation. To preserve the length, original bit ordering, and content of the information, the logical link control data layer is encapsulated by the MAC layer. Flag sequence and zero-bit stuffing techniques maintain data transparency and frame boundary delimitation. Forward error-correction coding is used to detect and correct transmission errors. Reed-Solomon encoding is used at the link layer to provide error correction in the received blocks.

MAC-Layer Management. The DSMA/CD access method is used to control the slotted reverse (i.e., mobile-to-base) channel. As previously stated, this technique is similar to the CSMA/CD protocol that is used in the IEEE 802.3 Ethernet standard.

Because the mobile receiver cannot sense the status of the reverse channel directly, periodic channel status flags on the forward (i.e., base-to-mobile) channel are used to signal the reverse channel. The two types of flags used on the forward channel to control the reverse channel are:

- *A block decode status flag.* This flag notifies the system that the previous forward error-correction block was successfully decoded by the mobile base station.
- *A channel idle/busy flag.* This flag notifies the system that the reverse channel is idle or busy.

Layer 3: The Subnetwork-Dependent Convergence Protocol (SNDCP).
SNDCP provides for connectionless-mode services and provides the following functions to OSI layer 3 (i.e., the network layer):

- Mapping of data primitives.
- Segmentation and reassembly of network protocol data units (NPDUs).
- Compression and recovery of redundant protocol control information from NPDUs using the TCP/IP protocol.
- Encryption and decryption of layer-3 NPDUs and exchange of encryption keys.
- Multiplexing of NPDUs from different layer-3 protocol entities onto a single data link connection.

Layer 3: The Mobile Data Link Protocol (MDLP). MDLP provides the link between layer 3 of the M-ES and the MD-IS system. It is based on International Telecommunications Union-Telecommunications Standards Sector (ITU-TSS) Q.920 and Q.921 specifications. The only variations are those required for the CDPD environment. The MDLP provides the following functions:

- Flow control.
- One or more logical data links on a channel stream (addresses contained in each stream). Connection between different logical connections.
- Sequential order of frames for the logical connection.
- Detection of format, operational, and transmission errors on a logical connection.
- Recovery from detected errors.
- Suspension of transmission during an idle data link, during which the M-ES is placed in sleep mode to conserve battery life.

TYPICAL COSTS AND TARIFFS

There is a one-time setup charge of $50. Monthly port connection charges are from $40 to $50. Packet transmission charges are offered in three payment plans:

- Plan 1: A monthly minimum of $15, plus $00058 per packet.
- Plan 2: A monthly minimum of $24, plus $00024 per packet.
- Plan 3: A monthly minimum of $49, plus $00021 per packet.

SUMMARY

CDPD is available in all major cities throughout the U.S. and is now beginning to be widely deployed. Many large national organizations are testing it for internal use. For example, American Airlines, Inc. uses CDPD in wireless handheld computers to enable gate attendants to communicate with agents throughout an airport; Federal Express personnel use CDPD to log package deliveries; and Price Waterhouse employs CDPD to send audit and tax files from wireless notebooks to a server.

With more than 36 million cellular phones in use today, the need for highly reliable mobile data communications is growing. CDPD is one solution that takes advantage of the existing cellular infrastructure as well as other hardwire networks already in place. Moreover, standardized access to CDPD ensures support of future data network services and facilities.

Section VII
Designing and Managing Multimedia Networks

An adage to electronics design engineers is that the power supply always gets designed last. How could you possibly design the power source until you know what the power requirements are? The management of complex network technology is much the same. Certainly engineering tools are provided along the way to assist in the design and development testing, but these tools are far from what is needed for the network manager.

Our current state of multimedia networking is a daunting set of protocol, transport, and media levels that defies a common management approach. However, we must acquire or be furnished tools from the technology vendors to provide as much common management as possible. Often these tools are created because of the specific demands of large networking users or user groups. We must have the technology to monitor, configure, and troubleshoot our networks. Network management and control are very important keys to optimal network operation. Without them, our network is merely a driverless vehicle with the means to deliver a payload of data, but no assurance of a timely, intact arrival.

This section contains chapters on managing a multimedia network, choosing an appropriate management tool, and simulating network operation for the design of multimedia networks. All of these are important topics, as successful multimedia networking will depend upon the network professionals who manage the network.

Chapter 21
Managing the Multimedia Network

Erik Fretheim

It is one thing to build a network and have it work once. It is quite another to have that network function continuously day after day. This is the domain of network management.

When conducted properly, network management serves four useful purposes. It:

- Confirms the validity of the network design.
- Discovers and leads to recovery from faults that occur in the network.
- Provides a guide for future expansion or changes in the network.
- Allows for the accurate allocation of the cost of the network.

These are significant requirements, yet network management has generally been approached more as an afterthought than as a guiding requirement.

In the multimedia wide area network environment, network management serves these same purposes; however, it also serves to establish a tie between the user and vendor networks. The qualities of this link to the network provider are critical in determining how well the LAN and WAN are able to work together to provide an effective network environment.

REASONS FOR NETWORK MANAGEMENT

Cost-of-Business Requirement

Three basic approaches can be taken to managing networks. The first, and perhaps most common, is that network management is a necessary cost of business. That is, it needs to be done to keep the network functioning.

Certain expenses and actions must be undertaken, but as long as these functions are adequately performed, further spending and efforts are not justified as network management. Adherents to this approach attempt to minimize the amount they spend on network management tools and training and deploy network management tools on an ad-hoc, as-needed basis.

Ensuring Network Success

The second approach is to view network management as a significant contribution to the success of the network. While it may not have value in itself, network management contributes to the value of the network through the optimization of resources. Users of this approach tend to have a coherent strategy, and although this approach is not state of the art, it uses a large variety of the tools available and deploys them methodically.

Maintaining Service Levels

The third approach is to view network management as a strategic component of maintaining service levels. Providing new services that are a result of management capabilities — and even providing products to support the business — are all characteristics of this approach to network management.

Organizations that operate at this level not only deploy the full set of management tools, they integrate these tools with each other and with other business systems. These organizations are always looking for new solutions, new approaches to using their existing tools, and new ways of creating value from their efforts. These are the organizations that are going to drive new developments in the network management field.

Focus on "Services," Not Circuits

Another way to characterize these approaches is to note what uses and business purposes the network supports. Users of the first approach essentially provide data transmission. Those who take the second approach provide data services, and those who take the third approach are able to provide their users with a comprehensive set of information services.

In this sense, data transmission is the movement of data from an input to an output location without regard to the content, or value of information other than the external values assigned by the selection of the transport mechanism. The appropriate measurements for data transmission are the bit error rates, the packets lost, and the delay through the network.

These are all valid measures, but in many cases they disclose little about the true quality of the information transmission. Additionally, the focus is on the line, the circuit, and the elements, not the service.

Measuring Data Services. The focus should, however, be on adding value within the network — not to the data itself, but to the way it is delivered. Data services take account of the fact there is more to the delivery of data than just the physical elements of the delivery.

Services are concerned about issues such as data integrity, rerouting, and other such service elements that come together to ensure timely and accurate delivery of the data. The measurements that are more appropriate to a data service are uptime, throughput, effective data rates, and reachability.

Information services deliver value from the network. Through the monitoring, evaluation, and analysis of data transported through the network, and through specific information-related services, they provide sources of information, as well as provide the service of data transport. The measures that are appropriate for information service are accuracy, response times, and consistency.

The approach that a particular organization takes is dictated by a number of factors. The first of these is the capabilities and attitudes of the people who run the network. The second is the amount of resources that the organization is willing to dedicate to network management, and the final consideration is how comfortable the management is in supporting the chosen approach. If the organization's leaders are not willing to commit themselves to fully supporting a strategic approach, the effort will be costly and will not succeed.

The requirements a customer will have for a vendor's customer network management (CNM) services will depend on the network management approach taken by the organization supporting the LAN environment. To support the simplest management approach, the CNM services provided need not be very sophisticated; reports on the quality of the transmission services provided and usage reports for predicting when the WAN links will require segmenting and augmenting are sufficient.

In a data services approach, the need for tighter links is beginning to be felt. In this environment, the manager of the multimedia network must have access to data in a timely and automated manner. This data will be integrated into the local management systems and will be used both for long-term planning and for immediate assessments and troubleshooting. In the information services environment, the link to the communications vendor has to be tight because the environments of the LAN and WAN merge, and the users of the WAN come to depend on services that are not necessarily local.

NETWORK MANAGEMENT STANDARDS

There have been several organized efforts to bring order to and set standards in the network management field. The Internet Engineering Task Force (IETF) Network Management group has promulgated a set of standards that collectively define a standard called the simple network management protocol (SNMP), which has recently been updated with a new set of standards known as SNMP version 2 (SNMPv2).

The other major set of standards has come from the same group that established the Open Systems Interconnection (OSI) network model. This group has defined the common management information protocol (CMIP).

Most of the work of other groups in the area has been to further define and specify what has been established in these protocols, to cover areas that have not been addressed in the standards, and to find common capabilities that the two sets of protocols have in common.

SNMP

SNMP as a management approach has two parts: the management information base (MIB) and the management protocol. The management information base is a definition of a set of objects or significant data items concerning a particular network device or system.

The objective of the MIB effort is to define as fully and generically as possible the information needed for management and control. As a result of these objectives, several common MIBs have been defined. Perhaps the most common of these is MIB II, which provides generic tables for devices and interfaces. Although SNMP was originally defined with routers and other networking devices in mind, significant work has been done in instrumenting not only computers, but also processes with SNMP capabilities.

MIBS

Any device that is going to be monitored has a number of characteristics that are of interest to the person doing the management. These may include such conditions as the current operational status of an interface, the number of packets or octets of data that have been sent through an interface, the current configuration parameters of a device, or the last time that a particular value has been changed.

For the SNMP MIB, these values are gathered into a collection of variables. Often these objects are grouped into tables of closely related values. The variables are defined very precisely using a language known as abstract syntax notation 1, or ASN1. The descriptions given in this language define a structure, names, and data types for the information that will be used to manage the device. The values of the objects are mapped to particular registers or software variables on the device.

Object Identifiers. Each object in the MIB has an object identifier. This is a way of uniquely identifying that particular object and distinguishing it from all other objects.

This unique identification is necessary because one of the goals of the groups sponsoring the development of SNMP is to create a number of common MIBs that can be implemented in similar devices. This can cause devices to appear, to the manager, to be identical, even though they may come from different manufacturers or even have different higher-order functions. The unique object identifier sorts out these problems.

The object identifier is built using a tree structure. The root of the tree is common for all objects. The early branches of the tree are used to differentiate a number of different organizations and means of grouping sets of MIBs. These include such organizations as the International Standards Organization (ISO), International Telecommunications Union (ITU), Department of Defense (DOD), and the Internet.

Later in the tree, the group that created a particular MIB is identified, or the MIB is classified by category, which could mean identifying an industry organization or a standards body (in the case of a standardized MIB, such as the ATM MIB or the T1 MIB, these are being developed by the IETF). The MIB may also be an enterprise-specific MIB as defined by a manufacturer for either a particular piece of equipment or even for a whole line of equipment.

These preliminary portions of the object identifier tree can be expressed both in a dotted numerical format (the official designation) or a dotted name format (a more readable version of what the values represent). A typical example is the identifier for the DS-1 MIB:

1.3.6.1.2.1.10.18
osi.org.dod.internet.mgmt.mib.transmission.dsl

SNMP Agents. Access to the information defined in the MIB is obtained through the use of an SNMP agent. This agent is a software entity that is implemented either on the managed device or on a server. The agent can access the status of the objects defined for the device. If the agent is not on the device it is referred to as a proxy agent. The agent interacts with external systems using the management protocol.

SNMP Message Protocol Types

The simplest use of the protocol is for the manager to observe the value associated with a particular object. This is done with an SNMP GET command.

The command is one of five SNMP message protocol types. These include the GET, GET-NEXT, and SET requests, as well as the GET-RESPONSE, an all-purpose acknowledgment message. This message is used in responding to a GET command with the data requested or in responding to a SET message by acknowledging the value to which the object is set.

GET-NEXT is used when polling information from tables to obtain subsequent table entries. This command requires knowledge of the state of the last request. When the next request for an object from the same table is received, the GET-NEXT command responds either with the requested values or an indication that the end of the table has been reached.

The fifth SNMP message protocol type is the TRAP. TRAP is a message that is sent unsolicited from the agent to one or more manager stations. A typical trap in ASN.1 format might be:

```
ts__busytrap TRAP-TYPE
    ENTERPRISE tuffstuf__boxes
    VARIABLES {
    tsPortid,
    tsChannelld,
    tsToneSpeed,
    tsSequence,
    tsSeverity,
    tsText}
    DESCRIPTION "This trap is sent any time a busy signal is detected the
    tone speed is used to identify the busy signal as a network or end device
    blockage."
    ::=5;
```

In this sample, the name of the trap is formed using a notation that keeps the object identifiers of different manufacturers consistent and unique, thereby preventing the use of the same identifiers for two unique data types and helping to maintain consistency. The name of the trap is also descriptive of the type of fault, which makes working with the trap easier for the people working on the fault monitoring system or otherwise trying to decode the meaning of a trap.

The ENTERPRISE definition identifies the kind of device sending the message. It may uniquely identify a particular type of equipment (e.g., a switch) or it may generically identify a family of products.

The first two object identifiers, tsPortid and tsChannelld, identify the specific location where the fault occurred.

The next object identifier (OID) is an example of additional information that is sent along with the trap to make it more meaningful. Whenever possible this additional information should be included.

Many manufacturers include a string variable that contains all of the relevant information. Although this is an easy way of implementing SNMP traps, it makes parsing and delimiting the data difficult, especially if the management station receiving the trap is doing some type of automated reaction based on the values of the data in the trap. Whatever data can be presented here to clarify the alert prevents the operator from having to poll the data from the network device.

The tsSequence OID is used to provide a sequence number of the traps sent from a particular agent. This OID is not found in all traps, but when it is used it can identify when a trap has been missed. The device can then be polled or error logs on the device checked to find what was missed when the trap was lost.

The final two data fields are added to allow the trap to convey useful information to non-fully functional management systems and for manual identification of the causes for the trap. In the case of the automated management systems, these attributes will be determined by the network management system itself. Some users may not have a system with this capability, in which case this data can be useful.

The description is used as documentation for the trap. In the ideal world, everything that a network manager would need to know to respond to the trap would be given in this field. That may include the exact source in the hardware or software that generates the trap, the conditions under which the trap is generated, and a list of suggested actions for resolving any faults that may be causing the generation of the trap. In practice, the use of this field is rarely that complete, but more and more manufacturers are beginning to provide a greater degree of detail here.

SNMPv2

SNMPv2 varies significantly only in a few aspects from SNMPv1. Most readily apparent is the addition of protocol formats to help alleviate the problems with bulk data transport — the GET-BULK request and response.

A second major change is the inclusion of a provision of manager-to-manager concepts. Another often wished-for advantage to SNMPv2 is the inclusion of a security mechanism of administration control, which, however, is not included in the final version adapted by the standards body. Work is continuing in this area.

The two major new features, however, have not proved to be significant enough to lure users away from the older version of SNMP. The GET-BULK command allows for the use of a consistent protocol when dealing with large amounts of data, but it does not offer all of the features of a more standard file transfer protocol (FTP). Missing features include flow control, compression, and dynamic restart,

In addition, the manager-to-manager feature has not attracted a large following. Likewise, the security features are difficult to manage on a large scale, and the option of choosing from multiple features has increased the implementation challenge.

On the positive side, SNMPv2 has added several features to the TRAP message that enhance its usefulness. These changes include the use of uniquely indexing traps sent to each manager and the ability to selectively determine which traps will be sent to each manager.

The TRAP format was also adjusted to be identical to the GET and SET formats, resulting in the loss of some information in the small set of generic traps that has been offered with the standard MIB. SNMPv2 also codifies some manager-to-manager functions.

Customer Concerns About Implementing SNMP

For managing the carrier portions of networks, different approaches can be taken to implementing the SNMP agent functions. These approaches are driven by several factors.

Privacy Expectations. One factor is that more than one customer shares the same resources on any particular switch. If all customers were granted full SNMP access to the switch, they would be able to find out information about another customer and potentially violate a customer's privacy expectations.

Equipment Concerns. Another factor is that the customer may not be concerned about the particular hardware that is used, but rather only about those logical components that make up the network of the customer. In addition, there is some equipment in which the SNMP implementation is so poorly done that the mere act of retrieving data can cause the loss of traffic or, worse yet, the crash of a switch.

"Commercial" Level of Service. Another significant factor driving the telecommunications industry is concern for being able to provide a commercial" level of service. Users of the Internet have over the years developed an expectation that they will receive a best-effort service.

For the most part, the service levels have been relatively high; nonetheless, it is not uncommon to have to make several attempts over a period of hours or days to download information from popular FTP archives and World Wide Web sites. These delays are expected and no one complains too much because these services are free to the user. The same level of service is not acceptable for customers who are paying for their information sources.

Solutions for SNMP's Limitations. SNMP does not include fairness or resource-sharing capabilities, nor have most network devices been made with these capabilities. Therefore, most service providers have taken another approach to providing this data. These approaches include modifying the management systems to accept data periodically via file transfer and installing proxy agents that collect data either periodically or on demand from network devices and deliver it to the user.

The advantage of using file transfers to provide data is that the transfer is done on a predictable fixed schedule. The transferred data is then loaded into a proxy agent at the customer's location from which it can be polled as needed. The disadvantages are numerous. The data may become stale between transfers. The customer's management station may need to have modifications made to access the data, and more data than is necessary may be transferred.

Having a proxy agent on the provider's premises rather than the customer's will reduce the amount of unused data that is transferred. The problem, then, is what happens if several customers access the system at the same time. If the system puts values periodically collected from the network into a data base, a number of schemes can be devised to distribute the access, including using multiple proxy agents — as many as one per customer — and implementing fairness algorithms in the proxy agents.

Although these solutions take care of the access problem, the potential still exists for the data to be stale. Some solutions pass requests directly to the network device after filtering to ensure that the customers can only obtain information directly related to their service, but doing so still poses a potential problem of placing too much demand on the device.

Most devices simply have not been designed to support the measurement load that multiple users require. Methods to get around these problems include both increasing the frequency with which the network information is stored (thus increasing its freshness) and limiting the number of accesses that are allowed in any time period. No solution, though, has yet proved entirely satisfactory. Either the data window size is too coarse for making observations at the desired granularity, or the potential for demand threatens the integrity of the data. The potential solution for both carriers and the consumers are with the device manufacturers, and this problem has not yet become their priority.

SNMP's Advantages

SNMP has been widely used for three primary reasons.

Simplicity. First, its relative simplicity makes it an easier protocol to implement on network devices, especially those that may not have extensive processor and other resources. As manufacturers of communications equipment are focused more on features such as higher bandwidth and adding more functionality, simplified implementation of management protocols has allowed them to focus more resources on other aspects of their products.

Tool Support. Second, many tools are available to support both the agent and manager implementations. This means that each effort is not a one-time effort. Thus fewer resources are required for the design of the management portions of any device, and a third-party system can be used to provided management support rather than the device manufacturer having to provide a complete suite of tools.

From the user point of view, having the tools available means that each user does not need to customize a new tool for each device, and that numerous types of devices for diverse purposes and from different vendors can be controlled from a single workstation.

Management of Heterogeneous Environments. Third, by using proxy agent technology, it is possible to retrofit devices that use other methods, thereby allowing the control of a large network of a heterogeneous nature to be controlled from a single platform with a single protocol.

Often, however, for bulk data transfer (e.g., the forwarding of large amounts of performance data), SNMP is not the preferred protocol. For large data sets, the overhead to support SNMP is inefficient. In addition, SNMP is based on the user datagram protocol (UDP) and does not have flow control, consistency checking, or security mechanisms.

CMIP

The common management information protocol (CMIP) was designed as the application layer of the OSI model. As such, it was principally designed to work using the OSI protocols for the transport of management information. Work has also been done, however, to make the applications work with an Internet Protocol stack. This is known as CMIP over TCP/ IP, or CMOT.

CMIP begins with a network management model. This model is divided into the five functional areas:

- Fault management.
- Security management.
- Performance management.
- Accounting management.
- Configuration management.

This division has been generally accepted even by those who do not subscribe to the CMIP model as a method for building and managing networks, in much the same way as the OSI seven-layer model has been adapted as a model with which to describe protocols other than those that are strict implementations of the model. Thus, both have proved useful, if for no other reason than their conceptual contributions.

Guidelines for the Definition of Managed Objects

The OMIP management model has additional divisions for system management functions. These may span multiple functional areas and represent the work that is actually done by a single system or set of systems.

CMIP uses as its management information base descriptions built using the Guidelines for the Definition of Managed Objects (GDMO). These descriptions are very similar in many respects to the SNMP MIBs in that they are an ASN.1 notion and contain definitions of the values that are available for managing devices.

The GDMO description may contain other information that would not normally be found in an SNMP MIB, such as descriptions of the functions that are available on a device. The functions of a device are often included in an SNMP MIB as well, though these are implicit rather than explicit.

Interaction Between Devices and Systems

Like SNMP, CMIP uses a set of functions for interaction between devices and systems. These are referred to as the common management information service elements, or CMISE.

Unlike SNMP, CMISE is officially defined for more than communications between the manager and device. There are also elements that are not included in SNMP. The elements are Initialize, Terminate, Abort, Event-Report, Get, Set, Action, Create, and Delete.

The Initialize element is used to establish a communications session. Terminate is used to close a management session. The uses of Event-Report, Set, and Get are similar to the SNMP equivalents. The major difference is that the Set and Get elements only establish the request.

The Action message is used to kick off the request. The Abort elements can be used to call off a Set or Get. The Create and Delete elements are used to manipulate objects. These objects can be either particular views of the management base or used to initiate a process on a device. Views of a management base enable users to see a particular subset of the data — for example, switches of the same type or devices in a region. The details of the view are defined as attributes of the view object, as is the list of who is allowed to access the view. Processes that are initiated through encapsulation in a created object may include test routines, provisioning routines, or other such uses.

TNM AND OMNIPOINT

The CMIP model has been further extended by other groups into the Telecommunication Network Management (TNM) model and the OMNIpoint model. The TNM model has worked at codifying those areas that fall outside of the standard model, especially as they relate to carriers and other communications service providers. Perhaps the most significant contribution of TNM has been defining layers for describing network management and the interfaces between network management systems. The layers that have been defined include:

- Network element layer.
- Element management layer.
- Network management layer.
- Service management layer.
- Business management layer.

The lowest layer is that which contains all of the equipment on the network. The element management layer is concerned with specialized functions needed to monitor and interact with each type of element.

The network management layer is concerned with performing network wide functions. This layer uses the element managers as mediation devices to communicate with each of the individual elements.

The service layer is concerned with those aspects of the network that are necessary to provide and maintain particular customer services. This is the layer that would include customer network management functions as well as call processing and service-level agreement monitoring.

The business layer is concerned with the creation and distribution of network services. This layer would include such things as order taking, market forecasting, and other activities more related to the business functions than the network itself,

The TNM model defines a number of functional blocks and the connections between these blocks. By formalizing the labeling and definition of the interfaces, the TNM model contributes to the ability to interconnect blocks of the model that have been constructed by different vendors.

The Network Management Forum, in producing the OMNIpoint model, has taken a somewhat more pragmatic approach than other groups. This industry-based group has been concerned not with providing an elegant theoretical model, but with the solving of the practical problem of having a set of standards that will allow them to carry on business. As a result, the forum has chosen to endorse other existing standards and to only add such new standards as needed to cover those areas that are not covered elsewhere.

OMNIpoint has adapted both CMIP and SNMP for use in network management. There is still a large amount of work that continues to be done. None of the models have yet been fully completed or accepted.

FAULT MANAGEMENT

Fault management can be divided into three processes:

- Fault monitoring.
- Fault isolation.
- Fault resolution.

In fault monitoring, a network is observed to detect when a fault occurs. This can either be done intrusively though the use of polling via SNMP get commands, CMIP get requests, or CMIP echo requests (pings) and other such devices, or passively through the use of SNMP traps, CMIP event notifications, and other unsolicited alarm mechanisms.

In fault isolation, the detected fault is located as precisely as possible, both in regard to position of occurrence physically and in regard to isolating the particular logical or physical type of fault within the possible taxonomy of faults. Once the fault has been identified and located, fault resolution — the actions that are taken to remove the fault from the network, to alleviate the effects of the fault, and to prevent the recurrence of the fault — occurs.

Automated Approaches

Of the three processes of fault management, fault monitoring is the one that is easiest to automate. Fault isolation and fault resolution require increasing degrees of abstract reasoning in order to be effective. This reasoning is usually introduced in the form of some type of an expert system or other artificial intelligence (AI) artifact.

As increasing levels of fault isolation and monitoring are introduced, these processes must in themselves be monitored. This is done both to assess the general health of the components of the network and to assess the effectiveness of the automation itself. The automation of fault management can be seen to involve a number of phases, each of which involves a higher degree of involvement with the later processes.

In the initial phase, almost all effort is directed toward fault monitoring, while in subsequent phases, more effort is directed toward fault isolation and finally to fault resolution. One useful method is to divide the implementation of fault management into three phases, each of which represents not only increasing levels of fault isolation and improvements in fault monitoring, but also describes increasing sophistication on the part of the managed devices themselves. This increased sophistication is necessary in order to report the data required for higher levels of fault management.

Phase 1 is the initial installation of a new piece of equipment in the network. The equipment is monitored primarily for large-scale failures with most isolation accomplished in a nonautomated fashion.

Phase 2 occurs when equipment has been in place for some time and its performance has become better understood. Increased attention is paid to performance degradation. Fault isolation is rather thorough for physical components of the equipment, and increased levels of problem identification are supported.

Phase 3 is when the equipment's fault monitoring has been integrated with that of other network components and increasingly sophisticated capabilities are available that help to isolate the fault logically as well as physically. Automated isolation to a particular cause is increasingly common. In many common or simple cases, automated fault resolution may be performed.

These definitions are rather fluid and any particular device may have characteristics associated with different phases. In determining what requirements are to be applied in evaluating the level of monitoring of a particular device, the portions of the device may be specified as meeting the requirements of one phase or another. For any supported phase, however, the portions that support that phase should also support all underlying functions.

Multimedia WANs

Isolating a fault in a multimedia WAN environment is more difficult than in a LAN because there are more components that can contribute to any problem and the entire transmission facility is not in the hands of the network manager. Furthermore, the nature of the modern network is such that problems in one layer of the network may show as symptoms in other layers.

For example, many network or data path layer problems with congestion may be symptoms of misconfiguration in the application layer. To resolve problems that may not be easily detected requires contributions from the telecommunications service providers, which means that they need to provide more than a periodic report stating that their service is excellent. Service providers should provide fault reports on a near-time basis whenever possible, as well as make available data needed to determine the cause of any problems that may have come to light.

CONFIGURATION MANAGEMENT

What distinguishes multimedia WANs from multimedia-ready LANs is that in addition to having a large amount of equipment, they have a significant logical infrastructure that needs to be configured. This logical infrastructure may include permanent virtual circuits (PVCs) and switched virtual circuits (SVCs) for frame relay and asynchronous transfer mode (ATM), routing tables, group address lists, and allowed and disallowed address screen tables. These logical components need to be managed actively as it is their configuration that determines the quality with which the network will service the users.

Several tools are available that provide for the tracking of physical assets. These tools have, to a large degree, automated the process by taking advantage of "discovery" algorithms on standard management platforms.

These algorithms work by either probing the network to determine if there are any devices at a particular address, or in a particular address range, or by passively listening to the network and recording the devices they hear transmitting. Some of the newer devices have included support for discovery that allows for the determination of more information than just the existence of a device at a particular address. This additional information could include the type of device being probed as well as important information about its configuration.

One of the most important functions in the high-speed broadband WANs used for multimedia is the need to be able to actively tune and adjust the network as the bandwidth requirements change. This is critical because of the large bandwidth requirements of some of the applications. With too little bandwidth the applications will not function optimally; however, too much bandwidth is an unnecessary expense.

Adding to the problem is the dynamic way applications are deployed — for example, an application may be used for only the brief period of a particular project. Other applications may cause network use to grow unpredictably. As a result, it is important for the consumer to have the ability to dynamically control the logical network in as near a real-time manner as possible. This type of a capability is useful for disaster recovery as well.

Prioritization of Multimedia Information

Adding to the complexity of the problem is the introduction of prioritization of data. Prioritization is often used in multimedia systems to tag the elements that must be delivered for a minimum quality of service, or to label the importance of elements of the information.

For example, real-time transmissions of drawing on a video bulletin board would be given a higher priority than passing e-mail messages. Likewise an image may have both higher and lower priority elements in which the image is delivered as the composition of low- and high-resolution elements. This kind of prioritization is valuable because it provides a quick first look while still delivering the complete image.

Bandwidth Implications. The use of data priorities introduces new requirements for controlling how much of the available bandwidth is given to each data priority. The distribution needs to be made in a manner that ensures that the higher-priority data is well serviced yet that the lower-priority data streams are not starved.

If this distribution were not done, the low-resolution image and the bulletin board updates that are tagged as low priority because of their time requirements, rather than their importance, would never be delved — a consequence that is not the intention of prioritization.

One way of gaining control over the distribution of resources to support bandwidth tuning and prioritization is to use SVCs over frame relay or ATM, or to use a connectionless protocol such as switched multimegabit data service (SMDS). These services, however, are not yet generally available, and they do not have all the characteristics that may be desired. The use of these services requires newer and more complex devices, as well as increased management capabilities for the decision-making processes used to invoke the applications.

Another drawback is that because the service parameters are negotiated with each call, there is no guarantee of availability or consistency of service with each use. As a result, there is a need to allow for direct control of PVCs.

Currently, most schemes that let the customer control the logical portion of the network are more manual in nature than automatic. This is a result of many factors. First, the back office systems in most carrier networks are not equipped to handle this kind of a transaction; second, controlling what each customer does so that it does not impact the entire network is of significant concern; and third, there is no standard accepted protocol or method for accomplishing this task.

ACCOUNTING MANAGEMENT

Accounting management is the process of tracking and controlling the costs of the network services. Important to accounting management is not simply the tracking and the paying of the bills, but also controlling those bills in such a manner that they are predictable, accurate, and representative of the true value of the network.

There are several ways in which these goals can be accomplished. First, network managers have to know and understand the full costs of services. They can then prevent the use of networked applications that consume high levels of bandwidth but are used simply because the bandwidth is available. They are also less likely to put applications on-line if it does not make good business sense.

Cost Models

Among the best ways to make apparent the true cost of the resources is to chargeback network costs to the departments with network users. Chargebacks for WAN costs are often done on a rather arbitrary basis, with the cost assigned either being a fixed percentage of the overall bandwidth costs or some allocation based on the relative size of the number of connections used to support the department.

With the usage-based billing options that many carriers are now providing for their broadband services, it is much easier to build a true cost model for individual applications. The billing data is even more useful if it is provided on a CD-ROM or some other electronic format.

Accounting data should always be verified by comparing it to another data source. These sources would include:

- Internal lists of the circuits and services a company subscribes to.
- Analysis of patterns.
- Network diagrams and logs and other tools for monitoring the services used.

Auditing Carrier Statements

The communications industry as a whole is known for its poor billing accuracy. A typical example is a line or a service that is removed from service at the request of the customer yet may continue to appear in the bill for a period of several months. Other services may have the wrong entry codes applied by the sales representative who is not completely familiar with the complete variety of service offered and all of their options. The misentered code may result in other excess charges. In fact, an industry has sprung up around auditing carrier bills. These consultants offer to perform the audit for a percentage of the savings they are able to obtain for the customer.

More important, if the figures on the carrier statement cannot be verified independently, either from a heuristic model or from other measurements, the door is open to fraud, waste, and abuse.

PERFORMANCE MANAGEMENT

There are three primary uses for performance monitoring:

- To validate the design of the network.
- To plan for growth and capacity expansions of the network.
- To identify developing problems in the network.

Many network managers begin with the question, "What data is available?" instead of focusing on these goals. The result is that they obtain a massive amount of data, which is a problem to process but that does not serve their purposes.

Data for data's sake is not nearly the same as art for art's sake. The choices of what to measure on a network are extensive, and the measures that fit one WAN do not fit another. At the other end of the spectrum from taking too much data, there is often pressure to sum up the health of the network in a single number (executives would prefer this to be a number between 1 and 10, as in "the network is a 9 today, sir").

Beware Availability Measures

One of the more commonly used criteria for a single measure of network health is availability. The use of this number became popular in the days of large computer systems that tended to be describable by binary states — the systems were either down and waiting to get fixed or up and waiting to go down. Availability was an easy thing to calculate, but in a multimedia network, availability becomes more difficult to measure, much less to attribute to any particular device or portion of the network. Carriers have a particular problem in providing this number to their customers for broadband network services.

The difficulty is how to measure this elusive number. If it is measured by the percentage of time that the access lines are functioning, the carrier has lost control of it. The customer can take down the access line for testing or the painter may unplug the router while trimming around a receptacle (a true story — it was interesting to see the brush lying there wet and deserted on top of the still-open paint can). If the carrier measures availability as being when its switched services are available, then the carriers can obtain credit for quite a bit of time when the customer actually does not have access to the network.

The other alternative is to measure when destinations and services are available. Attempting to do this internally to the network is another difficult, if not impossible task. There is no way in a high-speed switched network to precisely predict what points are reachable to a customer and what services at those points may be made unreachable by the current state of the network.

With a PVC-based service, some switches have a limited capability to measure when the PVC is connected end-to-end, but relying on this number ignores what is happening internally within the PVC. With SVC-type services, some measures can be derived from the call completion and call dropped records, but these again do not provide enough data to determine whether the call was not completed as a result of a network problem or because of a badly formed request.

To make accurate measurements, the carriers must place themselves into the role of a network user. This can be done either by directly contributing to the customer data stream or by using a test bed to model a typical customer configuration. In the first case, this may directly affect the quality of the customer network. In the second, what is measured is at best an estimate of the availability of any customer's network and not the complete picture.

Thus, any measure provided by a carrier and labeled availability is suspect and does not contribute to the three goals of performance management. Any true measurements of this statistic need to be made from the very edges of the network. Even then, the number may be suspect.

Other Measures

What the carriers can provide accurate data on is the amount of data carried across the WAN, the amount of data that was discarded at points within the WAN, and the measured delay between points in the WAN. When this data is assembled and trended, it can significantly contribute to the goals of performance management. As single point measures, these figures are fairly worthless.

The amount of traffic carried across the WAN needs to be measured at several points. These include application-level measurements at the end points, measurements of the traffic at the entry points, and measures of the WAN internal data carried.

The differences between the application-layer measures and the other measures indicate the efficiency of the encapsulation of the lower protocol levels. If the difference is too great or changes over time, it may indicate the need for tuning of the application. There may be either too little WAN bandwidth available, or there may be control-level traffic that has not been properly tuned.

Similarly, the amount of traffic lost within the network may indicate where the logical network design is inadequate. For example, if there is a large loss of traffic on entry into 56K links when sent from a T1 connection, this may indicate a problem that could be fixed by adding to the capacity of the smaller link or by tuning the flow control at the source.

Whatever the measurements are, summary reports are sufficient until a problem is found, but then greater detail is required. Ideally, the carrier should provide data to customers as a set of summaries, with the complete data available on request at a later date. This prevents the customer from having to maintain a large store of data for detailed analyses that may not need to be made. The network manager will still need to make measurements of the LAN portions of the network, so the format that is used to provide the detailed customer reports should be compatible with the format of the data in the customer's network management system.

SECURITY MANAGEMENT

Security management is ensuring that access to and use of the data and resources of the network are available to all authorized users and denied to unauthorized users. Security is often neglected until last and is ignored because it is too difficult, complex, and boring — unless, of course, it has been violated. The first thing anyone should do when considering connecting anything to a network is to obtain a book dedicated entirely to the subject of security and read it thoroughly.

The three areas of primary concern to the user are:

- Destruction of data.
- Integrity of data.
- Privacy of data.

During the early years of computing, it was easy to ensure all of these through the use of physical security. That is if one could control the ability to touch the computer and its attached devices, the data would be secure. With the advent of modern networking technology, it is no longer possible to build a fence around the computer and assume everything remains secure.

Physical Security

Physical security is still important, especially for the servers and other devices where data is stored and security systems are maintained. In many cases, if a threat has access to any large server, the electronic security measures on that system can be compromised.

In many cases the vulnerabilities of physical access apply even more strongly to smaller devices. This needs to be recognized as more devices are installed in locations close to the users in order to provide them with better support, and as more devices are left unattended to be operated remotely.

Electronic Security

Electronic security measures include passwords, request verification, firewalls, source address monitors, filtering, encryption, and electronic signatures. The most common of these measures, and perhaps the least secure, is the password.

Passwords. The password suffers a variety of weaknesses, some of which are inherent in the manner in which password systems function, and some of which are the result of their use by people. Systemic problems may include the transmission of passwords as clear text over the network and the shortness of most passwords, which makes them easy for others to guess.

People-related vulnerabilities of passwords usually stem from the inconvenience passwords impose. People may use an easily guessed password so it is easy for them to remember, they may use the same password on multiple systems, or they may use the same password for long periods of time, again so they can be easily remembered. Likewise, people may write passwords down or include them in script files where others can observe them.

Additionally, passwords are subject to other attacks, such as spoofing the login script of a system.

There have been a number of systems introduced to get around the vulnerability of passwords. These include one-time passwords, security cards, and time-dependent passwords. Although there are also a number of measures that can be taken to decrease the vulnerability of passwords, they all add increased complexity to accessing resources and thus are subject to user resistance.

Encryption Methods. Firewalls, filtering, and source address verification are methods for ensuring that unknown, or undesired, users are unable to access a network. These are attempts to limit services to only a known list of users. Like passwords, the application of each is important, but each requires an increased management load.

Encryption and electronic signatures are increasingly popular ways of controlling access and verifying the validity of data sent across a network. They make use of cipher technology to secure data.

Both techniques bring a large burden in terms of the administrative overhead to maintain the cipher keys in a dependable, controlled manner. Even with the use of a public–private key system, there is an element of risk in determining how to know if the key that is proffered is authentic.

As the volume and extent of financial transactions rises in the multimedia environment, this will become an increasingly important issue. Is there a need for national authenticating authorities who issue passports to the information highway, and even then how do we ensure that the passport is legitimate?

SUMMARY

This chapter should make it clear that the task of managing a multimedia network is not as simple as it would at first appear to be. The field of network management is full of challenges and incomplete answers. Most of the standards in the field are new and very few have been widely implemented. Those that have been implemented are often poorly executed.

What the carriers have to offer the WAN user is also not as much as one might wish. The situation is further complicated by the fact that the logical networks of today cannot be measured against the standards developed for fixed-line networks.

As the logical networks grow in complexity, the task will only get harder. For example, although service levels are included in the ATM standard, switches available today do not support the measurements needed to ensure that those requirements are met.

The most successful approach, then, is to take a cautious approach to the effort and carefully select a variety of tools. The tools should be chosen to complement each other's capabilities. They should also be chosen for being as flexible as possible so that they can have additional capabilities added as they become available. This means that the systems should meet open standards that are supported by a variety of vendors, are well documented, and are not proprietary. Systems that endorse open standards will not become immediately obsolete as the field advances and will help protect investments.

Another conservative strategy is to select the appropriate technology for sensitive and critical applications. Therefore, network managers may want to avoid state-of-the-art networks, as well as older legacy-type networks. In the first case, the management systems will not yet be fully developed. In the second case, new and superior techniques for network management will not be applied either because the technologies are not compatible or because of the cost of retrofitting the network for the new techniques.

Chapter 22
Issues in Managing Multimedia Networks

Luc T. Nguyen

With the quickened pace of technological advances in recent years, from telecommunications technologies, information technologies, and computing technologies to VLSI technologies, the telecommunications networks have become more advanced and complex than ever. To compound the issues, the traffic that is being carried on these networks is becoming more diverse. The percentage of nonvoice traffic is getting much larger, thus creating true multimedia networks. These realizations pose a challenge for many companies to look for ways to evolve their networks while still being able to manage them. To the telecommunications industry, this is both a challenge and an opportunity to provide new equipment and services.

More and more applications are being added to the networks. From intranet phone to Internet radio, from videoconferencing to entertainment video, from Web TV to movies on demand — all these will make some of the current network management methodologies obsolete. With multimedia, the definition of network performance will change; methodologies to measure and manage networks for peak performance will need to be revised.

In this chapter we will take a look at some of the issues in managing multimedia networks.

THE MULTIMEDIA NETWORKS

The network itself is changing. Service providers are widely deploying new technologies. These include very high-speed access technologies such as ADSL and cable modems, ATM switches, and ultra-fast servers that can provide instantaneous access to information. As the networks grow larger and more complex, new applications to be carried on these networks are being invented every day. Each of the new applications introduces new types of traffic characteristics that require new methodologies to manage.

With voice networks, we previously knew where the traffic came from, where it went, how long the average phone call was, and what statistical distribution could best describe its characteristics. With the introduction of data traffic, some of our knowledge of traffic engineering does not apply anymore. The average length of a data call is much longer than a voice call. The data traffic distribution is very different than that of voice traffic. In fact, each data application has its own traffic distribution that does not resemble any other. The network busy time of each type of traffic is very different, too. Voice networks tend to be busy in the morning, while Web-browsing traffic tends to peak in the early evening, and batch data transfer will pick up activities at night.

The various video applications contribute yet other types of traffic characteristics to the networks. Voice and video traffic are much more sensitive to network delay than data traffic. Video traffic also requires much higher bandwidth than either voice or data to produce a smooth picture.

When an application integrates more than one type of traffic characteristic, then the issues become even more complex. For a videoconferencing session, both the video and the voice must be sent simultaneously. Not only does each stream have to be sent in a time-sensitive manner to achieve a smoothness in delivery, they also have to be synchronized to match the movement of the picture with the appropriate sound.

To manage such multimedia networks, neither the voice network management system, the data network management system, nor the video network management system is adequate. The use of all three together is not even adequate because of the lack of coordination between the different systems. What is needed is an Integrated Network Management System.

THE INTEGRATED NETWORK MANAGEMENT SYSTEM (INMS)

As is apparent, managing a multimedia network is very complex. The network will be much faster, and the traffic mix is unpredictable. The equipment may be from multiple vendors using different technologies to support a multitude of applications. This presents a real challenge for network managers.

There are five primary areas of network management: fault management, security management, configuration management, performance management, and accounting management. Another network management area that has been receiving much interest recently is customer network management (CNM). This is when the customers are given the opportunity and tools to manage their part of the networks. We will discuss these network management areas in more detail and present options and issues involved with managing multimedia networks.

For large and complex networks, network management exceeds human capability to monitor and react to any event in the network in real time. The

INMS running on high-speed computers will have to be built to keep track of the status and state changes in the numerous devices, facilities, protocols, users, and applications in the network. The INMS must be smarter, more scalable, easier to use, and more adaptable to the changes in networks and technologies than conventional management schemes. For the following sections, we will discuss the capabilities of the typical INMS.

Fault Management

Fault management is the process of locating and correcting network problems. Fault management consists of identifying the occurrence of a fault, isolating the cause of the fault, and correcting or tracking the fault.

When a fault happens in the network, generally a change of state happens in some equipment. One or more alarms are generated. Ideally, we have to capture the alarms and filter them to determine the severity, the type, the devices or services affected, and even the number of occurrences.

Often a network error results in multiple alarms. As a simple example, when a link between two devices is cut, at least two alarms are generated, one from each end device. Potentially many more may be generated, from excessive packet loss, incomplete calls, sessions disconnected, and application time-outs. The amount of data generated from one of these network faults can be overwhelming for a person to look at and will often take a considerable amount of time to determine what the real problem is. One of the roles of an INMS is to correlate all these alarms to determine their cause.

In multimedia networks, the INMS has to recognize the interdependencies of alarms between various media. A disconnect in a voice network may not affect the video network unless the voice connection is part of a videoconference. Similarly, a remote slide presentation will not be very successful if the voice and the data on the slides do not correspond satisfactorily. The INMS should be able to correlate the various parts of a multimedia connection or set of connections and monitor it for irregularities and alarms.

Sometimes an alarm is not a cause for concern. But if the same alarm happens continuously or consistently over a period of time, then it may indicate a more serious problem. The INMS should be able to count the number of occurrences of an event, either over an absolute period of time or over a sliding interval of time. These occurrences can be a specific event, or event type, or a combination of several events or event types.

Some alarms are more severe than others. The INMS should be able to recognize the severity of the alarms and react accordingly. Some alarms may be ignored with only an increase in the statistics counter. Other service-affected alarms must be dealt with immediately. Service personnel must be paged or dispatched, and management must be notified.

Alarms can be displayed on an INMS console in one of several forms. They can be displayed on a colored map of the network where each colored location can determine the severity and the location of the alarm. They can also be displayed on a list, sorted by severity, location, type, or customer. They can also be propagated to multiple monitors under different formats for different people, depending on their functions.

Security Management

Security management involves protecting sensitive information found on devices attached to a network by controlling access to that information. Sensitive information is any data an organization wants to secure. Security management protects sensitive information by limiting access to hosts and network devices, and by notifying responsible personnel of attempted or successful breaches of security. Protection via security management is achieved through specific configurations of network hosts and devices to control-access points within a network. Access points may include software devices, hardware components, and network media.

An INMS should provide a means to control the security of the network. At any time, there can be two types of users accessing the INMS: the customers and the operators. The customers access the INMS to retrieve information about their network usage, their profile, and their connectivity. The customers' login profiles should provide them with limited access to their applications and their partitions of the network. Since several competing customers can use the same network provider, it is very important for this provider to keep their data separate and only viewable by them.

The operators should be organized into several hierarchical levels depending on their authorities and responsibilities. The operator levels can be set up in their login profiles. The authority profiles will determine which operator can access what system, data, or applications. Only the INMS administrator should be permitted to change these levels of authority.

Any successful or attempted security violation, based on system or connectivity, should be reported and analyzed. Security policy should be viewed and updated often to avoid gaps and weaknesses.

Configuration Management

Configuration management is the process of obtaining data from the network and using it to manage and set up network devices. It consists of (1) gathering information about the current network configuration, (2) using the data to modify the configuration of the network devices, and (3) storing the data, maintaining an up-to-date inventory, and producing reports based on the data.

In large and complex networks, it is a tedious job to keep track of the inventory of equipment, devices, and facilities, together with their locations, network addresses, software versions, and maintenance schedules. If a device, such as a switch, fails, and a replacement switch is brought in, it is of paramount importance to bring the new switch up to the same software version of the old switch, using the same switching table, the same addresses, and the same connectivity. This must be done for the network function in the same manner as before.

When a network upgrade is necessary, especially a software version upgrade, then an INMS with this configuration management feature will become invaluable. It can save countless hours of frustrated troubleshooting to bring the network up and functioning again.

In multimedia networks, the role of the end devices becomes more important to the satisfactory connections and services. For example, the ability to control, troubleshoot, and reset the cable modems or set-top boxes will greatly enhance the up-time of the cable service. Similarly, the ability for a videoconferencing service provider to control the camera and display devices would contribute to the service quality and consistency of a videoconference. These video end devices are complex, as is the network. The complexity of these devices exceeds most users' ability to understand and operate them effectively. The INMS must reach out to these devices, check the configurations, and ensure compatibility before setting up each videoconferencing connection.

Performance Management

Performance management ensures that a network remains accessible and uncongested for maximum efficiency. Performance management should monitor network devices and associated links to determine utilization and error rates. It should also ensure that capacities of devices and links are not overtaxed to the extent of adversely impacting performance.

In multimedia networks, performance management also ensures the effective functioning of the various media making up the services. The degradation in any part of a multimedia connection means the degradation of the whole connection. Even if the video comes through flawlessly, if the audio is less than clear, a videoconference session will be less than satisfactory. The INMS should be able to collect data on the interdependencies between various media in the same connection to evaluate overall performance.

Performance management should consist of:

1. Collecting data on utilization of network devices and links.
2. Analyzing relevant data to discern high utilization trends.
3. Setting utilization thresholds.

4. Using simulation to determine how the network can be altered to maximize performance.

5. Correlating between the collected data to infer the performance levels of multimedia applications.

The INMS must provide a process or processes that can collect many types of network performance data. Some of these types of data are:

- *Response time:* Time it takes for a datum to enter the network, be processed, and leave the network.
- *Rejection rate:* Percentage of times the network cannot transfer information because of a lack of network resources and performance.
- *Availability:* Percentage of times the network is available for use, often measured as mean time between failure (MTBF).

The INMS should be able to collect performance data on demand or on schedule. Collection time should be a function of devices, links, and absolute or relative times. Information may be collected for specific devices and links or device and link types. Information should also be collected for specific applications, especially multimedia applications.

The INMS should be able to provide performance statistic reports to help the network engineer in analyzing the network. These reports will also provide a long-term view of the overall health and efficiency of the network. There are three types of performance reports:

1. *The real-time operations reports:* Provide snapshots of some part of the network at a specific time. Example: switch usage report for Christmas Day.

2. *The summary or percentage reports:* Provide the general view of the performance of parts of the network during a certain time period. Example: average switch usage report.

3. *The trending reports:* Provide the view of the performance of parts of the network over time. Example: monthly average switch usage report.

The INMS should also have a process to set performance thresholds for various parts of the network. Thresholds are boundaries within which affected devices will function normally. Violation is when one of these boundaries is exceeded. A violation will automatically trigger procedures to collect data, generate reports, or create an alarm.

Accounting Management

Accounting management is the process of measuring network usage to establish metrics, check quotas, determine costs, and bill users. Accounting management includes the gathering of data about utilization of network resources, the setting of usage quotas using metrics, and the preparing of data for billing users for their use of the network.

The INMS should have processes to measure the usage of network resources for each customer. The measurement should be on demand and/or scheduled. Since different applications may incur different costs, the INMS should also be able to measure the network usage based on applications. Example: a user may only subscribe to basic Internet access with applications such as e-mail and Web access. At any time, this user may want to communicate with the INMS of the service provider to request in real time a higher priced bandwidth for videoconferencing. The INMS should detect the request and begin measuring the video traffic when it starts so that appropriate charges can be applied.

The INMS should also allow the administration of usage quotas for each customer. The quotas define the amount of network resources a customer is allowed to use under its contracts. The use of resources beyond the quotas will trigger separate measurements and traffic may be blocked or charged at a different price. Network resources should include the INMS and other customer support functions.

Billing is a complex process that involves taxes, special pricing, promotions, and various discounting schemes that can change frequently. Billing programs should be left to specialized billing companies for those reasons and because they differ from company to company and from one industry to the next. The INMS should be flexible enough to interface with any or all billing programs, especially nonstandard legacy ones. The INMS should provide its billing data in the right format to the appropriate billing programs.

Customer Network Management

Customer network management (CNM) allows the customers access to the INMS with applications to manage their own real or virtual networks. The simplest form of CNM is an application that allows the customers to see information (e.g., billing) for their parts of the network.

Even in this simple form, many issues can be raised in a large, complex multiuser network. Some examples are how to ensure that customers can only see their own data, how to keep the data fresh and up-to-date, and what interfaces to provide to the customer. Some trends on these issues have emerged and will likely continue into the future — trends such as Web or Java user interfaces and a standard application-to-application interface using SNMP.

The INMS should provide CNM functions for the customers to manage their own parts of the network. For example, without the service provider's involvement, it should allow the customers to:

1. Change their own network routes as needed.
2. Activate high-bandwidth multimedia applications.
3. Schedule changes or updates to their network services.
4. Request specialized reports on their network usage.

To do this, the INMS must maintain a customer network data base that contains all customer information pertinent to the network. This data base may contain information about ordering, provisioning, trouble handling, operation, maintenance contracts, and billing options, as well as information about carriers and equipment vendors. Other informational data that should be included in this data base are customer contacts, vendor services, responsible organizations, types of services used or on order, etc. More specifically, the data base must contain the exact equipment that the customer has, what their capabilities are, where they are located, who made them, what software version they have, and what network addresses they have.

The INMS will maintain all these data for each customer. It must have the ability to add, delete, or modify records in this data base. Depending on the services, some of these records may be changed by the customers themselves; some may be changed only by the network operators, depending on their security levels.

The CNM should also facilitate the communications between the human operators and the human customers. Communications by faxes, e-mail, and Web sites are all possible and should be maintained and used.

As technology advances are measured in months and days, compared to years and decades, the communications network is becoming far more complex and is exceeding the capability of humans to manage it in any reasonable manner without fully integrated network management tools. The challenge we face today and in the years ahead is to build flexible and feature-rich network management systems that can help us control and administer the multimedia networks on which we all depend for our day-to-day lives. The basic network management techniques and concepts will not change, but the integration of all these techniques and concepts into an INMS will be the theme of the future. As the networks get larger and more complex, only a cohesive INMS can help an organization master its applications and its services in a cost-effective and efficient manner.

Chapter 23
A Simulation Method for the Design of Multimedia Networks

G. Thomas Des Jardins

Vendors of network design tools usually provide ample documentation and examples concerning the use of the tool. What is often lacking, however, is a methodology for applying simulation techniques in general.

Multimedia networks and the tools that represent them are complex, and simple examples are often insufficient to impart an understanding of the process or methodology that a network designer needs to use to achieve accurate simulation results. This chapter describes one such methodology, which is applicable to the use of tools for the design and analysis of multimedia networks that carry voice, video, and data. The chapter provides the structure and approach that are missing from the user manuals.

Furthermore, the information is intended to be helpful regardless of the simulation tool chosen. The chapter also discusses approaches to solving particular modeling problems that arise in multimedia networks.

THE MODELING PROCESS

Networks that are complicated enough to have multimedia segments are frequently too complex and too large for simple rule-of-thumb calculations. Simulation is the best means of collecting performance data on networks that are in the planning and design stages.

Complexity requires a great deal of organization in data collection, model validation, and analysis of results. A defined process increases confidence in the results by increasing organization and thereby managing complexity.

0-8493-9949-1/99/$0.00+$.50
© 1999 by CRC Press LLC

This chapter specifically draws to the reader's attention the following aspects of simulation:

- Important data that will be required.
- Means for obtaining this data.
- Suggestions for modeling the data.
- Possible interpretations of results.
- How the modeling procedure might be segmented into tractable units.

Simulation results are highly dependent on the quality of data being input. The large amount of detailed data being handled increases the margin for error. By paying attention to the process, the network manager can maintain the data in an organized fashion, track the validation of the model, and increase the confidence in the results.

There is no such thing as being too organized. The corollary is that if there is any confusion about the results, the procedure should be interrupted and investigated until there is no longer any confusion. Bad data and bugs are the worst enemies of accurate simulations.

The process described in this chapter contains the following three basic phases:

- Phase I: Preparation.
- Phase II: Baseline.
- Phase III: Delta.

The tasks for each phase are outlined briefly here, then discussed in detail:

- Phase I tasks include:
  - *Goals.* These must be stated in measurable and clear terms.
  - *Data collection.* The topology and traffic of the existing network is captured.
- Phase II tasks include:
  - *Capture.* The collected data is captured in the model.
  - *Validation.* The captured model is validated.
- Phase III tasks include:
  - *Delta.* Changes are applied to the baselined network.
  - *Analysis.* The results are analyzed and summarized.

PHASE I: PREPARATION

This phase includes the definition of goals and the collection of topology and traffic data for the baseline network. The first task is identifying the goals.

Identifying Goals

A simulation should have clearly defined goals. For the hypothetical case discussed in this chapter, there are two principal goals: The first is to develop a validated baseline model of the network in its current configuration; the second is to model the introduction of an asynchronous transfer mode (ATM) backbone.

A brief summary of the modeling strategy entails the following actions:

1. Decide if modeling is appropriate.
2. Determine simulation goals.
3. Describe the network in one or two slides.
4. Combine each goal and its network description into a series of scenarios, each with a simple, testable model description and a clearly defined goal.
5. For each model description, define the data to be collected, the results expected, and how the model will be validated.
6. Combine these individual documents into a simulation notebook.
7. After the individual models have been validated, repeat the process by combining the models into more complex models and validating each in a stepwise, iterative fashion.

Sample Goals of a Modeling Project. Frequently, network managers embark on projects without ensuring that they have defined, achievable goals, although they may have an intuitive idea of what problem they seek to resolve and what steps might be useful to take. The difficulty is in translating these qualitative statements to quantitative goals based on known metrics. Without these goals, even beginning a modeling project is a waste of time.

Problem. Users are experiencing delays of 1.5 seconds running application X (problem could also be expressed in terms of low throughput).

Goal. The goals of a modeling project can often be stated simply. For example, the goal in solving the previous problem may be to "run application X, reducing delay to 0.5 seconds."

Experiments to consider to solve the problem include:

- *Segmentation.* Can further segmentation of the existing Ethernet LAN improve the performance to the desired level?
- *Backbone increase.* Can upgrading the backbone improve the performance to the desired level?
- *Segment upgrade.* Will upgrading the network improve the performance to the desired level?

Projecting Costs. Next, a spreadsheet for anticipated costs should be created. For example:

Experiments Considered	Cost of Experimental Upgrade
Segmentation	Bridges = $
	Routers = $
	Switching hubs = $
Backbone increase	New backbone hardware = $
	Plant (e.g., cabling) upgrade = $
Segment upgrade	Adapter cards = $

This step is usually followed by some qualitative analysis as to the amount of room for future growth, improvements in supportability, and so on.

Preparing a spreadsheet is relatively easy; however, it is not that easy to decide what precise changes are required to give needed quality of service. In addition, it is difficult to set parameters for wide area network interfaces because the answers to request for proposals for WAN services may use different sets of metrics.

Figures of Merit. The key is to define what measurements are important; these are often called figures of merit.

For example, is end-to-end delay the figure of merit that must be improved to provide users with the required quality of service? Are hardware costs more important than recurring costs? Is on-line transaction processing running across some segments? Voice? Video? For each set of users, there must be some number that can be extracted from the analysis that can quantitatively define the quality of service (QOS) being provided for each group.

To begin, a spreadsheet should be created for each group of supported users, showing the applications they are using currently or will be using in the future. For each of these applications, the metrics that describe the desired QOS should be defined (the network manager should already, to a large extent, be familiar with these).

Next, the available tools should be examined in light of the following questions:

- Can the modeling tool provide these measurements?
- Can these measurements be extracted from the network (for validation)?
- Do these measurements provide insight into users' satisfaction?

If the answer to any question is no, the tools, metrics, or decision to model should be reevaluated. If the modeling tool does not provide the desired reports, perhaps the manufacturer will modify the tool. If the network monitoring tools are inadequate, it may be necessary to add instrumentation to the network. The network manager may need to identify additional network monitoring hardware for acquisition or lease — or perhaps simulation is not the answer to the problem. Once these criteria are satisfied, the baseline should be defined by collecting the topology and traffic of the network.

Performance Metrics

In order to manage a network, its performance must be measurable and network goals must be specified in measurable metrics. Some of the more important metrics include:

- Queue buildup.
- End-to-end delay.
- Throughput.
- Jitter.
- Goodput.

Models must be instrumented according to the data collection requirements, by placing probes or turning on data collection routines in certain modules. The way that data collection is performed is unique to each simulation tool, but most tools will allow the collection of much of this information. The following paragraphs describe these metrics.

Buffer/Queue Size. Queue buildup is an important indicator of potential congestion points. Queue size is one of the largest factors in delays on ATM LANs. It is also the largest contributing factor to jitter.

Large queues always add to end-to-end delay and can indicate possible packet loss, which could adversely affect throughput by causing retransmission. When a network device such as an ATM switch has more traffic than it can send out on a given link, it is faced with two choices: either discard the traffic or save it in a buffer.

Assuming an infinite supply of buffers, frequently buffering is the optimal choice because it improves throughput. Buffering, however, creates queue buildup, and cells of a given quality of service must wait in turn to exit, in order to maintain first in, first out ordering. This means that the cell that arrives at the back of the line must wait for all of the cells in front of it to exit the switch before it can exit, increasing its latency.

Latency or End-to-End Delay. Latency is the amount of delay introduced by a particular device or link; end-to-end delay is the sum of all latencies experienced from source to destination. End-to-end delay is important because many applications require a specific quality of service. (The various quality of service levels are discussed in more detail in other chapters in this handbook.)

While buffering cells, rather than dropping them, can certainly improve throughput, this waiting increases latency and contributes to jitter. In ATM networks, latency is one of the QOS metrics that a committed bit rate (CBR) or variable bit rate (VBR) traffic stream may negotiate, and therefore may seek to minimize. In other types of networks it may simply be a design goal. In other words, some applications would rather have the data right away or not at all.

Jitter. Jitter is also an ATM QOS metric for which some CBR and VBR applications desire to negotiate a low value. If a cell arrives at a switch when it has a large number of cells in its buffer, and another cell arrives when the switch has a small number of cells in its buffer, the difference between the buffer sizes in these cases is that particular switch's contribution to a cell's total end-to-end jitter.

Jitter is minimized by maintaining constant buffer queue sizes. In general, ATM available bit rate (ABR) traffic expects to have a very low cell loss probability and higher latencies and jitter. Some switches address this problem by having multiple queues.

Utilization, Throughput, and Goodput. Utilization is the amount of time a link is idle, versus the amount of time it is in use. This calculation does not necessarily show how much data is reaching the end system.

Throughput defines how much data is delivered to the end system. Throughput needs to be determined to ensure that components and links are sized correctly.

The calculation of raw bandwidth is trivial, but does not include any bandwidth lost because of retransmission or other protocol and hardware interactions. Thus, throughput is important to measure because it allows the manager to estimate reserve capacity; it also reveals those interactions in the network that may lower overall throughput.

Goodput includes the actual upper-layer contributions to performance, such as whether TCP received the packets in a usable amount of time. In some instances, goodput is a preferred metric if it can be obtained. Some simulation tools, such as CACI's COMNET III, can measure goodput, throughput, and utilization.

Data Collection

Once metrics are defined, the actual characteristics of the network as it exists currently must be collected. This is the first step in baselining the network.

First, a topology data collection sheet is created. A sample is shown in Exhibit 1. Using the topology data collection spreadsheet, each hardware

Exhibit 1.   Example of a Topology Data Collection Sheet

Network Type	Node Description	ID
Data	10Base-T hub	DH1

Link Name	Link Type	Speed	From	To
WAN	Coaxial	DS-3	DH1	AT&T
Backbone	Fiber	SONET	DH1	DR1

device in the network and the links that connect them are documented. The number and rate of each link are identified.

This is also a good time to note all network costs. The cost of a link consists of the local component as well as the long-distance charges; some simulation tools are integrated with tariff data bases to some extent.

Most simulation tool manufacturers have or are planning interfaces to network management tools, which will simplify information collection on the data portions of the network. Tools have different levels of integration with network management. Some tools can collect topology information; others can also collect traffic information. There are three categories of traffic: voice, video, and data.

Traffic collection is the more difficult activity, especially for data and voice. Once again, a very careful, systematic approach yields the best results.

Some useful numbers for calculating propagation delay times in various media are:

Medium	*Propagation Delay*
Coaxial cable	4 µs/km
Fiber	5 µs/km

Voice Network Information. To collect the topology and traffic information for the voice portion of the network, here are some recommendations as to how the information might be represented in the model.

Topology. All segments of the voice network have to be described, including trunks, PBXs, and additional analog lines used by fax and data equipment for each location that is serviced by the network. Links to remote users also should be documented by listing the closest points of presence (POP) of any services that remote users will be calling. Quality of service and bandwidth required for each link should be noted.

Traffic. Billing information for any voice lines should be helpful in providing usage patterns for voice links. Most PBXs collect this information.

Any simple network management protocol (SNMP)-managed devices in the voice network may deliver usage information to the management tool.

This information may be expressed in several forms, but for the simulation a probability distribution function is needed to drive the traffic sources in the models. Because voice traffic exhibits a high degree of randomness, it is frequently viewed as a Poisson distribution. Depending on the modeling tool, there should be several distributions for voice traffic:

- The distribution of addresses (i.e., who is calling whom).
- The distribution of the length of the message (i.e., call holding time).
- The distribution of the number of calls (i.e., call attempts).
- The desired quality of service.

Modeling Recommendations. Typically, voice traffic is represented as a Poisson distribution. This method specifies the number of events that will occur over time. The exponential distribution is what is actually used to produce a Poisson distribution of traffic arrival because the exponential distribution determines the amount of time to the next event (i.e., the call to be generated).

Another method to simulate voice traffic is to use an interrupted Markov process to generate spurts of digitized speech packets. If the traffic is to be carried over a CBR circuit, it is entirely valid to use a constant source at the defined rate. Typical data rates for voice lines are as follows (because faxes are also essentially voice traffic, they are included in the table):

Traffic on Voice Circuit	Rate
Voice	64K bps
Group 3 fax	14.4K bps
Group 4 fax	64K bps

In ATM networks, voice traffic is usually represented as CBR traffic. Because it is CBR, it is tempting to subtract CBR traffic from the model in an attempt to speed it up; however, it is not recommended unless the manager is extremely familiar with the way the switch handles buffer allocation. Even though the CBR traffic is always there, some jitter may occur in the competition for buffer space, which will affect queue buildup.

Video Network Information. To collect the topology and traffic information for the video portion of the network, here are some recommendations as to how it might be represented in the model.

Topology. All video segments should be described, in the same fashion as the voice network, noting areas of overlap.

Traffic. Again, billing information may be of great assistance when determining the usage pattern for video links. Many video codecs (e.g.,

PictureTel's) use two switched 56K-bps lines. It can be safely assumed that current usage for such a link is at least 2x56K-bps multiplied by the holding time of the call in this case. The manufacturer of the video codec equipment should be able to provide a more accurate idea of the traffic the device generates. The holding times of the video sessions may be derived from billing or from equipment checkout logs.

For each video source there should be the following information:

- Maximum bit rate generated by the codec.
- Holding time for each session.
- Number of sessions for the sample period.
- Address distribution of sessions (i.e., who is calling whom).

The character of these sessions may vary a great deal; if so, developing several scenarios for the model may be appropriate. One scenario might be supporting a worst-case video session during the worst-case data session and worst-case voice; another scenario could show a more normal video session.

With improved network services, users may alter their habits and begin using the service at worst-case times. Because the network manager is usually interested in the worst-case behavior, maximum usage should be assumed for the video portion of the model.

If a model is a discrete event simulation of an ATM network, long periods will not be simulated. ATM simulations take a large amount of computer time. Therefore it is generally safe to simply presume that all of the video sessions are already established and in use for the length of the worst-case scenario. This is simpler than attempting to capture any periodic qualities they may have.

Modeling Recommendations. The data rate for a video codec can vary. Some produce constant bit rate traffic while others generate traffic with a bit rate that changes as the amount of data that can be compressed changes. Because all of the data is important, these can either be represented as a worst-case constant video source at the bit rate desired, or as "bursts of bursts."

Generally, Poisson distributions are extremely poor at representing this sort of traffic. If an ATM or frame relay network is to be the carrier for this data, one important consideration is what sort of QOS is anticipated. If this traffic will be sent over a CBR connection, then it would be appropriate to model it as a constant source. Some typical video data rates are shown in Exhibit 2.

Exhibit 2. Data Rates for Several Types of Video Traffic

Video Type	Uncompressed	Compressed
Real tlme, 30 fps ($128 \times 240 \times 9$)	8,294	2,000
Studio 30 fps ($640 \times 480 \times 24$)	221,184	4,000
MPEG	N/A	>1.86M b/s
H.261	N/A	> = 128K b/s

Data Network Information. To collect topology and traffic information for the data portion of the network, here are recommendations as to how it might be represented in the model.

Topology. Describe the network's topology, including virtual (e.g., source and destination of traffic) as well as physical aspects.

Traffic. The hardest type of traffic for which to get an accurate probability distribution is often data. To get a profile of the distribution of data, several techniques can be used. For the subnets that make up the WAN, one technique is to place a sniffer or similar device at each of the subnetwork WAN interface points and to measure the actual loading.

This method yields the most accurate and fastest-running simulation, because the actual LANs are not modeled, only the load they offer to the WAN. Many network managers only have equipment suitable for monitoring the LAN side of their interconnecting device. In this case, the capacity of the current link can be used with estimates of current user activities to derive profiles of the data traffic.

In addition, many devices have SNMP information bases that provide some useful information. Network management tools may also be useful. If frame relay or ATM is currently being used, information may be available from the provider regarding traffic patterns. For each interface (i.e., traffic source) to the WAN, the following traffic details are necessary:

- The data rate of sources.
- The size of the packets.
- The quality of service desired (as for voice channels).
- The distribution of the addresses.

Modeling Recommendations. The best way to model data sources is to think of them as bursts with some space between them. An example would be to have fixed burst sizes with some distribution of random delay between.

However, most tools (including COMNET III, BONeS, and Opnet) can drive the simulation to some extent from sniffer-collected traces. If there is a large amount of query-and-response type data, it may be better to define

Exhibit 3. Representative Packet Sizes for Use in Simulations

Network Type	Most Common Packet Size	Next Most Common Packet Size
Ethernet	64 bytes (50% of traffic)	1,500 bytes (50% of traffic)
Token Ring	64 bytes (75% of traffic)	
ATM	9,180 bytes (default for ATM)	
FDDI	4,352 bytes (default for FDDI)	

the applications' query response in the model, with the guidance of the sniffer-acquired data.

On ATM networks, data is generally sent as ABR or perhaps even as uncommitted bit rate (UBR). Ethernet packets are generally either the largest or the smallest that the Ethernet can handle; Token Ring packets are almost always small. Some packet size data for use in simulations is shown in Exhibit 3.

PHASE II: BASELINE MODEL POPULATION AND VALIDATION

After capturing the data required to construct the baseline, model design can begin. The goal now is to transform the collected information into a valid baseline.

Simple small steps, gradually increasing the complexity as each step has been validated, should be used. This way, data collection efforts can be validated, establishing confidence in the tool and modeling methodology.

Guidelines for Building Models

Creating Subnets. Preliminary steps should be modeling a portion of the network that the network manager understands very well — for instance, the simple case of determining the loading of the video portion of the net. Although it may not prove to be a very interesting model, it will give confidence in the use of the tool. Later, smaller separate models for portions of each type of traffic in the network (e.g., voice, video, and data) can be built. By keeping the problems simple and only gradually adding complexity, the overall quality of the work is greatly improved.

The following paragraphs provide more detailed, step-by-step guidelines. Vendors of network design tools provide considerable support for their products that can be of additional assistance.

Step 1: Tool Use and Data Collection Validation. During this step, the goal is to learn how to use the tool and to validate the data collection techniques.

It is likely that some data requirements of the problem or model will have been overlooked. A small representative of the network should be modeled, preferably using portions that are fairly well understood.

By validating knowledge of the tool and the manager's ability to capture raw data in a model, much work will be saved. Putting off gaining this intuitive understanding of how the modeling tool represents the network's components only postpones difficulties. Later, when the model has more data in it and more processes running, it will not be possible to see what happens with the very simple cases. The idea is to conduct simple experiments until the tool is completely understood.

Some suggestions for these early experiments are video only (this is probably the simplest part of the problem), a simple WAN link, or a very simple voice link. Most networks, when lightly loaded, are of little interest so it is a good idea to experiment by reducing the bandwidth at a random bottleneck point.

Validating Subnets

Once a subnet is built, it must be validated. The process of validation requires running the model and comparing the results against data collected for the real subnet. Validation should be in three steps:

- *Topology.* The topology of the subnetwork or network should be checked. For example, are all of the links connected to the correct devices? Are they of the correct type and bandwidth? Is each traffic source connected correctly?
- *Routing.* Are the router tables set up correctly? For the path of a packet traveling through the network, does it go where it should (and on the reverse path as well)?
- *Load.* Run the simulation with only one source turned on at a time. Is the correct amount of traffic sent to each destination? Is the delay close to what the network really experiences?

Step 2: Beginning to Validate the Data Network. At this point subnets (which later will be collected into a larger model) should be created. Start with subnets that can operate independently. Rather than spending time encoding large amounts of routing or other information for larger future networks, it is better to model a small subnet correctly. In doing so, tools and models will be built up for future use in other areas.

For instance, using COMNET III, application profiles (including message response pairs) may be built, which will be very useful when building up other models. At first, entries should have depth as opposed to breadth. Once a working subnet is created, it may be copied in its entirety. In brief, the steps are to build a subnet, validate it, and repeat.

All of the subnets that may possibly be built should be built and validated before moving on. Validation can have multiple meanings. A simple validation might be a data check: Was the correct information entered for the model? Next might be a sanity check: Does it make sense? A logical check might be next: Does it behave as expected? Do all sources reach their destinations? Are source message pairs coded correctly?

Only proceed when all of this work has been done. The more time spent testing the pieces, the easier the job will be when putting them together.

Integrating and Validating Subnets. When the subnets have been validated, they must be integrated and validated in a stepwise fashion. An example might be considering replacing a collapsed Ethernet backbone with a distributed ATM backbone that also carries video and contiguous portions of the voice network. First the data is integrated, then the video, and finally the voice.

Once again, there are three tips to successfully building an accurate simulation of a network:

- *Never proceed if there are any doubts about a result.* Stop immediately and investigate the problem until it is resolved. If the problem is not resolved, numerous bugs will creep in. This practice cannot be overemphasized.
- *Be organized.* There is a lot of data to compile. The spreadsheet can be the biggest asset.
- *Understand the network.* To this end, a good network analyzer is invaluable. If the expense of buying one cannot be justified, many leasing agencies and sometimes even the manufacturers rent them out.

The key to successful integration and validation is taking small steps, testing the results each time, and never proceeding if there are any doubts about a result. It is best to work up in complexity by beginning with the portions of the network that are best understood.

PHASE III: ALTERATION OF BASELINE TO ACQUIRE DATA

When a baseline with which to compare is completed and validated, alterations can be introduced. The alterations should be introduced with the same care that the baseline was constructed.

An example might be to compare the performance of both 100Base-T Ethernet and ATM backbone links. (Both should be able to handle the offered data load easily, but video traffic may be too much for the Ethernet backbone.) Loss and delay experienced by each traffic source should be measured, as well as the throughput on the backbone, to determine if these meet the required quality of service.

There are limits as to how much accuracy can be achieved by modeling. Efforts should focus on those areas that yield the highest return. Focusing on describing the offered load accurately will yield a more accurate simulation.

The goal is to have a model that yields valid information to guide decisions when doing experimentation on the network.

SUMMARY

This chapter has offered a brief description of a methodology that may be used to simulate a wide variety of networks using network design tools such as COMNET III. Because of the complexity of networks and the tools that represent them, simple examples are often insufficient to impart an understanding of the process or methodology that a network designer needs to use to achieve accurate simulation results.

Many steps described in this chapter are a necessary part of network analysis and design, yet they are often not found in the manuals of network design tools themselves. By focusing on the methodology rather than a particular tool's implementation, this chapter has attempted to provide the structure and approach that are missing from the users' manuals and to give readers insight into approaches they can use to solve some of the particular modeling problems that are expected in modeling multimedia networks.

There are many issues still untouched. Examples include parameter sensitivity analysis, confidence intervals, and length of time to run a simulation. Unfortunately, these issues are beyond the scope of this chapter. However, an excellent text on simulation that covers these issues is Dr. Raj Jam's book *The Art of Computer Systems Performance Analysis* (New York: Wiley, 1991).

Section VIII
A Multimedia Networking Future

Nobody can truly know the future, but we can already see some emerging technologies that will shape the future of multimedia networking. Perhaps we can learn a little about what likely course technology changes will take by looking forward from a point in the past.

It has been little more than a decade and a half since the world first laid eyes on the IBM PC. At that time, the idea of a personal computer on everyone's work desk was far-fetched to say the least. Most affordable remote computer connections were at 300 bps, and 1,200 bps was "high-speed" for most of us, although 4,800- and 9,600-bps leased-line modems were available, the latter at less than $10,000. Ethernet was quite new and required thick bulky cable as big around as your thumb. Token Ring was soon to be deployed, at a blinding speed of 4M bps. Color computer monitors for the personal computer were still in the lab. The Internet was a military-inspired link to educational research labs, primarily in the U.S.

Then the so-called "killer" software applications started to surface. It was often said that more people bought the business spreadsheet automation software VisiCalc than Apple computers. Of course, VisiCalc would only run on the Apple at the time. Nobody needed an Apple, but they sure needed the computational capability that an Apple with VisiCalc offered. So they bought both. The personal computer revolution was jump-started by a *capability* that everyone in business wanted.

Next came a rapid succession of productivity tools and operating environments, coupled with significant advances in hardware computing power, and enabled by companies with an "open architecture" philosophy. Almost overnight, computer applications such as dBase, Word Perfect, Excel, and PageMaker began to proliferate. Eventually, the need to connect the computers supporting those applications became paramount and the field of computer networking began to take off. Classic Ethernet begat twisted-pair 10BaseT, then 100Base-x (T4, TX, and Fx), and now 1000Base-x. Branches formed to other networking technologies, such as Token Ring 4 and 16M bps (and now 100M bps), FDDI, 100VG-AnyLAN, and Iso-Ethernet.

A MULTIMEDIA NETWORKING FUTURE

Why was there a push to higher and higher speed networks? The higher speed networks were needed to support more demanding network applications. There seems to be a common thread here! Computer and network advances have accelerated along lines predicted by specific *uses*. Business persons needed to automate spreadsheet-type calculation tasks. VisiCalc and a computer could do that. Office workers needed tools that would increase their personal productivity. A PC with word-processing software could do that. Later, graphic artists needed to create and process detailed graphic images and combine them into prepress artwork. High-speed personal computers, such as the Apple Macintosh, with appropriate graphics applications, could do that. Groups of computer users needed to be interconnected to share data, printers, and resources through a network and operating system. Network wiring, hubs, and servers could do that. People in all vocations across the world needed to communicate, share data, and do research. The network-connected computer and the Internet could do that.

Thus, basically, all of this computer revolution has been pushed along by a never-ending succession of significant user needs, enabled by key applications and empowered by advancing hardware. Thus, to know the multimedia networking future, we simply need to imagine a multimedia solution to significant communication needs we have now, for which the utility is broad, the applications reachable, and the technology near.

With this final section, let us look toward that multimedia future. There is a current need for much higher speed "last-mile" connectivity to internetworking resources, such as the Internet. The need is greater for speed outbound toward the user than inbound toward the network. Asymmetrical Digital Subscriber Lines (ADSL) supplies exactly this characteristic. Equipment vendors and service providers are already able to bring this service to limited markets. In addition, other leading-edge technologies offer to bring the last mile up to very respectable network speeds. These techniques include other xDSL methods, such as HDSL, VSAL, and RADSL in addition to ADSL; cable modems; basic-rate ISDN; and fiber to the curb (FTTC) methods. Let's see what the future has to offer.

Chapter 24
Choosing Asymmetrical Digital Subscriber Lines

Gilbert Held

Digital subscriber lines (DSLs) enable high-speed transmissions — including interLAN communications, videoconferencing, and mainframe access — over existing copper twisted-pair local loops. By determining the availability, operating rate of the service, and the capability of the carrier's internal broadband network, users can decide whether DSL service is a cost-effective transport replacement for their current service.

Although essentially all long-distance communications in North America are now transported via fiber-optic cable, the majority of what is referred to as "the last cable mile" — the 18,000-foot local loop from the telephone company central office (CO) to subscribers — continues to be twisted-pair copper cable. Because of the high cost of installing fiber cable from telephone company central offices to individual residential and business subscribers, communications carriers are exploring methods that enable high-speed transmission to occur over their existing copper twisted-pair local loops. The result is the development of a series of digital subscriber lines.

Although several DSL products, including high data-rate digital subscriber lines (HDSL), single-line digital subscriber lines (SDSL), and very high data-rate digital subscriber lines (VDSL) are discussed in this chapter, the focus is on asymmetrical digital subscriber line (ADSL) technology, because it is the most practical transmission facility. In addition, ADSL is being used in a series of field trials conducted by telephone companies around the world.

ASYMMETRICAL DIGITAL SUBSCRIBER LINES (ADSL)

ADSL is a technology for use over telephone twisted-pair loops in which data rates between 1.544 and 6M bps, and in some cases up to 8M bps, can

0-8493-9949-1/99/$0.00+$.50

be obtained from the carrier's central office to the subscriber (referred to as downstream transmission), while a transmission rate of 640K bps to 800K bps is obtained in the opposite direction (referred to as upstream transmission). Because the operating rate differs in each direction, this technique is referred to as asymmetrical transmission.

ADSL modems use either discrete multitone (DMT) or carrierless amplitude/phase(CAP) modulation. DMT was standardized by the American National Standards Institute (ANSI) as standard T1.413. CAP was developed by Paradyne, formerly a unit of AT&T and now an independent company. Although DMT is standardized, CAP is presently deployed in a number of field trials throughout the world for high-speed Internet access and has received high marks for its performance. It is quite possible that communications carriers will select both of the competitive methods to obtain an ADSL capability.

Discrete Multitone (DMT) Operation

DMT permits the transmission of high-speed data over conventional copper twisted-pair wire without adversely affecting voice communications. Through the use of frequency division multiplexing (FDM), a copper twisted-pair subscriber line is subdivided into three parts by frequency. One channel is assigned for downstream data transmission and a second is assigned for upstream data transmission. The first two channels have a variable amount of bandwidth based on the results of the ADSL modems communicating with one another. The third channel, which uses a fixed spectrum of bandwidth from 0 to 4 KHz, is used for normal telephone operations. Thus, an ADSL line simultaneously supports the bidirectional transmission of high-speed data and conventional voice connection.

In Exhibit 1,the ADSL modem is shown with two digital connections, one to a LAN and another to a mainframe. An ADSL modem can support virtually unlimited digital connections; however, most modems used in field trials have been limited to two to four connectors. The ADSL modem supports multiple digital devices through the use of time-division multiplexing (TDM), which can be used to subdivide the upstream and downstream data channels by time into independent digital connections.

Under the DMT standard, the frequency spectrum above 10 KHz is subdivided into a large number of independent subchannels. Because the amount of attenuation at high frequencies depends on the length of the subscriber line and its wire gauge, an ADSL modem based on DMT technology installed at a central office must first determine which subchannels are usable. The modem transmits tones to the remote modem installed at the customer's premises, where the tones are analyzed. The remote modem responds during this initiation process at a relatively low data rate, which

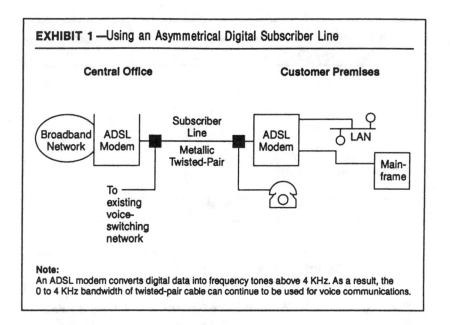

EXHIBIT 1—Using an Asymmetrical Digital Subscriber Line

Central Office   **Customer Premises**

Note:
An ADSL modem converts digital data into frequency tones above 4 KHz. As a result, the 0 to 4 KHz bandwidth of twisted-pair cable can continue to be used for voice communications.

significantly reduces the possibility of the signal analysis performed by the remote modem being misinterpreted.

On receipt of the returned signal analysis, the ADSL modem located in the telephone company's central office will use up to 256 4-KHz-wide subchannels for downstream transmissions. Through a reverse learning process, the remote modem will use up to 32 4-KHz-wide subchannels for upstream transmission. Exhibit 2 illustrates the use of the copper twisted-pair frequency spectrum by an ADSL modem. In Exhibit 2, f1, f2, and f3 are variables based on the results of the ADSL modem's discrete multitone handshaking process; however, the actual limit for f3 is 1.1 MHz, which represents the maximum usable bandwidth on a copper twisted-pair cable.

Benefits of DMT. One of the main benefits of DMT is its ability to take advantage of the characteristics of twisted-pair wire, which can vary from one local loop to another. This makes DMT modulation well suited for obtaining a higher data throughput than is possible through the use of a single carrier transmission technique. Because the transmission rate varies depending on the wire gauge and cable length as well as the physical characteristics of the cable, ADSL performance can vary considerably from one local loop to another. Ignoring bridge taps, which represent sections of unterminated twisted-pair cable connected in parallel across the twisted-pair cable under consideration, various tests of ADSL lines provide a general indication of their operating rate capability, which is summarized in Exhibit 3.

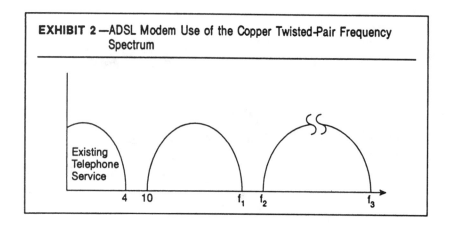

EXHIBIT 2—ADSL Modem Use of the Copper Twisted-Pair Frequency Spectrum

EXHIBIT 3—Generalized ADSL Performance

Wire Gauge	Subscriber Line Distance	Operating Rate
24 AWG	18,000 feet	1.5/2.0M bps
26 AWG	15,000 feet	1.5/2.0M bps
24 AWG	12,000 feet	6.1M bps
26 AWG	9,000 feet	6.1M bps

Note: AWG is the American Wire Gauge standard for measuring connectors.

Carrierless Amplitude/Phase (CAP) Modulation

CAP modulation is a derivative of quadrature amplitude modulation (QAM),which was developed by Paradyne when it was a subsidiary of AT&T and which is used in most modems today. Unlike DMT, which subdivides the bandwidth of the twisted-pair wire into 4-KHz segments, CAP uses the entire bandwidth in upstream and downstream channels.

Under CAP, serial data is encoded by mapping a group of bits into a signal constellation point using a two-dimensional, eight-state trellis coding with Reed-Solomon forward error correction. Reed-Solomon automatically protects transmitted data against impairments due to crosstalk, impulse noise, and background noise.

Exhibit 4 illustrates the CAP modulation process. Once a group of bits is mapped to a predefined point in the signal constellation, the in-phase and quadrature filters implement the positioning in the signal constellation. Because this technique simply adjusts the amplitude and phase without requiring a constant carrier, the technique is referred to as "carrierless."

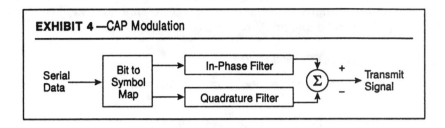

EXHIBIT 4 —CAP Modulation

The ADSL modem developed by Paradyne uses a 256-point signal constellation for downstream operations. This constellation pattern is in the 120 KHz to 1,224 KHz frequency range and produces a composite signaling rate of 960K baud, with 7 bits packed into each signal change. Although the resulting downstream operating rate is 6.72M bps, the use of the Reed-Solomon forward error correction code reduces the actual payload to 6.312M bps, plus a 64K-bps control channel. In the upstream direction, the Paradyne ADSL modem uses a CAP-16 line code in the 35-KHz to 72-KHz frequency band to obtain a composite signaling rate of 24K baud across 16 subchannels. By packing 3 bits per signal change, an upstream line rate of 72K bps is obtained, of which 64K bps is available for data. Similar to an ADSL DMT modem, an ADSL CAP modem can use time-division multiplexing to derive multiple channels on the upstream and downstream channels.

ADSL Developments and Field Tests

Although the ANSI DMT standard defines an operating rate of 6M bps on local loops up to 12,000 feet in length, some vendors now offer rates approaching 8M bps downstream and up to 800K bps upstream. This additional data rate is accomplished through an automatic rate adaptation capability that correlates the connected data rate to distance and line noise, enabling additional bandwidth to be gained–which translates into a higher operating rate.

In the U.S., GTE Telephone Operations (Stamford, CT) began testing the use of ADSL technology as part of a public data trial in the Dallas–Fort Worth area during 1996. This trial tests downstream data transmission at operating rates of up to 4M bps and upstream transmission at data rates up to 500K bps. The testing involves the Irving Public Library system, several bookstores, and area GTE employees. ADSL modems used during this trial are provided by Western Technologies of Oswego, IL, and Aware, Inc. of Bedford, MA.

On the West Coast, U.S. WEST (Olympia, WA) is testing ADSL-based services through its !NTERPRISE business unit and will use equipment from several vendors before deciding on which equipment to deploy commercially.

Other communications carriers are expected to announce field trials as well as commercial deployment of ADSL technology soon.

ADDITIONAL DSL TECHNOLOGIES

In addition to ADSL, three related technologies warrant a degree of discussion:

- High data-rate digital subscriber line (HDSL).
- Single-line digital subscriber line (SDSL).
- Very high data-rate digital subscriber line (VDSL).

HDSL modems are used on either end of one or more pairs of twisted-pair wires to obtain a T1 or E1 operating rate. Currently, a T1 operating rate requires two lines and E1 requires three. HDSL is primarily used on college campuses to provide a T1 or E1 link to interconnect LANs.

SDSL represents HDSL over a single telephone line and is used where multiple lines do not exist or would be expensive to install.

VDSL modems for twisted-pair access operate at data rates from 12.9 to 52.8M bps on 24-gauge cable. Because of the higher operating rate, the maximum transmission distance supported by VDSL is limited to under 4,000 feet. Higher rates over shorter distances may limit VDSL's ability to support communications carrier customers.

VDSL standards may not be finalized for several years. There are four VDSL line coding methods—discrete multitone, discrete wavelet multitone, carrierless amplitude/phase modulation, and simple line coding. DMT for VDSL is similar to the technology used in the ADSL standard, with more carriers(supporting ADSL) being the primary difference between the two. Discrete wavelet multitone coding represents a multicarrier system that uses wavelet transformers for individual carriers. The carrierless amplitude/phase modulation method under consideration is similar to Paradyne's CAP, representing a version of suppressed carrier quadrature amplitude modulation. The fourth coding technique, simple line coding, represents a baseband signaling and filtering system.

Based on the higher transmission capacity of VDSL, it will probably be deployed by communications carriers to businesses as a mechanism for asynchronous transfer mode (ATM) connectivity. The ATM Forum, which produced a 51.84M-bps standard for a private user-to-network interface, is currently examining the potential delivery of ATM via VDSL transmission.

CONCLUSION

From the viewpoint of a corporate network manager, ADSL is probably the only digital subscriber line technology that will be offered by enough carriers in the next few years to deserve consideration for interconnecting geographically separated locations. Although two different types of ADSL technology, based on either DMT or CAP modulation, are being considered by communications carriers, from the perspective of the end user the most important factors are:

- Availability of service.
- Operating rate of the service.
- Ability of the carrier's internal broadband network to provide connectivity.

The availability of ADSL will govern whether or not the technology can be used to interconnect LANs, provide remote access to mainframes, support videoconferencing between locations, or perform other communications functions. Although it may be possible, for example, to use an ADSL connection in one location and a conventional T1 connection in another location for communications, carriers still have not addressed the conversion of data between different transmission facilities.

The second area of concern is the operating rate of ADSL service. Because the transmission rate varies—depending on line quality, the distance of the user's location from a carrier's central office, and the wire gauge of the wire pair—users cannot fully appreciate its transmission capability until an ADSL line becomes operational. Vendor specifications should be used as a guide, and ADSL should be considered for applications that require a high data transmission capability but that can also be effectively performed if only a fraction of that capability is actually achieved.

Thus, videoconferencing or LAN access to the Internet are two applications for which ADSL may prove effective, even if the user achieves half or even a quarter of the theoretical ADSL rate due to a bad subscriber loop, long subscriber wire distance from the carrier's central office, or a similar factor.

A third area that should be examined before considering ADSL service is the scope of the carrier's internal broadband network. The user should determine whether the network interconnects only the ADSL offerings of that carrier, if it provides connectivity to other carriers, and if it provides connectivity to other data services offered by that carrier. By doing so, the user can determine if it will be possible to use ADSL services as a transport mechanism for such data services as X.25 and frame relay.

By contacting their communications carrier, users can ascertain when ADSL may be deployed in their areas and its projected cost. By asking the carrier key questions concerning the availability of the service in different areas where an organization may have offices, the operating rate of the service, and the capability of the carrier's internal broadband network, users can determine if ADSL service will be suitable for trial. If so, a test plan should be developed to compare ADSL with traditional T1 service to determine if it can be used as a cost-effective transport replacement.

Chapter 25
Access Architectures and Multimedia

Dale Smith

With the extremely rapid growth in the Internet, the requirement for high-speed, reliable access technologies for data networking service providers is not only in high demand, but becoming a competitive weapon in the network operator's ability to provide effective service delivery for multimedia applications. This chapter will explore the common technologies such as xDSL (ADSL, HDSL, etc.), cable modems, and dial services that are being touted for high-speed access today. The chapter will provide solution examples for those seeking to build or learn more about large-scale access networks that will support service areas into the millions of subscribers. The designs presented will be suitable for carriers, RBHOCs, cable companies, ISPs, and large enterprises wishing to construct access networks of this scale and complexity. The chapter will not cover wireless, cellular, and/or CDPD as access technologies, but the infrastructure presented in the chapter is still applicable to those wishing to design to this scale.

SERVICE PROVIDER SCALING AND CAPACITY REQUIREMENTS

What Is Large Scale?

Large-scale networks come in a variety of definitions, but for the purposes of this discussion, a large-scale network is one that introduces complexity for any of the following reasons:

- Topological complexity
- Data flow and routing complexity
- Complex security management, virtualization, and administration
- Large concentrations of users/subscribers (10^{3-6})
- Aggregation and concentration of broadband data [roughly defined as any data rate beyond Basic Rate ISDN (BRI) 128 Kb]

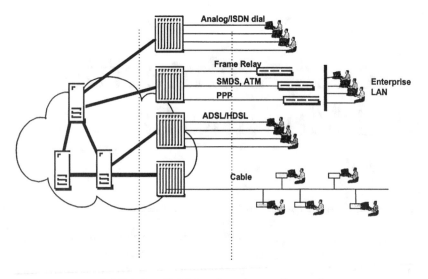

Exhibit 1. Multi-Services Access Network

Large scale does not inherently imply high and/or advanced technology, but due to the factors of large numbers, high speeds, and variable service levels, the scaling problems of such multimedia access networks create design complexity.

Multi-Service Access Networks

Multi-service access networks will allow for a variety of access technologies to be used as an access mechanism over a common transport network fabric. This will allow an operator to provide multiple services to a wide variety of subscribers who will have different types of access needs.

Exhibit 1 shows the notion of a "multi-services" access network where the core transport network will provide access connectivity for a variety of access technologies. The multi-services access network can be configured to provide general public access to the Internet, and Virtual Private Networks (VPN) using a variety of virtualization techniques such as tunneling.

Subscriber Densities

Large-scale multimedia access networks will require the distribution of access lines to large numbers of subscribers that will have subscriber densities ranging from as few as 500 to 1,000 subscribers in a small wire center to as many as 1,000,000 or more subscribers in an overall metropolitan area. With numbers in this order of magnitude, the data transport requirements of the access networks will be significant.

xDSL

A typical xDSL wire center will consist of a central office (CO) and wiring plant that will provide access lines to a specific number of subscribers within that serving area. The wire center will be constructed with local loops that will reach the customer directly from the CO and typically some number of remote terminals (RT) that pick up subscribers outside the distance limitations of a typical copper loop facility.

For example, consider an imaginary metropolitan area (i.e., a city) that consists of the following:

- ~3 M population
- ~1 M telephone (subscriber) lines
- ~50,000 subscribers for data service
- 20 central offices in serving area (out of total ~32)

Given these parameters, and a given "take rate" that is established by market studies (in this case 5%), the xDSL access network would consist of the following concentration requirements:

- Subscriber access lines = 2500 access ports per CO
- Maximum 250 active subscribers at any time per CO
- Maximum 25 subscribers bursting simultaneously (10% concurrency)

Assuming that a symmetrical HDSL (760 Kb full duplex) service has been implemented for this set of subscribers, then each CO would inject 19 Mb of data continuously into the core transport network of the service provider. Collectively, assuming that all COs were equivalently loaded, the transport network would at least be required to support 380 Mb of data that would be delivered to the Internet or other service provider at the egress points of the carrier network.

Cable Modems

Cable modems provide subscriber data access in the existing video distribution cable plant of a cable operator by allocating video channels (usually 2 to 6 Mhz) for data services. One channel is used for the "downstream" path and the other channel is used for the "upstream" path. This type of data over cable is known as two-way, where both the upstream and downstream data paths are implemented within the cable operator's plant.

Other schemes allow for traditional dial services upstream (14.4, 28.8, or 36.6 modems) where requests are sent to the service provider via a dial-up modem connection and a "cable return" downstream path over the cable modem facilities. This type of service can be implemented over older cable television infrastructures where it would be difficult to upgrade the cable plant for two-way service.

With 36Mhz (six 6Mhz channels) of bandwidth for a "typical" web browsing application, the cable subscriber density of a hypothetical metropolitan area would have the following characteristics:

- Subscriber clusters of 500 to 1500 sharing 30 Mbs of bandwidth
- Subscriber cluster node coax head ends would aggregrate to 20,000 head ends — in this case 14 head end clusters
- Groups of these aggregating head ends would form a "super" head end where management and content services would be provided
- Collectively, the head ends, and super head ends could support a metropolitan area of 200,000 subscribers.

Given these scaling parameters, this would allow a typical subscriber an average of 20 to 60 Kb of access bandwidth to the cable network. This carving of bandwidth would make the assumption that each subscriber would provide a sustained level of traffic. Cable modems act on a CSMACD "like" access protocol, so the transmitting and receiving subscriber modems would have full 10 Mb access once the cable modem gains access to the media. With 14 or so clustering node head end sytems, the core network of the super head end would be required to support up to 420 Mb of traffic, assuming sustained 20 to 60 Kb subscriber traffic.

Dial Services

Dial service subscriber concentrations vary widely with the various internet service providers (ISP) that are in play today. However, the same type of user population that would want high-speed multimedia access would be quite similar to those of xDSL as described above.

Thus assuming that the densities are the same as in xDSL:

- ~3 M population
- ~1 M telephone (subscriber) lines
- ~50,000 subscribers for data service
- 20 central offices in serving area (out of total ~32)

and a substantially higher take rate (25%):

- Subscriber access lines = 10,000 access ports per CO
- Maximum 1000 active subscribers at any time per CO
- Maximum 100 subscribers bursting simultaneously (10% concurrency)

then the bandwidth requirements at each of the access COs would be approximately 6.5 Mb per CO (100 × 64Kb), assuming that the maximum dial channel capacity is in 64Kb DS0 increments. This data would aggregrate up to 128 Mb of access data being injected into the transport network.

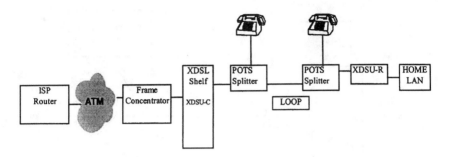

Exhibit 2.   DSL Wiring Configuration

ACCESS NETWORK TECHNOLOGIES

Digital Subscriber Line (xDSL)

Digital subscriber line technology (DSL) comes in a variety of formats all of which use various techniques to achieve higher effective bit rates over existing copper plant that is as ubiquitous as telephone service. DSL has a better bit error performance than NISDN and allows for the use of older legacy copper plant. With its ability to handle relative high bit rates over a large portion of existing copper facilities that match the demographics of dial services subscribers, DSL is a very attractive and cost-effective solution for TELCO service providers to provide high-speed access to the Internet and multimedia services between commercial subscribers operating in a SOHO manner.

DSL Technology. Most DSL technologies are based on some form of digital signaling and encoding over copper wire. For application as an access technology that will provide both data and voice services of the existing copper pair to a subscriber's residence, the encoding schemes must preserve the 4 Khz voice baseband channel that is available in the electromagnetic spectrum of the copper pair.

Exhibit 2 shows a typical DSL wiring configuration where a "life line" voice service is made available to the subscriber by the use of a POTS splitter which provides filtering of the voice and data frequencies.

There are currently widely accepted encoding techniques for DSL: CAP and DMT.

Exhibit 3 illustrates the line encoding mechanism for carrierless amplitude phase (CAP) modulation that is a proprietary technology of Paradyne Inc. While it is proprietary and not a formal standard, CAP is widely used in commercial applications of HDSL. Discrete multi-tone (DMT) line encoding, on the other hand, is a formal standard from ANSI T1.314. The line encoding mechanism for DMT is shown in Exhibit 4.

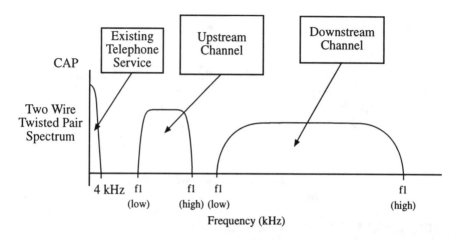

Exhibit 3.   Carrierless Amplitude Phase (CAP) Line Encoding Mechanism

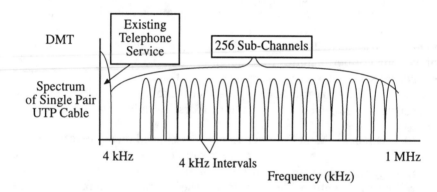

Exhibit 4.   Discrete Multi-Tone (DMT) Line Encoding Mechanism

Both CAP and DMT have different cost and performance characteristics which are in some cases competing. The specific discussion of the two encoding schemes is outside the scope of this chapter.

Regardless of the line encoding technique, available downstream bandwidth in DSL is a function of line quality and the distance of the receiver from the transmitter over the copper pair. Exhibit 5 shows the relative bandwidth vs. distance factors using DSL.

In most DSL applications 18 Kf is a nominal distance from the CO and is typically referenced as a "standard" loop reach. However, various DSL implementations may be tuned or optimized to achieve a greater loop

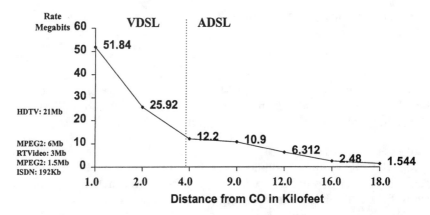

Exhibit 5. Relative Bandwidth Vs. Distance Factors Using DSL

reach in addition to various loop extension technologies such as digital loop carrier (DLC).

High Bit Rate DSL

HDSL (high bit rate DSL) and SDSL (symmetrical DSL) are DSL technologies that are in widespread use in TELCOs for what are known as pair gain applications. HDSL is used for multiplexing digital data over as few as one single pair of copper wires, whereas older technology may have used at least two pairs of copper wires — hence the "gain" or the recovery of a pair of copper wires in a distribution wiring sheath. HDSL and SDSL is a symmetrical service where both the uplink and downlink bandwidths are equal. SDSL typically operates at ½ T1 rates (760Kb full duplex) on a single copper pair, while HDSL operates at full T1 (1.5 Mb full duplex) over two copper pairs. HDSL/SDSL has the following characteristics:

- 760 Kb or 1.5 Mb uplink and downlink
- CAP line encoding

Asymmetric DSL. ADSL is a DSL implementation that was developed for video on demand applications that was deployed in a trial mode, but never successful as a commercial service. However, as a trial service, ADSL standards and implementations were significantly developed during the trial phases of video on demand. ADSL is suitable for a variety of high-speed access applications that support behaviors where there is a relatively small data request upstream toward a content provider and a relatively large response back to the requesting client (subscriber). Web browsing and multicasting applications are well suited for ADSL. ADSL has the following characteristics:

- 640 Kb uplink (toward CO)
- 1 to 2 Mb downlink (from CO)
- CAP or DMT line encoding

While not in vogue as a service, ADSL is suitable for multimedia applications that require NTSC-quality real-time video and audio. Compared to the best bandwidth available from dial services (128 Kb bonded NISDN), ADSL is a significant step up in access bandwidth.

Very High Speed DSL. VDSL has the same application characteristics as ADSL with higher speed uplinks and down links operating in an asymmetrical fashion. The tradeoff for this higher bandwidth is in the loop distance from the CO. VDSL has the following characteristics:

- Uplinks 1 to 2 megabits
- Downlinks 6+ megabits
- DMT line encoding

With its higher speed downlink capability, VDSL has the bandwidth to support MPEG 2 format video with sacrifice of shorter loop distances. VDSL is suitable (similar to cable) hybrid fiber to the curb (HFC) distribution plant for providing high-speed access for multimedia.

Rate Adaptive ADSL. RADSL (RADSL) is essentially an implementation of ADSL that will "tune" itself to the conditions of the local loop copper plant in a fashion similar to the way analog modems adjust to the line conditions of a dial up connection. The key benefit of RADSL modems is that they are "plug and play" from an installation perspective. Additionally, RADSL modems can provide preselected bit rates that can be negotiated as the subscriber's connection is being made. Different service levels (i.e., access bandwidths) can be achieved by programming the adaptive bit rates. RADSL has the following characteristics:

- Rate adaptive DSL
- Varying bit rates based on BER of line
- Can be used over a wide variety of plant
- Can be set for "selective" bit rates (i.e., different service levels)

Cable Modem

A cable modem is a bridge-like device (has layer 2 characteristics for forward and filter) that is located in the home. The cable modem converts RF signal to 10BT and connects to an Ethernet adapter card in a PC or other distribution mechanism in a home LAN. It is called a "modem" to leverage the existing residential user's perception that "modems" are used to connect to the outside world and is used generically to refer to the CPE that is in the home or small office.

The physical network infrastructure of a cable network involves the coaxial cable, fiber deployment, frequency assignments, and head end equipment. The physical plant varies from "trunk to trunk" and "city to city." Exhibit 6 shows a typical cable modem system for a metropolitan network.

Channel Managers. A channel manager (CM) is a cable modem multiplexor. These devices convert the RF signal back into Ethernet, where it is connected to an Ethernet network device such as a hub, router, or switch. Around 40 cable modems per CM is a typical network design assumption. They have the functionality of both a hub/bridge and router with an RF interface. In addition, frequency assignments and verification of line condition are accomplished by this device.

Distribution Hub. A distribution hub is a collection point in the cable infrastructure that feeds large head ends. There is generally a surplus of dark fiber between the head ends and distribution hubs that could be used to create a fiber backbone (FDDI, TLS, ATM) to connect the distribution hubs to the head end.

Head End. A cable modem head end is analogous to a TELCO central office. In large metropolitan areas, there may be more that one head end to serve the overall concentration of subscribers.

HFC-Hybrid Fiber Coax. Fiber cable is the network media from the cable operator's head end to the node, then coax from the node to the home. There is an RF cable television channel in the downstream direction and an RF subsplit CATV plant return.

RF/Ethernet. Because the cost of running fiber to the curb is not practical, the current trend in the industry is to run fiber to the distribution hub and the coax to the node and on to the home. This necessitates a data network architecture that allows for Ethernet to run over broadband RF.

Cable Modem Technology. Since cable modems must provide data service that is compatible and concurrent with existing video signals that are being distributed over a cable operator's cable plant, the data must be modulated in a format that will not interfere with adjacent video signals within the coaxial cable. Exhibit 7 shows how video is typically modulated on a coaxial cable. The video portion of the signal is modulated around the base of the 6Mhz channel with the upper portion reserved for an audio channel.

Data over cable, on the other hand, is typically modulated around the center of the 6Mhz channel, as shown in Exhibit 8.

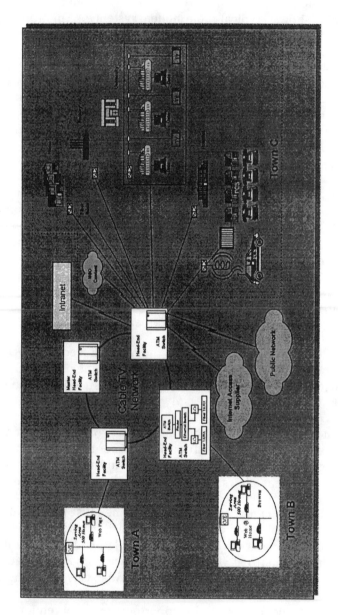

Exhibit 6. Typical Cable Modem System for a Metropolitan Network

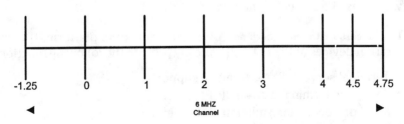

Exhibit 7. Modulation of Video on a Coaxial Cable

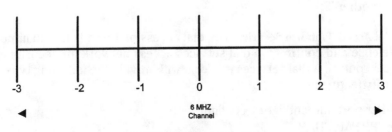

Exhibit 8. Data over Cable

Dial Services

Dial service is probably the most well understood access technology in existence. It is typically the dial-up modem paradigm for access networks that we all know and love. Usually dial service is generally categorized as both dial analog modem access and NISDN terminal equipment "dialing" into a circuit switched public network.

Dial service is a popular and widespread mechanism for access to data networks and the services provided over them. However, dial technology is almost at the limits of feasibility of providing bandwidths that are capable of supporting multimedia. Even with the new 56Kb digital modems that are available, full feature multimedia service levels are marginal. The current infrastructure of most if not all PSTN providers is designed for DS0 (i.e., 56Kb or 64Kb voice channel) access. Traditional dial services over the PSTN will be capped at this data rate unless an alternative access technology, such as xDSL or cable modem, is used.

Dial Access Platform Functions. A typical dial access platform, the concentration devices at the CO, will typically provide the following functions:

- Terminal server/ASYNC terminal support
- Serial line termination — SLIP, PPP, etc.
- Multi-protocol encapsulation: IP, IPX, etc.
- Layer 2 and layer 3 protocol support
- Bridging access ports to concentration media
- Routing of layer 3 protocols into core network
- Access control and security
- Tunneling features for virtual network services

The dial access platform will accept and control connections from the subscribers as they dial into the service provider's access network from the public switched telephone network (PSTN). Once this circuit switched connection is established, the data flows through a transport network to gain access to content and to external services such as the Internet at large and/or other ISPs.

Dial Access Platform Security. The dial access platform is the main point of defense and control in a dial services access network for security and access control. A dial services platform will provide the following types of security features:

- Per port authentication configuration
- PPP PAP/CHAP
- User level login/password
- RADIUS
- Session mapping to tunnel circuits

Call Flow Summary. Given the network topology in Exhibit 9, a typical user session using a typical tunneling technology to establish a virtual private network (VPN) can be set up in this fashion:

1. A remote user dials remote access server (RAS) where DNIS and/or user entered username.domain is received by RAS.
2. The RAS queries a centralized tunnel management system (TMS) with DNIS and/or domain name to find matching entry.

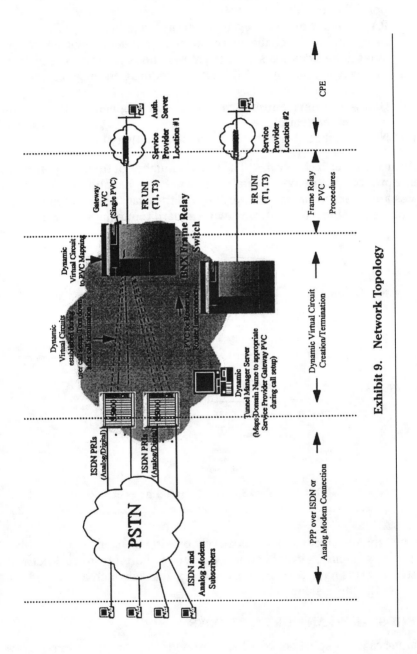

Exhibit 9. Network Topology

3. If the entry is found, the TMS responds to RAS with necessary information to build an IP "tunnel" from dial port to a specific frame relay port/DLCI or ATM port/VCI/VPI.
4. RAS sends mobile IP registration message including DLCI, username, and CHAP challenge response and IP address of service provider authentication server to gateway node (or same node).
5. Gateway sends out RADIUS access request message to specified authentication server.
6. Gateway passes authentication acknowledgment to RAS to complete authentication.
7. Normal subscriber data flow and billing activity begin.

Virtual Tunnel Technologies. There are a number of tunneling protocols being proposed to deliver virtual private network capabilities. The differences are layer 2 vs. layer 3 forwarding and the exact termination points of the tunnels. Exhibit 10 illustrates two standard tunneling scenarios.

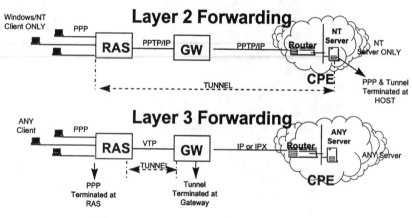

Exhibit 10.   Two Standard Tunneling Scenarios

The tunneling mechanisms effectively provide the same functionality of providing a secure, virtual connection over a shared transport network. Both scenarios have their benefits and drawbacks which are outside the scope of this discussion.

LARGE-SCALE TRANSPORT NETWORKS

A large-scale transport network has to provide the concentration, aggregation, and steering of data traffic once it is all collected at the access points within the network. Not only does the transport network have to support

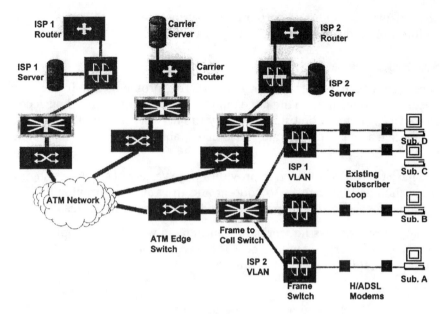

Exhibit 11.   Large-Scale Transport Network

the bandwidth and data flows of the subscriber data, it must also support the following functions in order to be useful:

- Quality of service (QOS)
- Service levels and feature sets
- Carrier selection (which ISP to choose)
- Content
- Access control, billing, and administration

Exhibit 11 is a diagram of a large-scale transport network. This particular network is based on a "layer 2" transport concept where the subscriber datagrams that are injected into the network are effectively bridged and/or repeated until they exit at a service provider egress point.

Exhibit 11 suggests xDSL as the access technology, but the functions would be the same for dial services and cable modems where the subscriber data is aggregated at the ingress CO.

As described in the sections above, this core network will be required to transport substantial amounts of subscriber traffic. In addition to the fundamental requirement of supporting large amounts of data, the core transport network will be required to provide mechanisms to support VPNs between subscribers who want service delivered in a virtual private line implementation such as a corporate subscriber needing to gain access to an internal corporate network in a secure fashion.

SUMMARY

Large-scale access networks bring interesting problems due to the complexities associated with the large numbers of subscribers needing access to services that will be transported by the network. For multimedia, the large-scale access network must also be capable of supporting high bandwidth.

These networks will need to provide a wide variety of service configurations such as VPN, access to content and the ability to provide flexible, dynamic access to service providers and other carrier networks.

Large-scale access networks for multimedia will offer not only the on ramps to the Internet, but also access to myriad services and content that true multimedia networks of the future promise.

Chapter 26

The Change Has Begun, The Future is Now

James Trulove

The world is about to experience a transcendent change in remote personal communications. In the past several generations, humankind has experienced several such changes. However, until now, revolutions in interpersonal communications have involved a single mode of communication, such as voice or electronic text. Image transmission of everything from digitized photographs to television has been primarily a one-way event, and not "communication" in the interpersonal sense. The coming revolution is in multimedia communication: the ability to share live-action images and audio in real time. To understand what social and economic effects this new technology will have, we can look to the past revolutions in communications.

THE PAST DAYS OF COMMUNICATIONS

Several preliminary steps occurred in human history which are a basis for all human communication. While it can be argued that the species has always had an underlying basis of verbal and nonverbal language, the organization of the verbal language into discrete components with a lexicon and syntax allowed the eventual development of forms of written communication, which progressed from symbolic drawings to phonemic symbols. A significant revolutionary step in the development of written communication was embodied in the printing press, which allowed a rapid reproduction of written thought and eventually the reproduction of drawings and photographs, as well. However, this means of communication is essentially one-way and/or nonreal time.

The first remote communications method that exhibited a real-time nature was telegraphy. The telegraph allowed an instantaneous transmission of text characters to a remote receiver. Telegraphy utilized a coded translation (via the Morse Code, among others) of letters and numbers into an on/off digital representation that could be easily decoded at the remote end by a trained human operator, who listened to the clicks of a remote solenoid. Later, telegraphy progressed to a constant-length code that was encoded and decoded by mechanical means. This coded representation became the basis for storage, retrieval, and transmission of text by computers. Although telegraphy provided an important means of communication for critical business and personal one-way communication, it created little change in everyday life.

The invention and proliferation of the telephone, on the other hand, did provide pervasive changes in everyday interpersonal communication. Unlike written correspondence or telegraphy, two parties could now give immediate feedback by responding to statements, answering questions, providing needed information, or taking needed action. In addition, the telephone added a critical component: One could not only recognize the other person's voice, but hear the tone, urgency, and emotion that is so important to effective interpersonal communication. Subsequently, the development of wireless voice communication through two-way radio equipment provided similar benefits without the need for fixed wiring.

The deployment telephone and two-way radio systems have brought us instantaneous voice communication. As a result, we can have quick and easy voice access to others around the country, around the world, and even in aircraft and ships at sea. For that matter, some of us regularly speak to craft in orbit around the planet.

Video communication has also moved quickly to influence our everyday lives. From the early beginnings of television, we have had the ability to communicate fixed and moving images in real time. One-way transmission of video and audio content are now second nature, although recent years have seen the addition of more extensive content selections through cable and direct satellite transmission. Now technological advances will allow new applications for video communication that are not limited to a single direction, one-to-many mode. We are beginning to experience communication as a multiple media event.

DAYS OF FUTURE PAST

We have long been looking forward to the future that will be realized by multimedia communications. Tellers of tales have painted word pictures of a time when communication from a distance would be almost commonplace. From ethereal visions to mystical crystal balls, from magic viewscreens to teleportation, we have often imagined a means of instant communications. Viewed from the past, this must have been very nearly a magical journey. Were ancient visitors to appear in our time, they could scarcely be convinced that our modern tele-conveniences were not real magic. Fortunately, current generations have been preparing themselves psychologically for this new future.

Long before the advent of color TV and the VCR, writers of fiction had been predicting the current communication revolution. The future, in print, was portrayed decades ago by such forward-looking authors as Jules Verne, Victor Appleton, and his "son" Victor Appleton, Jr. (To those who read the latter two authors, another shattered myth of youth is that a whole array of writers contracted to supply modernistic adventures under those pseudonyms.) Science fiction and fact writer Isaac Asimov inspired generations of readers with interesting technological tales of the future, including many references to two-way video and instant computer access to a vast knowledge-base. We also enjoyed the fanciful future of communications through the comic tales of Dick Tracy's wrist radio/TV, as well as Flash Gordon and others.

Hollywood, too, has prepared us well for the dawning future of communications through a cornucopia of films and television series. At the leading edge of the multimedia communications revolution, the film industry regaled us with science fiction jewels, such as the classic Jules Verne tales, the epic *2001 A Space Odyssey*, and the very successful *Star Wars* trilogy. But concentrating solely on the science fiction genre would ignore the subtle move of multimedia communications into more mainstream film fare. Examples abound in action movies with a technical edge, such as *The Net* or *Mission Impossible*. However, the presence of real-life multimedia communications has also been seen in a few comedy/dramas such as *Mother*, in which Debbie Reynolds is seen communicating with her son by picture-phone, albeit a fairly primitive model.

So, the future is upon us, whether we have realized it or not. In some ways, this future has caught up with our expectations. Much of the current voice/video/data technology has been available in some means for many years, if one had enough money. But now the price has begun to plummet on this marvelous convenience of instant communications in multiple media. Now every business can easily justify the expense if they have a business need. Soon businesses may begin to adopt the technology simply for business convenience. Home use will lag behind that of business, as it does with most other technologies, but we will begin to see more and more multimedia in that environment as well.

USES FOR THE FUTURE

The difference between plausible science fantasy and science reality is often that an idea must be practical, not merely possible, to reach the market. In fact, we frequently mistake impractical extensions of trends for true future plausibilities. For example, popular magazines in the '50s and '60s projected trends in fixed- and rotary-winged aircraft into a personal flying machine that all of us would be driving long before now. This, of course, has not happened for a variety of really practical reasons. First and foremost, is that such flying cars, at this point in economic history, would be very expensive to own and operate. They simply would not make it to market. In addition, imagine the disarray in the skies if there were no roadways to manage traffic, as there is for wheeled vehicles. Flying machines also have a nasty habit of encountering the ground with great force when their ability to fly is suddenly removed. Cars do not. On the other hand, automatic control of cars along a roadway specially equipped for on-board sensors is being tested on experimental roads right now. Such a vehicle would be economically feasible and practical to tightly pack roadways with automatically controlled vehicles. The expense of the roadway modifications would be made up by the reduced need for more lanes, and more highways, and fewer delays.

It is therefore important that the future be useful. For multimedia networking's future, fortunately most of the present and proposed uses are beneficial and quite practical. From this vantage point, we have had several technological breakthroughs that may allow us to predict the near-term future for multimedia.

The most significant application for mixing multiple means of communication is undoubtedly videoconferencing. Videoconferencing is a technology that has been available at high cost for quite some time. Television journalist Edward R. Murrow conducted what were essentially videoconferenced interviews nearly four decades ago. However, the conference was one-way for video, and accomplished through more than a little TV magic. Over the past decade, we have seen the rise of several high-end videoconferencing companies, such as V-Tel, Picture-Tel, and the newest edition, PolyCom. In addition, PC-based applications have appeared, yielding low-resolution videoconferencing capabilities over the LAN, the Internet, or point-to-point. In many cases, data-sharing applications are included with these video products so that distant video callers can share PC application screens, medical images, or classroom slides.

Videoconferencing, as an application, is truly multimedia. Carried on a network or WAN, it may be voice/video-over-IP, voice/video-over-frame relay, or voice/video-over ATM. It requires high-bandwidth, temporal quality-of-service guarantees, and error-free delivery. Videoconferencing is the multimedia "worst case" scenario, in many ways. It mixes all three major modes of communications, in real time, with a time-sensitive interdependence. In addition, videoconferencing is a bandwidth hog, has intermittent connection-oriented needs, and is cost-sensitive. Left to its own, the initial capital investment, bandwidth requirements, and operating costs of a conventional videoconferencing network are so significant that one could expect a rather lengthy introduction of this technology. The bandwidth requirements for a satisfactory image size and frame rate are well above that available to most businesses, without installing T-carrier access or multiple ISDN/BRI lines.

Fortunately, other emerging high-bandwidth technologies are giving videoconferencing a helping hand. Initiatives to deliver services such as high-speed Internet access and digital television programming are in process throughout the industrialized world. ADSL (and its relatives), cable modems, fiber-to-the-curb, and even digital satellites are making the "big pipe" available to home and business alike. The costs are well within reason, particularly with respect to the delivery of multiple services. The technology is ready now. The applications, including videoconferencing, either are ready to be moved to these technologies, or are waiting in the wings. The backbones that will transport the vast new amounts of data-as-voice/video are being deployed today.

The net result of this rapid expansion in bandwidth available to the user is that applications such as Internet access and videoconferencing will become so practical that they will be deployed in great numbers.

THE FUTURE IMPACTS THE BACKBONE

The vast bandwidth increases and the multiple modes of communications that are to be carried on the backbone of the future will necessitate a complete restructuring of network backbone transmission. The term backbone must be viewed in two contexts: the local network within an enterprise, and the far-reaching traffic consolidation and interconnecting pathways of the wide area.

In the enterprise, two technology divisions are evident. First is the ability to transport voice and data (and perhaps video) on the same physical media from a switching or concentration point to a work area. At the central concentration point, this scheme would allow, for example, a single voice/data/video switch to take the place of the conventional analog PBX, the data router, and the video switch. At the work area, a multiple-media communications device, perhaps in combination with computer hardware, would provide the user with access to any of the three modes of communication. Conversely, a stand-alone device could be employed to break out each mode to the appropriate interface, whether an analog POTS line for a telephone or a computer network connection. Video users would utilize a device that also provided multiple BRIs or an FT1 interface.

The second technology division in the enterprise is the need to provide multiple-mode content embedded in a conventional networking environment, enhanced to provide multimedia transport. Two examples of this are embedded IP multimedia traffic and LAN-emulating ATM. Each would utilize specialized computer-based work station access node that used conventional networking protocols to provide transport and end-connectivity of voice/data/video signals. Again, a stand-alone device could be provided to allow the use of existing legacy voice and data equipment. The central concentration device would be a network router or layer 2/layer 3 switch with provisions for maintaining high quality-of-service virtual connections for those applications that are delivery-time sensitive.

Both of these enterprise technologies require an extensive upgrade in bandwidth, switching equipment, and work area devices. Intermediate backbones and nodal equipment may be replaced, as may the horizontal transport to each work area. A goal of the multimedia networking practitioner will be to optimize the scarce resources of time, money, and materials to provide a workable multimedia network that will meet reasonable future needs.

The wide area backbone presents additional challenges, both for local service providers and inter-regional backbone providers. It would not be out of line to expect the bandwidth requirements for networking multimedia to the user to increase by a factor of 10 or 20 above the currently available levels that are used for POTS and ISDN connections. Certainly, to provide multichannel broadcast access to the user level requires another bandwidth surge of 10x to 100x, depending upon whether digital or analog signals are broadcast.

THE CHANGE HAS BEGUN

Once the capability for a multimedia signal has been made available to the business and home user, the matter of interconnecting transport remains. The careful implementation and deployment of multimedia networking through high-bandwidth fiber optic networking is another key to providing innovative new services to the user. Much of the long-span fiber that is now in place can be converted to even higher bandwidth transmission. Bandwidth in this respect is somewhat like the proverbial ballpark: build it and they will come. Whether the super-backbone that is now under continuous construction is targeted at the Internet or at some other esoteric application, users will be able to grab some of the excess bandwidth (which is expected to be considerable) for additional uses that will enhance interpersonal and extrapersonal (meaning computer-centric) communication to a degree we can only imagine.

For the first time, a merging of communications media is becoming practical. Properly implemented, this will make immediately available the vast knowledge base we have been busy computerizing. It will also make direct voice and video communication ubiquitous. Data sharing, with adequate security and safeguards, will allow information and commerce to flow freely. We will create a true global village, with instantaneous multimedia communication which will provide substantial increases in productivity, a better quality of life, enhancements in education and recreation, and cross-cultural understanding.

Multimedia networking is beginning to change the world. Today we can easily communicate with our peers around the globe. Persons in vastly different regions can collaborate and communicate on research, projects, education, or recreation. Do you want the latest weather in Alaska? How about in Auckland? What are the ski conditions in Vail ... or in Switzerland? Would you like to see a picture of the slopes, right now? You might rather listen to a concert at Carnegie Hall, or perhaps a chamber music ensemble in Munich. Do you want to travel? You can find hotel and attraction information, compare prices, and even purchase your tickets instantly over the Internet. Currently, you can have a video meeting with customers or employees around the globe. Soon, you will be able to do the same type of video conversing from your home, with your geographically distributed family and friends.

For multimedia networking and its related communications applications, the change has begun, and it is revolutionary. Multimedia communications will indeed change the world. It has already begun. The future is now.

About the Editor

James Trulove has more than 20 years of experience in data and telecommunications with companies such as AT&T, Motorola, and Intel. He has a background in designing and configuring multimedia communications systems for local and wide area networks, using a variety of technologies from manufacturers such as Cisco, Ascend, Fore, Madge, RAD, and Adtran. He writes on networking topics and is the author of *A Guide to Fractional T1* and *LAN Wiring: An Illustrated Guide to Network Cabling*.

Index

principles of videoconferencing and multimedia communications, **14**-2-**14**-5
qualitative QOS experience, **14**-4-**14**-5
quantitative quality of service parameters, **14**-2-**14**-4
pros and cons of, **14**-5-**14**-8
  bandwidth allocation, **14**-5-**14**-6
  IP network advantages, **14**-6-**14**-7
  IP network disadvantages, **14**-7-**14**-8
video-ready networks, **14**-11-**14**-14
  billing and related issues, **14**-14
  end-point performance, **14**-12-**14**-13
  evolving bandwidth management protocols, **14**-13-**14**-14
  network upgrade and management issues, **14**-11-**14**-12
Virtual area network (VAN), **14**-8
Virtual circuit (VC), **17**-19
Virtual connections, **10**-8
Virtual path (VP) multiplexer, **9**-9
Virtual Private Network (VPN), **25**-2
Virtual shopping malls, **1**-7
Virtual tributary (VT), **18**-17
Visual sensitivity, **15**-3
VLSI, see Very large scale integration
Vocoder, **7**-6
Voice
  activity detection (VAD), **7**-7, **7**-8
  channel monitoring, **20**-5
  communications, history of, **5**-1
  digitization standards, **13**-5
  quality
    benchmark for, **7**-4
    potential, **5**-4
  services, **17**-7
  Telephony over ATM (VTOA), **4**-7
  traffic, method to simulate, **23**-8
  transmission quality, **18**-4
Voice compression, silence suppression and, **7**-1-**7**-10
  ADPCM, **7**-4-**7**-5
  advances in new networks, **7**-1
  assessing different voice compression schemes, **7**-2

CELP, **7**-6-**7**-7
current implementations, **7**-9-**7**-10
  Internet voice, **7**-10
  narrowband ATM compression techniques, **7**-9-**7**-10
  true speech, **7**-9
CVSD, **7**-5-**7**-6
PCM, **7**-2-**7**-4
techniques and guidelines for voice compression through silence suppression, **7**-7-**7**-9
VP multiplexer, see Virtual path multiplexer
VPN, see Virtual Private Network
VSELP, see Variable slope excited linear predictive
VT, see Virtual tributary
VTOA, see Voice Telephony over ATM

W

WAN, see Wide area network
Web
  browsing, **25**-7
  services, **17**-7
  sites, **22**-8
  TV, **22**-1
Whiteboard capabilities, **14**-9
Wide area network (WAN), **7**-4, **9**-2
  access, **14**-11
  amount of traffic carried across, **21**-19
  file transfer sent over, **11**-4
  high-speed broadband, **21**-15
  link, **23**-12
  multimedia, **21**-14
  point-to-point, **19**-2
  private, **9**-5
  rates, **9**-3
  transferring images through, **13**-9
Work
  environments, cooperative, **1**-5
  -at-home jobs, **1**-4

X

X bit, **18**-14